HOLLYWOOD
POWER
STATS

By Christopher Reynolds

CINEVIEW
PUBLISHING

Hollywood Power Stats
by Christopher Reynolds

Published by: **Cineview Publishing**
4804 Laurel Canyon Blvd., Suite #203
Valley Village, CA 91607
Fax: (818) 509-1349

Printed by Griffin Printing & Lithograph Co., Inc., Glendale, CA
Manufactured in the United States of America.

Publisher's Cataloging in Publication Data
Reynolds, Christopher
Hollywood Power Stats: The Essential Facts and Figures of the Motion Picture Industry by Christopher Reynolds. — 1st Edition
Includes Index.
1. Moving-Pictures. — Handbooks, Manuals, etc.
2. Moving-Pictures. — Dictionaries. I. Title
LC# 93-73776

ISBN 0-9638748-4-5 $18.95 Softcover

Table of Contents

Warning-Disclaimer

*For **FREE** update information see back page!*

Top 150
Blockbusters

Top 150 Blockbusters

Top 150
Blockbusters

The following movies represent the all-time megahits in the motion picture industry and they are ranked by their reported domestic (U.S. & Canada) rental figures from theatrical release. Films are ranked by their rental figures as opposed to their box office gross because rentals are more verifiable and have been better kept throughout the years. Overseas and ancillary markets are not figured in because they cannot be verified. The rank is followed by the title of the picture, the distribution company that released it, the year in which it was first released, the box office gross, the rental figure and finally the rental-to-gross percentage. These statistics have been compiled from a variety of sources and inflation has <u>not</u> been accounted for. For more information about film rentals and how they relate to box office gross please see page 76.

*Indicates estimated %.

**Indicates estimated gross or rental figure.

***Indicates film still in release at time of publication.

Rank	Title	Gross	Rental	%
1	**E.T. The Extra-Terrestrial (U, 1982)**	$399,800,000	$228,618,940	57.18%
2	**Jurassic Park (U, 1993)*****	$327,871,950	$196,723,170**	60%*
3	**Star Wars (Fox, 1977)**	$323,000,000	$193,777,000	59.99%
4	**Return of the Jedi (Fox, 1983)**	$264,000,000	$169,193,000	64.08%
5	**Batman (WB, 1989)**	$251,188,924	$150,500,000	59.91%
6	**The Empire Strikes Back (Fox, 1980)**	$223,000,000	$141,672,000	63.53%
7	**Home Alone (Fox,1990)**	$281,493,907	$140,099,000	49.76%
8	**Ghostbusters (Col, 1984)**	$220,855,498	$132,720,000	60.09%
9	**Aladdin (BV, 1992)**	$217,042,825	$130,225,695**	60%*
10	**Jaws (U, 1975)**	$215,915,392**	$129,549,325	60%*
11	**Raiders of the Lost Ark (Par, 1981)**	$210,178,181**	$115,598,000	55%*
12	**Indiana Jones and the Last Crusade (Par, 1989)**	$197,035,089	$115,500,000	58.61%
13	**Terminator II (TriStar, 1991)**	$203,764,837	$112,500,000	55.21%
14	**Indiana Jones and the Temple of Doom (Par, 1984)**	$175,083,524	$109,000,000	62.25%
15	**Beverly Hills Cop (Par,1984)**	$229,909,722	$108,000,000	46.97%
16	**Back to the Future (U, 1985)**	$200,132,594	$105,496,270	52.71%
17	**Home Alone II (Fox, 1992)**	$172,667,450	$102,000,000	59.07%
18	**Batman Returns (WB, 1992)**	$162,831,700	$100,100,000	61.47%
19	**Ghost (Par, 1990)**	$216,818,693	$98,200,000	45.29%
20	**Grease (Par, 1978)**	$185,192,307**	$96,300,000	52%*
21	**Tootsie (Col, 1982)**	$176,188,774	$94,910,000	53.86%
22	**The Fugitive (WB, 1993)*****	$172,494,360	$89,697,067**	52%*
23	**The Exorcist (WB, 1973)**	$171,153,846**	$89,000,000	52%*
24	**Rain Man (MGM/UA, 1988)**	$171,188,895	$86,813,000	50.71%
25	**The Godfather (Par, 1972)**	$165,913,461**	$86,275,000	52%*
26	**Robin Hood: Prince of Thieves (WB, 1991)**	$164,045,251	$86,000,000	52.42%

Rank	Title	Gross	Rental	%
27	Snow White and Seven Dwarfs (RKO/BV, 1937)***	$178,685,986	$83,982,413**	47%*
28	Superman (WB, 1978)	$159,230,769**	$82,800,000	52%*
29	Close Encounters of the Third Kind (Col, 1977)	$159,134,615**	$82,750,000	52%*
30	Pretty Woman (BV, 1990)	$178,088,702	$81,905,530	45.99%
31	Dances With Wolves (Orion, 1990)	$183,243,347	$81,537,970	44.49%
32	Three Men and a Baby (BV, 1987)	$167,780,960	$81,313,000	48.46%
33	Who Framed Roger Rabbit (BV, 1988)	$152,715,105	$81,244,000	53.19%
34	Beverly Hills Cop II (Par, 1987)	$153,651,824	$80,857,775	52.62%
35	The Firm (Par, 1993)***	$155,186,342	$80,696,897**	52%*
36	Lethal Weapon III (WB, 1992)	$144,624,387	$80,000,000	55.31%
37	The Sound of Music (Fox, 1965)	$153,798,076**	$79,975,000	52%*
38	Gremlins (WB, 1984)	$148,117,285	$79,500,000	53.67%
39	Lethal Weapon II (WB, 1989)	$147,253,986	$79,500,000	53.98%
40	Top Gun (Par, 1986)	$176,750,705	$79,400,000	44.92%
41	Gone With the Wind (MGM/UA/TEC, 1939)	$152,644,385**	$79,375,080	52%*
42	Rambo:First Blood Part II (TriStar, 1985)	$150,415,432	$78,919,250	52.46%
43	The Sting (U, 1973)	$150,407,692**	$78,212,000	52%*
44	Rocky IV (MGM/UA, 1985)	$127,800,000	$76,023,250	59.48%
45	Saturday Night Fever (Par, 1977)	$142,500,000**	$74,100,000	52%*
46	A Few Good Men (Col, 1992)	$141,340,178	$73,496,892**	52%*
47	Back to the Future Pt II (U, 1989)	$116,425,676	$72,319,630	62.11%
48	Honey, I Shrunk the Kids (BV, 1989)	$130,150,514	$72,007,000	55.32%
49	National Lampoon's Animal House (WB, 1985)	$136,203,846**	$70,826,000	52%*
50	Crocodile Dundee (Par, 1986)	$174,634,806	$70,227,000	40.21%
51	Fatal Attraction (Par, 1987)	$156,645,693	$70,000,000	44.68%
52	Platoon (Orion, 1986)	$137,900,000	$69,937,100	50.71%
53	Beauty and the Beast (BV, 1991)	$141,018,356	$69,415,000	49.22%
54	Look Who's Talking (TriStar, 1989)	$138,054,925	$68,872,000	49.88%
55	101 Dalmatians (BV, 1961)	$144,880,014	$68,648,000	47.38%
56	Teenage Mutant Ninja Turtles (New Line, 1990)	$133,145,682	$67,650,000	50.80%
57	Die Hard II (Fox, 1990)	$115,288,665	$67,512,000	58.55%
58	Rocky III (MGM/UA, 1982)	$120,252,948	$66,262,800	55.10%
59	Superman II (WB, 1981)	$108,100,000	$65,100,000	60.22%
60	Coming to America (Par, 1988)	$128,113,607	$65,000,000	50.73%
61	Hook (TriStar, 1991)	$118,965,084	$65,000,000	54.63%
62	Total Recall (TriStar, 1990)	$118,272,498	$63,511,050	53.69%
63	Sleepless in Seattle (TriStar, 1993)***	$120,277,388	$62,544,241**	52%*
64	Sister Act (BV, 1992)	$138,477,418	$62,420,000	45.07%
65	On Golden Pond (U/AFD, 1981)	$118,700,000	$61,175,030	51.53%
66	The Jungle Book (BV, 1967)	$128,745,619	$60,964,000	47.35%
67	City Slickers (Col, 1991)	$120,735,850	$60,750,000	50.31%
68	Dick Tracy (BV, 1990)	$103,738,726	$60,611,145	58.42%

Rank	Title	Gross	Rental	%
69	Ghostbusters II (Col, 1989)	$111,932,094	$60,490,000	54.04%
70	Kramer Vs. Kramer (Col, 1979)	$115,358,337**	$59,986,335	52%*
71	One Flew Over the Cuckoo's Nest (UA, 1975)	$115,268,654**	$59,939,700	52%*
72	The Silence of the Lambs (Orion, 1991)	$130,726,716	$59,882,870	45.80%
73	9 to 5 (Fox, 1980)	$104,000,000	$59,068,000	56.79%
74	Smokey and the Bandit (U, 1977)	$113,365,269**	$58,949,940	52%*
75	The Hunt for Red October (Par, 1990)	$120,617,004	$58,500,000	48.50%
76	Stir Crazy (Col, 1980)	$101,300,000	$58,364,420	57.61%
77	The Karate Kid Pt II (Col, 1986)	$114,878,000	$58,310,000	50.75%
78	Good Morning, Vietnam (BV, 1987)	$123,922,370	$58,083,110	46.87%
79	The Bodyguard (WB, 1992)	$121,936,132	$58,000,000	47.56%
80	Twins (U, 1988)	$110,618,737	$57,715,130	52.17%
81	Crocodile Dundee II (Par, 1988)	$109,201,624	$57,300,000	52.47%
82	Star Trek IV: The Voyage Home (Par, 1986)	$109,692,882	$56,820,070	51.79%
83	Rocky (UA, 1976)	$108,701,865**	$56,524,970	52%*
84	The Addams Family (Par, 1991)	$113,379,166	$56,200,000	49.56%
85	Star Trek (Par, 1979)	$107,692,307	$56,000,000	.52*
86	Porky's (Fox, 1982)	$105,492,483	$55,559,000	52.66%
87	An Officer and a Gentleman (Par, 1982)	$127,311,797	$55,223,000	43.37%
88	American Graffiti (U, 1973)	$110,256,350**	$55,128,175	50%*
89	Wayne's World (Par, 1992)	$121,631,114	$54,000,000	44.39%
90	Big (Fox, 1988)	$113,596,430	$53,700,000	47.27%
91	In the Line of Fire (Col, 1993)***	$102,243,874	$53,166,814**	52%*
92	A League of their Own (Col, 1992)	$107,404,544	$53,100,000	49.43%
93	Basic Instinct (TriStar, 1992)	$117,208,217	$53,000,000	45.21%
94	Unforgiven (WB, 1992)	$101,101,229	$52,572,639**	52%*
95	Every Which Way But Loose (WB, 1978)	$99,807,692**	$51,900,000	51%*
96	Driving Miss Daisy (WB, 1989)	$106,368,291	$50,500,000	47.47%
97	Jaws II (U, 1978)	$96,984,557**	$50,431,970	51%*
98	Terms of Endearment (Par, 1983)	$105,237,012	$50,250,000	47.74%
99	Parenthood (U, 1989)	$95,565,783	$50,004,367	52.32%
100	The Color Purple (WB, 1985)	$94,100,000	$49,800,000	52.92%
101	Heaven Can Wait (Par, 1978)	$95,000,000	$49,400,000	52%*
102	Back to the Future Pt III (U, 1990)	$86,498,961	$49,072,000	56.73%
103	The Towering Inferno (Fox/WB, 1974)	$93,919,230**	$48,838,000	52%*
104	Love Story (Par, 1970)	$93,653,846**	$48,700,000	52%*
105	Dead Poets Society (BV, 1989)	$94,544,861	$48,427,510	51.22%
106	Blazing Saddles (WB, 1974)	$91,923,076**	$47,800,000	52%*
107	Kindergarten Cop (U, 1990)	$90,272,872	$47,365,485	52.46%
108	The Best Little Whorehouse in Texas (U, 1982)	$69,701,637	$47,333,927	67.90%
109	Bambi (RKO/BV, 1942)	$102,247,150	$47,265,000	46.22%
110	Doctor Zhivago (MGM, 1965)	$94,507,520**	$47,253,760	50%*

Rank	Title	Gross	Rental	%
111	Bram Stoker's Dracula (Col, 1992)	$82,416,928	$47,200,000	57.26%
112	Sleeping With the Enemy (Fox, 1991)	$100,294,830	$46,000,000	45.86%
113	Butch Cassidy and the Sundance Kid (Fox, 1969)	$91,906,000**	$45,953,000	50%*
114	Airport (U, 1970)	$90,440,240**	$45,220,120	50%*
115	Mary Poppins (BV, 1964)	$91,500,000	$45,000,000	49.18%
116	The Naked Gun 2 1/2 (Par, 1991)	$86,816,416	$44,200,000	50.91%
117	The Graduate (Avemb,1968)	$88,181,460**	$44,090,730	50%*
118	Presumed Innocent (WB, 1990)	$86,266,757	$43,800,000	50.77%
119	Aliens (Fox, 1986)	$78,720,655	$43,753,000	55.58%
120	Out of Africa (U, 1985)	$86,896,510**	$43,448,255	50%*
121	The Karate Kid (Col, 1984)	$90,815,558	$43,120,000	47.48%
122	Father of the Bride (BV, 1991)	$88,192,752	$43,027,000	48.78%
123	The Ten Commandments (Par, 1956)	$86,000,000**	$43,000,000	50%*
124	The Jerk (U, 1979)	$85,979,320**	$42,989,660	50%*
125	Rocky II (UA, 1979)	$84,338,780**	$42,169,390	50%*
126	Arthur (Orion/WB, 1981)	$95,400,000	$42,000,000	44.02%
127	The Poseidon Adventure (Fox, 1972)	$84,000,000**	$42,000,000	50%*
128	Back to School (Orion, 1986)	$90,424,432	$41,948,385	46.39%
129	Teenage Mutant Ninja Turtles II (New Line, 1991)	$78,391,796	$41,900,000	53.44%
130	The Goodbye Girl (MGM/WB, 1977)	$83,678,340**	$41,839,170	50%*
131	When Harry Met Sally (Col, 1989)	$92,247,887	$41,790,000	45.30%
132	Fantasia (RKO/BV, 1940)	$78,356,105	$41,660,000	53.16%
133	The War of the Roses (Fox, 1989)	$84,130,763	$41,400,000	49.20%
134	Cinderella (RKO/BV, 1949)	$93,201,149	$41,087,000	44.08%
135	Stripes (Col, 1981)	$81,773,180**	$40,886,590	50%*
136	Airplane (Par, 1980)	$81,220,000**	$40,610,000	50%*
137	Trading Places (Par, 1983)	$88,621,914	$40,600,000	45.81%
138	Any Which Way You Can (WB, 1980)	$81,000.000**	$40,500,000	50%*
139	Pinocchio (RKO/BV, 1940)	$89,277,597	$40,442,000	45.29%
140	Alien (Fox, 1979)	$62,000,000	$40,300,000	65.00%
141	Backdraft (U, 1991)	$77,593,978	$40,260,680	51.88%
142	The Lady and the Tramp (BV, 1955)	$87,629,082	$40,249,000	45.93%
143	The Little Mermaid (BV, 1989)	$83,728,073	$40,227,000	48.04%
144	Another 48 Hours (Par, 1990)	$80,786,874	$40,100,000	49.63%
145	Cocoon (Fox, 1985)	$76,113,124	$40,000,000	52.55%
146	Days of Thunder (Par, 1990)	$82,663,996	$40,000,000	48.38%
147	Star Trek II: The Wrath of Khan (Par, 1982)	$78,912,963	$40,000,000	50.68%
148	Steel Magnolias (TriStar, 1989)	$81,004,509	$40,000,000	49.37%
149	Under Siege (WB, 1992)	$83,550,855	$40,000,000	47.87%
150	The Golden Child (Par, 1986)	$79,793,282	$39,723,090	49.78%

For those films reporting both box office gross and rentals the average rental-to-gross percentage for the top 150 blockbusters is 51.7%.

1994 Film Preview

The following movies are scheduled to be released in 1994. Some films listed are in development at the time of this printing and may or may not make it into production. Movies that have made it into production will have a start date next to the title which is followed by the production company name, the cast, the executive producer, the producer, the director, the screenwriter and finally the U.S. distributor (all upon availability). A quick list of movies being released, grouped by distributors, is at the end of this section on page 14.

Ace Ventura: Pet Detective
(5/10/93)
Ace Productions
Cast: *Jim Carrey, Sean Young, Courteney Cox, Tone Loc, Dan Marino*
ExPrd., Gary Barber; Prd., James G. Robinson; Dir., Tom Shadyac; Scr., Jack Bernstein, Tom Shadyac, Jim Carrey
US Distrib., Warner Bros.

Airheads (6/21/93)
Twentieth Century Fox
Cast: *Brendan Fraser, Steve Buscemi, Adam Sandler, Joe Mantegna, Michael McKean, Ernie Hudson, Marshall Bell, Amy Locane, Chris Farley, Michael Richards*
ExPrd., Todd Baker; Prd., Robert Simonds, Mark Burg; Dir., Michael Lehmann; Scr., Richard Wilkes
Distrib., 20th Century Fox.

Angels In The Outfield (10/5/93)
Caravan Pictures
Cast: *Danny Glover, Brenda Fricker, Tony Danza, Christopher Lloyd, Ben Johnson, Joseph Gordon-Levitt, Milton Davis Jr., Jay O. Sanders, Taylor Negron*
Exprd., Gary Stutman; Prod., Joe Roth, Roger Birnbaum, Irby Smith; Dir., William Dear; Scr., Holly Goldberg Sloan
Distrib., Buena Vista

The Apostle (10/4/93)
City Lights International Inc.
Cast: *Robert Duvall, June Carter Cash, Wilford Brimley, Arliss Howard*
ExPrd., Kenneth Schur; Prd., Carl Clifford, Danny Fisher, Jack Fisher; Dir/Scr., Robert Duvall

Baby's Day Out (8/17/93)
Hughes Entertainment
Cast: *Joe Mantegna, Joe Pantoliano, Brian Haley, John Neville, Laura Flynn Boyle, Matthew Glave, Fred Dalton Thompson*
ExPrd., Bill Ryan; Prd., John Hughes, Richard Vane; Dir., Patrick Read Johnson; Scr., John Hughes
Distrib., 20th Century Fox.

Bad Girls (6/21/93)
Echo City Prods
Cast: *Madeleine Stowe, Drew Barrymore, Mary Stuart Masterson, Andie MacDowell, Dermot Mulroney, James LeGros, James Russo*
ExPrd., Lynda Obst; Prd., Albert S. Ruddy, Andre E. Morgan, Charles Finch; Dir., Jonathan Kaplan; Scr., Yolande Finch, Becky Johnston

The Bee (10/93)
Warner Bros.
Prd/Dir/Scr., John Hughes
Distrib., Warner Bros.

Beresford Untitled (9/20/93)
Eastern Shore Prods.
Cast: *Richard Dreyfuss, John Lithgow, Linda Hamilton, J.T. Walsh, Liv Tyler, Ben Faulkner*
ExPrd., Gary Barber;, Prd., James G. Robinson; Dir., Bruce Beresford; Scr., Akiva Goldsman.

Betty Boop (Animated) (5/3/93)
The Zanuck Co./MGM
ExPrd., Richard D. Zanuck, Lili Fini Zanuck, Richard Fleisher; Prd., Jerry Rees, Steven Paul Leiva; Dir., Stephen Moore; Scr., Jerry Rees
Distrib., MGM

Beverly Hills Cop III (9/8/93)
Paramount Pictures
Cast: *Eddie Murphy, Theresa Randle*
ExPrd., Mark Lipsky; Prd., Mace Nuefeld, Robert Rehme; Dir., John Landis; Scr., Steven de Souza
Distrib., Paramount.

Billie's Song (8/30/93)
Billie Films Inc.
Cast: *Niki Harris, Bruce Willis*
ExPrd., J. David Williams; Prd., Gregory Marquette, Terry Carr; Dir/Scr., Gregory Marquette

Black Beauty (8/2/93)
Warner Bros.
Cast: *Sean Bean, David Thewlis, Andrew Knott, Jim Carter, Alan Armstrong, Elearnor Bron, Peter Cook, Peter Davison, John McEnery, Niall O'Brien*
Prd., Robert W. Shapiro; Dir/Scr., Caroline Thompson
Distrib., Warner Bros.

Blankman (9/14/93)
Columbia Pictures
Cast: *Damon Wayans, David Alan Grier, Robin Givens*
ExPrd., Damon Wayans; Prd., Eric Gold, Doc Erickson; Dir., Mike Binder; Scr., Damon Wayans, J.F. Lawton
Distrib., Columbia

Blown Away (8/23/93)
Trilogy Enter./MGM
Cast: *Jeff Bridges, Tommy Lee Jones,*

Lloyd Bridges, Forest Whitaker, Suzy Amis, Loyd Catlett, Caitlan Clarke, Ruben Santiago-Hudson
ExPrd., Lloyd Segan; Prd., John Watson, Richard Lewis, Pen Densham; Dir., Stephen Hopkins; Scr., Joe Batteer, John Rice
Distrib., MGM

Blue Chips (5/10/93)
Paramount Pictures
Cast: *Nick Nolte, Mary McDonnell, Shaquille O'Neal, Ed O'Neill, J.T. Walsh*
ExPrd., Wolfgang Glattes, Ron Shelton; Prd., Michelle Rappaport; Dir., William Friedkin; Scr., Ron Shelton
Distrib., Paramount.

The Browning Version (7/5/93)
Percy Main Prods.
Cast: *Albert Finney, Greta Scacchi, Matthew Modine, Ben Silverstone*
Prd., Ridley Scott, Mimi Polk; Dir., Mike Figgis; Scr., Ronald Harwood
Distrib., Paramount.

Cabin Boy (3/10/93)
Cabin Boy Productions
Cast: *Chris Elliott, Rich Brinkley, James Gammon, Brian Doyle Murray, Russ Tamblyn, Brion James, Ann Magnuson*
ExPrd., Steve White, Barry Bernardi; Prd., Denise DiNovi, Tim Burton; Dir/Scr., Adam Resnick

The Californians (Dev. for 94)
Red Hots Entertainment/ Parkway Prods.
Cast: *Liam Neeson*
ExPrd., Penny Marshall; CoPrd., Chip Miller; Dir., Ted Bessell; Scr., Chip Miller, Rex Maurice Oppenheimer

Camilla (4/19/93)
Camilla Films Inc.
Cast: *Jessica Tandy, Bridget Fonda, Elias Koteas, Maury Chaykin, Graham Greene, Howie Mandel, Hume Cronyn*
ExPrd., Jonathan Barker; Prd., Christina Jennings, Simon Relph; Dir., Deepe Mehta; Scr., Paul Quarrington

Canadian Bacon (10/29/93)
Manhattan Project/Maverick Film/Pro-paganda Films
Cast: *John Candy, Rhea Perlman, Alan Alda*
ExPrd., Freddie DeMann, Sigurjon Sighvatsson; Prd., David Brown, Ron Rotholz, Steve Golin, Michael Moore; Dir/Scr., Michael Moore

The Chase (7/20/93)
C.P.C. Prods., Inc.
Cast: *Charlie Sheen, Kristy Swanson, Henry Rollins, Josh Mostel, Claudia Christian, Rocky Carroll, Anthony Kiedis, Michael Balzary, Joe Segal*
ExPrd., Edward Sarlui., Prd., Cassian Elwes, Brad Wyman; Dir/Scr., Adam Rifkin
Distrib., 20th Century Fox.

Chasers (5/17/93)
Roadway Productions
Cast: *Tom Berenger, Erika Eleniak, William McNamara*
ExPrd., Gary Barber; Prd., James G. Robinson; Dir., Dennis Hopper; Scr., Joe Batteer, John Rice, Dan Gilroy, Joe Gayton
Distrib., Warner Bros.

City Slickers II: The Legend of Curly's Gold (8/3/93)
Castle Rock Entertainment
Cast: *Billy Crystal, Daniel Stern, Jon Lovitz, Jack Palance, David Paymer*
ExPrd., Peter Schindler; Prd., Billy Crystal; Dir., Paul Welland; Scr., Billy Crystal, Babaloo Mandel, Lowell Ganz
Distrib., Columbia

Clear and Present Danger (Oct. 5)
Neufeld-Rehme Prods.
Cast: *Harrison Ford, Anne Archer, James Earl Jones*
Prd., Mace Neufeld, Robert Rehme; Dir., Phillip Noyce; Scr., Donald E. Stewart
Distrib., Paramount.

The Client (7/6/93)
Client Prods.
Cast: *Susan Sarandon, Tommy Lee Jones, Anthony LaPaglia, Brad Renfro, Mary-Louise Parker*
Prd., Arnon Milchan, Steven Reuther; Dir., Joel Schumacher; Scr., Robert

Getchell, Akiva Goldsman
Distrib., Warner Bros.

Color Of Night (4/19/93)
Color of Night Prods.
Cast: *Bruce Willis, Jane March, Scott Bakula, Lesley Ann Warren, Lance Henriksen, Kevin J. O'Conner, Andrew Lowery, Ruben Blades, Brad Dourif*
Prd., Andy Vajna, David Matalon, Buzz Feitshans; Dir., Richard Rush; Scr., Billy Ray, Matthew Chapman
Distrib., Hollywood Pictures, Buena Vista

Conneticut Yankee in King Arthur's Court (Dev. for 94)
Warner Bros.
Prd., Jerry Weintraub; Dir., Terry Gilliam; Scr., Robert Kamen
Distrib., Warner Bros.

Cop Gives Waitress $2 Million Dollar Tip (8/2/93)
Cop Gives Waitress Prods. Inc.
Cast: *Nicolas Cage, Bridget Fonda, Rosie Perez, Red Buttons, Isaac Hayes, Seymour Cassel, Richard Jennings, Ann Dowd, Stanley Tucci, Wendell Pierce*
ExPrd., Craig Baumgarten, Gary Adelson, Joseph Hartwick; Prd., Mike Lobell; Dir., Andrew Bergman; Scr., Jane Anderson, Stephen Metcalf, Andrew Bergman
Distrib., TriStar.

Cop and Robbersons (3/8/93)
Dweezil Prods. Inc.
Cast: *Chevy Chase, Jack Palance, Dianne Wiest, Robert Davi, David Barry Gray, Fay Masterson*
Prd., Ned Tanen, Nancy Graham Tanen, Ronald L. Schwary; Dir., Michael Ritchie; Scr., Bernie Somers
Distrib., TriStar.

Corrina, Corrina (9/27/93)
Hughes Avenue Films
Cast: *Whoopi Goldberg, Ray Liotta*
ExPrd., Bernie Goldmann; Prd., Steve Tisch; Dir/Scr., Jesse Nelson

The Cowboy Way (9/9/93)
Imagine Films Entertainment
Cast: *Woody Harrelson, Kiefer Suth-*

erland, Dylan McDermott, Ernie Hudson, Cara Buono, Tomas Milian, Marg Heigenberger, Luis Guzman, Travis Tritt, Joaquin Martinez
Prd., Brian Grazer; Dir., Gregg Champion; Scr., William Witliffe, Joe Gayton
Distrib., Universal.

Crooklyn (6/30/93)
Crooklyn's In Da House, Inc.
Cast: *Alfre Woodard, Delroy Lindo*
ExPrd., John Kilik, Preston Holmes; Prd., Spike Lee; Dir., Spike Lee; Scr., Spike Lee
Distrib., Universal.

Dark Blood (9/21/93)
Fine Line Features/Scala Prods.
US Distrib: Fine Line Features
Cast: *River Phoenix, Judy Davis, Jonathan Pryce, Nik Powell, Stephen Wooley*
ExPrd., Nik Powell, Stephen Woolley; Prd., Joanne Sellar; Dir., George Sluizer; Scr., James Barton

Ed Wood (8/5/93)
Casual Pictures Inc.
Cast: *Johnny Depp, Martin Landau, Bill Murray, Jim Myers, Patricia Arquette, Sarah Jessica Parker, Jeffrey Jones, Lisa Marie , Vincent D'Onofrio*
ExPrd., Michael Lehmann; Prd., Denise DiNovi; Dir., Tim Burton; Scr., Scott Alexander, Larry Karaszewski
Distrib., Touchstone Pictures, Buena Vista

Exit to Eden (9/15/93)
Savoy Pictures Entertainment Inc./ Henderson Prods.
Cast: *Dana Delaney, Paul Mercurio, Rosie O'Donnell, Dan Aykroyd*
Prd., Alexandra Rose, Garry Marshall; Dir., Garry Marshall; Scr., Debrah Amelon
Dist: Savoy Pictures Enter.

Fair Game (9/93)
Silver Pictures
Cast: *Sylvester Stallone*
Prd., Joel Silver; Scr., Charlie Fletcher
Distrib., Warner Bros.

Fire Down Below (Dev. for 94)
Columbia Pictures/Peters Entertain-

ment Co.
Cast: *Steven Seagal*
Prd., Jon Peters, Steven Seagal; Scr., Jeb Stuart
Distrib., Columbia

The Flintstones (5/17/93)
Amblin Entertainment
Cast: *John Goodman, Rick Moranis, Elizabeth Perkins, Rosie O'Donnell, Kyle MacLachlan, Halle Berry, Elizabeth Taylor, Richard Moll, Irwin Keyes, Dann Florek, Melanie & Elaine Silver, Hlynur & Marino Sigurdsson*
ExPrd., Steven Spielberg, Kathleen Kennedy, Gerald R. Molen, Bill Hanna, Joseph Barbera, David Kirshner; Prd., Bruce Cohen; Dir., Brian Levant
Distrib., Universal.

Forrest Gump (8/27/93)
Paramount Pictures
Cast: *Tom Hanks, Sally Field, Gary Sinise, Robin Wright, Mykelti Williamson*
Prd., Steve Starkey, Steve Tisch, Wendy Fineman; Dir., Robert Zemeckis, Scr., Eric Roth
Distrib., Paramount.

F.T.W. (8/9/93)
Big Truck Prods.,
Cast: *Mickey Rourke, Lori Singer, Aaron Neville, Charlie Sexton, John Enos, Stella Stevens, Rodney Grant*
ExPrd., Ron Altbach, Avi Lerner, Danny Dimbort; Prd., Tom Mickel; Dir., Michael Karbeinikoff; Scr., Mari Komhauser

Galatea (8/93)
Scala Prods./Balthazar Pictures
Cast: *Val Kilmer, Virginia Madsen, Christopher Walken*
Prd., Stephen Woolley, Kerry Boyle, Janet Jacobson; Dir., Julien Temple; Scr., John Kamps, Mark Horowitz

The Getaway (4/5/93)
Largo Entertainment/Turman-Foster Co./Discovery Prod.
Cast: *Alec Baldwin, Kim Basinger, Michael Madsen, James Woods*
Prd., David Foster, Lawrence Turman, John Alan Simon; Dir., Roger Donaldson; Scr., Walter Hill

Distrib., Buena Vista

Getting Even With Dad (7/8/93)
MGM/Jacobs/Gardner Prods.
Cast: *Macaulay Culkin, Ted Danson, Glenne Headly, Saul Rubinek, Gailard Sartain, Sam McMurray, Katherine Wilhoit*
ExPrd., Richard Hashimoto; Prd., Katie Jacobs, Pierce Gardner; Dir., Howard Deutch; Scr., Tom S. Parker, Jim Jennewein
Distrib., MGM

Greedy (6/21/93)
Imagine Films Entertainment
Cast: *Michael J. Fox, Kirk Douglas, Nancy Travis, Olivia d'Abo, Bob Balaban, Ed Begley Jr., Jere Burns, Colleen Camp, Slobhan Fallon, Phil Hartman, Joyce Hyser, Mary Ellen Trainor*
ExPrd., David Friendly, George Folsey Jr.; Prd., Brian Grazer; Dir., Jonathan Lynn; Scr., Lowell Ganz, Babaloo Mandel
Distrib., Universal.

The High Crusade (6/6/93)
Overseas Film Group
Cast: *John Rhys-Davies, Rick Overton, Patrick Brymer, Debbie Lee Carrington, Michael Des Barres*
ExPrd., Roland Emmerich; Prd., Ute Emmerich, Jakob Claussen, Thomas Woebke; Dir., Holger Neuhauser, Klaus Knoesel; Scr., Robert Gerard Brown, River Pegnitz
Distrib., Overseas Film Group

Highlander III (9/93)
Davis/Panzer Prods.
Cast: *Christopher Lambert*
Prd., Peter Davis, William Panzer; Dir., Andrew Morahan

Him (Working Title) (8/30/93)
Fried/Woods Films/TriStar Pictures
Cast: *Marisa Tomei, Robert Downey Jr., Bonnie Hunt, Fisher Stevens*
Prd., Rob Fried, Cary Woods, Norman Jewison, Chuck Mulvehill; Dir., Norman Jewison; Scr., Diane Drake

Holy Matrimony (7/19/93)
Colony Inc.
Cast: *Patricia Arquette, Joseph Gordon-Levitt, Lois Smith, John Schuck, Tate Donovan*
ExPrd., Ted Field, Robert W. Cort; Prd., William Stuart, David Madden, Diane Nabatoff; Dir., Leonard Nimoy; Scr., Douglas S. Cook, David Weisberg, Gina Wendkos
Distrib., Buena Vista

I Love Trouble (10/4/93)
Touchstone Pictures/Caravan Pictures
Cast: *Julia Roberts, Nick Nolte*
ExPrd., Joe Roth, Roger Birnbaum; Prd., Nancy Meyers; Dir., Charles Shyer; Scr., Charles Shyer, Nancy Meyers
Distrib., Touchstone Pictures, Buena Vista

Interview with the Vampire (10/18/93)
Geffen Pictures/ Warner Bros.
Cast: *Tom Cruise, Brad Pitt, Antonio Banderas, Stephen Rea, River Phoenix, Miranda Richardson*
Prd., David Geffen, Stephen Woolley; Dir., Neil Jordan; Scr., Anne Rice, Neil Jordan
Distrib., Warner Bros.

In the Mouth of Madness (8/23/93)
New Line
Cast: *Sam Neill, Julie Carmen, Jurgen Prochnow, Charlton Heston*
Prd., Sandy King; Dir., John Carpenter; Scr., Michael De Luca, Desmond Caters
Distrib., New Line

It's Pat (8/2/93)
Ruth and Barbara's Film Inc.
Cast: *Julia Sweeney, Dave Foley, Charles Rocket, Harvey Keitel, Kathy Griffin, Julie Hayden, Tim Meadows, Arleen Sorkin*
ExPrd., Teri Schwartz; Prd., Charles Wessler; Dir., Adam Bernstein; Scr., Jim Emerson, Stephen Hibbert, Julia Sweeney
Distrib., Touchstone Pictures, Buena Vista

Jason's Lyric (9/22/93)
Jackson-McHenry Prods.
Cast: *Forest Whitaker, Allen Payne, Jada Pinkett, Bokeem Woodbine, Treach*
ExPrd., Clarence Avant, Suzanne Broderick; Prd., George Jackson, Doug McHenry; Dir., Doug McHenry; Scr., Bobby Smith Jr.

Jefferson In Paris (Dev. for 94)
Merchant Ivory Prods.
Cast: *Greta Scacchi*
Prd., Ismail Merchant; Dir., James Ivory; Scr., Ruth Prawer Jhabvala
Distrib., Buena Vista

Judge Dredd (2/1/94)
Cinergi Prods./Edward R. Pressman Prods.
Cast: *Sylvester Stallone*
Prd., Andy Vajna, Edward R. Pressman, Charles Lipincott; Dir., Danny Dannon; Scr., William Wisher
Distrib., Buena Vista

The Lane Frost Story (5/1/93)
Jersey Films/ New Line Cinema
Cast: *Luke Perry, Cynthia Geary, Stephen Baldwin, James Rebhorn*
ExPrd., Danny DeVito, Cyd Levin, Jeffrey Swab; Prd., Michael Shamberg; Dir., John G. Avildsen; Scr., Monte Merrick, Larry Brothers

Legends of the Fall (6/14/93)
TriStar Pictures
Cast: *Brad Pitt, Anthony Hopkins, Aldan Quinn, Julia Ormond, Henry Thomas, Karina Lombard*
ExPrd., Patrick Crowley; Prd., Edward Zwick, William Wittliff, Marshall Herskovitz; Dir., Edward Zwick; Scr., William Wittliff, Susan Shilliday
Distrib., TriStar.

Leon (6/10/93)
Les Films du Dauphin/Gaumont
Cast: *Gary Oldman, Jeanne Reneau*
Prd., Luc Besson; Dir/Scr., Luc Besson
Distrib., Columbia

Lightning Jack (8/7/93)
Lightning Ridge Prods.
Cast: *Paul Hogan, Cuba Gooding Jr., Beverly D'Angelo, Pat Hingle, Kamaia Dawson, Richard Richle, Karen Austin, Frank McRae, L.Q. Jones*
ExPrd., Paul Hogan, Graham Burke; Prd., Simon Wincer, Greg Coote; Dir., Simon Wincer; Scr., Paul Hogan

The Lion King (Animated) (6/15/93)
Walt Disney Pictures
ExPrd., Tom Schumacher, Sarah McArthur; Prd., Don Hahn; Dir., Roger Allers, Rob Minkoff; Scr., Irene Mecchi, Jonathan Roberts
Distrib., Walt Disney, Buena Vista.

Little Big League (8/23/93)
Castle Rock Enter. in assn. with Lobell/Bergman Prods.
Cast *Jonathan Silverman, Brad Johnson, Scott Patterson, Jason Robards, Luke Edwards, Timothy Busfield, John Ashton, Ashley Crow, Dennis Farina, Billy L. Sullivan, Miles Feulner*
ExPrd., Andrew Bergman; Prd., Mike Lobell; Dir., Andy Scheinman; Scr., Gregory Pincus, Adam Schelnman
Distrib., Columbia

Love Affair (Working Title) (8/11/93)
Warner Bros.
Cast: *Warren Beatty, Annette Bening, Kate Capshaw, Paul Mazursky, Brenda Vaccaro, Garry Shandling, Pierce Brosnan*
Prd., Warren Beatty; Dir., Glenn Gordon Caron; Scr., Robert Towne
Distrib., Warner Bros.

Love is a Gun (8/23/93)
Trimark Pictures
Cast: *Eric Roberts, Kelly Preston, Eliza Roberts, Joe Sirole*
Prd., Jonathan Krane, Kaniel Berk; Dir/Scr., David Hartwell
Distrib., Trimark

Low Fives (Dev. for 94)
Jersey Films
Cast: *Danny DeVito*
Prd., Danny DeVito, Michael Shamberg; Scr., William Goldman
Distrib., TriStar.

Lying in Wait (6/28/93)
Republic Pictures in Assn. with Magic

Hour Prod.
Cast: *Brian Dennehy, JoBeth Williams*
ExPrd., Laurie Levit; Prd., Jay Benson; Dir., Eric Till; Scr., Phil Rosenberg

Major League II (9/14/93)
Home Run Prods.
Cast: *Tom Berenger, Charlie Sheen, Corbin Bernsen, James Gammon, Dennis Haysbert, Omar Epps, David Keith, Margaret Whitten*
ExPrd., Gary Barber; Prd., James G. Robinson, David Ward; Dir., David Ward; Scr., R.J. Stewart
Distrib., Warner Bros.

Mary Shelley's Frankenstein (10/93)
Zoetrope/TriStar
Cast: *Kenneth Branagh, Robert De Niro, Helena Bonham-Carter*
ExPrd., Fred Fuchs; Prd., Francis Ford Coppola, James V. Hart, John Veitch; Dir., Kenneth Branagh; Scr., Frank Darabont
Distrib., TriStar.

The Mask (8/93)
New Line Cinema
Cast: *Jim Carrey, Richard Jeni, Richard Greene*
ExPrd., Mike Richardson; Dir., Chuck Russell; Scr., Michael Werb

Maverick (8/16/93)
Garthorpe Inc.
Cast: *Mel Gibson, James Garner, Jodie Foster, Graham Greene, Linda Hunt, James Coburn, Alfred Molina, Margot Kidder*
ExPrd., Bruce Davey; Dir., Richard Donner; Scr., William Goldman
Distrib., Warner Bros.

Mesmer (8/8/93)
Levergreen Ltd., Accent Enter.
Cast: *Alan Rickman, Gillian Barge, Simon McBurney, Amanda Ooms*
ExPrd., David Bowie; Prd., Lance Reynolds, Wieland Schulz-Keil, Robert F. Goodale; Dir., Roger Spottiswoode; Scr., Dennis Potter
Distrib., Mayfair Entertainment

The Mighty Ducks II (7/7/93)
Bombay Films Inc.
Cast: *Emilio Estevez, Kathryn Erbe,*

Jan Rubes, Michael Tucker, Brandon Adams, Matt Doherty, Garette Ratliff Henson, Josh Jackson, Colombe Jacobsen, Vincent La Russo
ExPrd., Doug Claybourne; Prd., Jordan Kemer, Jon Avnet; Dir., Sam Weisman; Scr., Steven Brill
Distrib., Buena Vista

Milk Money (8/9/93)
The Kennedy/Marshall Co. Paramount Pictures
Cast: *Melanie Griffith, Ed Harris, Malcolm McDowell, Michael Patrick Carter, Brian Christopher, Adam La Vorgna, Casey Siemaszko, Anne Heche, Kevin Scannell, Kati Powell, Margaret Nagle*
ExPrd., Patrick Palmer; Prd., Kathleen Kennedy, Frank Marshall; Dir., Richard Benjamin; Scr., John Mattson
Distrib., Paramount.

Mirror Image (5/11/93)
Ugly Sisters Productions Inc.
Cast: *Gary Busey, Kim Cattrall*
ExPrd., Gary Delfiner, Avi Lerner, Michael Strange; Prd., Robert Vince, William Vince; Dir., Paul Ziller; Scr., Michael Berlin, Eric Estrin
Distrib., Worldvision.

Morgan Parker (9/93)
Michaelangelo Prods. Inc.
Cast: *Scott Baio, Martin Kove, Mike Connors, Michael Horse, Chris Compton, Tom Tayback*
Prd., Fritz Manes; Line Prd., James Etter; Dir., William Gereghty; Scr., Camille Fadia

Mrs. Parker & the Round Table (6/12/93)
Fine Line Features
US Dist: Fine Line
Cast: *Jennifer Jason Leigh, Campbell Scott, Matthew Broderick, Andrew McCarthy, Tom McGowan, Nick Cassavetes, James LeGross, Jake Johhannsen*
ExPrd., Scott Bushnell; Prd., Robert Altman; Dir., Alan Rudolph; Scr., Alan Rudolph, Randy Sue Coburn

My Father The Hero (6/2/93)
Father Prods., Inc.
Cast: *Gerard Depardieu, Katherine Heigi, Dalton James, Faith Prince, Lauren Hutton*
ExPrd., Edward S. Feldman; Prd., Jean-Louis Livi, Jacques Bar; Dir., Steve Miner; Scr., Francis Veber
Distrib., Buena Vista

My Girl II (6/14/93)
Columbia Pictures
Cast: *Anna Chlumsky, Dan Aykroyd, Jamie Lee Curtis, Austin O'Brien, Richard Masur, Christine Ebersole, Angeline Ball, J.D. Souther, Aubrey Morris, Gerrit Graham*
ExPrd., Joe Caracciolo Jr., David Friendly; Prd., Brian Grazer; Dir., Howard A. Zieff; Scr., Janet Kovaicik
Distrib., Columbia

My Summer Story (8/2/93)
MGM
Cast: *Charles Grodin, Kieran Culkin, Mary Steenburgen*
Prd., Rene DuPont; Dir., Bob Clark; Scr., Jean Shepherd, Leigh Brown, Bob Clark
Distrib., MGM

Murder in the First (11/15/93)
Hexagon Films
Cast: *Christian Slater, Kevin Bacon*
ExPrd., David L. Wolper; Prd., Marc Frydman, Mark Wolper; Dir., Marc Rocco; Scr., Dan Gordon
Distrib., Warner Bros.

Naked Gun 33 1/3: The Final Insult (8/9/93)
Zucker Bros. Prods./Paramount Pic.
Cast: *Leslie Nielsen, Priscilla Presley, George Kennedy, O.J. Simpson*
ExPrd., Jerry Zucker, Jim Abrahams, Gil Netter; Prd., David Zucker, Robert K. Weiss; Dir., Peter Segal; Scr., Pat Proft
Distrib., Paramount.

National Lampoon's Scuba School (5/26/93)
Rose & Ruby Prods.
Cast: *Corey Feldman, Corey Haim*
ExPrd., Ashok Amritraj, Jim Jimmaro; Prd./Dir., Damian Lee; Scr., Damian Lee, Patrick Labyorteaux

Natural Born Killers (5/25/93)
NBK Inc./LeStudio Canal Plus/Alcor Films Prods.
Cast: *Woody Harrelson, Robert Downey Jr., Juliette Lewis, Tommy Lee Jones, Tom Sizemore, Rodney Dangerfield, Ashley Judd, Rachel Ticotin, Arliss Howard, Steven Wright, Denis Leary*
ExPrd., Arnon Milchan, Oliver Stone, Thom Mount; Prod., Jane Hamsher, Don Murphy, Clayton Townsend; Dir., Oliver Stone; Scr., Quentin Tarantino
Distrib., Warner Bros.

The Neverending Story III (8/9/93)
CineVox Entertainment/NES III Prod.
Cast: *Jason James Richter*
Prd., Dieter Geissler, Tim Hampton; Dir., Peter MacDonald; Scr., Jeff Lieberman

The Next Karate Kid (6/26/93)
Jerry Weintraub Prods.
Cast: *Pat Morita, Hillary Swank*
ExPrd., R.J. Louis; Prd., Jerry Weintraub; Dir., Chris Cain; Scr., Mark Lee
Distrib., Columbia

The Night and the Moment (10/20/93)
Arthur Pictures Ltd.
Cast: *Willem Dafoe, Lena Olin, Miranda Richardson*
ExPrd., Philippe Martinez, Ernst Goldschmidt; Prd., Pierre Novat; Dir., Anna Maria Tato; Scr., Jean-Claude Carriere, Ana Maria Tato

Nobody's Fool (11/93)
Paramount Pictures/Scott Rudin Prod.
Cast: *Paul Newman*
CoPrd., Scott Rudin, Arlene Donovan, Michael Hausman; Dir/Scr., Robert Benton
Distrib., Paramount.

North (5/4/93)
Castle Rock Entertainment
Cast: Elijah Wood, Bruce Willis, Jon Lovitz, Julia Louis-Dreyfus, Jason Alexander, Kathy Bates
ExPrd., Jeffrey Stott; Prd., Rob Reiner, Alan Zweibel; Dir., Rob Reiner; Scr., Alan Zeibel, Andrew Scheinman

Distrib., Columbia

On Deadly Ground (5/18/93)
Seagal-Nasso Prods.
Cast: *Steven Seagal, Michael Caine, Joan Chen, John C. McGinley*
ExPrd., Robert Watts; Prd., Steven Seagal, Julius R. Nasso, A. Kitman Ho; Dir., Steven Seagal; Scr., Ed Horowitz, Robin Ruscin, David Goyer, Chris Gerolmo, Mitchell Kapner
Distrib., Warner Bros.

One Night Stand (7/12/93)
New Horizons/New World
Cast: *Ally Sheedy, A. Martinez, Frederic Forrest, Don Novello*
ExPrd., Jack Schwartzman, Roger Corman; Prd., Alida Camp; Dir., Talia Shire; Scr., Marty Casella

Our Father (Dev. for 94)
Prelude Pictures/ Frostbacks Prods.
Cast: *John Candy*
Scr., Gene Quintano
Distrib., TriStar.

The Pagemaster (Animated)
9/21/92
Voices: *Macaulay Culkin, Christopher Lloyd, Whoopi Goldberg, Patrick Stewart, Leonard Nimoy, Charles Fleischer, Phil Hartman, Frank Welker, George Hearn, Robert Picardo*
Prd., David Kirchner, Michael R. Joyce; Dir., Joe Johnston; Scr., David Kirschner, Ernie Contreras; Anim. Dir., Maurice Hunt
Distrib., 20th Century Fox.

The Paper (7/19/93)
Imagine Films Entertainment
Cast: *Michael Keaton, Glenn Close, Marisa Tomei, Randy Quaid, Robert Duvall*
ExPrd., Todd Hallowell, Dylan Sellers; Prd., Brian Grazer, Frederick Zollo; Dir., Ron Howard; Scr., David Koepp, Stephen Koepp
Distrib., Universal.

The Penal Colony (5/17/93)
Platinum Pictures Pty. Ltd.
US Dist: Savoy Pic. Entertainment
Cast: *Ray Liotta, Lance Henriksen, Stuart Wilson, Kevin Dillon, Ernie*

Hudson, Michael Lerner, Kevin J. O'Conner, Ian McNiece, Brian Logan, Cheuk Fal Chan, Don Henderson, Jack Shepherd
ExPrd., Jake Eberts; Prd., Gale Anne Hurd; Dir., Martin Campbell; Scr., Michael Gaylin, Joel Gross

The Pebble and the Penquin (Animated) (4/15/93)
Voices: *Martin Short, Jim Belushi, Tim Curry, Annie Golden*
Prd.;, Don Bluth, Gary Goldman; Dir., Don Bluth, Gary Goldman; Scr., Rachel Koretsky, Steven Whitestone

Pet (5/18/93)
Percy Main Prods.
US Dist: New Line Pictures
Cast: *Thora Birch, Harvey Keitel, Mimi Rogers, Christopher McDonald*
ExPrd., Ridley Scott; Prod., Mimi Polk Sotela, Heidi Rufus Isaacs; Dir., Franco Amurri; Scr., Franco Amurri, Stu Kreiger

Pet People (Dev. for 94)
Amblin Entertainment
Prd., Steven Spielberg; Dir., Diane Keaton; Scr., Alice Hoffman
Distrib., Warner Bros.

Police Academy VI: Mission to Moscow (9/13/93)
Warner Bros.
Cast: *George Gaynes, Leslie Easterbrook, David Graf, Michael Winslow, G.W. Balley, Christopher Lee, Ron Perlman, Charlie Schlatter, Claire Foriani, Gregg Berger*
Prd., Paul Maslansky; Dir., Alan Metter; Scr., Randolph Davis, Michele Chodos
Distrib., Warner Bros.

Princess Caraboo (9/13/93)
Beacon Pictures/Longfellow Pictures/ Artisan Films
Cast: *Phoebe Cates, Kevin Kline, Wendy Hughes, Stephen Rea, John Malkovich, John Lithgow, Jerry Hall, John Wells*
ExPrd., Armyan Bernstein, Tom Rosenberg, Marc Abraham; Prd., Andrew Karsch, Simon Bosenquet; Dir., Michael Austin; Scr., Michael Austin, John Wells

Pulp Fiction (9/93)
Jersey Films
Cast: *John Travolta, Samuel L. Jackson, Uma Thurman, Harvey Keitel, Tim Roth, Amanda Plummer, Maria De Madelros, Ving Rhames, Bruce Willis*
ExPrd., Danny DeVito, Stacey Sher, Michael Shamberg; Prod., Lawrence Bender; Dir/Scr., Quentin Tarantino,

The Quick and the Dead (11/93)
TriStar Pictures/Indie Prod. Co.
Cast: *Sharon Stone*
Prd., Dan Melnick, Josh Donen, Sam Raimi, Robert Tapert; Dir., Sam Raimi., Scr., Simon Moore
Distrib., TriStar.

Quiz Show (5/27/93)
The Quiz Show Co.
Cast: *John Turturro, Rob Morrow, Ralph Fiennes, David Paymer, Hank Azaria, Christopher McDonald*
ExPrd., Frederick Zollo, Richard Dreyfuss, Judith James; Prd., Michael Jacobs, Julian Krainin, Michael Nozik; Dir., Robert Redford; Scr., Paul Attanasio
Distrib., Hollywood Pictures, Buena Vista

Reality Bites (6/16/93)
Jersey Films
Cast: *Winona Ryder, Ethan Hawke, Janeane Garofalo, Steve Zahn, Ben Stiller, Joe Don Baker, Swoosie Kurtz*
ExPrd., Clay Malcom, Stacey Sher; Prd., Michael Shamberg, Danny DeVito; Dir., Ben Stiller; Scr., Helen Childress
Distrib., Universal.

The Ref (6/23/93)
The Old Saybrook Co. Inc.
Cast: *Denis Leary, Judy Davis, Kevin Spacey, Glynis Johns, Raymond J. Barry, Robert Steinmiller, Christine Baranski, Richard Bright*
ExPrd., Don Simpson, Jerry Bruckheimer; Prd., Richard LaGravenese, Jeff Weiss, Ron Bozman; Dir., Ted Demme; Scr., Richard LaGravenese, Marie Weiss
Distrib., Buena Vista

Renaissance Man (9/10/93)
Cinergi Prods.
Cast: *Danny DeVito, Marky Mark, Stacey Dash, Gregory Hines, Ed Begley Jr., James Remar, Stacey Dash, Kadeem Hardison, Richard T. Jones, Kahill Kain, Greg Sporleder, Peter Simmons*
Prd., Penny Marshall, Sara Colleton, Elliot Abbott, Robert Greenhut; Dir., Penny Marshall; Scr., Jim Burnstein
Distrib., Buena Vista

Richie Rich (Dev. for 94)
Silver Pictures In assn. with Davis Entertainment
Cast: *Macaulay Culkin*
ExPrd., Jon Shapiro, Joe Bilella; Prd., Joel Silver, John Davis; Scr., Jim Jennewein, Tom S. Parker
Distrib., Warner Bros.

Rita Hayworth & Shawshank Redemption (6/16/93)
Castle Rock Pictures Inc.
Cast: *Tim Robbins, Morgan Freeman, Bob Gunton, William Sadler, Clancy Brown, Gil Bellows, James Whitmore*
ExPrd., Liz Glotzer, David Lester; Prd., Niki Marvin; Dir/Scr., Frank Darabont
Distrib., Columbia.

The River Wild (7/25/93)
Universal Pictures
Cast: *Meryl Streep, David Strathairn, Kevin Bacon, Joseph Mazzello, John C. Riley*
Prd., David Foster, Lawrence Turman; Dir., Curtis Hanson; Scr., Dennis O'Neill, Raynold Gideon, Bruce Evans
Distrib., Universal.

Road Flower (5/10/93)
Silver Lion Films
Cast: *Christopher Lambert, David Arquette, Joseph Gordon-Levitt, Adrienne Shelly, Craig Sheffer, Michele Forbes, Josh Brolin, Christopher McDonald, Alexandra Lee, John Pyper-Ferguson*
ExPrd., Conrad Hool; Prod., Lance Hool, John Flock; Dir, Deran Sarafian; Scr., Tedi Sarafian

Serial Mom (4/12/93)
Blizzard Film Inc. Prods.
Cast: *Kathleen Turner, Sam Waterston, Rickie Lake*
ExPrd., Joe Caracciolo Jr.; Prd., John Fiedler, Mark Tarlov; Dir./Scr., John Waters

The Seventh Floor (6/23/93)
Rutherford Films Holdings
Cast: *Brooke Shields, Masayo Kato, Linda Cropper, Craig Pearce*
ExPrd., Victor Glynn, Susumu Kondo, Yoshinori Watanabe, Alan Bateman; Prod., Chris Brown, Hiroyuki Ikeda, John Sexton; Dir., Ian Barry; Scr., Tony Morphett

The Shadow (9/27/93)
Bregman/Baer Prods./Universal Pictures
Cast: *Alec Baldwin, John Lone, Penelope Ann Miller, Peter Boyle, Tim Curry, Ian Mckellen, Jonathan Winters*
ExPrd., Louis Stroller, Ortwin Freyermuth; Prd., Martin Bregman, Willy Baer, Michael Bregman; Dir., Russell Mulcahy; Scr., David Koepp
Distrib., Universal.

Shadowlands (4/23/93)
Shadowlands Productions
Cast: *Anthony Hopkins, Debra Winger*
ExPrd., Terence Clegg; Prod., Brian Eastman, Richard Attenborough; Dir., Richard Attenborough; Scr., William Nicholson
Distrib., Savoy Pictures.

Shattered Image (5/3/93)
Rysher Productions
Cast: *Jack Scalla, Bo Derek, John Savage, Dorian Haywood, David McCallum, Carol Lawrence, Ramon Franco, Michael Harris*
ExPrd., Keith Samples, William Hart; Prd., Bruce Cohn Curtis, Dir., Fritz Kiersch; Scr., William Delligan
Distrib., Savoy Pictures

Significant Other (5/17/93)
Avnet/Kerner Co.
Cast: *Andy Garcia, Meg Ryan, Tina Majorino, Mae Whitman, Lauren Tom, Al Franken, Ellen Burstyn*
Prd., Jon Avnet, Jordan Kerner; Dir., Luis Mandoki; Scr., Ronald Bass, Al

Franken, Susan Shilliday
Distrib., Touchstone Pictures, Buena Vista

Sleep With Me (8/16/93)
Sleep With Me Prods.
Cast: *Eric Stoltz, Meg Tilly, Craig Scheffer, Todd Field, Susan Taylor, Thomas Gibson, Dean Cameron, Tegan West, Amaryills Borrego*
ExPrd., Joel Castleberg., Prd., Michael Steinberg, Roger Hedden, Eric Stoltz; Dir., Rory Kelly; Scr., Roger Hedden, Neal Jimenez, Rory Kelly.

Snowballs (Animated) (3/15/93)
Amblimation/ Universal Pictures
ExPrd., Steven Spielberg, Kathleen Kennedy; Prd., Steven Hickner; Dir., Simon Wells
Distrib., Universal.

Speed (9/7/93)
Twentieth Century Fox
Cast: *Keanu Reeves, Sandra Bullock, Jeff Daniels, Joe Morton*
ExPrd., Ian Bryce; Prd., Mark Gordon; Dir., Jan De Bont; Scr., Graham Yost
Distrib., 20th Century Fox.

Stargate (9/13/93)
Hexagon Films/Centropolis in assn with Carolco Pictures
Cast: *Kurt Russell, James Spader*
ExPrd., Mario Kassar; LinePrd., Ramsey Thomas; Dir., Roland Emmerich; Scr., Dean Devlin, Roland Emmerich

Surviving the Game (8/16/93)
New Line Cinema/Permut Pres. Inc.
US Dist: New Line Cinema
Cast: *Rutger Hauer, Ice-T, Charles Dutton, John C. McGinley, William McNamara, Jeff Corey, Gary Busey, F. Murray Abraham*
Prd., David Permut, Kevin Messick; Dir., Ernest Dickerson; Scr., Eric Bernt
Distrib., New Line

Tall Tale (9/12/93)
Caravan Pictures
Cast: *Scott Glenn, Oliver Platt, Nick Stahl, Patrick Swayze, Aaron Brown, Catherine O'Hara, Stephen Lang, Jared Harris, William H. Macy, Moira Harris*

ExPrd., Tom Schulman; Prd., Joe Roth, Roger Birnbaum; Dir., Jeremiah Chechik; Scr., Steven Bloom, Robert Rodat
Distrib., Buena Vista

Teresa's Tattoo (7/15/93)
CineTel Films Inc.
US Dist: Trimark Pictures
Cast: *Adrienne Shelly, C. Thomas Howell, Nancy McKeon, Lou Diamond Phillips, Casey Siemaszko, Jonathan Silverman*
ExPrd., Paul Hertzberg, Marc Rocco; Prd., Philip McKeon, Lisa Hansen; Dir., Julie Cypher; Scr., Georgie Huntington

Terminal Velocity (12/93)
Interscope Communications/Hollywood Pictures
Cast: *Charlie Sheen*
ExPrd., Ted Field, David Twohy, Robert Cort; Prd., Scott Kroopf, Tom Engelman; Dir., Deran Sarafian; Scr., David Twohy
Distrib., Hollywood Pictures, Buena Vista

30 Wishes (Dev. for 94)
Universal Pictures/Snowback Prods.
Cast: *Michael J. Fox*
Prd., Matthew Tolmach; Dir., Michael J. Fox; Scr., Elisa Bell
Distrib., Universal.

Thumbelina (Animated) 2/1/91)
Don Bluth Ireland Ltd.
Voices: *Jodi Benson, Carol Channing, Gino Confortl, Barbara Cook, June Foray, Gilbert Gottfried, John Hurt, Gary Imhoff, Kenneth Mars, Charo*
Prd., Don Bluth, Gary Goldman, John Pomeroy; Dir., Don Bluth, Gary Goldman; Scr., Don Bluth, Kevin Gollaher, Rowland Wilson, Mark Swan

Time Cop (9/12/93)
Largo Entertainment/Signature Entertainment Group/Raimi/Tapert/Dark Horse
Cast: *Jean-Claude Van Damme, Ron Silver, Mia Sara, Gloria Reuben, Bruce McGill, Jason Schombing*
ExPrd., Mike Richardson; Prd., Moshe Diamant, Robert Tapert, Sam

Raimi; Dir., Peter Hyams; Scr., Mark Verheiden
Distrib., Universal.

Tom and Viv (7/11/93)
New Era Entertainment/I.R.S. Media Inc.
US Dist: I.R.S. Releasing Inc.
Cast: *Willem Dafoe, Miranda Richardson, Tim Dutton, Nickolas Grace, Clare Holman, Rosemary Harris, Philip Locke, Hugh Simon, Roberta Taylor, Joseph O'Conor*
ExPrd., Paul Colichman, Miles Copeland; Prd., Marc Samuelson, Peter Samuelson, Harvey Kass; Dir., Brian Gilbert; Scr., Adrian Hodges, Michael Hastings

Tombstone (5/17/93)
Cinergi Prods.
Cast: *Kurt Russell, Val Kilmer, Charlton Heston, Dana Delaney, Sam Elliott, Bill Paxton, Powers Boothe, Michael Blehn, Stephen Lang, Michael Rooker, Jason Priestley, Jon Tenney*
Prd., Jim Jacks, Sean Daniel, Bob Misiorowski; Dir., George Cosmatos; Scr., Kevin Jarre
Distrib., Buena Vista

The Tool Shed (8/12/93)
Tool Shed Prods./Jazz Pictures
Cast: *Larry Fishburne, Ellen Barkin, Frank Langella, David Ogden Stiers, Michael Beach, Spalding Gray, Michael Murphy, Gia Carides, B.D. Wong*
Prd., Amedeo Ursini, Jeffrey Chernov; Dir., Damian Harris; Scr., Ross Thomas
Distrib., Buena Vista

Totally London (Dev. for 94)
Hollywood Pictures
Cast: *Pauly Shore*
Prd., Bob Beitcher, Brad Weston, Michael Rotenberg; Scr., Ryan Rowe
Distrib., Hollywood Pictures, Buena Vista

Trial By Jury (8/3/93)
TBJ Prods. Inc.
Cast: *Joanne Whalley-Kilmer, William Hurt, Armand Assante, Gabriel Byrne*
ExPrd., Gary Barber; Prd., James G.

Robinson, Mark Gordon, Chris Meledandri; Dir., Heywood Gould; Scr., Jordan Katz, Heywood Gould Distrib., Warner Bros.

True Lies (8/25/93)
Lightstorm Entertainment
Cast: *Arnold Schwarzenegger, Jamie Lee Curtis, Tom Arnold,Bill Paxton, Eliza Dushku, Grant Heslou, Art Malik, Karina Lombard*
ExPrd., Bobby Shriver, Rae Sanchini; Prd., James Cameron, Stephanie Austin; Dir/Scr., James Cameron
Distrib., 20th Century Fox.

Twist of Fate (Dev. for 94)
Touchstone Pictures
Cast: *Steve Martin*
Dir., Gilles Mackinnon; Scr., Steve Martin
Distrib., Touchstone Pictures, Buena Vista

Two Bits (7/26/93)
Arthur Cohn Prods.
Dist: Capella Intl.
Cast: *Al Pacino, Mary Elizabeth Mastrantonio, Gerlando Barone, Patrick Borriello, Andy Romano*
ExPrd., Joseph Stefano, Willy Baer, David Korda; Prd., Arthur Cohn; Dir., James Foley; Scr., Joseph Stefano

Untitled Barry Levinson (8/15/93)
Baltimore Pictures
Cast: *Joe Pesci, Christian Slater, Victoria Abril*
Prd., Mark Johnson; Dir/Scr., Barry Levinson
Distrib., Paramount.

Vampire in Brooklyn
(Dev. for 94)
Eddie Murphy Productions
Cast: *Eddie Murphy, Charles Murphy*
Prd., Eddie Murphy; Dir., Wes Craven; Scr., Eddie Murphy, Charles Murphy
Distrib., Paramount

The War (8/19/93)
Avnet/Kerner Co., Island, World Group Pictures, Pipeline
Cast: *Elijah Wood, Kevin Costner,Mare Winningham, Lexi Randall*

ExPrd., Eric Eisner, Todd Baker; Prd., Jon Avnet, Jordan Kerner; Dir., Jon Avnet; Scr., Kathy McWorter
Distrib., Universal.

White Fang II - The Myth of the White Wolf (7/19/93)
Walt Disney Pictures
Cast: *Scott Bairstow, Charmaine Craig, Al Harrington, Victoria Racimo, Alfred Molina, Paul Coeur*
Prd., Preston Fischer; Dir., Ken Olin; Scr., David Fallon
Distrib., Walt Disney, Buena Vista

Widow's Peak (7/19/93)
Jo Manuel Prods. in assn. with The Production Center
US Dist: Fine Line Features
Cast: *Mia Farrow, Joan Plowright, Natasha Richardson, Adrian Dunbar, Jim Broadbent*
ExPrd., Michael White; Prd., Jo Manuel; Dir., John Irvin; Scr., Hugh Leonard

Without a Word (Dev. for 94)
Pelemele Pictures/Troph Prods.
Cast: *Patrick Swayze, Lisa Niemi*
Dir., Percy Adlon; Scr., Lisa Niemi

Wolf (4/7/93)
Red Wagon Prods
Cast: *Jack Nicholson, Michelle Pfeiffer, James Spader, Kate Nelligan*
ExPrd., Robert Greenhut, Neil Machlis; Prd., Douglas Wick; Dir., Mike Nichols; Scr., Jim Harrison
Distrib., Columbia

Woody Allen Fall Project (9/27/93)
TriStar Pictures
Cast: *Joan Cusack, Mary Louise Parker, Jennifer Tilly, Dianne Wiest, Carl Reiner, Tracey Ullman, Alan Arkin, Jack Warden, Joe Vitereitt,Chazz Palminteri*
ExPrd., Jack Rollins, Charles Joffe; Prd., Robert Greenhut; Dir/Scr., Woody Allen
Distrib., TriStar.

Wyatt Earp (7/19/93)
Earp Prods. Inc.
Cast: *Kevin Costner, Dennis Quaid,*

Gene Hackman, Todd Allen, David Andrews, Linden Ashby, Adam Baldwin, Jeff Fahey, Michael Madsen, Bill Pullman, JoBeth Williams, Mare Winningham, Rex Linn, Mary Steenburgen, Mark Harmon, John Furlong, Betty Buckley , Heath Kizzier, Martin Kove, Tom Sizemore
ExPrd., Dan Gordon, Jon Slan, Charlie Okun, Michael Grillo; Prd., Jim Wilson, Kevin Costner, Lawrence Kasdan; Dir., Lawrence Kasdan; Scr., Lawrence Kasdan, Dan Gordon
Distrib., Warner Bros.

Yellow Dog (8/13/93)
20th Century Fox
Cast: *Jesse Bradford, Bruce Davison, Mimi Rogers*
Prd., Peter O'Brian; Dir/Scr., Phillip Borsos
Distrib., 20th Century Fox.

Zorro (11/93)
Amblin Entertainment
ExPrd., Steven Spielberg; Dir., Mikael Salomon; Scr., Kathleen King
Distrib., TriStar.

Quick List of New Films for 1994 Release

Buena Vista

Angels In The Outfield
Beauty
Color Of Night
Ed Wood
The Getaway
Holy Matrimony
I Love Trouble
Indian Warrior
It's Pat
Jefferson In Paris
Judge Dredd
The Lion King (Animated)
The Mighty Ducks II
My Father The Hero
The Ref
Renaissance Man
Significant Other
Tall Tale
Terminal Velocity
The Tool Shed
Tombstone
Totally London
Twist of Fate
Quiz Show
White Fang II

Columbia

Blankman
City Slickers II
Fire Down Below
Leon
Little Big League
My Girl II
The Next Karate Kid
North
Rita Hayworth & Shawshank
  Redemption
Wolf

MGM

Betty Boop (Animated)
Blown Away
Getting Even With Dad
My Summer Story

Paramount

Beverly Hills Cop III
Blue Chips
The Browning Version
Clear and Present Danger
Forrest Gump
Milk Money
Naked Gun 33 1/3
Nobody's Fool

Untitled Barry Levinson
Vampire in Brooklyn

TriStar

Cop and Robbersons
Cop Gives Waitress $2 million Tip
Him (Working Title)
Legends of the Fall
Low Fives
Mary Shelley's Frankenstein
Our Father
The Quick and the Dead
Zorro
Woody Allen Fall Project

20th Century Fox

Airheads
Baby's Day Out
The Chase
The Pagemaster (Animated)
Speed
True Lies
Yellow Dog

Universal

The Cowboy Way
Crooklyn
The Flintstones
Greedy
Reality Bites
The Paper
The River Wild
The Shadow
Snowballs (Animated)
Time Cop
30 Wishes
The War

Warner Bros.

Ace Ventura: Pet Detective
Black Beauty
The Bee
Chasers
The Client
Connecticut Yankee in King Arthur's
 Court
Dead Reckoning
Fair Game
Interview with the Vampire
Love Affair
Major League II
Maverick
Murder in the First
On Deadly Ground
Police Academy; Mission to Moscow

Natural Born Killers
Pet People
Richie Rich
Trial By Jury
Wyatt Earp

Independents

The Apostle
Bad Girls
Beresford Untitled
Billie's Song
The Californians
Cabin Boy
Camilla
Canadian Bacon
Corrina, Corrina
Dark Blood
Exit to Eden
F.T.W.
Galatea
The High Crusade
Highlander III
In the Mouth of Madness
Jason's Lyric
The Lane Frost Story
Lightning Jack
Love is a Gun
Lying in Wait
The Mask
Mesmer
Mirror Image
Morgan Parker
Mrs. Parker & the Round Table
National Lampoon's Scuba School
The Neverending Story III
The Night and the Moment
One Night Stand
The Penal Colony
The Pebble and the Penquin (Animated)
Pet
Princess Caraboo
Pulp Fiction
Road Flower
Sleep With Me
Stargate
Serial Mom
The Seventh Floor
Shadowlands
Shattered Image
Surviving the Game
Thumbelina (Animated)
Teresa's Tattoo
Tom and Viv
Two Bits
Widow's Peak
Without a Word

1993 Film Grosses

1993 Alphabetical Listing

This alphabetical list of movies represents the reported domestic box office gross (U.S. & Canada) of films that were released in 1993 up to the time of the publication of this book. *For a FREE update of this information please see the back page!* The title of the picture is followed by its distribution company, the Motion Picture Association of America rating, the day it was released, the last day grosses were reported, how many days it was in release and finally the total box office revenue received at the theaters. These statistics have been compiled from a variety of sources. ***Indicates still in release.

Title	Distributor	MPAA	Open	Last	Days	Gross
The Adventures of Huck Finn	(Buena Vista)	PG	4/2/93	7/11/93	193	$23,838,687
The Age of Innocence***	(Columbia)	PG	9/17/93	10/17/93	31	$22,288,476
Airborne	(Warner Bros.)	N/A	9/17/93	10/10/93	24	$2,432,104
Alive	(Buena Vista)	R	1/15/93	5/2/93	108	$36,299,670
American Heart	(Triton)	R	5/7/93	8/22/93	108	$325,220
Amongst Friends	(Fine Line)	R	7/23/93	8/22/93	31	$202,702
Amos & Andrew	(Columbia)	PG-13	3/5/93	6/6/93	94	$9,693,633
Another Stakeout***	(Buena Vista)	PG-13	7/23/93	10/17/93	87	$20,066,343
Army of Darkness	(Universal)	R	2/19/93	3/21/93	31	$10,482,305
Aspen Extreme	(Buena Vista)	PG-13	1/22/93	3/28/93	66	$7,875,498
Bad Behaviour	(October Films)	NR	9/3/93	9/12/93	10	$54,489
The Ballad of Little Jo	(Fine Line)	NR	8/20/93	9/26/93	38	$339,827
Baraka ***	(Goldwyn)	NR	9/24/93	10/17/93	24	$201,394
Benefit of the Doubt	(Miramax)	N/A	7/16/93	7/25/93	10	$135,602
Benny & Joon	(MGM)	PG	4/16/93	8/1/93	108	$23,286,270
Best of the Best II	(20th Fox)	R	3/5/93	4/4/93	31	$6,044,652
The Beverly Hillbillies ***	(20th Fox)	PG	10/15/93	10/17/93	3	$9,525,375
Black Diamond Rush ***	(Warren Miller)	NR	10/12/93	10/17/93	6	$213,047
Bodies, Rest & Motion	(Fine Line)	R	4/9/93	6/14/93	66	$685,216
Body of Evidence	(MGM)	R	1/15/93	2/7/93	24	$13,739,239
Boiling Point	(Warner Bros.)	R	4/16/93	6/20/93	66	$10,023,598
Bopha!	(Paramount)	PG-13	9/24/93	10/10/93	17	$179,962
Born Yesterday	(Buena Vista)	PG	3/26/93	6/27/93	94	$17,807,759
Bound by Honor	(Buena Vista)	R	4/16/93	6/20/93	66	$4,028,555
Boxing Helena	(Orion Classics)	R	9/3/93	9/26/93	24	$1,664,331
A Bronx Tale***	(Savoy Pic)	R	9/29/93	10/17/93	19	$10,723,720
Calendar Girl	(Columbia)	PG-13	9/3/93	9/19/93	17	$2,501,113
Carnosaur***	(Concorde)	R	5/21/93	10/17/93	142	$1,677,493
CB4	(Universal)	R	3/12/93	5/2/93	52	$17,642,060
The Cemetary Club	(Buena Vista)	PG-13	2/3/93	3/28/93	54	$5,613,673
Chain of Desire	(Mad Dog Pic)	NR	6/25/93	8/15/93	52	$197,180
Children of the Corn II	(Dimension)	R	1/29/93	3/21/93	52	$6,980,986
Cliffhanger***	(TriStar)	R	5/25/93	10/17/93	143	$83,798,348
Coneheads	(Paramount)	PG	7/23/93	8/29/93	38	$21,274,717
Cool Runnings***	(Buena Vista)	PG	10/1/93	10/17/93	17	$26,566,902
Cop and a Half	(Universal)	PG	4/2/93	8/8/93	129	$31,206,321
Crush	(Strand Rel)	NR	8/27/93	9/6/93	11	$39,753
The Crush	(Warner Bros.)	R	4/2/93	6/14/93	73	$13,589,383

Title	Distributor	MPAA	Open	Last	Days	Gross
The Dark Half	*(Orion)*	R	4/23/93	7/25/93	94	$9,568,795
Dave	*(Warner Bros.)*	PG-13	5/7/93	9/12/93	129	$63,254,274
Dazed and Confused***	*(Gramercy Pic)*	R	9/24/93	10/17/93	24	$3,639,241
Dead Alive	*(Trimark)*	NR	2/12/93	8/15/93	184	$204,742
Demolition Man***	*(Warner Bros.)*	R	10/8/93	10/17/93	10	$29,554,832
Dennis the Menace	*(Warner Bros.)*	PG	6/25/93	10/3/93	101	$51,255,463
Dragon	*(Universal)*	PG-13	5/7/93	8/8/93	94	$34,979,305
El Mariachi	*(Columbia)*	R	2/26/93	6/14/93	108	$1,860,870
Equinox	*(IRS)*	R	6/12/93	8/15/93	66	$194,026
Especially on Sunday	*(Miramax)*	N/A	8/13/93	9/12/93	31	$312,351
Ethan Frome	*(Miramax)*	PG-13	3/12/93	4/4/93	24	$296,081
Excessive Force	*(New Line)*	R	5/14/93	7/18/93	66	$1,146,520
Falling Down	*(Warner Bros.)*	R	2/26/93	6/20/93	115	$40,878,731
A Far Off Place	*(Buena Vista)*	PG	3/12/93	5/31/93	81	$12,874,686
Farewell My Concubine***	*(Miramax)*	NR	10/15/93	10/17/93	3	$69,408
Father Hood	*(Buena Vista)*	PG-13	8/27/93	9/26/93	31	$3,255,577
Fearless***	*(Warner Bros.)*	N/A	10/15/93	10/17/93	3	$144,044
Fire in the Sky	*(Paramount)*	PG-13	3/12/93	4/25/93	45	$19,885,552
The Firm***	*(Paramount)*	R	6/30/93	10/17/93	110	$155,186,342
For a Lost Soldier	*(Strand Rel)*	NR	5/7/93	8/22/93	108	$194,312
For Love or Money***	*(Universal)*	PG	10/1/93	10/17/93	17	$9,113,795
Fortress	*(Miramax)*	R	9/3/93	10/3/93	31	$6,723,318
Free Willy***	*(Warner Bros.)*	PG	7/16/93	10/17/93	94	$74,648,459
The Fugitive***	*(Warner Bros.)*	PG-13	8/6/93	10/17/93	73	$172,494,360
Gettysburg***	*(New Line)*	PG	10/8/93	10/17/93	10	$2,085,017
The Good Son***	*(20th Fox)*	R	9/24/93	10/17/93	24	$35,165,875
Groundhog Day	*(Columbia)*	PG	2/12/93	8/1/93	171	$70,835,374
Guilty as Sin	*(Buena Vista)*	R	6/4/93	9/6/93	95	$22,710,579
Happily Ever After	*(1st Nat'l Film)*	G	5/25/93	6/14/93	17	$3,229,522
Hard Target***	*(Universal)*	R	8/20/93	10/17/93	59	$31,485,750
Hear No Evil	*(20th Fox)*	R	3/26/93	4/18/93	24	$5,319,479
Hearts and Souls***	*(Universal)*	PG-13	8/13/93	10/17/93	66	$16,423,215
Hexed	*(Columbia)*	R	1/22/93	2/28/93	38	$2,693,248
Hocus Pocus***	*(Buena Vista)*	PG	7/16/93	10/17/93	94	$37,714,871
Hold Me, Thrill Me, Kiss Me	*(Mad Dog)*	NR	7/30/93	8/22/93	24	$74,436
Homeward Bound: Incredible Journey	*(Buena Vista)*	G	2/3/93	7/5/93	153	$41,633,185
Hot Shots! Part Deux	*(20th Fox)*	PG-13	5/21/93	8/29/93	101	$38,612,933
House of Angels	*(Sony Classics)*	NR	8/6/93	10/17/93	73	$121,773
House of Cards	*(Miramax)*	PG-13	6/25/93	8/1/93	38	$309,831
Household Saints***	*(Fine Line)*	R	9/15/93	10/17/93	33	$290,905
In the Line of Fire***	*(Columbia)*	R	7/9/93	10/17/93	101	$102,243,874
Indecent Proposal	*(Paramount)*	R	4/7/93	8/29/93	145	$105,935,860
Indian Summer	*(Buena Vista)*	PG-13	4/23/93	7/25/93	94	$14,663,905
Into the West***	*(Miramax)*	PG	9/17/93	10/17/93	31	$4,160,999
Jack the Bear	*(20th Fox)*	PG-13	4/2/93	4/18/93	17	$4,693,167
Jason Goes to Hell-Final Friday	*(New Line)*	R	8/13/93	10/10/93	59	$15,554,508
The Joy Luck Club***	*(Buena Vista)*	R	9/8/93	10/17/93	40	$14,865,329
The Judas Project***	*(R.S. Enter.)*	PG-13	5/9/93	10/17/93	241	$1,721,237
Judgment Night***	*(Universal)*	R	10/15/93	10/17/93	3	$4,088,955
Jurassic Park***	*(Universal)*	PG-13	6/12/93	10/17/93	129	$327,871,950
Just Another Girl on the IRT	*(Miramax)*	N/A	3/19/93	4/18/93	31	$435,300
Kalifornia	*(Gramercy Pics)*	R	9/3/93	10/3/93	31	$2,373,406
King of the Hill***	*(Gramercy)*	PG-13	8/20/93	10/17/93	59	$989,786
Knight Moves	*(Interstar)*	N/A	1/22/93	2/7/93	17	$853,554

Title	Distributor	MPAA	Open	Last	Days	Gross
Last Action Hero	(Columbia)	PG-13	6/18/93	9/6/93	81	$50,016,394
Last Days of Chez Nouz	(Fine Line)	NR	2/26/93	7/11/93	136	$752,814
Leolo	(Fine Line)	NR	4/2/93	6/20/93	80	$515,834
Leprachaun	(Trimark)	R	1/8/93	5/16/93	129	$8,530,048
Life with Mikey	(Buena Vista)	PG	6/4/93	8/15/93	73	$12,252,196
Like Water for Chocolate***	(Miramax)	R	2/17/93	10/17/93	243	$18,476,345
The Long Day Closes	(Sony Classics)	PG	5/25/93	8/8/93	73	$109,768
Lost In Yonkers	(Columbia)	PG	5/14/93	7/25/93	73	$9,149,433
Love Field	(Orion)	N/A	2/5/93	3/7/93	31	$825,731
Love Your Mama	(Hemdale)	N/A	3/5/93	4/14/93	10	$101,920
M. Butterfly***	(Warner Bros.)	R	10/1/93	10/17/93	17	$759,615
Mac	(Goldwyn)	R	1/19/93	4/4/93	45	$363,769
Mad Dog and Glory	(Universal)	R	3/5/93	4/11/93	38	$10,666,090
Made In America	(Warner Bros.)	PG-13	5/25/93	9/12/93	108	$44,904,674
Malice***	(Columbia)	R	10/1/93	10/17/93	17	$27,159,464
Man Bites Dog	(Roxie Rel.)	NC-17	1/15/93	2/15/93	32	$71,020
The Man Without a Face***	(Warner Bros.)	PG-13	8/25/93	10/17/93	54	$23,246,244
Manhattan Murder Mystery***	(TriStar)	PG	8/18/93	10/17/93	61	$10,817,282
Map of the Human Heart	(Miramax)	R	4/23/93	8/1/93	101	$2,805,759
Married to It	(Orion)	R	3/26/93	4/18/93	24	$1,961,562
Matinee	(Universal)	PG	1/29/93	3/14/93	45	$8,902,915
Menace II Society	(New Line)	R	5/23/93	10/10/93	138	$27,710,300
The Meteor Man***	(MGM)	PG	8/6/93	10/17/93	73	$7,982,817
Money for Nothing	(Buena Vista)	R	9/10/93	9/19/93	10	$917,588
Mr. Jones***	(TriStar)	R	10/8/93	10/17/93	10	$6,003,516
Mr. Nanny***	(New Line)	PG	10/8/93	10/17/93	10	$3,415,712
Mr. Wonderful***	(Warner Bros.)	PG-13	10/15/93	10/17/93	3	$1,177,311
Much Ado About Nothing***	(Goldwyn)	PG-13	5/7/93	10/17/93	164	$22,197,968
The Music of Chance	(IRS)	NR	6/4/93	9/6/93	95	$257,330
My Boyfriend's Back	(Buena Vista)	PG-13	8/6/93	8/22/93	17	$3,193,322
Nat'l Lampoon's Loaded Weapon 1	(New Line)	PG-13	2/5/93	5/16/93	101	$27,967,603
Needful Things	(Columbia)	R	8/27/93	9/26/93	31	$14,594,114
Nemesis	(Imperial)	R	1/29/93	5/16/93	105	$1,468,232
The Night We Never Met	(Miramax)	R	4/30/93	5/23/93	24	$1,806,589
The Nightmare Before Christmas ***	(Buena Vista)	PG	10/13/93	10/17/93	5	$210,648
No Place to Hide	(Cannon)	N/A	4/16/93	4/18/93	3	$91,000
Nowhere To Run	(Columbia)	R	1/15/93	5/23/93	129	$22,066,143
Okoge	(Cinevista)	N/A	4/2/93	8/1/93	122	$203,464
Olivier, Olivier	(Sony Pics)	R	3/3/93	8/8/93	159	$1,016,411
Once Upon a Forest	(20th Fox)	G	6/18/93	7/18/93	31	$6,134,380
Only the Strong	(20th Fox)	PG-13	8/27/93	9/12/93	17	$2,861,927
The Opposite Sex	(Miramax)	R	3/26/93	4/4/93	10	$690,966
Orlando***	(Sony Pics)	PG-13	6/10/93	10/17/93	131	$5,108,850
The Pickle	(Columbia)	R	4/30/93	5/2/93	3	$45,570
Poetic Justice	(Columbia)	R	7/23/93	9/6/93	46	$27,515,786
Point of No Return	(Warner Bros.)	R	3/19/93	7/11/93	115	$30,008,534
Posse	(Gramercy Pic)	R	5/14/93	8/1/93	80	$18,250,630
The Program***	(Buena Vista)	R	9/24/93	10/17/93	24	$18,948,276
The Real McCoy	(Universal)	PG-13	9/10/93	10/10/93	31	$6,305,945
Rich in Love	(MGM)	PG-13	3/5/93	4/11/93	38	$1,964,019
Riff-Raff	(Fine Line)	N/A	2/12/93	4/25/93	73	$225,559
Rising Sun	(20th Fox)	R	7/30/93	10/10/93	73	$61,438,872
Road Scholar	(Goldwyn)	NR	7/16/93	9/19/93	66	$420,762
Robin Hood: Men in Tights	(20th Fox)	PG-13	7/27/93	10/10/93	75	$35,135,906

Title	Distributor	MPAA	Open	Last	Days	Gross
Romper Stomper	*(Academy)*	NC-17	6/9/93	7/5/93	27	$72,946
Rookie of the Year	*(20th Fox)*	PG	7/7/93	10/10/93	96	$52,911,548
Ruby in Paradise***	*(October Films)*	NR	10/8/93	10/17/93	10	$77,609
Rudy***	*(TriStar)*	PG	10/13/93	10/17/93	5	$1,041,326
The Sandlot	*(20th Fox)*	PG	4/7/93	7/25/93	110	$31,709,974
Searching for Bobby Fisher ***	*(Paramount)*	PG	8/11/93	10/17/93	68	$7,190,131
The Secret Garden***	*(Warner Bros.)*	G	8/13/93	10/17/93	66	$29,489,794
Shadow of the Wolf	*(Triumph)*	PG-13	3/5/93	3/28/93	24	$1,335,515
Short Cuts***	*(Fine Line)*	R]	10/3/93	10/17/93	15	$200,452
Sidekicks	*(Triumph)*	PG	4/9/93	7/25/93	107	$17,180,393
Sleepless in Seattle***	*(TriStar)*	PG	6/25/93	10/17/93	115	$120,277,388
Sliver	*(Paramount)*	R	5/21/93	7/5/93	46	$36,156,008
Sniper	*(Tri Star)*	R	1/29/93	4/11/93	73	$18,556,563
Snow White and Seven Dwarfs (Re)***	*(Buena Vista)*	G	7/2/93	10/17/93	108	$41,078,082
So I Married an Axe Murderer	*(TriStar)*	PG-13	7/30/93	10/3/93	66	$11,565,025
Sommersby	*(Warner Bros.)*	PG-13	2/5/93	8/15/93	192	$50,052,806
Son of the Pink Panther	*(MGM)*	PG	8/27/93	9/12/93	17	$2,365,290
Son-In-Law***	*(Buena Vista)*	PG-13	7/2/93	10/17/93	108	$35,644,772
Splitting Heirs	*(Universal)*	PG-13	4/30/93	5/23/93	24	$3,138,625
Stolen Children	*(Goldwyn)*	N/A	3/3/93	5/31/93	90	$903,884
The Story of Qiu Ju	*(Sony Pics)*	PG	4/16/93	9/6/93	144	$1,368,735
Street Knight	*(Cannon)*	R	3/12/93	3/14/93	3	$507,656
Strictly Ballroom	*(Miramax)*	NR	2/12/93	8/15/93	185	$11,649,577
Striking Distance***	*(Columbia)*	R	9/17/93	10/17/93	31	$22,459,850
Super Mario Bros.	*(Buena Vista)*	PG	5/25/93	8/15/93	80	$20,765,082
Surf Ninjas	*(New Line)*	PG-13	8/20/93	10/10/93	52	$4,907,077
Swing Kids	*(Buena Vista)*	PG-13	3/5/93	4/11/93	38	$5,371,714
Teenage Ninja Mutant Turtles III	*(New Line)*	PG	3/17/93	7/18/93	124	$42,265,465
The Temp	*(Paramount)*	R	2/12/93	3/7/93	24	$6,307,876
The Thing Called Love	*(Paramount)*	N/A	8/27/93	9/12/93	17	$943,567
This Boy's Life	*(Warner Bros.)*	R	4/9/93	6/14/93	66	$4,094,747
Three of Hearts	*(New Line)*	R	4/30/93	6/27/93	59	$5,471,155
Tokyo Decadence	*(Northern Arts)*	N/A	4/30/93	10/17/93	173	$273,813
Tom and Jerry: The Movie	*(Miramax)*	G	7/30/93	9/6/93	39	$3,532,083
True Romance***	*(Warner Bros.)*	R	9/10/93	10/17/93	38	$11,847,701
Un Coeur en Hiver	*(Octorber Films)*	NR	6/4/93	10/3/93	122	$1,485,249
Undercover Blues***	*(MGM)*	PG-13	9/10/93	10/17/93	38	$12,043,775
Untamed Heart	*(MGM)*	PG-13	2/12/93	5/2/93	80	$18,762,104
The Vanishing	*(20th Fox)*	R	2/5/93	3/7/93	31	$13,441,821
Visions of Light	*(Kino Int'l)*	N/A	2/24/93	8/22/93	180	$770,968
Volere Volare	*(Fine Line)*	NR	2/3/93	2/21/93	19	$60,186
Warlock, The Armageddon***	*(Trimark)*	R	9/24/93	10/17/93	24	$3,620,442
The Wedding Banquet ***	*(Goldwyn)*	NR	8/4/93	10/17/93	75	$4,712,009
Weekend at Bernie's II	*(TriStar)*	PG	7/9/93	9/19/93	73	$12,725,631
What's Love Got to Do With It***	*(Buena Vista)*	R	6/10/93	10/17/93	131	$38,887,009
Who's the Man	*(New Line)*	R	4/23/93	8/1/93	101	$11,292,808
Wide Sargossa Sea	*(Fine Line)*	NC-17	4/16/93	8/8/93	115	$1,427,240
Wilder Napalm	*(TriStar)*	PG-13	8/20/93	8/29/93	10	$56,239
Witchboard II	*(Blue Rider)*	R	9/10/93	9/19/93	10	$118,631

*For **FREE** update information see back page!*

The following movies are ranked by their reported domestic box office gross (U.S. & Canada). The list represents films that were released in 1992 and shows the entire longevity of the release not just the calendar year it was released in. The rank is followed by the title of the picture, its distribution company, the Motion Picture Association of America rating, the day it was released, the last day grosses were reported, how many days it was in release and finally the total box office revenue received at the theaters. These statistics have been compiled from a variety of sources.

Rank	Title	Distributor	MPAA	Open	Last	Days	Gross
1	Aladdin	(Buena Vista)	G	11/11/92	9/26/93	320	$217,042,825
2	Home Alone II	(20th Fox)	PG	11/20/92	4/18/93	150	$172,667,450
3	Batman Returns	(Warner Bros.)	PG-13	6/19/92	10/22/92	126	$162,831,698
4	Lethal Weapon III	(Warner Bros.)	R	5/15/92	11/15/92	185	$144,624,387
5	A Few Good Men	(Columbia)	R	12/11/92	7/25/93	227	$141,340,178
6	Sister Act	(Buena Vista)	PG	5/29/92	11/15/92	171	$138,477,418
7	The Bodyguard	(Warner Bros.)	R	11/25/92	5/23/93	180	$121,936,132
8	Wayne's World	(Paramount)	PG-13	2/14/92	8/2/92	171	$121,631,114
9	Basic Instinct	(TriStar)	R	3/20/92	10/4/92	199	$117,208,217
10	A League of their Own	(Columbia)	PG	7/1/92	1/3/93	187	$107,404,544
11	Unforgiven	(Warner Bros.)	R	8/7/92	7/11/93	339	$101,101,229
12	The Hand that Rocks the Cradle	(Buena Vista)	R	1/10/92	7/5/92	178	$87,512,809
13	Under Siege	(Warner Bros.)	R	10/9/92	3/14/93	157	$83,550,855
14	Patriot Games	(Paramount)	R	6/5/92	9/13/92	101	$82,690,527
15	Bram Stoker's Dracula	(Columbia)	R	11/13/92	1/10/93	59	$82,416,928
16	The Last of the Mohicans	(20th Fox)	R	9/25/92	2/7/93	136	$72,155,275
17	White Men Can't Jump	(20th Fox)	R	3/27/92	7/12/92	108	$71,969,454
18	Boomerang	(Paramount)	R	7/1/92	9/7/92	69	$66,659,378
19	Scent of a Woman	(Universal)	R	12/23/92	8/3/93	229	$63,091,398
20	The Crying Game	(Miramax)	R	11/25/92	8/1/93	250	$62,544,123
21	Far and Away	(Universal)	PG-13	5/22/92	10/12/92	144	$58,836,800
22	Honey, I Blew Up the Kid	(Buena Vista)	PG	7/17/92	1/3/93	171	$58,662,452
23	Housesitter	(Universal)	PG	6/12/92	10/12/92	123	$58,479,975
24	Death Becomes Her	(Universal)	PG-13	7/31/92	11/29/92	122	$58,407,350
25	Beethoven	(Universal)	PG	4/3/92	9/27/92	170	$56,970,868
26	Unlawful Entry	(20th Fox)	R	6/26/92	10/4/92	101	$55,916,298
27	Forever Young	(Warner Bros.)	PG	12/16/92	4/11/93	117	$55,394,658
28	Alien III	(20th Fox)	R	5/22/92	8/2/92	73	$54,780,116
29	My Cousin Vinny	(20th Fox)	R	3/13/92	7/12/92	122	$51,101,559
30	The Mighty Ducks	(Buena Vista)	PG	10/2/92	2/28/93	150	$50,727,056
31	Sneakers	(Universal)	PG-13	9/9/92	1/3/93	117	$50,560,948
32	Malcolm X	(Warner Bros.)	PG-13	11/18/92	4/11/93	149	$48,140,191
33	Single White Female	(Columbia)	R	8/14/92	1/3/93	143	$48,017,402
34	The Distinguished Gentleman	(Buena Vista)	R	12/4/92	4/11/93	129	$46,486,415
35	Medicine Man	(Buena Vista)	PG-13	2/7/92	6/28/92	143	$45,031,441
36	Passenger 57	(Warner Bros.)	R	11/6/92	2/21/93	108	$44,041,843
37	A River Runs Through It	(Columbia)	PG	10/9/92	5/31/93	235	$43,406,504
38	Mo' Money	(Columbia)	R	7/24/92	11/29/92	129	$40,224,901

Rank	Title	Distributor	MPAA	Open	Last	Days	Gross
39	**Encino Man**	(Buena Vista)	PG	5/22/92	9/20/92	122	$40,028,108
40	**Universal Soldier**	(TriStar)	R	7/10/92	10/4/92	87	$36,168,043
41	**Honeymoon in Vegas**	(Columbia)	PG-13	8/28/92	1/3/93	129	$35,208,854
42	**The Lawnmower Man**	(New Line)	R	2/14/92	7/5/92	143	$32,100,816
43	**3 Ninjas**	(Buena Vista)	PG	8/7/92	1/3/93	150	$29,000,301
44	**Sleepwalkers**	(Columbia)	R	4/10/92	6/28/92	80	$28,594,754
45	**Final Analysis**	(Warner Bros.)	R	2/7/92	4/19/92	73	$27,640,345
46	**The Muppet Christmas Carol**	(Buena Vista)	G	12/11/92	2/21/93	73	$27,274,107
47	**Stop! Or My Mom Will Shoot**	(Universal)	PG-13	2/21/92	5/17/92	87	$26,613,295
48	**Howards End**	(Sony Classics)	PG	3/13/92	7/5/93	480	$25,915,540
49	**Candyman**	(TriStar)	R	10/16/92	1/31/93	108	$25,540,672
50	**Hoffa**	(20th Fox)	R	12/25/92	1/31/93	38	$23,265,190
51	**The Cutting Edge**	(MGM)	PG	3/27/92	6/7/92	73	$22,977,689
52	**Captain Ron**	(Buena Vista)	PG-13	9/18/92	1/18/93	127	$22,503,440
53	**Thunderheart**	(TriStar)	R	4/3/92	8/2/92	122	$22,261,508
54	**Leap of Faith**	(Paramount)	PG-13	12/18/92	2/7/93	52	$22,257,579
55	**The Player**	(Fine Line)	R	4/10/92	3/7/93	332	$21,657,020
56	**Consenting Adults**	(Buena Vista)	R	10/16/92	1/18/93	95	$21,577,791
57	**Toys**	(20th Fox)	PG-13	12/18/92	1/24/93	38	$21,326,485
58	**Raising Cain**	(Universal)	R	8/7/92	10/18/92	73	$21,143,810
59	**FernGully: The Last Rain Forest**	(20th Fox)	G	4/10/92	6/14/92	66	$20,906,175
60	**Shining Through**	(20th Fox)	R	1/31/92	3/8/92	38	$20,655,388
61	**Mr. Baseball**	(Universal)	PG-13	10/2/92	12/13/92	73	$20,316,385
62	**Juice**	(Paramount)	R	1/17/92	4/19/92	94	$20,128,178
63	**Straight Talk**	(Buena Vista)	PG	4/3/92	7/5/92	94	$20,125,295
64	**Kuffs**	(Universal)	PG-13	1/10/92	3/8/92	59	$19,585,735
65	**Prelude to A Kiss**	(20th Fox)	PG-13	7/10/92	8/30/92	52	$19,343,600
66	**Hero**	(Columbia)	PG-13	10/2/92	1/3/93	94	$19,161,476
67	**Pinocchio (Re)**	(Buena Vista)	G	6/26/92	9/13/92	80	$18,693,516
68	**Singles**	(Warner Bros.)	PG-13	9/18/92	12/6/92	80	$17,829,560
69	**Used People**	(20th Fox)	PG-13	12/16/92	2/28/93	75	$17,130,101
70	**Pet Sematary II**	(Paramount)	R	8/28/92	11/29/92	94	$17,092,453
71	**The Babe**	(Universal)	PG	4/17/92	7/12/92	87	$17,026,195
72	**Freejack**	(Warner Bros.)	R	1/17/92	3/15/92	59	$16,812,927
73	**Deep Cover**	(New Line)	R	4/15/92	8/23/92	131	$16,627,648
74	**Pure Country**	(Warner Bros.)	PG	10/23/92	2/7/93	108	$15,105,784
75	**Ladybugs**	(Paramount)	PG-13	3/27/92	5/10/92	45	$14,579,141
76	**City of Joy**	(TriStar)	PG-13	4/15/92	8/2/92	110	$14,360,321
77	**Buffy The Vampire Slayer**	(20th Fox)	PG-13	7/31/92	8/30/92	31	$14,132,507
78	**School Ties**	(Paramount)	PG-13	9/18/92	11/29/92	73	$14,107,964
79	**Cool World**	(Paramount)	PG-13	7/10/92	8/9/92	31	$14,024,772
80	**Rapid Fire**	(20th Fox)	R	8/21/92	9/27/92	38	$13,575,684
81	**Memoirs of an Invisible Man**	(Warner Bros.)	PG-13	2/28/92	4/26/92	59	$13,405,114
82	**Mr. Saturday Night**	(Columbia)	R	9/23/92	12/13/92	82	$13,336,262
83	**Enchanted April**	(Miramax)	PG	7/31/92	3/28/93	241	$13,178,794
84	**Great Mouse Detective (Re)**	(Buena Vista)	G	2/14/92	4/26/92	73	$13,021,114
85	**Trespass**	(Universal)	R	12/25/92	2/7/93	45	$12,640,985
86	**Hellraiser III**	(Dimension)	R	9/11/92	12/13/92	94	$12,534,961
87	**Class Act**	(Warner Bros.)	PG-13	6/5/92	8/9/92	66	$12,304,991
88	**A Stranger Among Us**	(Buena Vista)	PG-13	7/17/92	9/20/92	66	$12,079,497
89	**Rock-A-Doodle**	(Goldwyn)	G	4/3/92	7/19/92	108	$11,638,724
90	**American Me**	(Universal)	R	3/13/92	4/26/92	45	$11,318,310
91	**Jennifer Eight**	(Paramount)	R	11/6/92	12/13/92	38	$11,237,313

Rank	Title	Distributor	MPAA	Open	Last	Days	Gross
92	Stay Tuned	(Warner Bros.)	PG	8/14/92	11/8/92	87	$10,699,907
93	Glengarry Glen Ross	(New Line)	R	9/30/92	3/7/93	159	$10,685,924
94	Husbands and Wives	(TriStar)	R	9/18/92	11/22/92	66	$10,310,847
95	Whispers in the Dark	(Paramount)	R	8/7/92	9/7/92	32	$10,214,596
96	Chaplin	(TriStar)	PG-13	12/25/92	3/21/93	87	$9,329,605
97	White Sands	(Warner Bros.)	R	4/24/92	7/12/92	80	$8,939,665
98	Once Upon a Crime	(MGM)	PG	3/6/92	4/5/92	31	$8,508,961
99	Christopher Columbus	(Warner Bros.)	PG-13	8/21/92	11/1/92	73	$8,240,257
100	Dr. Giggles	(Universal)	R	10/23/92	12/13/92	52	$8,172,110
101	Gladiator	(Columbia)	R	3/6/92	3/29/92	24	$8,098,005
102	Bebe's Kids	(Paramount)	PG-13	7/31/92	8/30/92	31	$7,910,080
103	Damage	(New Line)	R	12/23/92	5/9/93	138	$7,522,045
104	Mississippi Masala	(Goldwyn)	R	2/5/92	5/17/92	99	$7,299,996
105	Sarafina	(Buena Vista)	PG-13	9/16/92	12/6/92	82	$7,284,413
106	1492: Conquest Of Paradise	(Paramount)	PG-13	10/9/92	11/29/92	52	$7,148,891
107	Lorenzo's Oil	(Universal)	PG-13	12/30/92	4/25/93	117	$7,126,465
108	The Mambo Kings	(Warner Bros.)	R	2/28/92	5/10/92	73	$6,678,641
109	Article 99	(Orion)	R	3/13/92	4/5/92	24	$6,222,754
110	Night and the City	(20th Fox)	R	10/16/92	11/29/92	45	$6,190,239
111	Folks	(20th Fox)	PG-13	5/1/92	5/31/92	31	$5,870,761
112	Split Second	(Interstar)	R	5/1/92	7/26/92	87	$5,430,082
113	Wind	(TriStar)	PG-13	9/11/92	10/12/92	32	$5,293,346
114	Indochine	(Sony Classics)	PG-13	12/23/92	8/8/93	229	$5,236,942
115	Of Mice and Men	(MGM)	PG-13	10/2/92	12/6/92	66	$5,031,254
116	Innocent Blood	(Warner Bros.)	R	9/25/92	11/29/92	66	$4,928,062
117	Passion Fish	(Miramax)	R	12/18/92	5/16/93	150	$4,810,619
118	The Playboys	(Goldwyn)	PG-13	4/22/92	9/13/92	145	$4,805,197
119	Mediterraneo	(Miramax)	NR	3/22/92	10/4/92	197	$4,532,791
120	Diggstown	(MGM)	R	8/14/92	9/7/92	25	$4,432,789
121	Bob Roberts	(Paramount)	R	9/4/92	11/29/92	87	$4,382,265
122	Radio Flyer	(Columbia)	PG-13	2/21/92	3/15/92	24	$4,232,502
123	Twin Peaks: Fire Walk With Me	(New Line)	R	8/28/92	10/4/92	38	$4,152,201
124	The Lover	(MGM)	R	10/30/92	2/7/93	101	$4,143,501
125	Peter's Friends	(Goldwyn)	NR	12/25/92	4/4/93	101	$3,992,157
126	Passed Away	(Buena Vista)	PG-13	4/24/92	5/25/92	32	$3,772,179
127	Blade Runner (Re)	(Warner Bros.)	R	9/11/92	11/29/92	80	$3,740,330
128	The Gun in Betty Lou's Handbag	(Buena Vista)	PG-13	8/21/92	9/20/92	31	$3,562,623
129	Man Trouble	(20th Fox)	R	7/17/92	7/26/92	10	$3,525,384
130	Traces of Red	(Goldwyn)	R	11/11/92	1/10/93	61	$3,188,572
131	Tous les Matins du Monde	(Oct. Films)	NR	11/13/92	6/6/93	206	$3,060,347
132	K2	(Paramount)	R	5/1/92	5/31/92	31	$2,997,055
133	Blame It on the Bellboy	(Buena Vista)	PG-13	3/6/92	4/5/92	31	$2,986,511
134	The Public Eye	(Universal)	R	10/14/92	11/15/92	33	$2,979,110
135	Reservoir Dogs	(Miramax)	R	10/23/92	3/21/93	150	$2,817,798
136	This is My Life	(20th Fox)	PG-13	2/21/92	3/29/92	38	$2,809,802
137	The Power of One	(Warner Bros.)	PG-13	3/27/92	5/10/92	45	$2,808,950
138	Newsies	(Buena Vista)	PG	4/8/92	4/26/92	17	$2,706,352
139	Crisscross	(MGM)	R	5/8/92	5/31/92	24	$2,657,325
140	Raise the Red Lantern	(Orion Classics)	PG	3/13/92	10/18/92	220	$2,603,061
141	Year of the Comet	(Columbia)	PG-13	4/24/92	5/10/92	17	$2,575,460
142	Aces: Iron Eagle III	(New Line)	R	6/12/92	8/9/92	59	$2,513,979
143	Shadows and Fog	(Orion)	PG-13	3/20/92	4/5/92	17	$2,447,000
144	Flirting	(Goldwyn)	NR	11/6/92	4/4/93	150	$2,354,815

Rank	Title	Distributor	MPAA	Open	Last	Days	Gross
145	**Love Crimes**	*(Millimeter)*	R	1/24/92	2/9/92	17	$2,287,928
146	**Noises Off**	*(Buena Vista)*	PG-13	3/20/92	4/5/92	17	$2,228,003
147	**A Brief History of Time**	*(Triton)*	NR	8/21/92	2/15/93	179	$2,220,586
148	**Gate II**	*(Triumph)*	R	2/28/92	4/5/92	38	$2,026,041
149	**Night on Earth**	*(Fine Line)*	R	5/1/92	9/20/92	142	$2,011,294
150	**Bad Lieutenant**	*(Aries)*	NC-17	11/20/92	5/16/93	178	$1,936,592
151	**Poison Ivy**	*(New Line)*	R	5/8/92	8/16/92	101	$1,818,929
152	**Mom and Dad Save the World**	*(Warner Bros.)*	PG	7/24/92	8/2/92	10	$1,814,852
153	**Delicatessen**	*(Miramax)*	R	4/3/92	8/23/92	143	$1,787,746
154	**The Waterdance**	*(Goldwyn)*	R	5/13/92	7/26/92	75	$1,714,515
155	**Casablanca (Re)**	*(MGM)*	NR	4/8/92	7/19/92	103	$1,711,189
156	**Out on a Limb**	*(Universal)*	PG	9/4/92	9/20/92	17	$1,599,655
157	**One False Move**	*(IRS)*	R	5/8/92	9/27/92	143	$1,524,759
158	**A Midnight Clear**	*(Interstar)*	R	4/24/92	7/12/92	80	$1,521,743
159	**Leaving Normal**	*(Universal)*	R	4/29/92	5/25/92	27	$1,409,652
160	**Lovers**	*(Aries)*	NR	3/27/92	11/1/92	220	$1,407,309
161	**Little Nemo (Re)**	*(Hemdale)*	G	8/21/92	11/29/92	101	$1,370,262
162	**South Central**	*(Warner Bros.)*	R	9/18/92	11/22/92	66	$1,368,770
163	**Gas, Food, Lodging**	*(IRS)*	R	8/8/92	3/7/93	212	$1,342,613
164	**Brothers Keeper*****	*(Creative Think)*	NR	9/9/92	9/12/93	369	$1,305,915
165	**The Best Intentions**	*(Goldwyn)*	NR	7/10/92	11/1/92	115	$1,249,489
166	**The Hairdresser's Husband**	*(Triton)*	NR	6/19/92	2/15/93	242	$1,210,406
167	**Toto Le Heros**	*(Triton)*	PG-13	3/6/92	8/16/92	164	$1,198,603
168	**Where Angels Fear to Tread**	*(New Line)*	PG	2/28/92	5/17/92	80	$1,136,194
169	**Mistress**	*(Rainbow Rel.)*	R	8/7/92	1/31/93	178	$1,093,877
170	**Waterland**	*(Fine Line)*	R	10/30/92	1/24/93	87	$1,090,872
171	**Freddie As F.R.O.7.**	*(Miramax)*	PG	8/28/92	9/7/92	11	$1,081,209
172	**Steeper and Deeper**	*(Warren Miller)*	NR	10/1/92	11/22/92	53	$1,076,685
173	**Light Sleeper**	*(Fine Line)*	R	8/21/92	12/6/92	108	$1,047,724
174	**Ruby**	*(Triumph)*	R	3/27/92	4/5/92	10	$890,313
175	**Brain Doners**	*(Paramount)*	PG	4/17/92	4/26/92	10	$860,365
176	**35 Up**	*(Goldwyn)*	NR	1/16/92	5/17/92	124	$823,262
177	**Zentropa**	*(Miramax)*	NR	5/22/92	10/4/92	136	$812,662
178	**Cabeza De Vaca**	*(Concorde)*	R	4/18/92	11/29/92	226	$789,127
179	**Rampage**	*(Miramax)*	R	10/30/92	12/13/92	45	$784,008
180	**Turtle Beach**	*(Warner Bros.)*	R	5/1/92	5/10/92	10	$708,444
181	**The Living End**	*(October Films)*	NR	8/14/92	10/25/92	73	$692,585
182	**Claire of the Moon**	*(Strand Rel.)*	NR	10/9/92	6/6/93	234	$660,656
183	**Love Potion #9**	*(20th Fox)*	R	11/13/92	11/22/92	10	$656,681
184	**Venice/Venice**	*(Rainbow Rel.)*	NR	10/9/92	9/19/93	347	$645,346
185	**Into the Sun**	*(Trimark)*	R	1/31/92	2/23/92	24	$632,099
186	**Johnny Stecchino**	*(New Line)*	R	10/9/92	2/15/93	130	$616,854
187	**Zebrahead**	*(Triumph)*	R	10/24/92	10/25/92	3	$609,000
188	**Wild Orchid II**	*(Triumph)*	R	5/8/92	5/17/92	10	$534,849
189	**Edward II**	*(Fine Line)*	R	3/20/92	5/17/92	59	$459,325
190	**Crossing the Bridge**	*(Buena Vista)*	R	9/11/92	9/20/92	10	$430,447
191	**The Adjuster**	*(Orion Classics)*	R	5/29/92	9/7/92	102	$396,573
192	**Danzon**	*(Sony Classics)*	PG-13	9/25/92	2/15/93	144	$391,908
193	**A Woman's Tale**	*(Orion Classics)*	PG-13	5/1/92	8/23/92	115	$384,376
194	**Where the Day Takes You**	*(New Line)*	R	9/11/92	9/27/92	17	$380,110
195	**Close to Eden**	*(Miramax)*	NR	10/30/92	12/20/92	52	$377,832
196	**Othello (Re)**	*(Castle Hill)*	NR	3/6/92	6/14/92	101	$377,401
197	**Frozen Assets**	*(RKO)*	PG-13	10/23/92	11/15/92	24	$376,008

Rank	Title	Distributor	MPAA	Open	Last	Days	Gross
198	Storyville	*(20th Fox)*	R	8/28/92	10/14/92	48	$356,476
199	Voyager	*(Castle Hill)*	PG-13	1/30/92	4/26/92	88	$348,272
200	Incident at Oglala	*(Miramax)*	PG	5/8/92	7/26/92	80	$344,018
201	Swoon	*(Fine Line)*	R	9/11/92	12/20/92	101	$340,147
202	Monster in a Box	*(Fine Line)*	PG-13	5/15/92	8/16/92	94	$308,844
203	Highway 61	*(Skouras)*	R	4/24/92	8/23/92	122	$294,645
204	Hard Promises	*(Columbia)*	PG	1/31/92	2/9/92	10	$277,686
205	Becoming Colette	*(Castle Hill)*	R	11/20/92	2/15/93	88	$272,931
206	Big Girls Don't Cry, They Get Even	*(New Line)*	PG	5/8/92	5/31/92	24	$270,399
207	Alan and Naomi	*(Triton)*	PG	1/31/92	3/8/92	38	$238,021
208	L A Discrete	*(MK2USA)*	NR	8/14/92	12/20/92	129	$229,160
209	Terminal Bliss	*(Cannon)*	R	3/6/92	3/8/92	3	$215,500
210	Adam's Rib	*(October Films)*	NR	5/8/92	8/23/92	108	$212,244
211	In the Soup	*(Triton)*	NR	11/6/92	1/31/93	87	$200,512
212	Under Suspicion	*(Columbia)*	R	2/28/92	4/19/92	52	$197,821
213	Proof	*(Fine Line)*	R	3/20/92	5/10/92	52	$184,024
214	The 4th Animation Celebration	*(Expanded Ent.)*	NR	4/1/92	5/3/92	33	$179,377
215	London Kills Me	*(Fine Line)*	R	8/7/92	10/4/92	59	$169,027
216	Tale of Springtime	*(Orion Classics)*	PG	7/17/92	9/7/92	53	$156,848
217	My New Gun	*(IRS)*	R	10/26/92	1/31/93	98	$147,128
218	The Match Factory	*(Kino Int'l)*	NR	11/6/92	2/21/93	108	$145,767
219	Simple Men	*(Fine Line)*	R	10/14/92	12/20/92	68	$141,554
220	Intervista	*(Castle Hill)*	NR	11/28/92	2/28/93	93	$138,608
221	Falling from Grace	*(Columbia)*	PG-13	2/21/92	3/15/92	24	$136,185
222	Roadside Prophets	*(Fine Line)*	R	3/27/92	4/19/92	24	$131,340
223	American Dream	*(Miramax)*	NR	3/18/92	5/17/92	61	$126,414
224	Favor, The Watch & The VB Fish	*(Trimark)*	R	5/6/92	5/31/92	24	$124,965
225	Laws of Gravity	*(RKO)*	NR	8/26/92	11/1/92	68	$117,480
226	The Quarrel	*(RKO)*	NR	10/28/92	1/24/93	89	$117,139
227	Van Gogh	*(Sony Classics)*	R	10/30/92	2/15/93	109	$111,548
228	The Efficiency Expert	*(Miramax)*	PG	11/6/92	11/22/92	17	$106,899
229	Shakes the Clown	*(IRS)*	R	3/13/92	3/29/92	17	$97,360
230	In the Heat of Passion	*(Concorde)*	R	2/4/92	2/6/92	3	$96,225
231	For Sasha	*(MK2USA)*	NR	6/5/92	7/12/92	38	$90,264
232	I Don't Buy Kisses Anymore	*(Skouras)*	PG	2/14/92	5/3/92	80	$76,750
233	Double Trouble	*(MPCA)*	PG-13	2/14/92	2/23/92	10	$69,570
234	The Station	*(Aries)*	NR	1/3/92	9/20/92	5	$62,478
235	Brenda Starr	*(Triumph)*	PG	4/15/92	4/26/92	12	$60,906
236	Cold Heaven	*(Hemdale)*	R	5/29/92	7/5/92	38	$58,340
237	The Legend of Wolf Mountain	*(Hemdale)*	PG	11/20/92	12/6/92	17	$56,699
238	The Lunatic	*(Triton)*	R	2/7/92	3/15/92	38	$55,913
239	Johnny Suede	*(Miramax)*	R	8/14/92	9/13/92	31	$53,709
240	Afraid of the Dark	*(Fine Line)*	R	7/24/92	8/23/92	31	$52,708
241	The Silk Road	*(Trimark)*	PG-13	1/31/92	3/1/92	31	$48,304
242	Broadway Bill (Reissue)	*(Paramount)*	NR	5/15/92	6/14/92	31	$48,007
243	The Human Shield	*(Independent)*	R	5/29/92	5/31/92	3	$43,161
244	Time Will Tell	*(IRS)*	NR	6/4/92	6/28/92	25	$42,552
245	Bloodfist III	*(Concorde)*	R	1/3/92	1/5/92	3	$35,154
246	Beautiful Dreamers	*(Hemdale)*	PG-13	6/12/92	6/28/92	24	$34,858
247	Nat'l Canada Animation Fest	*(Expanded Ent.)*	NR	1/5/92	2/6/92	33	$33,292
248	Secret Friends	*(Briar Patch)*	NR	2/14/92	2/23/92	10	$29,316
249	Breaking the Rules	*(Miramax)*	PG-13	10/9/92	10/12/92	4	$27,375
250	Highway to Hell	*(Hemdale)*	R	3/13/92	3/22/92	10	$26,326

Rank	Title	Distributor	MPAA	Open	Last	Days	Gross
251	Together Alone	*(Frame Line)*	NR	9/24/92	10/4/92	11	$26,260
252	Singin' in the Rain (Re)	*(MGM)*	NR	2/21/92	3/1/92	10	$23,894
253	Love Field	*(Orion)*	PG-13	12/11/92	12/13/92	3	$21,895
254	Dark Horse	*(Line Ent.)*	PG	7/17/92	7/26/92	10	$21,855
255	Center of the Web	*(AIP)*	R	5/15/92	6/21/92	38	$18,357
256	The Tune	*(October Films)*	NR	9/4/92	9/13/92	10	$17,087
257	Rubin and Ed	*(IRS)*	PG-13	5/15/92	5/31/92	17	$15,675
258	The Bachelor	*(Greycat)*	NR	10/2/92	10/18/92	17	$14,087
259	Complex World	*(Hemdale)*	R	2/27/92	3/8/92	10	$12,490
260	Drive	*(Megagiant Rel.)*	NR	8/7/92	8/16/92	10	$11,637
261	All the Vermeers in New York	*(Strand Rel.)*	NR	5/1/92	5/3/92	3	$10,576
262	Bed and Breakfast	*(Hemdale)*	PG-13	8/7/92	8/16/92	10	$9,486
263	There Goes the Neighborhood	*(Paramount)*	PG-13	10/30/92	11/1/92	3	$8,233
264	Magical World of Chuck Jones	*(Warner Bros.)*	PG	10/23/92	11/1/92	10	$6,154
265	Jumpin' at the Boneyard	*(20th Fox)*	R	9/18/92	9/20/92	3	$5,875
266	Once Upon a Time in Amer. (Re)	*(Warner Bros.)*	R	10/23/92	10/25/92	3	$5,186
267	The Vagrant	*(MGM)*	R	5/15/92	5/17/92	3	$5,000

1991 Film Grosses

The following movies are ranked by their reported domestic box office gross (U.S. & Canada). The list represents films that were released in 1991 and shows the entire longevity of the release not just the calendar year it was released in. The rank is followed by the title of the picture, its distribution company, the Motion Picture Association of America rating, the day it was released, the last day grosses were reported, how many days it was in release and finally the total box office revenue received at the theatres. These statistics have been compiled from a variety of sources.

Rank	Title	Distributor	MPAA	Open	Last	Days	Gross
1	Terminator II	(TriStar)	R	7/3/91	12/8/91	160	$203,764,837
2	Robin Hood: Prince of Thieves	(Warner Bros.)	PG-13	6/14/91	10/27/91	136	$164,045,251
3	Beauty and the Beast	(Buena Vista)	G	11/13/91	6/21/92	222	$141,018,356
4	The Silence of the Lambs	(Orion)	R	2/14/91	10/6/91	235	$130,726,716
5	City Slickers	(Columbia)	PG-13	6/7/91	11/3/91	150	$120,735,850
6	Hook	(TriStar)	PG	12/11/91	5/25/92	168	$118,965,084
7	The Addams Family	(Paramount)	PG-13	11/22/91	4/26/92	157	$113,379,166
8	Sleeping with the Enemy	(20th Fox)	R	2/8/91	7/21/91	164	$100,294,830
9	Father of the Bride	(Buena Vista)	PG	12/20/91	5/25/92	158	$88,192,752
10	The Naked Gun 2 1/2	(Paramount)	PG-13	6/28/91	11/10/91	136	$86,816,416
11	Fried Green Tomatoes	(Universal)	PG-13	12/27/91	8/9/92	229	$81,192,860
12	Teenage Mutant Ninja Turtles II	(New Line)	PG	3/22/91	7/21/91	122	$78,391,796
13	Backdraft	(Universal)	R	5/24/91	11/3/91	164	$77,593,978
14	Cape Fear	(Universal)	R	11/13/91	4/12/92	152	$77,314,612
15	Star Trek VI	(Paramount)	PG	12/6/91	4/26/92	143	$74,739,913
16	The Prince of Tides	(Columbia)	R	12/25/91	4/19/92	117	$72,705,397
17	JFK	(Warner Bros.)	R	12/20/91	5/10/92	143	$70,180,458
18	Hot Shots	(20th Fox)	PG-13	7/31/91	11/17/91	110	$68,251,753
19	What About Bob?	(Buena Vista)	PG	5/17/91	10/14/91	151	$63,536,619
20	101 Dalmations (Re)	(Buena Vista)	G	7/12/91	11/10/91	122	$60,679,097
21	The Last Boy Scout	(Warner Bros.)	R	12/13/91	3/15/92	94	$58,926,549
22	My Girl	(Columbia)	PG	11/27/91	3/22/92	117	$57,896,291
23	Boyz N the Hood	(Columbia)	R	7/12/91	11/3/91	115	$56,128,283
24	Doc Hollywood	(Warner Bros.)	PG-13	8/2/91	12/8/91	129	$54,706,335
25	Bugsy	(TriStar)	R	12/13/91	5/25/92	165	$49,091,562
26	New Jack City	(Warner Bros.)	R	3/8/91	7/28/91	143	$47,322,863
27	The Rocketeer	(Buena Vista)	PG	6/21/91	10/14/91	116	$46,551,856
28	Thelma & Louise	(MGM)	R	5/24/91	9/29/91	129	$43,295,821
29	Regarding Henry	(Paramount)	PG-13	7/10/91	11/10/91	124	$42,685,761
30	The Fisher King	(TriStar)	R	9/20/91	2/23/92	157	$41,864,521
31	Point Break	(20th Fox)	R	7/12/91	9/22/91	73	$40,516,810
32	The Doctor	(Buena Vista)	PG-13	7/24/91	1/5/92	166	$38,120,905
33	Out for Justice	(Warner Bros.)	R	4/12/91	6/23/91	73	$37,866,491
34	Bill & Ted's Bogus Journey	(Orion)	PG	7/19/91	9/29/91	73	$37,244,270
35	Dead Again	(Paramount)	R	8/23/91	11/24/91	53	$36,816,234
36	Soapdish	(Paramount)	PG-13	5/31/91	9/2/91	95	$36,416,994
37	White Fang	(Buena Vista)	PG	1/18/91	5/19/91	122	$34,576,736
38	The Doors	(TriStar)	R	3/1/91	6/23/91	115	$34,156,467

Rank	Title	Distributor	MPAA	Open	Last	Days	Gross
39	Freddy's Dead: Final Nightmare	(New Line)	R	9/13/91	11/17/91	66	$34,015,591
40	King Ralph	(Universal)	PG	2/15/91	6/30/91	136	$33,512,735
41	Grand Canyon	(20th Fox)	R	12/25/91	3/29/92	96	$32,301,451
42	Dying Young	(20th Fox)	R	6/21/91	8/25/91	66	$32,280,097
43	Jungle Fever	(Universal)	R	6/7/91	9/2/91	88	$31,724,045
44	Curly Sue	(Warner Bros.)	PG	10/25/91	12/22/91	59	$29,934,051
45	Double Impact	(Columbia)	R	8/9/91	10/14/91	67	$29,066,674
46	L.A. Story	(TriStar)	PG-13	2/8/91	6/23/91	136	$28,838,380
47	Deceived	(Buena Vista)	PG-13	9/27/91	1/20/92	116	$28,712,056
48	Necessary Roughness	(Paramount)	PG-13	9/27/91	1/12/92	108	$25,986,632
49	Don't Tell Mom Babysitter's Dead	(Warner Bros.)	PG-13	6/7/91	10/6/91	122	$25,122,195
50	Little Man Tate	(Orion)	PG	10/9/91	3/1/92	145	$25,010,896
51	Other People's Money	(Warner Bros.)	R	10/18/91	12/22/91	66	$24,542,633
52	The Hard Way	(Universal)	R	3/8/91	5/19/91	73	$24,497,730
53	Problem Child II	(Universal)	PG-13	7/3/91	10/6/91	96	$24,411,267
54	Class Action	(20th Fox)	R	3/15/91	6/2/91	80	$23,940,341
55	Oscar	(Buena Vista)	PG	4/26/91	8/11/91	108	$23,548,772
56	Lionheart	(Universal)	R	1/11/91	3/31/91	80	$22,519,735
57	Frankie & Johnny	(Paramount)	R	10/11/91	12/15/91	66	$22,002,243
58	Pure Luck	(Universal)	PG	8/9/91	10/20/91	73	$21,944,730
59	The People Under the Stairs	(Universal)	R	11/1/91	1/12/92	73	$21,911,645
60	Ricochet	(Warner Bros.)	R	10/4/91	12/22/91	80	$21,658,471
61	FX2	(Orion)	PG-13	5/10/91	8/4/91	87	$21,047,744
62	American Tail: Fievel Goes West	(Universal)	G	11/22/91	2/23/92	94	$20,206,498
63	Only the Lonely	(20th Fox)	PG-13	5/24/91	7/14/91	52	$19,931,682
64	Mobsters	(Universal)	R	7/26/91	10/6/91	73	$19,826,478
65	House Party II	(New Line)	R	10/23/91	1/26/92	96	$19,421,634
66	Paradise	(Buena Vista)	PG-13	9/18/91	1/12/92	117	$18,595,037
67	Mortal Thoughts	(Columbia)	R	4/19/91	6/9/91	52	$18,169,263
68	For the Boys	(20th Fox)	R	11/22/91	2/23/92	94	$17,664,229
69	The Neverending Story II	(Warner Bros.)	PG	2/8/91	5/27/91	109	$17,363,690
70	Hudson Hawk	(TriStar)	R	5/24/91	8/4/91	73	$17,187,525
71	Defending Your Life	(Warner Bros.)	PG	3/22/91	6/9/91	80	$16,353,618
72	Billy Bathgate	(Buena Vista)	R	11/1/91	1/5/92	66	$15,538,407
73	Toy Soldiers	(TriStar)	R	4/26/91	8/4/91	101	$15,062,424
74	Truth or Dare	(Miramax)	R	5/10/91	9/2/91	116	$15,012,935
75	Shipwrecked	(Buena Vista)	PG	3/1/91	5/19/91	80	$14,927,504
76	All I Want For Christmas	(Paramount)	G	11/8/91	1/5/92	59	$14,784,045
77	Switch	(Warner Bros.)	R	5/10/91	6/23/91	45	$14,758,352
78	A Kiss Before Dying	(Universal)	R	4/26/91	6/9/91	45	$14,743,575
79	Once Around	(Universal)	R	1/18/91	3/17/91	59	$14,291,475
80	Flight of the Intruder	(Paramount)	PG-13	1/18/91	4/21/91	94	$14,290,469
81	Child's Play III	(Universal)	R	8/30/91	10/20/91	52	$14,220,380
82	Ernest Scared Stupid	(Buena Vista)	PG	10/11/91	1/12/92	94	$14,132,671
83	Highlander II	(Interstar)	R	11/1/91	12/8/91	38	$14,082,334
84	Not Without My Daughter	(MGM)	PG-13	1/11/91	3/10/91	59	$13,993,018
85	The Commitments	(20th Fox)	R	8/14/91	11/17/91	96	$13,931,633
86	Drop Dead Fred	(New Line)	PG-13	4/19/91	9/2/91	137	$13,870,896
87	The Perfect Weapon	(Paramount)	R	3/15/91	5/27/91	74	$12,833,672
88	The Grifters	(Miramax)	R	1/18/91	3/31/91	117	$12,811,516
89	The Marrying Man	(Buena Vista)	R	4/5/91	5/19/91	45	$12,424,745
90	One Good Cop	(Buena Vista)	R	5/3/91	8/4/91	94	$11,265,710
91	V.I. Warshawski	(Buena Vista)	R	7/26/91	9/29/91	66	$11,091,649

Rank	Title	Distributor	MPAA	Open	Last	Days	Gross
92	Shattered	(MGM)	R	10/11/91	12/1/91	52	$11,087,368
93	Career Opportunities	(Universal)	PG-13	3/29/91	5/19/91	52	$10,979,645
94	The Super	(20th Fox)	R	10/4/91	11/17/91	45	$10,627,423
95	A Rage in Harlem	(Miramax)	R	5/3/91	8/4/91	94	$10,438,504
96	He Said, She Said	(Paramount)	PG-13	2/22/91	5/27/91	95	$9,658,673
97	Guilty By Suspicion	(Warner Bros.)	PG-13	3/15/91	5/27/91	74	$9,473,176
98	The Butcher's Wife	(Paramount)	PG-13	10/25/91	12/15/91	52	$9,256,829
99	Scenes from a Mall	(Buena Vista)	R	2/22/91	3/24/91	31	$9,236,937
100	Warlock	(Trimark)	R	1/11/91	5/19/91	129	$9,079,056
101	Late for Dinner	(Columbia)	PG	9/20/91	10/20/91	31	$8,566,948
102	Nothing But Trouble	(Warner Bros.)	PG-13	2/15/91	4/28/91	73	$8,470,191
103	Stone Cold	(Columbia)	R	5/17/91	6/16/91	31	$8,442,527
104	Body Parts	(Paramount)	R	8/2/91	9/2/91	32	$8,366,538
105	Black Robe	(Goldwyn)	R	10/4/91	3/29/92	178	$8,201,410
106	Bingo	(TriStar)	PG	8/9/91	9/29/91	52	$8,136,139
107	If Looks Could Kill	(Warner Bros.)	PG-13	3/15/91	5/27/91	74	$7,781,025
108	Strictly Business	(Warner Bros.)	R	11/8/91	12/8/91	31	$7,367,117
109	The Five Heartbeats	(20th Fox)	R	3/29/91	5/12/91	45	$7,301,006
110	Wild Hearts Can't Be Broken	(Buena Vista)	G	5/24/91	8/11/91	80	$7,255,939
111	Harley Davidson & Marlboro Man	(MGM)	R	8/23/91	9/29/91	38	$6,972,669
112	Rush	(MGM)	R	12/22/91	2/23/92	64	$6,580,574
113	Suburban Commando	(New Line)	PG	6/21/91	11/17/91	150	$6,574,850
114	Defenseless	(New Line)	R	8/23/91	10/27/91	66	$6,411,877
115	My Own Private Idaho	(New Line)	R	9/29/91	3/8/92	162	$6,382,667
116	Rambling Rose	(New Line)	R	9/20/91	1/14/92	115	$6,254,095
117	Mystery Date	(Orion)	PG-13	8/16/91	10/6/91	52	$6,141,446
118	Barton Fink	(20th Fox)	R	8/21/91	11/17/91	89	$5,708,393
119	Livin' Large!	(Goldwyn)	R	9/20/91	11/10/91	52	$5,459,902
120	Europa, Europa	(Orion Classics)	R	6/28/91	5/10/92	318	$5,372,072
121	The Object of Beauty	(Avenue)	R	4/12/91	7/21/91	101	$5,136,759
122	La Femme Nikita	(Goldwyn)	R	3/8/91	9/2/91	179	$4,985,789
123	Delirious	(MGM)	PG	8/9/91	9/2/91	25	$4,721,931
124	Eve of Destruction	(Orion)	R	1/18/91	2/10/91	24	$4,698,076
125	True Identity	(Buena Vista)	R	8/23/91	9/29/91	38	$4,676,035
126	The Hitman	(Cannon)	R	10/25/91	12/1/91	38	$4,568,498
127	Run	(Buena Vista)	R	2/1/91	3/3/91	31	$4,294,183
128	Dutch	(20th Fox)	PG-13	7/19/91	8/11/91	24	$4,233,008
129	Hear My Song	(Miramax)	R	12/27/91	5/10/92	136	$3,879,613
130	Life Stinks	(MGM)	PG-13	7/26/91	8/11/91	17	$3,785,481
131	Paris is Burning	(Prestige)	NR	3/13/91	11/24/91	257	$3,779,620
132	Popcorn	(Studio 3)	R	2/1/91	2/10/91	10	$3,751,629
133	My Heroes Have Al. Been Cowboys	(Goldwyn)	PG	3/1/91	5/5/91	66	$3,596,338
134	Impromptu	(Hemdale)	PG-13	4/12/91	7/21/91	101	$3,564,947
135	Shout	(Universal)	PG	10/4/91	11/3/91	31	$3,448,785
136	Mannequin II	(20th Fox)	PG	5/17/91	6/2/91	17	$3,225,056
137	Homicide	(Triumph)	R	10/9/91	12/1/91	54	$2,971,661
138	Straight out of Brooklyn	(Goldwyn)	R	5/22/91	10/14/91	146	$2,707,969
139	Another You	(TriStar)	R	7/26/91	8/4/91	10	$2,516,301
140	Return to the Blue Lagoon	(Columbia)	PG-13	8/2/91	8/11/91	10	$2,330,621
141	Naked Lunch	(20th Fox)	R	12/27/91	2/23/92	59	$2,233,860
142	The Man in the Moon	(MGM)	PG	10/4/91	12/22/91	80	$2,203,909
143	Showdown in Little Tokyo	(Warner Bros.)	R	8/23/91	10/14/91	53	$2,128,013
144	Cadence	(New Line)	PG-13	1/18/91	5/12/91	115	$2,028,171

Rank	Title	Distributor	MPAA	Open	Last	Days	Gross
145	Madame Bovary	(Goldwyn)	NR	12/25/91	3/29/92	96	$1,936,215
146	Slacker	(Orion Classics)	R	7/5/91	12/22/91	171	$1,906,659
147	29th Street	(20th Fox)	R	11/1/91	12/8/91	38	$1,840,532
148	Everybody's Fine	(Miramax)	NR	5/31/91	9/29/91	122	$1,739,310
149	My Father's Glory	(Orion Classics)	G	1/14/91	3/1/92	262	$1,722,298
150	High Heels	(Miramax)	NR	12/20/91	4/5/92	108	$1,710,057
151	Spartacus	(Universal)	NR	4/26/91	7/14/91	80	$1,659,554
152	Ju Dou	(Miramax)	NR	3/6/91	6/2/91	89	$1,561,758
153	Prospero's Books	(Miramax)	R	11/15/91	2/2/92	80	$1,560,417
154	Truly, Madly, Deeply	(Goldwyn)	NR	5/3/91	10/6/91	157	$1,547,309
155	Life is Sweet	(October Films)	NR	10/25/91	4/21/92	178	$1,516,414
156	The Double Life of Veronique	(Miramax)	NR	11/24/91	4/12/92	141	$1,512,310
157	My Mothers Castle	(Orion Classics)	PG	1/21/91	3/8/92	227	$1,471,218
158	Company Business	(MGM)	R	9/6/91	10/27/91	52	$1,443,690
159	Mister Johnson	(Avenue)	PG	3/22/91	7/21/91	122	$1,395,547
160	City of Hope	(Goldwyn)	R	10/11/91	1/26/92	108	$1,339,620
161	Book of Love	(New Line)	PG-13	2/1/91	3/17/91	73	$1,299,069
162	The Rapture	(Fine Line)	R	10/4/91	1/14/92	101	$1,269,394
163	At Play in the Fields of the Lords	(Universal)	R	12/6/91	4/5/92	122	$1,269,005
164	The Comfort of Strangers	(Skouras)	R	3/15/91	9/2/91	172	$1,244,381
165	Kickboxer II	(Trimark)	R	6/14/91	7/14/91	31	$1,193,837
166	Daughters of the Dust	(Kino Int'l)	NR	12/24/91	5/17/92	146	$1,176,779
167	Citizen Kane (Re)	(Paramount)	NR	5/1/91	6/23/91	54	$1,140,769
168	The Story of Boys and Girls	(Aries)	NR	8/23/91	12/15/91	115	$1,091,330
169	Year of the Gun	(Triumph)	R	11/1/91	11/10/91	10	$1,072,333
170	Daddy Nostalgia	(Avenue)	PG	4/12/91	7/21/91	101	$1,065,618
171	An Angel at my Table	(Fine Line)	R	5/19/91	9/29/91	134	$1,032,167
172	Cool as Ice	(Universal)	PG	10/18/91	11/3/91	17	$1,023,320
173	Meeting Venus	(Warner Bros.)	PG-13	11/15/91	2/9/92	87	$985,877
174	Whore	(Trimark)	NC-17	10/4/91	12/15/91	73	$919,458
175	Kafka	(Miramax)	PG-13	12/4/91	4/19/92	138	$903,671
176	The 23rd Tournee of Animation	(Expanded Ent.)	NR	8/28/91	10/27/91	59	$853,656
177	The Talking of Beverly Hills	(Columbia)	R	10/11/91	10/20/91	10	$845,057
178	The Miracle	(Miramax)	NR	7/3/91	10/6/91	96	$835,519
179	Antonia & Jane	(Miramax)	NR	10/11/91	2/2/92	115	$800,021
180	Beastmaster II	(New Line)	PG	8/30/91	9/27/91	24	$766,286
181	Rosencrantz & Guildenstern Dead	(Cinecom)	PG	2/8/91	6/2/91	115	$739,104
182	Thousand Pieces of Gold	(Greycat)	NR	4/27/91	10/27/91	185	$717,772
183	Mindwalk	(Triton)	PG	10/11/91	4/21/92	192	$638,544
184	Dice Rules	(Blossom)	NC-17	5/17/91	6/2/91	17	$637,327
185	British Animation Invasion	(Expanded Ent.)	NR	3/1/91	6/23/91	115	$621,199
186	The Inner Circle	(Columbia)	PG-13	12/25/91	3/15/92	82	$586,171
187	The Pope Must Die(t)	(Miramax)	R	8/30/91	9/22/91	24	$555,668
188	Search for Intelli. Signs of Life	(Orion Classics)	PG-13	9/27/91	1/5/92	101	$547,012
189	Sex, Drugs, Rock & Roll	(Avenue)	R	9/6/91	11/10/91	66	$527,397
190	Hangin' With the Homeboys	(New Line)	R	4/5/91	10/6/91	185	$516,855
191	Rhapsody in August	(Orion Classics)	PG	12/20/91	3/15/92	87	$516,431
192	Kiss Me a Killer	(Califilm)	R	4/5/91	6/16/91	73	$479,662
193	The Unborn	(Califilm)	R	3/29/91	6/9/91	66	$439,783
194	Meet the Applegates	(Triton)	R	2/1/91	2/10/91	10	$425,017
195	Until the End of the World	(Warner Bros.)	R	12/25/91	2/2/92	40	$419,264
196	Le Belle Noiseuse	(MK2USA)	NR	10/26/91	4/12/92	170	$408,571
197	True Colors	(Paramount)	R	3/15/91	5/19/91	66	$385,230

Rank	Title	Distributor	MPAA	Open	Last	Days	Gross
198	Rich Girl	(Studio 3)	R	5/3/91	5/5/91	3	$368,056
199	Sweet Talker	(New Line)	PG	5/10/91	5/19/91	10	$364,297
200	Iron and Silk	(Prestige)	NR	2/15/91	5/5/91	80	$356,077
201	Uranus	(Prestige)	NR	8/23/91	11/24/91	94	$342,198
202	Trust	(Fine Line)	R	7/26/91	9/29/91	66	$342,069
203	And You Thought Your Parents...	(Trimark)	PG	11/15/91	12/15/91	31	$341,681
204	McBain	(Shapiro)	R	9/20/91	9/22/91	3	$320,000
205	Queens Logic	(New Line)	R	2/1/91	3/3/91	31	$299,811
206	Ay Carmela	(Prestige)	NR	2/8/91	5/5/91	87	$299,090
207	Drowning by Numbers	(Prestige)	R	4/26/91	6/16/91	52	$297,366
208	Ambition	(Miramax)	R	5/31/91	6/2/91	3	$282,503
209	Heaven and Earth	(Triton)	PG-13	2/8/91	5/5/91	87	$280,127
210	American Ninja IV	(Cannon)	R	3/8/91	3/10/91	3	$277,462
211	Pastime	(Miramax)	PG	8/23/91	9/29/91	38	$267,265
212	Two Evil Eyes	(Tauras)	R	10/25/91	10/27/91	3	$260,410
213	Superstar! Life of Andy Warhol	(Aries)	NR	2/22/91	4/28/91	66	$259,297
214	Twenty-One	(Triton)	R	10/4/91	12/15/91	73	$256,521
215	Tatie Danielle	(Prestige)	NR	5/24/91	6/16/91	31	$251,238
216	Stepping Out	(Paramount)	PG	10/4/91	11/3/91	31	$242,014
217	Dogfight	(Warner Bros.)	R	9/13/91	10/14/91	32	$234,859
218	Delusions	(IRS)	R	6/7/91	10/14/91	130	$229,221
219	Exposure	(Miramax)	R	10/30/91	12/8/91	40	$228,304
220	Closet Land	(Universal)	R	3/6/91	3/17/91	12	$225,671
221	Journey of Hope	(Miramax)	NR	4/26/91	6/2/91	38	$170,411
222	Taxi Blues	(MK2USA)	NR	1/18/91	3/10/91	52	$169,410
223	The Indian Runner	(MGM)	R	9/20/91	11/10/91	52	$147,981
224	Talent for the Game	(Paramount)	PG	4/26/91	5/19/91	24	$140,689
225	Close My Eyes	(Castle Hill)	R	11/8/91	3/1/92	45	$134,134
226	Eminent Domain	(Triumph)	PG-13	4/12/91	4/21/91	10	$133,270
227	Hearts of Darkness	(Triton)	R	11/27/91	5/3/92	159	$127,670
228	Open Doors	(Orion Classics)	R	3/8/91	5/21/91	73	$123,470
229	Men of Respect	(Columbia)	R	1/18/91	1/27/91	10	$119,801
230	End of Innocence	(Skouras)	R	1/18/91	3/3/91	45	$116,779
231	Liebestraum	(MGM)	R	9/13/91	11/17/91	66	$101,631
232	Overseas	(Aries)	NR	11/8/91	12/15/91	38	$93,546
233	Blade Runner (Re)	(Warner Bros.)	R	9/27/91	10/6/91	10	$89,017
234	Bright Angel	(Hemdale)	R	6/14/91	7/21/91	38	$88,686
235	Naked Tango	(New Line)	R	8/23/91	10/6/91	45	$80,938
236	Good Woman of Bangkok	(Roxie)	NR	11/15/91	12/8/91	24	$77,172
237	Fires Within	(MGM)	R	6/28/91	7/7/91	10	$67,299
238	Scanners II: The New Order	(Triton)	R	6/28/91	7/7/91	10	$64,985
239	Iron Maze	(Castle Hill)	R	11/1/91	11/3/91	3	$64,218
240	Timebomb	(MGM)	R	9/27/91	10/6/91	10	$60,780
241	Prisoners of the Sun	(Skouras)	R	7/19/91	9/2/91	46	$60,231
242	Firehead	(AIP)	R	1/25/91	3/17/91	52	$57,139
243	Too Much Sun	(New Line)	R	1/25/91	2/10/91	17	$51,798
244	Shadow of China	(New Line)	NR	3/10/91	3/31/91	22	$51,758
245	Talkin' Dirty After Dark	(New Line)	R	11/27/91	12/1/91	5	$50,634
246	Young Soul Rebels	(Prestige)	NR	12/6/91	12/15/91	10	$50,099
247	Let Him Have It	(Fine Line)	R	12/6/91	1/5/92	31	$43,408
248	King of the Kickboxers	(Imperial)	R	8/9/91	9/2/91	25	$42,808
249	Prime Target	(Hero Films)	R	9/27/91	9/29/91	3	$41,378
250	Susan Brink's Arirany	(Cine Korea)	NR	12/8/91	12/22/91	15	$28,521

Rank	Title	Distributor	MPAA	Open	Last	Days	Gross
251	Julia Has Two Lovers	(South Gate)	R	3/21/91	3/31/91	10	$28,289
252	The Park Backward	(Greycat)	R	7/26/91	8/18/91	24	$27,049
253	Requiem for Dominic	(Hemdale)	R	4/19/91	5/5/91	17	$26,846
254	Deep Blues	(Tara Rel.)	NR	11/15/91	8/9/92	131	$22,405
255	Final Approach	(Trimark)	R	12/6/91	3/22/92	108	$19,902
256	Every Other Weekend	(MK2USA)	NR	6/17/91	6/30/91	12	$19,804
257	Ski School	(Moviestore)	R	1/11/91	1/13/91	3	$18,476
258	Born to Ride	(Warner Bros.)	PG	5/3/91	5/5/91	3	$17,680
259	Noir Et Blanc	(Greycat)	NR	5/24/91	6/2/91	10	$15,082
260	Voyeur	(Prestige)	NR	8/2/91	8/11/91	10	$14,750
261	Crossing the Line	(Miramax)	R	8/9/91	8/18/91	10	$11,790
262	Raw Nerve	(AIP)	R	6/28/91	6/30/91	3	$10,732
263	Robot Carnival	(Streamline)	NR	3/15/91	3/17/91	3	$10,642
264	Get Back	(New Line)	PG	10/25/91	10/27/91	3	$8,906
265	Blood and Concrete	(IRS)	R	9/13/91	9/22/91	17	$8,780
266	Crooked Hearts	(MGM)	R	5/31/91	6/16/91	17	$8,534
267	The Reflecting Skin	(Miramax)	R	12/18/91	12/22/91	5	$8,188
268	Don Juan, My Love	(IFEX)	NR	7/12/91	7/14/91	3	$6,501
269	Horseplayer	(Greycat)	NR	7/12/91	7/14/91	3	$5,355
270	Pizza Man	(Megalomania)	NR	12/6/91	12/8/91	3	$4,781
271	Love & Murder	(Hemdale)	R	11/8/91	11/10/91	3	$4,630
272	George's Island	(Fine Line)	PG	10/25/91	10/27/91	3	$1,652
273	Cheap Shots	(Hemdale)	PG-13	11/15/91	11/17/91	3	$1,380

1990 Numerical Ranking   1990 Nu...   1990 ...ical   1990 Numerical Ranking

1990 Film Grosses

The following movies are ranked by their reported domestic box office gross (U.S. & Canada). The list represents films that were released in 1990 and shows the entire longevity of the release not just the calendar year it was released in. The rank is followed by the title of the picture, its distribution company, the Motion Picture Association of America rating, the day it was released, the last day grosses were reported, how many days it was in release and finally the total box office revenue received at the theatres. These statistics have been compiled from a variety of sources.

Rank	Title	Distributor	MPAA	Open	Last	Days	Gross
1	Home Alone	(20th Fox)	PG	11/16/90	8/11/91	271	$281,493,907
2	Ghost	(Paramount)	PG-13	7/13/90	3/3/91	262	$216,818,693
3	Dances With Wolves	(Orion)	PG-13	11/9/90	8/25/91	290	$183,243,347
4	Pretty Woman	(Buena Vista)	R	3/23/90	11/4/90	227	$178,088,702
5	Teenage Mutant Ninja Turtles	(New Line)	PG	3/30/90	9/30/90	185	$133,145,682
6	The Hunt for Red October	(Paramount)	PG	3/2/90	9/16/90	199	$120,617,004
7	Total Recall	(TriStar)	R	6/1/90	10/14/90	136	$118,272,498
8	Die Hard II	(20th Fox)	R	7/4/90	12/16/90	167	$115,288,665
9	Dick Tracy	(Buena Vista)	PG	6/15/90	9/3/90	81	$103,738,726
10	Kindergarten Cop	(Universal)	PG-13	12/21/90	6/16/91	178	$90,272,872
11	Back to the Future Pt III	(Universal)	PG	5/25/90	11/4/90	164	$86,498,961
12	Presumed Innocent	(Warner Bros.)	R	7/27/90	12/16/90	143	$86,266,757
13	Days of Thunder	(Paramount)	PG-13	6/27/90	11/25/90	152	$82,663,996
14	Another 48 Hours	(Paramount)	R	6/8/90	11/11/90	157	$80,786,874
15	Three Men and a Little Lady	(Buena Vista)	PG	11/21/90	5/12/91	173	$71,481,438
16	Bird on a Wire	(Universal)	PG-13	5/18/90	9/23/90	129	$70,283,925
17	The Godfather, Pt III	(Paramount)	R	12/25/90	5/19/91	146	$66,661,321
18	Misery	(Columbia)	R	11/30/90	5/12/91	164	$61,633,748
19	Flatliners	(Columbia)	R	8/10/90	12/16/90	129	$61,308,153
20	Edward Scissorhands	(20th Fox)	PG-13	12/7/90	4/7/91	122	$54,155,571
21	Arachnophobia	(Buena Vista)	PG-13	7/18/90	1/6/91	173	$53,194,144
22	Awakenings	(Columbia)	PG-13	12/20/90	5/12/91	145	$51,570,513
23	Problem Child	(Universal)	PG	7/27/90	11/4/90	101	$50,317,125
24	Hard to Kill	(Warner Bros.)	R	2/9/90	7/10/90	150	$47,381,386
25	Goodfellas	(Warner Bros.)	R	9/19/90	6/9/91	264	$46,685,343
26	Look Who's Talking Too	(TriStar)	PG-13	12/14/90	5/19/91	157	$46,602,276
27	Robocop II	(Orion)	R	6/22/90	9/30/90	101	$45,367,609
28	The Jungle Book (Re)	(Buena Vista)	G	7/13/90	11/11/90	122	$44,575,321
29	Marked for Death	(20th Fox)	R	10/5/90	12/9/90	66	$43,120,554
30	Gremlins II	(Warner Bros.)	PG-13	6/15/90	10/8/90	116	$41,476,097
31	Young Guns II	(20th Fox)	PG-13	8/1/90	10/8/90	69	$40,478,635
32	Rocky V	(United Artist)	PG-13	11/16/90	2/18/91	95	$40,123,474
33	Joe Versus the Volcano	(Warner Bros.)	PG	3/9/90	7/10/90	122	$39,381,963
34	Postcards from the Edge	(Columbia)	R	9/12/90	12/16/90	96	$37,804,453
35	Mermaids	(Orion)	PG-13	12/14/90	4/14/91	122	$35,124,004
36	Darkman	(Universal)	R	8/24/90	11/4/90	73	$32,942,739
37	Air America	(TriStar)	R	8/10/90	11/4/90	87	$30,506,847
38	Green Card	(Buena Vista)	PG-13	12/23/90	5/19/91	148	$29,754,169

Rank	Title	Distributor	MPAA	Open	Last	Days	Gross
39	**Predator II**	*(20th Fox)*	R	11/21/90	1/21/91	62	$28,317,513
40	**Pacific Heights**	*(20th Fox)*	R	9/28/90	11/18/90	52	$27,892,883
41	**The Rescuers Down Under**	*(Buena Vista)*	G	11/16/90	4/2/91	157	$27,792,655
42	**Internal Affairs**	*(Paramount)*	R	1/12/90	5/20/90	129	$27,661,878
43	**Cadillac Man**	*(Orion)*	R	5/18/90	8/5/90	80	$27,257,086
44	**Child's Play II**	*(Universal)*	R	11/9/90	1/6/91	59	$26,874,812
45	**House Party**	*(New Line)*	R	3/9/90	9/3/90	179	$26,385,627
46	**Memphis Belle**	*(Warner Bros.)*	PG-13	10/12/90	12/16/90	66	$26,142,623
47	**Jacob's Ladder**	*(TriStar)*	R	11/2/90	2/10/91	111	$25,972,896
48	**Ernest Goes to Jail**	*(Buena Vista)*	PG	4/6/90	9/3/90	151	$25,029,569
49	**The Exorcist III**	*(20th Fox)*	R	8/17/90	10/8/90	53	$25,011,739
50	**Navy Seals**	*(Orion)*	R	7/20/90	10/8/90	59	$24,830,689
51	**Fantasia (Re)**	*(Buena Vista)*	NR	10/5/90	12/16/90	73	$24,764,877
52	**My Blue Heaven**	*(Warner Bros.)*	PG-13	8/17/90	12/9/90	115	$23,584,024
53	**Ghost Dad**	*(Universal)*	PG	6/29/90	11/4/90	129	$23,145,682
54	**The Russia House**	*(MGM)*	R	12/19/90	3/10/91	82	$22,583,018
55	**The First Power**	*(Orion)*	R	4/6/90	6/3/90	59	$21,365,321
56	**The Freshman**	*(TriStar)*	PG	7/20/90	10/14/90	87	$21,267,167
57	**Hamlet**	*(Warner Bros.)*	PG	12/19/90	6/9/91	173	$20,684,776
58	**Madhouse**	*(Orion)*	PG-13	2/16/90	5/6/90	80	$20,438,179
59	**The Adv.s of Ford Fairlane**	*(20th Fox)*	R	7/11/90	8/12/90	33	$20,423,389
60	**The Rookie**	*(Warner Bros.)*	R	12/7/90	1/21/91	46	$20,419,506
61	**Quigley Down Under**	*(MGM)*	PG-13	10/19/90	1/6/91	80	$20,273,701
62	**Stella**	*(Buena Vista)*	PG-13	2/2/90	5/6/90	94	$20,062,347
63	**Betsy's Wedding**	*(Buena Vista)*	R	6/22/90	9/3/90	31	$19,740,070
64	**Jetsons: The Movie**	*(Universal)*	G	7/6/90	10/28/90	115	$19,543,985
65	**Taking Care of Business**	*(Buena Vista)*	R	8/17/90	11/4/90	80	$19,476,362
66	**Duck Tales: The Movie**	*(Buena Vista)*	G	8/3/90	11/11/90	101	$18,075,331
67	**Sibling Rivalry**	*(Columbia)*	PG-13	10/26/90	1/1/91	68	$17,711,483
68	**White Palace**	*(Universal)*	R	10/19/90	12/16/90	59	$16,756,073
69	**Tales from the Dark Side: The Movie**	*(Paramount)*	R	5/4/90	7/1/90	59	$16,305,883
70	**Men at Work**	*(Triumph)*	PG-13	8/24/90	11/18/90	87	$16,151,032
71	**The Guardian**	*(Universal)*	R	4/27/90	6/17/90	52	$16,140,440
72	**Mo' Better Blues**	*(Universal)*	R	8/3/90	10/21/90	80	$15,897,125
73	**Avalon**	*(TriStar)*	PG	10/5/90	2/10/91	129	$15,698,797
74	**I Love You to Death**	*(TriStar)*	R	4/6/90	6/10/90	66	$15,600,149
75	**Revenge**	*(Columbia)*	R	2/16/90	4/8/90	52	$15,535,771
76	**Tremors**	*(Universal)*	PG-13	1/19/90	4/1/90	73	$15,475,065
77	**Reversal of Fortune**	*(Warner Bros.)*	R	10/17/90	6/23/91	250	$15,441,766
78	**The Bonfire of the Vanities**	*(Warner Bros.)*	R	12/21/90	2/3/91	45	$15,396,803
79	**Death Warrant**	*(MGM)*	R	9/14/90	10/28/90	45	$15,394,200
80	**Spaced Invaders**	*(Buena Vista)*	PG	4/27/90	9/3/90	130	$15,369,573
81	**Mr. Destiny**	*(Buena Vista)*	PG-13	10/12/90	1/13/91	94	$15,355,313
82	**Quick Change**	*(Warner Bros.)*	R	7/13/90	10/8/90	24	$15,255,554
83	**Fire Birds**	*(Buena Vista)*	PG-13	5/25/90	9/3/90	102	$14,760,451
84	**Wild at Heart**	*(Goldwyn)*	R	8/17/90	11/25/90	101	$14,535,649
85	**Lord of the Flies**	*(Columbia)*	R	3/16/90	5/28/90	74	$13,812,230
86	**Crazy People**	*(Paramount)*	R	4/11/90	6/24/90	75	$13,204,459
87	**Bad Influence**	*(Triumph)*	R	3/9/90	5/20/90	73	$12,626,043
88	**Graveyard Shift**	*(Paramount)*	R	10/26/90	12/16/90	52	$11,578,883
89	**Pump Up the Volume**	*(New Line)*	R	8/22/90	11/11/90	82	$11,534,231
90	**Henry & June**	*(Universal)*	NC-17	10/5/90	12/25/90	82	$11,003,353
91	**Wild Orchid**	*(Triumph)*	R	4/27/90	7/29/90	94	$10,976,117

Rank	Title	Distributor	MPAA	Open	Last	Days	Gross
92	Cinema Paradiso	(Miramax)	NR	2/2/90	1/18/91	290	$10,779,325
93	Q&A	(TriStar)	R	4/27/90	6/10/90	45	$10,738,946
94	Narrow Margin	(TriStar)	R	9/21/90	11/18/90	59	$10,650,478
95	Opportunity Knocks	(Universal)	PG-13	3/30/90	5/28/90	60	$10,525,505
96	The Witches	(Warner Bros.)	PG	8/24/90	12/9/90	297	$10,349,306
97	The Adv.s of Milo and Otis (Re)	(Columbia)	NR	6/15/90	8/19/90	65	$10,141,029
98	The Two Jakes	(Paramount)	R	8/10/90	10/8/90	60	$9,995,033
99	Nuns on the Run	(20th Fox)	PG-13	3/16/90	5/20/90	66	$9,978,475
100	Miami Blues	(Orion)	R	4/20/90	6/24/90	66	$9,654,290
101	Havana	(Universal)	R	12/12/90	1/27/91	47	$9,178,629
102	Nightbreed	(20th Fox)	R	2/16/90	3/25/90	38	$8,871,183
103	Ski Patrol	(Triumph)	PG	1/12/90	4/8/90	87	$8,448,158
104	Funny About Love	(Paramount)	PG-13	9/21/90	11/11/90	52	$8,105,538
105	Cry-Baby	(Universal)	PG-13	4/6/90	5/28/90	53	$7,735,790
106	Blue Steel	(MGM)	R	3/16/90	4/15/90	31	$7,701,707
107	Mr. & Mrs. Bridge	(Miramax)	PG	11/23/90	5/27/91	186	$7,698,010
108	Cook, Thief, His Wife & Her Lover	(Miramax)	NR	4/6/90	9/16/90	164	$7,407,995
109	Alice	(Orion)	PG-13	12/25/90	3/24/91	90	$6,759,247
110	Almost an Angel	(Paramount)	PG	12/19/90	1/13/91	26	$6,519,481
111	Flashback	(Paramount)	R	2/2/90	3/25/90	52	$6,476,134
112	Delta Force II	(MGM)	R	8/24/90	9/23/90	31	$6,154,944
113	Men Don't Leave	(Warner Bros.)	PG-13	2/2/90	4/1/90	59	$6,050,018
114	The Gods Must Be Crazy II	(Columbia)	PG	4/13/90	6/17/90	66	$5,938,663
115	Cyrano de Bergerac	(Orion Classics)	PG	11/16/90	7/7/91	235	$5,804,286
116	Leatherface: Tex Chain Mass III	(New Line)	R	1/12/90	2/19/90	39	$5,758,627
117	Night of the Living Dead	(Columbia)	R	10/19/90	11/11/90	24	$5,659,571
118	Welcome Home Roxy Carmichael	(Paramount)	PG-13	10/12/90	11/11/90	31	$5,659,571
119	Hardware	(Millimeter)	R	9/14/90	10/28/90	45	$5,649,801
120	Stanley & Iris	(MGM)	PG-13	2/9/90	3/11/90	31	$5,473,047
121	The Handmaid's Tale	(Cinecom)	R	3/9/90	8/5/90	150	$4,960,388
122	Miller's Crossing	(20th Fox)	R	9/22/90	11/18/90	58	$4,693,759
123	The Long Walk Home	(Miramax)	PG	12/21/90	5/12/91	143	$4,686,540
124	Longtime Companion	(Goldwyn)	R	5/11/90	9/3/90	116	$4,609,953
125	Graffiti Bridge	(Warner Bros.)	PG-13	11/2/90	12/16/90	45	$4,538,113
126	Loose Cannons	(TriStar)	R	2/9/90	2/25/90	17	$4,463,085
127	I Come in Peace	(Triumph)	R	9/28/90	11/11/90	45	$4,348,368
128	Lambada	(Warner Bros.)	PG	3/16/90	4/15/90	31	$4,248,622
129	China Cry	(Penland)	PG-13	11/2/90	5/19/91	197	$4,170,065
130	Heart Condition	(New Line)	R	2/2/90	3/11/90	38	$4,134,992
131	Lisa	(United Artists)	PG-13	4/20/90	6/24/90	66	$4,067,725
132	Tie Me Up! Tie Me Down!	(Miramax)	NR	5/4/90	9/30/90	150	$3,961,773
133	Short Time	(20th Fox)	PG-13	5/4/90	5/28/90	25	$3,537,478
134	A Shock to the System	(Cosair)	R	3/23/90	5/20/90	59	$3,417,056
135	The Lemon Sisters	(Miramax)	PG-13	8/31/90	9/30/90	17	$3,399,773
136	Mountains of the Moon	(TriStar)	R	2/23/90	6/10/90	108	$3,334,092
137	Metropolitan	(New Line)	PG-13	8/3/90	2/18/91	200	$2,923,846
138	After Dark, My Sweet	(Avenue)	R	8/24/90	11/4/90	73	$2,668,414
139	Desperate Hours	(MGM)	R	10/5/90	10/21/90	17	$2,624,629
140	Impulse	(Warner Bros.)	R	4/6/90	6/17/90	73	$2,531,528
141	King of New York	(New Line)	R	9/28/90	12/16/90	80	$2,389,850
142	Blind Fury	(TriStar)	R	3/16/90	4/8/90	24	$2,345,628
143	White Hunter, Black Heart	(Warner Bros.)	PG	9/14/90	11/25/90	73	$2,319,124
144	The Nasty Girl	(Miramax)	Dramedy	10/26/90	6/2/91	220	$2,281,569

Rank	Title	Distributor	MPAA	Open	Last	Days	Gross
145	Downtown	(20th Fox)	R	1/12/90	2/25/90	45	$2,205,486
146	Texasville	(Columbia)	R	9/28/90	11/4/90	38	$2,188,065
147	Vincent and Theo	(Hemdale)	PG-13	11/2/90	3/24/91	143	$2,154,787
148	The Krays	(Miramax)	R	11/9/90	12/16/90	38	$2,035,562
149	The Sheltering Sky	(Warner Bros.)	R	12/12/90	2/18/91	69	$1,977,308
150	Dreams	(Warner Bros.)	PG	8/24/90	11/25/90	94	$1,963,207
151	State of Grace	(Orion)	R	9/14/90	10/28/90	45	$1,869,451
152	Tune in Tomorrow	(Cinecom)	PG-13	10/26/90	12/16/90	52	$1,794,601
153	Too Beautiful For You	(Orion Classics)	NR	3/2/90	8/19/90	171	$1,776,440
154	The Forbidden Dance	(Columbia)	PG-13	3/16/90	4/8/90	24	$1,719,538
155	Last Exit to Brooklyn	(Cinecom)	R	5/4/90	8/26/90	115	$1,696,046
156	The Nutcracker Prince	(Warner Bros.)	G	11/21/90	12/16/90	26	$1,654,163
157	Jesus of Montreal	(Orion Classics)	R	5/25/90	11/11/90	171	$1,583,261
158	May Fools	(Orion Classics)	R	6/22/90	11/25/90	157	$1,565,594
159	A Cry in the Wild	(Concorde)	PG	6/1/90	11/4/90	157	$1,494,969
160	The Field	(Avenue)	PG-13	12/20/90	4/28/91	129	$1,494,399
161	Monsieur Hire	(Orion Classics)	PG-13	4/20/90	9/23/90	157	$1,417,030
162	Body Chemistry	(Concorde)	R	3/9/90	5/13/90	66	$1,406,900
163	The Last of the Finest	(Orion)	R	3/9/90	4/8/90	31	$1,395,694
164	Repossessed	(New Line)	PG-13	9/14/90	11/11/90	59	$1,376,061
165	Born to Ski	(Warren Miller)	NR	10/1/90	12/8/91	69	$1,366,043
166	Everybody Wins	(Orion)	R	1/19/90	2/19/90	32	$1,339,681
167	Courage Mountain	(Triumph)	PG	2/16/90	3/4/90	17	$1,263,739
168	Slumber Party Massacre III	(Concorde)	R	9/7/90	10/21/90	45	$1,242,995
169	The Fourth War	(Cannon)	R	3/23/90	4/1/90	10	$1,232,285
170	Icicle Thief	(Aries)	NR	8/24/90	2/24/91	121	$1,228,801
171	Without You I'm Nothing	(New Line)	R	5/11/90	8/26/90	108	$1,218,730
172	Love at Large	(Orion)	R	3/9/90	4/22/90	45	$1,214,295
173	The Hot Spot	(Orion)	R	10/12/90	11/18/90	38	$1,206,153
174	Robot Jox	(Triumph)	PG	11/21/90	12/16/90	26	$1,203,061
175	Daddy's Dyin'...Who's Got the Will?	(MGM)	PG-13	5/4/90	7/1/90	59	$1,169,941
176	To Sleep with Anger	(Goldwyn)	PG	10/12/90	2/18/91	130	$1,158,989
177	Up Against the Wall	(African Amer)	PG-13	10/26/90	3/3/91	129	$1,085,345
178	Don't Tell Her It's Me	(Hemdale)	PG-13	9/21/90	10/8/90	18	$1,036,933
179	Where the Heart Is	(Buena Vista)	R	2/23/90	3/11/90	17	$1,034,006
180	Bloodfist II	(Concorde)	R	10/12/90	11/11/90	31	$1,021,306
181	Hidden Agenda	(Hemdale)	R	11/21/90	2/24/91	96	$948,195
182	Sweetie	(Avenue)	R	1/19/90	7/22/90	185	$938,065
183	The Blood of Heros	(New Line)	R	2/23/90	3/11/90	17	$882,290
184	Corporate Affairs	(Concorde)	R	10/5/90	11/11/90	38	$862,292
185	Angel Town	(Taurus)	R	2/23/90	3/25/90	31	$855,810
186	Def By Temptation	(Troma)	R	3/23/90	6/10/90	55	$854,603
187	Come See the Paradise	(20th Fox)	R	12/23/90	2/3/91	43	$850,563
188	C'Est La Vie	(Goldwyn)	NR	11/2/90	2/18/91	109	$801,787
189	Waiting for the Light	(Triumph)	PG	11/1/90	11/25/90	24	$797,264
190	Vital Signs	(20th Fox)	R	4/13/90	4/29/90	17	$779,107
191	Listen Up: Lives Of Quincy Jones	(Warner Bros.)	PG-13	10/5/90	11/25/90	52	$774,902
192	The 22nd Tournee of Animation	(Expanded Ent.)	NR	3/30/90	6/17/90	80	$768,304
193	Strapless	(Miramax)	R	5/18/90	9/16/90	122	$745,744
194	My 20th Century	(Aries)	NR	11/9/90	4/28/91	171	$682,016
195	The Return of Superfly	(Triton)	R	11/9/90	11/25/90	17	$610,402
196	Henry: Portrait of a Serial Killer	(Greycat)	NR	1/5/90	9/23/90	262	$609,939
197	Coupe De Ville	(Universal)	PG-13	3/9/90	4/1/90	24	$592,089

Rank	Title	Distributor	MPAA	Open	Last	Days	Gross
198	Overexposed	(Concorde)	R	3/9/90	4/22/90	52	$577,701
199	Rosalie Goes Shopping	(Four Seasons)	PG	2/9/90	6/24/90	136	$574,080
200	Strike It Rich	(Miramax)	PG	1/26/90	2/19/90	25	$552,800
201	Rain Killer	(Concorde)	R	9/14/90	9/23/90	10	$504,607
202	How to Make Love to a Negro	(Angelika)	NR	6/8/90	9/23/90	108	$491,193
203	Shrimp on the Barbie	(Unity Pic)	PG-13	9/2/90	9/11/90	10	$458,996
204	The Unbelievable Truth	(Miramax)	R	7/20/90	9/16/90	59	$452,598
205	The Tall Guy	(Miramax)	R	9/21/90	11/4/90	45	$438,458
206	Life and Nothing But	(Orion Classics)	PG	9/14/90	2/10/91	149	$423,440
207	Welcome to Oblivion	(Concorde)	R	3/16/90	4/8/90	24	$410,880
208	Side Out	(TriStar)	PG-13	3/30/90	4/8/90	10	$403,357
209	Brain Dead	(Concorde)	R	1/19/90	2/11/90	24	$334,417
210	The Mahabarata	(MK2USA)	NR	4/27/90	9/16/90	143	$334,077
211	Outside Chance f Maximillian	(South Gate)	G	1/17/90	5/4/90	108	$317,670
212	Full Fathom Five	(Concorde)	PG	9/7/90	9/16/90	10	$313,214
213	Streets	(Concorde)	R	1/19/90	2/11/90	24	$309,060
214	The Plot Against Harry	(New Yorker)	NR	1/12/90	3/18/90	66	$274,182
215	Mama, There's a Man in Your Bed	(Miramax)	NR	4/13/90	5/20/90	38	$266,347
216	In the Spirit	(Castle Hill)	R	4/6/90	6/24/90	80	$265,481
217	Time of the Gypsies	(Columbia)	R	2/9/90	3/25/90	45	$263,482
218	Frankenhooker	(Shapiro)	R	5/11/90	10/8/90	130	$205,068
219	Imported Bridegroom	(ASA Comm)	NR	3/16/90	7/29/90	136	$203,417
220	Torn Apart	(Castle Hill)	R	4/20/90	6/24/90	66	$199,271
221	Life is a Long Quiet River	(MK2USA)	NR	7/13/90	9/30/90	80	$194,456
222	A Show of Force	(Paramount)	R	5/11/90	6/10/90	31	$150,028
223	Martians Go Home	(Taurus)	PG-13	4/20/90	4/22/90	3	$129,778
224	Haunting of Morella	(Concorde)	R	2/9/90	2/11/90	3	$125,940
225	Reincarnation of Golden Lotus	(East West)	NR	2/16/90	7/22/90	157	$123,254
226	L'Atalante (Re)	(New Yorker)	NR	10/19/90	12/9/90	52	$120,778
227	Ben-Hur (Re)	(MGM/UA)	NR	7/9/90	9/16/90	70	$114,936
228	Mortal Passions	(MGM)	R	1/26/90	1/28/90	3	$109,036
229	Torrents of Spring	(Millimeter)	NR	2/9/90	3/4/90	24	$101,855
230	Life is Cheap, TP is Expensive	(Silverlight)	NR	8/24/90	9/16/90	24	$98,226
231	A Man Called Sarge	(Cannon)	PG-13	2/2/90	2/4/90	3	$92,706
232	Chicago Joe and the Showgirl	(New Line)	R	7/27/90	8/19/90	24	$85,395
233	Far Out Man	(New Line)	R	5/11/90	5/13/90	3	$81,990
234	Raging Bull (Re)	(United Artists)	R	1/5/90	2/4/90	31	$80,307
235	The Misadventures of Mr. Wilt	(Goldwyn)	R	6/22/90	8/5/90	45	$74,483
236	Fools of Fortune	(New Line)	PG-13	9/14/90	10/28/90	45	$73,120
237	Happy Together	(Borde Rel.)	PG-13	5/4/90	5/13/90	10	$70,912
238	Santa Sangre	(Expanded Ent.)	R	3/30/90	4/29/90	31	$66,110
239	The Big Bang	(Triton)	R	5/11/90	9/11/90	122	$59,173
240	Spontaneous Combustion	(Taurus)	R	2/23/90	2/25/90	3	$50,367
241	Why Me?	(Triumph)	R	4/20/90	4/22/90	3	$49,933
242	Honeymoon Academy	(Triumph)	PG-13	5/11/90	5/13/90	3	$47,714
243	Leningrad Cowboys Go Amer.	(Orion Classics)	PG-13	11/1/90	11/25/90	24	$47,013
244	The Spirit of '76	(Columbia)	PG-13	10/12/90	3/10/91	151	$44,567
245	Frankenstein Unbound	(20th Fox)	R	11/2/90	11/4/90	3	$37,017
246	Driving In	(Skouras)	PG-13	9/21/90	9/23/90	3	$35,821
247	Twister	(Greycat)	PG-13	8/8/90	9/16/90	40	$33,455
248	Sonny Boy	(Triumph)	R	10/26/90	10/28/90	3	$32,623
249	Mr. Frost	(Triumph)	R	11/9/90	11/18/90	10	$32,326
250	Chattahoochee	(Hemdale)	R	4/20/90	4/29/90	10	$31,417

Rank	Title	Distributor	MPAA	Open	Last	Days	Gross
251	Mack the Knife	(21st Century)	PG-13	2/2/90	2/19/90	18	$30,833
252	The Sound of Music (Re)	(20th Fox)	NR	8/24/90	8/26/90	3	$30,108
253	The Man Inside	(New Line)	PG	10/26/90	11/11/90	17	$28,892
254	Lensman	(Streamline)	NR	8/31/90	9/16/90	17	$21,163
255	Encounter at Raven's Gate	(Hemdale)	R	1/26/90	2/25/90	31	$19,468
256	The Big Dis	(Olympia Pic)	NR	6/29/90	7/15/90	17	$17,842
257	Hollywood Mavericks	(Roxie)	NR	9/7/90	9/16/90	10	$17,102
258	Ghosts Can't Do It	(Triumph)	R	6/1/90	6/3/90	3	$16,626
259	Baxter	(Backstreet)	NR	11/7/90	11/11/90	5	$13,315
260	Diamond Edge	(Castle Hill)	PG	11/30/90	12/2/90	3	$12,751
261	Instant Karma	(MGM)	R	4/27/90	4/29/90	3	$12,047
262	Camp De Thiaroye	(New Yorker)	NR	9/5/90	9/16/90	12	$10,298
263	Freeze-Die-Come to Life	(IFEX)	NR	12/7/90	12/9/90	3	$6,258
264	Old Explorers	(Taurus)	PG	9/28/90	9/30/90	3	$6,157
265	Love Without Pity	(Orion Classics)	R	5/31/90	6/2/91	3	$5,534
266	Landscape in the Mist	(New Yorker)	NR	9/14/90	9/16/90	3	$5,106
267	Soul Taker	(AIP)	R	10/24/90	10/28/90	5	$4,206
268	Elliot Favman PHD	(Taurus)	PG-13	3/23/90	3/25/90	3	$3,128
269	The Fifth Monkey	(Columbia)	PG-13	10/5/90	10/8/90	4	$1,604
270	Wait Until Spring Bandini	(Orion Classics)	PG	6/29/90	7/1/90	3	$1,168

1989 Numerical Ranking   1989 Numerical Ranking   1989 Numerical Ranking   1989 Numerical Ranking

1989 Film Grosses

The following movies are ranked by their reported domestic box office gross (U.S. & Canada). The list represents films that were released in 1989 and shows the entire longevity of the release not just the calendar year it was released in. The rank is followed by the title of the picture, its distribution company, the Motion Picture Association of America rating, the day it was released, the last day grosses were reported, how many days it was in release and finally the total box office revenue received at the theatres. These statistics have been compiled from a variety of sources.

Rank	Title	Distributor	MPAA	Open	Last	Days	Gross
1	Batman	(Warner Bros.)	PG-13	6/23/89	12/14/89	175	$251,188,924
2	Indiana Jones & The Last Crus.	(Paramount)	PG-13	5/24/89	1/28/90	250	$197,035,089
3	Lethal Weapon II	(Warner Bros.)	R	7/7/89	12/14/89	161	$147,253,986
4	Look Who's Talking	(TriStar)	PG-13	10/13/89	5/13/90	213	$138,054,925
5	Honey, I Shrunk the Kids	(Buena Vista)	PG	6/23/89	1/1/90	193	$130,150,514
6	Back to the Future Pt II	(Universal)	PG	11/22/89	3/11/90	110	$116,425,676
7	Ghostbusters II	(Columbia)	PG	6/16/89	10/15/89	122	$111,932,094
8	Driving Miss Daisy	(Warner Bros.)	PG	12/13/89	7/29/90	229	$106,368,291
9	Parenthood	(Universal)	PG-13	8/2/89	1/1/90	153	$95,565,783
10	Dead Poets Society	(Buena Vista)	PG	6/2/89	1/1/90	214	$94,544,861
11	When Harry Met Sally...	(Columbia)	R	7/12/89	1/7/90	180	$92,247,887
12	The War of the Roses	(20th Fox)	R	12/8/89	4/1/90	115	$84,130,763
13	The Little Mermaid	(Buena Vista)	G	11/15/89	5/13/90	180	$83,728,073
14	Steel Magnolias	(TriStar)	PG	11/15/89	5/13/90	180	$81,004,509
15	Nat'l Lampoon's Christmas Vac.	(Warner Bros.)	PG-13	12/1/89	4/1/90	122	$71,303,526
16	Turner & Hooch	(Buena Vista)	PG	7/28/89	1/1/90	158	$70,469,935
17	Born on the Fourth of July	(Universal)	R	12/20/89	7/29/90	222	$70,001,698
18	Uncle Buck	(Universal)	PG	8/16/89	1/1/90	139	$63,914,578
19	Tango & Cash	(Warner Bros.)	R	12/22/89	5/20/90	150	$63,399,930
20	Field of Dreams	(Universal)	PG	4/21/89	11/5/89	199	$62,195,103
21	Harlem Nights	(Paramount)	R	11/17/89	5/13/90	178	$60,857,262
22	Pet Sematary	(Paramount)	R	4/21/89	10/22/89	185	$57,468,142
23	Sea of Love	(Universal)	R	9/15/89	1/1/90	109	$56,630,705
24	The Abyss	(20th Fox)	PG-13	8/9/89	10/29/89	82	$54,243,125
25	Star Trek V	(Paramount)	PG	6/9/89	11/19/89	164	$52,206,498
26	Major League	(Paramount)	R	4/7/89	10/1/89	178	$49,793,054
27	Black Rain	(Paramount)	R	9/22/89	2/4/90	136	$45,892,212
28	See No Evil, Hear No Evil	(TriStar)	R	5/12/89	7/30/89	80	$45,407,791
29	Always	(Universal)	PG	12/22/89	4/1/90	101	$41,843,630
30	Three Fugitives	(Buena Vista)	PG-13	1/27/89	6/4/89	129	$40,003,746
31	Bill & Ted's Excellent Adventure	(Orion)	PG	2/17/89	7/16/89	150	$39,916,091
32	K-9	(Universal)	PG-13	4/28/89	7/9/89	73	$38,859,189
33	The Karate Kid Pt III	(Columbia)	PG	6/30/89	9/24/89	87	$38,793,278
34	The Burbs	(Universal)	PG	2/17/89	7/2/89	136	$35,382,246
35	Fletch Lives	(Universal)	PG	3/17/89	7/9/89	115	$33,266,859
36	Licence To Kill	(United Artists)	PG-13	7/14/89	9/4/89	53	$33,197,509
37	The Bear	(TriStar)	PG	10/25/89	2/19/90	118	$30,861,336
38	Lean on Me	(Warner Bros.)	PG-13	3/3/89	5/14/89	73	$29,823,140

Rank	Title	Distributor	MPAA	Open	Last	Days	Gross
39	Weekend at Bernie's	(20th Fox)	PG-13	7/5/89	10/15/89	103	$29,433,521
40	Peter Pan (Reissue)	(Buena Vista)	NR	7/14/89	11/5/89	115	$29,341,498
41	Road House	(United Artists)	R	5/19/89	7/9/89	52	$27,362,103
42	The Dream Team	(Universal)	PG-13	4/7/89	7/9/89	94	$27,092,920
43	Glory	(TriStar)	R	12/14/89	5/13/90	151	$26,593,580
44	All Dogs Go To Heaven	(United Artists)	G	11/17/89	4/1/90	136	$26,220,877
45	Do the Right Thing	(Universal)	R	6/30/89	10/29/89	122	$26,004,026
46	sex, lies, and videotape	(Miramax)	R	8/4/89	3/4/90	213	$24,681,553
47	Lock Up	(TriStar)	R	8/4/89	10/15/89	73	$21,717,616
48	Cousins	(Paramount)	PG-13	2/10/89	4/23/89	73	$21,707,236
49	A Nightmare on Elm Street V	(New Line)	R	8/11/89	10/29/89	80	$21,584,039
50	The Rescuers (Reissue)	(Buena Vista)	G	3/17/89	7/2/89	108	$21,174,014
51	Say Anything	(20th Fox)	PG-13	4/14/89	6/18/89	66	$20,036,737
52	Dad	(Universal)	PG	10/27/89	1/1/90	67	$19,738,015
53	The Fly II	(20th Fox)	R	2/10/89	4/16/89	66	$19,628,219
54	Skin Deep	(20th Fox)	R	3/3/89	4/30/89	59	$19,418,324
55	An Innocent Man	(Buena Vista)	R	10/6/89	1/1/90	88	$19,397,847
56	Blaze	(Buena Vista)	R	12/13/89	3/18/90	96	$19,049,727
57	Casualties of War	(Columbia)	R	8/18/89	10/15/89	59	$18,468,714
58	Prancer	(Orion)	G	11/17/89	1/21/90	66	$18,358,242
59	The Fabulous Baker Boys	(20th Fox)	R	10/13/89	3/18/90	157	$18,121,297
60	Crimes and Misdemeanors	(Orion)	PG-13	10/13/89	3/18/90	157	$18,001,168
61	Her Alibi	(Warner Bros.)	PG	2/3/89	3/19/89	45	$17,195,050
62	No Holds Barred	(New Line)	PG-13	6/2/89	8/6/89	64	$16,093,651
63	Chances Are	(TriStar)	PG	3/10/89	4/30/89	52	$15,939,663
64	Shocker	(Universal)	R	10/27/89	12/17/89	52	$15,549,707
65	Leviathan	(MGM/UA)	R	3/17/89	5/7/89	52	$15,363,560
66	Next of Kin	(Warner Bros.)	R	10/20/89	11/26/89	38	$15,362,628
67	She-Devil	(Orion)	PG-13	12/8/89	3/11/90	94	$14,997,150
68	Kickboxer	(Cannon)	R	9/8/89	12/3/89	87	$14,533,681
69	Friday the 13th Pt VIII	(Paramount)	R	7/28/89	10/15/89	80	$14,335,525
70	My Left Foot	(Miramax)	R	11/10/89	5/20/90	192	$14,041,353
71	Great Balls of Fire	(Orion)	PG-13	6/30/89	8/27/89	59	$13,691,550
72	The Wizard	(Universal)	PG	12/15/89	1/28/90	45	$12,321,070
73	Family Business	(TriStar)	R	12/15/89	2/19/90	67	$12,149,190
74	Pink Cadillac	(Warner Bros,)	PG-13	5/26/89	7/2/89	38	$12,080,458
75	She's Out of Control	(Columbia)	PG	4/14/89	6/18/89	66	$12,060,942
76	Halloween V	(Galaxy Int'l)	R	10/13/89	11/12/89	31	$11,642,254
77	Gross Anatomy	(Buena Vista)	PG-13	10/20/89	1/1/90	74	$11,346,186
78	Who's Harry Crumb?	(TriStar)	PG-13	2/3/89	4/2/89	59	$10,982,364
79	Police Academy VI	(Warner Bros.)	PG	3/10/89	4/2/89	24	$10,612,345
80	New York Stories	(Buena Vista)	PG	3/1/89	6/4/89	96	$10,608,884
81	We're No Angels	(Paramount)	PG-13	12/15/89	2/19/90	67	$10,553,477
82	Yaaba	(New Yorker)	NR	8/4/89	9/4/89	32	$10,357,223
83	Young Einstein	(Warner Bros.)	PG	8/4/89	9/4/89	32	$10,357,223
84	The Package	(Orion)	R	8/25/89	11/19/89	87	$10,276,500
85	Henry V	(Goldwyn)	NR	11/8/89	8/12/90	278	$10,161,099
86	Cyborg	(Cannon)	R	4/7/89	6/25/89	80	$10,030,875
87	Criminal Law	(Hemdale)	R	4/28/89	6/25/89	59	$9,443,550
88	Tap	(TriStar)	PG-13	2/10/89	4/9/89	59	$9,114,702
89	True Believer	(Columbia)	R	2/17/89	3/26/89	38	$8,713,708
90	Troop Beverly Hills	(Columbia)	PG	3/22/89	4/30/89	40	$8,455,880
91	Scandal	(Miramax)	R	4/28/89	8/20/89	115	$8,366,874

Rank	Title	Distributor	MPAA	Open	Last	Days	Gross
92	Renegades	(Universal)	R	6/2/89	7/9/89	38	$8,244,915
93	Adv.s of Baron Munchausen	(Warner Bros.)	PG	3/10/89	7/9/89	122	$8,040,008
94	Cheetah	(Buena Vista)	G	8/18/89	10/9/89	53	$7,882,250
95	Deepstar Six	(TriStar)	R	1/13/89	2/20/89	39	$7,856,017
96	Enemies, A Love Story	(20th Fox)	R	12/13/89	4/1/90	110	$7,815,403
97	Dead Bang	(Warner Bros.)	R	3/24/89	4/16/89	24	$7,392,289
98	Disorganized Crime	(Buena Vista)	R	4/14/89	6/4/89	52	$7,378,042
99	Dead Calm	(Warner Bros.)	R	4/7/89	4/30/89	24	$7,032,915
100	Relentless	(New Line)	R	8/30/89	10/22/89	52	$6,985,999
101	Lawrence of Arabia (Reissue)	(Columbia)	NR	2/8/89	9/4/89	209	$6,789,292
102	Roger & Me	(Warner Bros.)	R	12/20/89	4/15/90	117	$6,692,893
103	Johnny Handsome	(TriStar)	R	9/29/89	10/22/89	24	$6,622,465
104	Shag	(Hemdale)	PG	7/21/89	9/4/89	46	$6,593,957
105	UHF	(Orion)	PG-13	7/21/89	10/9/89	81	$6,151,582
106	Shirley Valentine	(Paramount)	R	8/30/89	2/19/90	172	$6,016,374
107	Immediate Family	(Columbia)	PG-13	10/27/89	12/10/89	45	$5,841,286
108	Millennium	(20th Fox)	PG-13	8/25/89	10/15/89	52	$5,675,353
109	Dream a Little Dream	(Vestron)	PG-13	3/3/89	6/11/89	100	$5,552,441
110	The Music Box	(TriStar)	PG-13	12/25/89	2/25/90	63	$5,417,303
111	Second Sight	(Warner Bros.)	PG	11/3/89	11/26/89	24	$5,315,874
112	Let It Ride	(Paramount)	PG-13	8/18/89	10/15/89	59	$4,971,088
113	Drugstore Cowboy	(Avenue)	R	10/6/89	5/6/90	213	$4,457,027
114	See You In The Morning	(Warner Bros.)	PG-13	4/21/89	5/14/89	24	$4,356,260
115	The January Man	(MGM/UA)	R	1/13/89	2/5/89	24	$4,323,966
116	Listen To Me	(Columbia)	PG-13	5/5/89	6/11/89	38	$4,238,544
117	Staying Together	(Hemdale)	R	11/10/89	11/26/89	17	$4,084,213
118	The Mighty Quinn	(MGM/UA)	R	2/16/89	4/2/89	46	$3,992,420
119	The Phantom of the Opera	(21st Century)	R	11/3/89	11/17/90	15	$3,953,745
120	Earth Girls Are Easy	(Vestron)	PG	5/12/89	6/25/89	45	$3,916,303
121	Loverboy	(TriStar)	PG-13	4/28/89	5/21/89	24	$3,887,852
122	Worth Winning	(20th Fox)	PG-13	10/27/89	11/12/89	17	$3,621,762
123	Fat Man and Little Boy	(Paramount)	PG-13	10/20/89	12/3/89	45	$3,560,942
124	In Country	(Warner Bros.)	R	9/15/89	10/29/89	45	$3,531,971
125	Red Scorpion	(Shapiro)	R	4/19/89	4/30/89	12	$3,509,726
126	Physical Evidence	(Columbia)	R	1/27/89	2/26/89	31	$3,507,050
127	Camille Claudel	(Orion Classics)	R	12/19/89	7/29/90	221	$3,331,297
128	A Dry White Season	(MGM/UA)	R	9/20/89	11/12/89	54	$3,282,890
129	Rude Awakening	(Orion)	R	8/16/89	10/9/89	55	$3,165,362
130	Kinjite (Forbidden Subjects)	(Cannon)	R	2/3/89	4/16/89	73	$3,151,839
131	976-Evil	(New Line)	R	3/22/89	6/4/89	75	$2,955,917
132	Speed Zone	(Orion)	PG	4/21/89	5/29/89	39	$2,937,126
133	The Adv.s of Milo and Otis	(Columbia)	G	8/25/89	10/15/89	52	$2,893,685
134	Old Gringo	(Columbia)	R	10/6/89	10/29/89	24	$2,589,463
135	Gleaming The Cube	(20th Fox)	PG-13	1/13/89	2/26/89	45	$2,454,580
136	Farewell to the King	(Orion)	PG-13	3/3/89	4/2/89	31	$2,361,132
137	Fright Night: Part II	(New Century)	R	5/19/89	6/18/89	31	$2,350,289
138	Chocolat	(Orion Classics)	PG-13	3/10/89	12/10/89	276	$2,317,091
139	Sing	(TriStar)	PG-13	3/31/89	4/16/89	17	$2,202,233
140	Scenes Fm Class Struggle in B.H.	(Cinecom)	R	6/2/89	9/4/89	95	$2,156,471
141	Jacknife	(Cineplex)	R	3/10/89	6/4/89	87	$2,049,769
142	Communion	(New Line)	R	11/10/89	12/10/89	31	$1,895,988
143	Miss Firecracker	(Corsair)	PG	4/28/89	7/23/89	87	$1,852,655
144	Breaking In	(Goldwyn)	R	10/13/89	11/19/89	38	$1,847,143

Rank	Title	Distributor	MPAA	Open	Last	Days	Gross
145	Winter People	(Columbia)	PG-13	4/14/89	5/29/89	46	$1,811,580
146	Bloodfist	(Concorde)	R	9/19/89	12/17/89	87	$1,770,082
147	Rooftops	(New Visions)	R	3/17/89	3/26/89	10	$1,764,255
148	Cookie	(Warner Bros.)	R	8/23/89	10/9/89	48	$1,755,480
149	Erik the Viking	(Orion)	PG-13	9/22/89	11/19/89	59	$1,538,972
150	Mystery Train	(Orion Classics)	R	11/11/89	6/10/90	207	$1,531,855
151	Stepfather II	(Millimeter)	R	11/3/89	1/28/90	87	$1,483,050
152	The 2nd Animation Celebration	(Expanded Ent.)	NR	7/28/89	1/14/90	171	$1,456,852
153	The Horror Show	(MGM/UA)	R	4/28/89	5/7/89	10	$1,379,660
154	The Navigator	(Circle)	PG	3/3/89	11/26/89	269	$1,333,379
155	Romero	(Four Seasons)	PG-13	8/25/89	12/3/89	101	$1,316,495
156	Babar: The Movie	(New Line)	G	7/28/89	9/10/89	45	$1,305,187
157	How I Got Into College	(20th Fox)	PG-13	5/19/89	5/29/89	11	$1,298,357
158	Apartment Zero	(Skouras)	NR	9/15/89	3/4/90	171	$1,267,578
159	Little Vera	(Int'l Films)	NR	4/21/89	10/22/89	192	$1,262,598
160	Queen Of Hearts	(Cinecom)	NR	9/20/89	3/4/90	157	$1,236,844
161	Gone With the Wind (Reissue)	(MGM/UA)	NR	1/31/89	5/7/89	97	$1,223,671
162	High Hopes	(Skouras)	NR	2/24/89	8/13/89	171	$1,192,322
163	Murmur of the Heart (Re)	(Orion Classics)	NR	1/4/89	11/12/89	313	$1,160,784
164	Lost Angels	(Orion)	R	5/5/89	5/29/89	25	$1,150,986
165	Heathers	(New World)	R	3/31/89	4/30/89	31	$1,108,462
166	Heart of Dixie	(Orion)	PG	8/25/89	10/9/89	46	$1,093,011
167	Miracle Mile	(Hemdale)	R	5/19/89	7/16/89	59	$1,092,822
168	The Music Teacher	(Orion Classics)	PG	7/7/89	3/11/90	248	$1,086,894
169	Wired	(Tauras)	R	8/25/89	9/10/89	17	$1,083,635
170	True Love	(United Artists)	R	9/15/89	1/14/90	122	$1,043,303
171	Best of the Best	(Tauras)	PG-13	11/10/89	11/12/89	3	$990,000
172	The Little Thief	(Miramax)	NR	8/25/89	1/1/90	130	$971,981
173	Getting It Right	(MCEG)	R	5/5/89	10/1/89	150	$960,385
174	Valmont	(Orion)	R	11/17/89	2/19/90	95	$944,427
175	Welcome Home	(Columbia)	R	9/29/89	10/22/89	24	$913,781
176	Parents	(Vestron)	R	1/27/89	6/18/89	143	$870,532
177	The Terror Within	(Concorde)	R	2/20/89	5/14/89	85	$858,591
178	Toxic Avenger II	(Troma)	R	2/22/89	9/17/89	206	$792,966
179	The Girl in a Swing	(Millimeter)	NR	9/29/89	2/25/90	150	$744,459
180	La Lectrice	(Orion Classics)	R	5/8/89	12/10/89	234	$699,397
181	American Ninja III: Blood Hunt	(Cannon)	R	2/24/89	4/2/89	38	$679,980
182	Vampire's Kiss	(Hemdale)	R	6/2/89	7/16/89	45	$600,804
183	Wuthering Heights (Reissue)	(Goldwyn)	NR	4/7/89	10/9/89	186	$593,914
184	For All Mankind	(Circle)	NR	11/2/89	4/8/90	159	$568,720
185	Little Monsters	(United Artists)	PG	8/25/89	9/4/89	11	$542,939
186	Eddie and the Cruisers II	(Scotti Bros.)	PG-13	8/18/89	8/20/89	3	$536,508
187	War Party	(Hemdale)	R	9/29/89	10/9/89	11	$536,314
188	Distant Voices, Still Lives	(Avenue)	PG-13	7/28/89	11/5/89	101	$527,929
189	Crack House	(Canon)	R	11/10/89	12/3/89	24	$509,402
190	Story of a Woman	(New Yorker)	NR	10/10/89	1/28/90	108	$486,711
191	Tom Jones (Re)	(Goldwyn)	NR	9/23/89	3/18/90	185	$481,390
192	The Rainbow	(Vestron)	R	5/5/89	6/25/89	52	$444,055
193	Akira	(Streamline)	NR	12/25/89	7/22/90	210	$439,162
194	Cage	(New Century)	R	9/1/89	9/10/89	10	$430,943
195	Out of the Dark	(New Line)	R	3/10/89	5/7/89	58	$419,428
196	How to Get Ahead in Advertising	(Warner Bros.)	R	5/5/89	7/2/89	59	$415,503
197	Thirty-Six Fillette	(Circle)	NR	1/13/89	4/9/89	94	$410,109

Rank	Title	Distributor	MPAA	Open	Last	Days	Gross
198	Thelonius Monk	(Warner Bros.)	PG-13	9/29/89	12/17/89	80	$392,363
199	Triumph of the Spirit	(TriStar)	R	12/8/89	2/11/90	66	$387,361
200	Toxic Avenger III	(Troma)	R	11/7/89	3/4/90	115	$363,561
201	Slaves of New York	(TriStar)	R	3/17/89	4/30/89	45	$336,519
202	A Taxing Woman Returns	(New Yorker)	NR	6/27/89	9/4/89	70	$333,584
203	Crusoe	(Island)	PG-13	3/31/89	6/18/89	80	$315,421
204	Out Cold	(Hemdale)	R	3/3/89	3/12/89	10	$294,266
205	Powwow Highway	(Warner Bros.)	R	2/24/89	5/14/89	80	$276,698
206	Heavy Petting	(Skouras)	NR	9/22/89	12/10/89	80	$272,371
207	Paperhouse	(Vestron)	PG-13	2/17/89	6/18/89	122	$241,278
208	River of Death	(Cannon)	R	9/29/89	10/1/89	3	$237,548
209	Weapons of the Spirit	(First Run)	NR	8/28/89	4/22/90	225	$232,323
210	Eat a Bowl of Tea	(Columbia)	PG-13	7/21/89	10/9/89	81	$230,769
211	Night Game	(Trans World)	R	9/15/89	9/17/89	3	$228,108
212	Fist Fighter	(Tauras)	R	5/12/89	5/14/89	3	$221,163
213	Cold Feet	(Avenue)	R	5/19/89	7/9/89	52	$216,917
214	A Chorus of Disapproval	(South Gate)	PG	8/18/89	1/7/90	143	$216,373
215	Four Adv.s Of Reinette & Mira	(New Yorker)	NR	7/21/89	9/24/89	68	$215,073
216	Fast Food	(Fries Ent.)	PG-13	4/28/89	4/30/89	3	$212,160
217	Beverly Hills Brats	(Independent)	PG-13	10/6/89	10/9/89	4	$192,561
218	For Queen & Country	(Atlantic)	R	5/19/89	6/4/89	17	$191,051
219	Hell High	(JGM)	R	5/19/89	6/25/89	38	$166,411
220	Rachel Papers, The	(MGM/UA)	R	5/12/89	10/1/89	143	$154,582
221	Under the Boardwalk	(New World)	R	4/14/89	4/23/89	10	$147,542
222	Sidewalk Stories	(Island)	R	11/3/89	12/17/89	45	$131,433
223	Macho Dancer	(Strand Rel.)	NR	9/1/89	12/10/89	101	$129,581
224	Depeche Mode 101	(Westwood One)	R	5/5/89	11/1/89	156	$129,310
225	Michelangelo	(Roxie)	NR	2/23/89	12/3/89	285	$120,513
226	The Big Picture	(Columbia)	PG-13	9/15/89	10/9/89	25	$116,146
227	I, Madman	(Trans World)	R	10/13/89	10/15/89	3	$114,782
228	Night Visitor	(MGM/UA)	R	5/12/89	5/14/89	3	$108,415
229	No Retreat, No Surrender II	(Shapiro)	R	1/27/89	1/29/89	3	$108,154
230	Edge of Sanity	(Millimeter)	R	4/14/89	4/23/89	10	$102,219
231	Hanussen	(Columbia)	R	3/8/89	4/16/89	40	$81,741
232	Bert Rigby, You're a Fool	(Warner Bros.)	R	2/24/89	3/12/89	17	$75,049
233	Dealers	(Skouras)	R	11/3/89	11/12/89	10	$72,460
234	Heart of Midnight	(Goldwyn)	R	3/3/89	3/5/89	3	$71,145
235	Under the Sun of Satan	(Alive)	NR	1/20/89	4/2/89	73	$68,765
236	The Wizard of Oz (Re)	(MGM/UA)	NR	5/19/89	5/29/89	11	$68,429
237	Race for Glory	(New Century)	R	11/3/89	11/5/89	3	$67,000
238	Kill Me Again	(MGM/UA)	R	10/27/89	10/29/89	3	$66,013
239	Cohen & Tate	(Hemdale)	R	1/27/89	2/12/89	17	$64,227
240	Wonderland	(Vestron)	R	4/28/89	6/18/89	52	$64,137
241	Rachel River	(Tauras)	PG-13	1/21/89	3/5/89	44	$60,698
242	After Midnight	(MGM/UA)	R	11/3/89	11/5/89	3	$59,260
243	Penn & Teller Get Killed	(Warner Bros.)	R	9/22/89	10/9/89	18	$57,951
244	Bye Bye Baby	(Borde Rel.)	R	5/12/89	5/29/89	18	$56,564
245	Les Liaisons Dangerous	(Interama)	NR	7/19/89	8/27/89	40	$56,275
246	The Everlasting Secret Family	(Int'l Film)	NR	10/7/89	12/10/89	66	$55,288
247	A Flame in My Heart	(Roxie)	NR	4/28/89	12/10/89	157	$55,005
248	All's Fair	(Moviestore)	PG-13	2/3/89	2/5/89	3	$52,907
249	84 Charlie Mopic	(New Century)	R	4/7/89	4/16/89	10	$50,503
250	Wicked Stepmother	(MGM/UA)	PG-13	2/3/89	2/5/89	3	$43,749

Rank	Title	Distributor	MPAA	Open	Last	Days	Gross
251	Season of Fear	(MGM/UA)	R	5/12/89	5/14/89	3	$41,835
252	Warm Nights on Slow Mov Train	(Miramax)	R	3/31/89	4/9/89	10	$40,460
253	Mindgames	(MGM/UA)	R	3/3/89	3/5/89	3	$38,658
254	Manifesto	(Cannon)	R	1/27/89	2/26/89	31	$37,611
255	When the Whales Came	(20th Fox)	PG	10/20/89	10/22/89	3	$37,030
256	Checking Out	(Warner Bros.)	R	4/21/89	5/14/89	24	$30,474
257	Survival Quest	(MGM/UA)	R	11/10/89	11/12/89	3	$29,453
258	The Magic Toy Shop	(Roxie)	NR	7/28/89	10/17/89	82	$27,092
259	Bloodhounds of Broadway	(Columbia)	PG	11/3/89	11/12/89	10	$25,772
260	Twice Dead	(Concorde)	R	2/3/89	2/12/89	10	$25,477
261	Buying Time	(MGM/UA)	R	5/12/89	5/14/89	3	$24,621
262	Echoes of Paradice	(Quartet)	R	3/31/89	4/16/89	17	$23,717
263	I Went to the Dance	(Brazos Film)	NR	10/13/89	10/22/89	10	$22,752
264	Hawks	(Skouras)	R	11/10/89	11/12/89	3	$21,664
265	Animal Behavior	(Millimeter)	PG	10/27/89	10/29/89	3	$20,361
266	Murphy's Fault	(Triax)	PG-13	1/6/89	1/8/89	3	$19,711
267	To Kill a Priest	(Columbia)	R	10/13/89	10/22/89	10	$19,494
268	On the Black Hill	(Roxie)	NR	7/19/89	8/6/89	19	$18,590
269	Valentino Returns	(Skouras)	R	7/21/89	7/30/89	10	$15,954
270	Homer & Eddie	(Skouras)	R	12/25/89	2/11/90	49	$13,570
271	Veiled Threat	(Daystar)	NR	11/3/89	11/5/89	3	$12,381
272	Far From Home	(Vestron)	R	6/2/89	6/25/89	24	$11,859
273	Dance to Win	(MGM/UA)	R	12/1/89	12/3/89	3	$11,344
274	Trust Me	(Cinecom)	R	11/10/89	11/19/89	10	$9,390
275	Ginger Ale Afternoon	(Skouras)	R	8/25/89	8/27/89	3	$9,216
276	Meet the Hollowheads	(Moviestore)	PG-13	11/15/89	12/3/89	19	$9,042
277	Me and Him	(Columbia)	R	8/4/89	8/13/89	10	$6,948
278	We Think the World of You	(Cinecom)	PG	1/20/89	1/24/89	4	$6,135
279	Shuttlecock	(Stutz Co.)	NR	11/5/89	11/12/89	8	$5,713
280	The Rose Garden	(Cannon)	PG-13	12/22/89	1/1/90	11	$5,245
281	Fear, Anxiety and Depression	(Goldwyn)	R	12/8/89	12/10/89	3	$4,212
282	Hit List	(Cinetel)	R	3/3/89	3/5/89	3	$3,195
283	To Die For	(Skouras)	R	5/12/89	5/14/89	3	$3,032
284	Field of Honor	(Orion Classics)	PG	1/27/89	1/29/89	3	$2,737
285	Mutant on the Bounty	(Skouras)	PG-13	8/18/89	9/24/89	38	$2,029
286	Berlin Blues	(Cannon)	NR	8/25/89	8/27/89	3	$1,650

1988 Film Grosses

The following movies are ranked by their reported domestic box office gross (U.S. & Canada). The list represents films that were released in 1988 and shows the entire longevity of the release not just the calendar year it was released in. The rank is followed by the title of the picture, its distribution company, the Motion Picture Association of America rating, the day it was released, the last day grosses were reported, how many days it was in release and finally the total box office revenue received at the theatres. These statistics have been compiled from a variety of sources.

Rank	Title	Distributor	MPAA	Open	Last	Days	Gross
1	Rain Man	(United Artists)	R	12/16/88	8/6/89	234	$171,188,895
2	Who Framed Roger Rabbit	(Buena Vista)	PG	6/22/88	3/5/89	257	$152,715,105
3	Coming to America	(Paramount)	R	6/29/88	11/27/88	152	$128,113,607
4	Big	(20th Fox)	PG	6/3/88	2/12/89	255	$113,596,430
5	Twins	(Universal)	PG	12/9/88	7/2/89	181	$110,618,737
6	Crocodile Dundee II	(Paramount)	PG	5/25/88	10/30/88	159	$109,201,624
7	Die Hard	(20th Fox)	R	7/15/88	2/5/89	206	$80,707,729
8	The Naked Gun	(Paramount)	PG-13	12/2/88	4/12/89	122	$77,946,551
9	Cocktail	(Buena Vista)	R	7/29/88	1/15/89	171	$77,284,301
10	Beetlejuice	(Warner Bros.)	PG	3/30/88	11/6/88	222	$73,707,461
11	Working Girl	(20th Fox)	R	12/21/88	4/30/89	131	$62,152,437
12	Scrooged	(Paramount)	PG-13	11/23/88	2/20/89	90	$60,240,839
13	A Fish Called Wanda	(MGM)	R	7/15/88	11/27/88	136	$59,991,944
14	Beaches	(Buena Vista)	PG-13	12/21/88	8/6/89	229	$56,444,103
15	Willow	(MGM)	PG	5/20/88	9/25/88	129	$55,782,590
16	Rambo III	(TriStar)	R	5/25/88	9/18/88	117	$53,715,611
17	Oliver & Company	(Buena Vista)	G	11/18/88	3/5/89	108	$53,141,469
18	Bull Durham	(Orion)	R	6/15/88	10/30/88	138	$50,780,427
19	A Nightmare on Elm Street IV	(New Line)	R	8/19/88	12/18/88	122	$49,361,796
20	Colors	(Orion)	R	4/15/88	8/28/88	136	$46,158,157
21	The Land Before Time	(Universal)	G	11/18/88	4/23/89	157	$46,052,460
22	Young Guns	(20th Fox)	R	8/12/88	11/20/88	101	$43,396,497
23	Biloxi Blues	(Universal)	PG-13	3/25/88	6/12/88	80	$41,946,750
24	Dirty Rotten Scoundrels	(Orion)	PG	12/14/88	4/2/89	110	$41,412,820
25	Tequila Sunrise	(Warner Bros.)	R	12/2/88	2/20/89	81	$39,703,427
26	Big Business	(Buena Vista)	PG	6/10/88	10/16/88	129	$39,638,616
27	Bambi (Reissue)	(Buena Vista)	G	7/15/88	10/16/88	94	$38,136,595
28	The Great Outdoors	(Universal)	PG	6/17/88	8/21/88	66	$38,049,958
29	The Dead Pool	(Warner Bros.)	R	7/13/88	9/18/88	68	$37,814,698
30	Midnight Run	(Universal)	R	7/20/88	9/25/88	68	$37,195,662
31	Red Heat	(TriStar)	R	6/17/88	9/18/88	94	$34,944,648
32	Mississippi Burning	(Orion)	R	12/9/88	6/11/89	185	$34,603,943
33	Child's Play	(United Artists)	R	11/9/88	3/5/89	117	$32,842,703
34	Dangerous Liaisons	(Warner Bros.)	R	12/21/88	5/14/89	145	$32,663,833
35	The Accidental Tourist	(Warner Bros.)	PG	12/23/88	4/2/89	101	$30,260,987
36	The Accused	(Paramount)	R	10/14/88	1/2/89	81	$29,591,167
37	Shoot To Kill	(Buena Vista)	R	2/12/88	5/15/88	94	$29,292,015
38	Ernest Saves Christmas	(Buena Vista)	PG	11/11/88	1/15/89	65	$28,062,539

Rank	Title	Distributor	MPAA	Open	Last	Days	Gross
39	Funny Farm	(Warner Bros.)	PG	6/3/88	7/17/88	45	$25,271,734
40	Betrayed	(United Artists)	R	8/26/88	10/23/88	59	$24,967,366
41	Alien Nation	(20th Fox)	R	10/7/88	12/11/88	66	$24,674,171
42	The Fox and the Hound (Re)	(Buena vista)	G	3/25/88	7/4/88	102	$23,556,988
43	Gorillas in the Mist	(Universal)	PG-13	9/23/88	11/27/88	66	$22,597,541
44	Married to the Mob	(Orion)	R	8/19/88	12/11/88	115	$21,306,476
45	License To Drive	(20th Fox)	PG-13	7/6/88	10/10/88	97	$21,066,484
46	Punchline	(Columbia)	R	9/30/88	1/8/89	101	$21,016,294
47	Short Circuit II	(TriStar)	PG	7/6/88	10/16/88	103	$20,882,577
48	Presidio, The	(Paramount)	R	6/10/88	8/31/88	83	$20,036,242
49	Action Jackson	(Lorimar)	R	2/12/88	4/3/88	52	$19,606,142
50	Tucker: The Man and his Dream	(Paramount)	PG	8/12/88	10/30/88	80	$19,598,944
51	Police Academy V	(Warner Bros.)	PG	3/18/88	5/15/88	59	$19,449,527
52	Friday The 13th Part VII	(Paramount)	R	5/13/88	7/4/88	53	$19,170,001
53	The Serpent and the Rainbow	(Universal)	R	2/5/88	3/27/88	52	$19,020,107
54	Cocoon: The Return	(20th Fox)	PG	11/23/88	2/20/89	90	$18,828,121
55	Above the Law	(Warner Bros.)	R	4/8/88	5/30/88	53	$18,622,684
56	The Seventh Sign	(TriStar)	R	4/1/88	5/22/88	52	$18,392,605
57	Halloween IV	(Galaxy)	R	10/21/88	11/13/88	24	$17,768,757
58	For Keeps	(TriStar)	PG-13	1/15/88	4/3/88	80	$17,514,533
59	Frantic	(Warner Bros.)	R	2/26/88	4/3/88	38	$17,481,135
60	Johnny Be Good	(Orion)	PG-13	3/25/88	6/12/88	80	$17,162,556
61	She's Having A Baby	(Paramount)	PG-13	2/5/88	4/17/88	73	$16,008,564
62	Crossing Delancey	(Warner Bros.)	PG	8/24/88	2/5/89	165	$15,899,538
63	Bright Lights, Big City	(United Artists)	R	4/1/88	5/22/88	52	$15,667,402
64	Big Top Pee-Wee	(Paramount)	PG	7/22/88	9/18/88	59	$15,098,410
65	Arthur II: On The Rocks	(Warner Bros.)	PG	7/8/88	8/7/88	31	$14,553,319
66	Masquerade	(MGM)	R	3/11/88	4/17/88	38	$14,449,944
67	School Daze	(Columbia)	R	2/12/88	6/19/88	129	$14,138,388
68	Stand and Deliver	(Warner Bros.)	PG	3/11/88	7/4/88	116	$13,740,075
69	Return To Snowy River II	(Buena Vista)	PG	4/15/88	7/4/88	81	$13,687,027
70	Vice Versa	(Columbia)	PG	3/11/88	4/17/88	38	$13,563,669
71	Poltergeist III	(MGM)	PG-13	6/10/88	7/24/88	45	$13,057,249
72	The Milagro Beanfield War	(Universal)	R	3/18/88	6/26/88	101	$12,916,626
73	My Stepmother is an Alien	(Columbia)	PG-13	12/9/88	2/7/89	62	$12,897,014
74	Mystic Pizza	(Goldwyn)	R	10/21/88	3/5/89	136	$12,784,088
75	D.O.A.	(Buena Vista)	R	3/18/88	5/15/88	59	$12,653,462
76	Everybody's All-American	(Warner Bros.)	R	11/4/88	12/11/88	38	$12,570,653
77	They Live	(Universal)	R	11/4/88	11/27/88	24	$12,250,223
78	Hellbound: Hellraiser II	(New World)	R	12/23/88	2/5/89	43	$11,867,397
79	I'm Gonna Git You Sucka	(United Artists)	R	12/14/88	4/2/89	110	$11,827,798
80	Bloodsport	(Cannon)	R	2/26/88	6/26/88	122	$11,633,865
81	Caddyshack II	(Warner Bros.)	PG	7/22/88	8/7/88	17	$11,260,104
82	The Couch Trip	(Orion)	R	1/15/88	3/6/88	52	$10,921,486
83	Moving	(Warner Bros.)	R	3/4/88	4/3/88	31	$10,709,192
84	Iron Eagle II	(TriStar)	PG	11/11/88	1/2/89	53	$10,497,324
85	Moon Over Parador	(Universal)	PG-13	9/9/88	10/2/88	24	$10,082,905
86	Unbearable Lightness of Being	(Orion)	R	2/5/88	7/17/88	164	$10,006,806
87	Shakedown	(Universal)	R	5/6/88	5/30/88	25	$9,296,262
88	Casual Sex	(Universal)	R	4/22/88	5/8/88	17	$9,231,651
89	Dead Ringers	(20th Fox)	R	9/23/88	11/6/88	45	$9,134,733
90	Switching Channels	(TriStar)	PG	3/4/88	4/24/88	52	$9,129,999
91	Bad Dreams	(20th Fox)	R	4/8/88	5/1/88	24	$8,932,837

Rank	Title	Distributor	MPAA	Open	Last	Days	Gross
92	Salsa	(Cannon)	PG	5/6/88	6/26/88	52	$8,778,479
93	Clean and Sober	(Warner Bros.)	R	8/10/88	9/18/88	40	$8,584,258
94	U2 Rattle And Hum	(Paramount)	PG-13	11/4/88	12/4/88	31	$8,551,640
95	High Spirits	(TriStar)	PG-13	11/18/88	1/2/89	46	$8,478,231
96	Without a Clue	(Orion)	PG	10/21/88	1/8/89	80	$8,399,417
97	The Last Temptation of Christ	(Universal)	R	8/12/88	11/20/88	101	$8,165,112
98	The Blob	(TriStar)	R	8/5/88	10/10/88	67	$8,152,409
99	Return Of The Living Dead Pt II	(Lorimar)	R	1/15/88	1/31/88	17	$7,913,521
100	Satisfaction	(20th Fox)	PG-13	2/12/88	3/27/88	45	$7,878,504
101	A New Life	(Paramount)	PG-13	3/25/88	4/24/88	31	$7,668,187
102	Stealing Home	(Warner Bros.)	PG-13	8/26/88	9/18/88	24	$7,319,865
103	Woman On The Verge of Ner...	(Orion Classics)	R	11/11/88	1/1/90	417	$7,174,507
104	Off Limits	(20th Fox)	R	3/11/88	4/3/88	24	$6,913,419
105	A Cry in the Dark	(Warner Bros.)	PG-13	11/11/88	2/20/89	102	$6,903,809
106	Hairspray	(New Line)	PG	2/26/88	8/14/88	171	$6,663,014
107	Fresh Horses	(Columbia)	PG-13	11/18/88	12/11/88	24	$6,606,136
108	Phantasm II	(Universal)	R	7/8/88	7/24/88	17	$6,557,045
109	Hot To Trot	(Warner Bros.)	PG	8/26/88	9/18/88	24	$6,362,336
110	Mac And Me	(Orion)	PG	8/12/88	10/2/88	52	$6,275,415
111	The Unholy	(Vestron)	R	4/22/88	6/19/88	59	$6,204,947
112	Missing In Action III (Braddock)	(Cannon)	R	1/22/88	3/6/88	45	$6,126,726
113	Night In Life Of Jimmy Reardon	(20th Fox)	R	2/26/88	3/27/88	31	$6,015,567
114	1969	(Atlantic)	R	11/18/88	4/16/89	80	$5,979,011
115	The Rescue	(Buena Vista)	PG	8/5/88	10/10/88	66	$5,780,427
116	Eight Men Out	(Orion)	PG	9/2/88	11/20/88	80	$5,571,869
117	Heartbreak Hotel	(Buena Vista)	PG-13	9/30/88	11/27/88	59	$5,366,348
118	Hero and the Terror	(Cannon)	R	8/26/88	10/16/88	52	$5,236,737
119	Monkey Shines	(Orion)	R	7/29/88	9/11/88	45	$5,195,588
120	Clara's Heart	(Warner Bros.)	PG-13	10/7/88	11/27/88	52	$5,158,949
121	Elvira, Mistress of the Dark	(New World)	PG-13	9/30/88	10/30/88	31	$5,038,971
122	Torch Song Trilogy	(New Line)	R	12/14/88	5/29/89	167	$4,865,997
123	The Good Mother	(Buena Vista)	R	11/4/88	12/4/88	31	$4,574,816
124	Au Revoir Les Enfants	(Orion Classics)	NR	2/12/88	10/30/88	262	$4,542,825
125	Babette's Feast	(Orion Classics)	G	3/11/88	2/26/89	360	$4,398,938
126	Sunset	(TriStar)	R	4/29/88	5/22/88	24	$4,279,848
127	Pumpkinhead	(United Artists)	R	10/14/88	2/12/89	123	$4,150,460
128	Bat 21	(TriStar)	R	10/21/88	11/27/88	38	$3,832,728
129	Feds	(Warner Bros.)	PG-13	10/28/88	11/27/88	31	$3,811,309
130	Critters II	(New Line)	PG-13	4/29/88	7/4/88	67	$3,806,349
131	Sweet Hearts Dance	(TriStar)	R	9/23/88	11/13/88	52	$3,723,177
132	Imagine: John Lennon	(Warner Bros.)	R	10/7/88	11/6/88	31	$3,709,865
133	Memories Of Me	(MGM)	PG-13	9/28/88	10/30/88	33	$3,618,467
134	Tougher Than Leather	(New Line)	R	9/16/88	12/18/88	94	$3,574,760
135	Bagdad Cafe	(Island)	PG	4/22/88	3/5/89	318	$3,568,886
136	Things Change	(Columbia)	PG	10/21/88	2/20/89	123	$3,527,759
137	Dead Heat	(New World)	R	5/6/88	5/22/88	17	$3,511,819
138	Talk Radio	(Universal)	R	12/21/88	2/12/89	54	$3,395,181
139	Madame Sousatzka	(Universal)	PG-13	10/14/88	12/18/88	66	$3,358,839
140	Wings of Desire	(Orion Classics)	PG-13	5/20/88	5/29/89	373	$3,210,139
141	Night of the Demons	(Paragon)	R	9/9/88	6/11/89	273	$3,109,904
142	Messenger Of Death	(Cannon)	R	9/16/88	11/13/88	59	$3,065,608
143	Big Blue, The	(Columbia)	PG	8/19/88	8/28/88	10	$2,834,237
144	Running on Empty	(Warner Bros.)	PG-13	9/9/88	11/6/88	59	$2,809,806

Rank	Title	Distributor	MPAA	Open	Last	Days	Gross
145	White Mischief	(Columbia)	R	4/22/88	6/19/88	59	$2,348,327
146	Kansas	(Trans World)	R	9/23/88	10/2/88	10	$2,336,709
147	A World Apart	(Atlantic)	PG	6/17/88	1/29/89	197	$2,326,860
148	New Adv. Of Pippi Longstocking	(Columbia)	G	7/29/88	8/7/88	10	$2,314,019
149	18 Again	(New World)	PG	4/8/88	4/17/88	10	$2,312,877
150	House of Games	(Orion)	NR	10/14/87	2/28/88	56	$2,306,559
151	Dominick and Eugene	(Orion)	PG-13	3/18/88	6/19/88	94	$2,166,710
152	Bird	(Warner Bros.)	R	9/30/88	2/20/89	144	$2,163,327
153	Salaam Bombay	(Cinecom)	NR	10/9/88	5/7/89	213	$2,080,046
154	Pelle the Conqueror	(Miramax)	NR	12/21/88	5/14/89	145	$2,053,931
155	The Moderns	(Alive)	R	4/15/88	9/25/88	164	$2,011,497
156	Cop	(Atlantic)	R	2/5/88	6/5/88	122	$1,984,315
157	Manchurian Candidate (Reissue)	(United Artists)	NR	2/12/88	6/12/88	122	$1,975,927
158	Permanent Record	(Paramount)	PG-13	4/22/88	5/8/88	17	$1,842,861
159	Stormy Monday	(Atlantic)	R	4/22/88	11/13/88	206	$1,790,089
160	The Kiss	(TriStar)	R	10/14/88	11/6/88	24	$1,775,578
161	Little Nikita	(Columbia)	PG	3/18/88	4/3/88	17	$1,681,080
162	Vincent: Van Gogh	(Roxie)	NR	8/15/88	11/5/89	447	$1,577,480
163	A Handful of Dust	(New Line)	PG	6/24/88	11/20/88	150	$1,559,516
164	Lady in White	(New Century)	PG-13	4/22/88	6/19/88	59	$1,548,455
165	Two Moon Juction	(Lorimar)	R	4/29/88	6/12/88	45	$1,547,397
166	Pascali's Island	(Avenue)	PG-13	7/22/88	10/30/88	101	$1,451,857
167	Platoon Leader	(Cannon)	R	10/7/88	11/20/88	45	$1,347,587
168	Midnight Crossing	(Vestron)	R	5/13/88	6/5/88	24	$1,316,204
169	Patty Hearst	(Atlantic)	R	9/23/88	11/13/88	52	$1,222,741
170	Another Woman	(Orion)	PG	10/14/88	1/8/89	87	$1,213,923
171	A Time of Destiny	(Columbia)	PG-13	4/22/88	6/19/88	59	$1,211,796
172	Thin Blue Line, The	(Miramax)	NR	8/26/88	1/29/89	157	$1,209,846
173	The Lair of the White Worm	(Vestron)	R	10/21/88	3/26/89	157	$1,142,119
174	Mr. North	(Goldwyn)	PG	7/22/88	11/6/88	108	$1,128,046
175	High Season	(Hemdale)	R	3/25/88	10/2/88	192	$1,094,000
176	Aria	(Miramax)	R	3/18/88	8/7/88	143	$1,028,679
177	Little Dorrit	(Cannon)	G	10/21/88	5/29/89	221	$1,006,238
178	The Wrong Guys	(New World)	PG	5/13/88	5/22/88	10	$982,622
179	Vibes	(Columbia)	PG	8/5/88	8/7/88	3	$916,482
180	Appointment With Death	(Cannon)	PG	4/15/88	4/24/88	10	$831,064
181	Boyfriends And Girlfriends	(Orion Classics)	PG	7/22/88	2/20/89	214	$823,243
182	Bulletproof	(Cinetel)	R	5/13/88	6/5/88	24	$807,947
183	Waxwork	(Vestron)	R	6/27/88	12/11/88	178	$794,683
184	The Boost	(Hemdale)	R	12/23/88	1/29/89	37	$784,990
185	Julia And Julia	(Cinecom)	R	2/5/88	2/15/88	11	$782,151
186	The Grand Highway	(Miramax)	R	1/22/88	8/7/88	199	$760,539
187	And God Created Woman	(Vestron)	NR	3/4/88	6/5/88	94	$744,594
188	Five Corners	(Cineplex)	R	1/22/88	3/20/88	59	$706,818
189	Scavengers	(Triax)	PG-13	1/8/88	2/28/88	52	$699,118
190	Maniac Cop	(Shapiro)	R	5/6/88	5/30/88	25	$671,382
191	Sellbinder	(MGM)	R	9/23/88	9/25/88	3	$657,446
192	Da	(Film Dallas)	PG	4/29/88	8/7/88	101	$644,532
193	Spike Of Bensonhurst	(Film Dallas)	R	11/11/88	11/27/88	17	$623,112
194	Buster	(Hemdale)	R	11/23/88	12/26/88	32	$520,104
195	Pound Puppies/Legend of Big Paw	(TriStar)	G	3/18/88	4/24/88	38	$504,636
196	Jack's Back	(Palisades)	R	4/29/88	5/22/88	24	$492,619
197	A Summer Story	(Atlantic)	PG-13	7/22/88	11/27/88	129	$462,813

Rank	Title	Distributor	MPAA	Open	Last	Days	Gross
198	Watchers	(Universal)	R	12/2/88	12/11/88	10	$457,035
199	September	(Orion)	NR	12/18/87	2/21/88	49	$454,936
200	Full Moon in Blue Water	(Trans World)	R	11/23/88	1/29/89	83	$450,726
201	A Month in the Country	(Orion Classics)	PG	3/10/88	10/10/88	214	$443,524
202	Split Decisions	(New Century)	R	11/11/88	11/13/88	3	$423,303
203	Tiger Warsaw	(CEG)	R	9/2/88	12/4/88	94	$422,667
204	Aloha Summer	(Spectra)	PG	2/26/88	3/6/88	10	$418,379
205	21st Tournee Of Animation	(Expanded Ent.)	NR		10/10/88		$411,356
206	Track 29	(Island)	R	9/9/88	1/2/89	116	$399,256
207	Shy People	(Cannon)	NR	3/11/88	3/27/88	17	$397,148
208	Powaqqatsi	(Cannon)	G	4/29/88	6/26/88	59	$391,078
209	Commissar	(IFEX)	NR	6/17/88	10/2/88	108	$388,029
210	Paramedics	(Vestron)	NR	6/3/88	11/13/88	164	$384,893
211	Decline of Western Civil. Pt II	(New Line)	R	6/3/88	11/20/88	171	$373,743
212	Light Years	(Miramax)	PG	1/29/88	5/22/88	115	$370,698
213	Some Girls	(MGM/UA)	R	9/10/88	5/14/89	248	$352,634
214	The Deceivers	(Cinecom)	PG-13	9/2/88	10/10/88	39	$346,297
215	Patti Rocks	(Film Dallas)	R	1/15/88	3/20/88	66	$345,000
216	Sister Sister	(New World)	R	2/5/88	2/7/88	3	$316,420
217	The House on Carroll Street	(Orion)	PG	3/4/88	3/13/88	10	$312,851
218	You Can't Hurry Love	(Vestron)	R	1/29/88	2/7/88	10	$305,409
219	The Chocolate War	(MCEG)	R	11/23/88	2/12/89	81	$303,624
220	Promised Land	(Vestron)	R	1/22/88	6/5/88	136	$301,595
221	The Family	(Vestron)	PG	1/22/88	7/10/88	171	$297,473
222	Rent-A-Cop	(Kings Road)	R	1/15/88	1/17/88	3	$295,000
223	World Gone Wild	(Lorimar)	R	4/22/88	5/22/88	31	$274,530
224	Salome's Last Dance	(Vestron)	R	5/6/88	7/10/88	66	$247,823
225	Anguish	(Spectra)	R	1/29/88	1/31/88	3	$228,789
226	Bellman And True	(Island)	R	4/1/88	8/21/88	143	$226,944
227	Plain Clothes	(Paramount)	PG	4/15/88	4/17/88	3	$222,681
228	Judgement in Berlin	(New Line)	PG	5/6/88	5/30/88	25	$218,429
229	The Year My Voice Broke	(Avenue)	PG-13	8/31/88	10/30/88	61	$213,901
230	Sticky Fingers	(Spectra)	PG-13	5/6/88	5/15/88	10	$208,633
231	Matador	(Cinevista)	NR	7/1/88	10/10/88	102	$206,952
232	Tapeheads	(Avenue)	R	10/21/88	10/30/88	10	$199,773
233	Eat the Rich	(New Line)	NR	5/20/88	8/14/88	87	$199,005
234	Mondo New York	(Island)	NR	4/15/88	8/28/88	136	$193,209
235	Miles From Home	(Cinecom)	R	9/16/88	10/10/88	25	$188,964
236	Call Me	(Vestron)	R	5/20/88	6/19/88	31	$184,182
237	Ground Zero	(Avenue)	PG-13	9/23/88	10/30/88	38	$175,806
238	My Best Friend Is A Vampire	(Island)	PG	5/6/88	5/8/88	3	$174,380
239	It Takes Two	(United Artists)	PG-13	7/13/88	7/17/88	5	$157,294
240	Rocket Gibraltar	(Columbia)	PG	9/2/88	9/25/88	24	$154,423
241	Party Line	(SVS Films)	R	10/28/88	12/11/88	45	$154,167
242	Far North	(Alive)	PG-13	11/9/88	1/8/89	60	$147,234
243	Distant Thunder	(Paramount)	R	11/11/88	11/20/88	10	$145,973
244	The Wizard of Loneliness	(Skouras)	PG-13	9/2/88	9/11/88	10	$144,566
245	Beatrice	(Goldwyn)	R	3/4/88	6/5/88	94	$140,579
246	Apprentice to Murder	(New World)	PG-13	2/5/88	2/7/88	3	$140,332
247	High Tide	(TriStar)	NR	1/22/88	3/27/88	66	$138,288
248	Illegally Yours	(United Artists)	PG	5/13/88	5/15/88	3	$138,000
249	Hanna's War	(Cannon)	PG-13	11/23/88	12/11/88	19	$137,057
250	Big Time	(Island)	PG	9/30/88	12/4/88	66	$133,024

Rank	Title	Distributor	MPAA	Open	Last	Days	Gross
251	Rikky And Pete	(United Artists)	R	5/20/88	7/17/88	59	$127,999
252	Tokyo Pop	(Spectra)	R	4/15/88	4/24/88	10	$125,345
253	The In Crowd	(Orion)	PG	2/5/88	2/15/88	11	$124,880
254	Burning Secret	(Vestron)	PG	12/23/88	2/26/89	66	$123,251
255	Shame	(Skouras)	R	7/15/88	8/21/88	38	$122,739
256	The Blue Iguana	(Paramount)	R	4/22/88	4/24/88	3	$114,930
257	The Beast	(Columbia)	R	9/16/88	9/25/88	10	$108,246
258	Freeway	(New World)	R	9/2/88	9/5/88	4	$106,030
259	Hotel Terminus	(Goldwyn)	NR	10/21/88	11/13/88	24	$105,286
260	Stars And Bars	(Columbia)	R	3/18/88	6/19/88	94	$102,823
261	Pass The Ammo	(New Century)	R	3/4/88	3/6/88	3	$98,159
262	Amsterdamned	(Vestron)	R	11/23/88	2/26/89	94	$95,694
263	A Tiger's Tale	(Atlantic)	R	2/12/88	3/6/88	24	$88,895
264	White of the Eye	(Palisades)	R	6/3/88	6/5/88	3	$86,840
265	Heat and Sunlight	(Silverlight)	NR	11/1/88	4/9/89	160	$86,776
266	Biggles	(New Century)	PG	1/29/88	1/31/88	3	$85,692
267	The Forgotten Tune for the Flute	(Fries Ent.)	NR	12/22/88	4/30/89	131	$85,360
268	Not of this Earth	(Concorde)	R	5/20/88	5/22/88	3	$82,578
269	Seven Hours to Judgement	(Trans World)	R	9/16/88	9/18/88	3	$66,352
270	The Kitchen Toto	(Cannon)	PG-13	5/13/88	6/5/88	24	$60,823
271	Consuming Passions	(Goldwyn)	R	4/15/88	6/5/88	52	$56,206
272	The Telephone	(New World)	R	1/22/88	1/24/88	3	$54,811
273	Zelly & Me	(Columbia)	PG	4/15/88	6/9/88	55	$54,686
274	Half of Heaven	(Skouras)	NR	1/20/88	2/21/88	33	$48,549
275	Dakota	(Miramax)	PG	12/2/88	12/4/88	3	$34,733
276	Blueberry Hill	(MGM)	R	12/2/88	12/4/88	3	$31,652
277	Business as Usual	(Cannon)	PG	10/21/88	10/23/88	3	$28,238
278	Assault of the Killer Bimbos	(Crown Int'l)	R	5/6/88	5/8/88	3	$28,094
279	Into the Fire	(Movestar)	R	9/16/88	9/18/88	3	$21,411
280	Saturday The 14th Strikes Back	(Concorde)	PG	12/2/88	12/4/88	3	$21,004
281	A Killing Affair	(Hemdale)	R	7/15/88	7/24/88	10	$20,503
282	Purple People Eater	(Concorde)	R	12/16/88	12/18/88	3	$16,500
283	Slugs	(New World)	R	2/5/88	2/7/88	3	$15,842
284	Cherry 2000	(Orion)	PG-13	2/5/88	2/15/88	11	$13,936
285	The Wash	(Skouras)	NR	8/17/88	8/21/88	5	$13,479
286	Travelling North	(Cineplex Odeon)	PG-13	2/12/88	2/21/88	10	$10,238
287	Haunted Summer	(Cannon)	R	12/16/88	12/26/88	11	$8,946
288	Candy Mountain	(Int'l Film Ex.)	R	6/17/88	6/19/88	3	$8,607
289	The Beat	(Vestron)	R	6/3/88	6/5/88	3	$7,168
290	The Lighthorsemen	(Cinecom)	PG	5/20/88	5/22/88	3	$7,049
291	The Courier	(Vestron)	R	12/16/88	12/18/88	3	$1,506

Top Film Rentals

The following films are in alphabetical order and represent the domestic (U.S. & Canada) rental figures for the most profitable motion pictures released as well as some selected independent films. Sequels are listed in consecutive order under the original title. Rental figures are more accurate and have been better kept throughout the years than box office grosses and are used to determine "All-Time Box Office Champs" statistics. For a discussion on how film rentals relate to box office gross and for a complete listing of the abbreviations used in this section please turn to page 76.
***Indicates still in release.

Title (Distributor, Year Released)	$ Rentals	Title (Distributor, Year Released)	$ Rentals
Abby (AIP, 1974)	$2,600,000	Alice Doesn't Live Here Anymore (WB, 1975)	$7,900,000
Abominable Dr. Phibes, The (AIP, 1971)	$1,827,000	Alice in Wonderland (RKO/BV, 1951)	$7,196,000
About Last Night (TriStar, 1986)	$16,206,000	Alice in Wonderland (GNE, 1976)	$9,100,000
Above the Law (WB, 1988)	$8,200,000	Alice's Restaurant (UA, 1969)	$6,418,385
Absense of Malice (Col, 1981)	$19,688,775	Alien (Fox, 1979)	$40,300,000
Absent-Minded Professor, The (BV, 1961)	$11,426,000	Aliens (Fox, 1986)	$43,753,000
Abyss, The (Fox, 1989)	$28,700,000	Alien 3 (Fox, 1992)	$31,762,000
Accidental Tourist, The (WB, 1988)	$15,900,000	Alien Nation (Fox, 1988)	$11,700,000
Accused, The (Par, 1988)	$13,300,000	Alive (BV, 1993)	$17,000,000
Across 110th Street (UA, 1972)	$3,400,000	All About Eve (Fox, 1950)	$3,100,000
Across the Great Divide (PIE, 1977)	$8,107,000	All Dogs Go to Heaven (MGM/UA, 1989)	$10,961,000
Action Jackson (Lorimar, 1988)	$8,500,000	All of Me (U, 1984)	$15,214,390
Adam's Rib (MGM, 1949)	$3,000,000	All That Heaven Allows (U, 1955)	$3,100,000
Addams Family, The (Par, 1991)	$56,200,000	All That Jazz (Fox, 1979)	$20,030,000
Adv. of the Great Mouse Detective (BV, 1986)	$17,101,000	All the President's Men (WB, 1976)	$30,000,000
Adv. of the Wilderness Family, The (PIE, 1976)	$14,971,000	All the Right Moves (1983)	$8,000,000
Adv.s of Sher. Holmes Smarter Bro. (Fox, 1975)	$9,400,000	Allan Quatermain & Lost City of Gold (Can, 1987)	$1,400,000
Adventure (MGM, 1945)	$4,236,250	Aloha, Bobby and Rose (Col, 1975)	$6,730,000
Adventurers, The (Par, 1970)	$7,750,000	Alone In the Dark (NL, 1982)	$1,441,000
Adventures in Babysitting (BV, 1987)	$14,727,000	Altered States (WB, 1980)	$12,500,000
Adventures of Buckaroo Banzai (Fox, 1984)	$3,000,000	Always (U, 1989)	$23,256,055
Adventures of Ford Fairlane, The (Fox, 1990)	$11,500,000	Amadeus (Orion, 1984)	$23,034,449
Affair to Remember, An (Fox, 1957)	$3,800,000	Amarcord (NW, 1974)	$2,300,000
African Queen, The (UA, 1951)	$4,129,510	Amateur, The (Fox, 1982)	$4,000,000
After Dark My Sweet (Ave, 1990)	$1,300,000	Ambushers, The (Col, 1968)	$4,700,000
After Hours (Geffen/WB, 1985)	$4,400,000	American Anthem (Col, 1986)	$2,135,000
Against All Odds (Col, 1984)	$10,340,000	American Dreamer (WB, 1984)	$2,200,000
Agnes of God (Col, 1985)	$12,470,000	American Gigolo (Par, 1980)	$11,500,000
Agony and the Ecstasy, The (Fox, 1965)	$4,000,000	American Graffiti (U, 1973)	$55,128,175
Air America (TriStar, 1990)	$13,500,000	American Hot Wax (Par, 1978)	$5,532,000
Airplane (Par, 1980)	$40,610,000	American in Paris, An (MGM, 1951)	$4,212,776
Airplane Pt 2 (Par, 1982)	$11,341,000	American Ninja (Cannon, 1985)	$3,875,675
Airport (U, 1970)	$45,220,120	American Ninja 2 (Cannon, 1987)	$1,400,000
Airport 1975 (U, 1974)	$25,305,575	American Tail, An (U, 1986)	$22,879,105
Airport "77" (U, 1977)	$15,087,475	American Tail, An: Fievel Goes West (U, 1991)	$10,484,555
Airport '79, The Concorde (U, 1979)	$7,235,177	American Werewolf in London, An (U, 1981)	$13,764,200
Aladdin (BV, 1992)***	$103,680,000	American Wilderness (PIE, 1972)	$5,663,966
Alamo, The (UA, 1960)	$7,918,776	Americanization of Emily, The (MGM, 1964)	$3,800,000
Alfie (Par, 1966)	$8,500,000	Amityville Horror, The (AIP/FWS, 1979)	$35,000,000

Title (Distributor, Year Released)	$ Rentals	Title (Distributor, Year Released)	$ Rentals
Amityville II: The Posession (Orion, 1982)	$6,055,345	Baby Boom (MGM/UA, 1987)	$12,079,000
Anastasia (Fox, 1956)	$4,309,106	Baby—Secret of the Lost Legend (BV, 1985)	$6,832,000
Anatomy of a Murder (Col, 1959)	$5,500,000	Bachelor and the Bobby-Soxer, The (RKO, 1947)	$5,500,000
Anchors Aweigh (MGM, 1945)	$4,778,700	Bachelor Party (Fox, 1984)	$19,070,000
And God Created Woman (Kingsley, 1957)	$3,000,000	Back Roads (WB, 1981)	$6,300,000
And Justice for All (Col, 1979)	$14,514,906	Back Street (U, 1961)	$3,000,000
Anderson Tapes, The (Col, 1971)	$5,000,000	Back to School (Orion, 1986)	$41,948,385
Andromeda Strain, The (U, 1971)	$7,912,740	Back To The Beach (Par, 1987)	$5,666,392
Angel (NW, 1984)	$7,000,000	Back to the Future (U, 1985)	$105,496,270
Angel Heart (TriStar, 1987)	$6,500,000	Back to the Future Pt 2 (U, 1989)	$72,319,630
Angelo My Love (Cinecom, 1983)	$1,350,000	Back to the Future Pt 3 (U, 1990)	$49,072,000
Animal Crackers (Par/U, 1930)	$3,100,000	Backdraft (U, 1991)	$40,260,680
Anna and the King of Siam (Fox, 1946)	$3,500,000	Bad Boys (U, 1983)	$5,451,000
Anne of the Thousand Days (U, 1970)	$5,876,070	Bad News Bears, The (Par, 1976)	$24,888,000
Annie (Col, 1982)	$37,480,000	Bad News Bears: Breaking Training (Par, 1977)	$15,052,000
Annie Get Your Gun (MGM, 1950)	$4,919,400	Bad News Bears Go to Japan, The (Par, 1978)	$7,305,000
Annie Hall (UA, 1977)	$19,002,370	Bad Seed, The (WB, 1956)	$4,100,000
Another 48 Hours (Par, 1990)	$40,100,000	Bagdad Cafe (Island, 1988)	$1,500,000
Any Which Way You Can (WB, 1980)	$40,500,000	Bambi (RKO/BV, 1942)	$47,265,000
Apache (UA, 1954)	$3,500,000	Bananas (UA, 1971)	$3,500,000
Apartment, The (UA, 1960)	$6,680,040	Band of the Hand (TriStar, 1986)	$2,000,000
Apocalypse Now (UA, 1979)	$37,980,170	Bandit of Sherwood Forest, The (Col, 1946)	$3,000,000
Apple Dumpling Gang, The (BV, 1975)	$16,580,000	Bandolero (Fox, 1968)	$5,500,000
Apple Dumpling Gang Rides Again (BV, 1979)	$9,468,000	Barbarella (Par, 1968)	$5,500,000
April Fool's Day (Par, 1986)	$5,300,000	Barefoot Contessa, The (UA, 1954)	$3,300,000
April Fools, The (NGP/WB, 1969)	$5,000,000	Barefoot Executive, The (BV, 1971)	$3,500,000
April Love (Fox, 1957)	$3,700,000	Barefoot in the Park (Par, 1967)	$9,000,000
Arabesque (U, 1966)	$4,000,000	Barfly (Cannon, 1987)	$1,380,000
Arachnophobia (BV, 1990)	$31,366,000	Barkleys of Broadway, The (MGM, 1949)	$3,200,000
Aristocrats, The (BV, 1970)	$26,462,000	Barry Lyndon (WB, 1975)	$9,200,000
Armed and Dangerous (Col, 1986)	$6,604,080	Basic Instinct (TriStar, 1992)	$53,000,000
Armed Response (Cinetel, 1986)	$1,102,000	Bathing Beauty (MGM, 1944)	$3,500,000
Around the World in 80 Days (UA/WB, 1956)	$23,120,000	Batman (WB, 1989)	$150,500,000
Arrangement, The (WB, 1969)	$4,000,000	Batman Returns (WB, 1992)	$100,100,000
Art of Love, The (U, 1965)	$3,500,000	Battelground (MGM,1949)	$5,051,145
Arthur (Orion/WB, 1981)	$42,000,000	Batteries Not Included (U, 1987)	$15,416,100
Arthur 2 On The Rocks (WB, 1988)	$7,500,000	Battle Beyond the Stars (NW, 1980)	$3,600,000
Artists and Models (Par, 1955)	$3,800,000	Battle Cry (WB, 1955)	$8,100,000
Assassination (Cannon, 1987)	$2,200,000	Battle for the Planet of the Apes (Fox, 1973)	$4,027,000
At the Earth's Core (AIP, 1976)	$3,000,000	Battle Hymn (U, 1957)	$3,900,000
At the Max (IMAX/BCL, 1991)	$3,000,000	Battle of the Bulge (CRC/WB, 1965)	$5,100,000
At War With the Army (Par, 1950)	$3,300,000	Battlestar Galactica (U, 1978)	$6,396,020
Atlantic City (Par, 1981)	$5,000,000	Beach Girls, The (Crown, 1982)	$2,700,000
Ator (Comworld, 1983)	$1,200,000	Beaches (BV, 1988)	$24,900,000
Auntie Mame (WB, 1958)	$9,300,000	Bear, The (TriStar, 1989)	$13,500,000
Author! Author! (Fox, 1982)	$7,500,000	Bears and I, The (BV, 1974)	$4,000,000
Autumn Sonata (NW, 1978)	$2,000,000	Beast Within, The (MGM, 1982)	$2,640,000
Avenging Angel (NW, 1985)	$3,000,000	Beastmaster, The (MGM/UA, 1982)	$5,093,875
Avenging Force (Cannon, 1986)	$1,500,000	Beat Street (Orion, 1984)	$7,105,000
Awakening, The (Orion/WB, 1980)	$4,250,000	Beauty and the Beast (BV, 1991)	$69,415,000
Awakenings (Col, 1990)	$23,240,000	Beavers-IMAX (Stephen Low Prods, 1988)	$2,500,000
Away All Boats (U, 1956)	$3,500,000	Becket (Par, 1964)	$5,000,000
Babes in Toyland (RKO/BV, 1961)	$4,600,000	Bedknobs and Broomsticks (BV, 1972)	$11,426,000
Babette's Feast (Orion Classics, 1988)	$2,000,000	Bedroom Window, The (DEG, 1987)	$4,700,000

Title (Distributor, Year Released)	$ Rentals	Title (Distributor, Year Released)	$ Rentals
Beethoven (U, 1992)	$26,450,910	Bishop's Wife, The (RKO, 1948)	$3,000,000
Beetlejuice (WB, 1988)	$33,200,000	Bite the Bullet (Col, 1975)	$5,274,000
Behind the Green Door (Mitchell Bros., 1972)	$5,000,000	Black Cauldron, The (BV, 1985)	$9,542,000
Being There (UA, 1979)	$11,014,470	Black Godfather, The (Cinemation, 1974)	$1,300,000
Believers, The (Orion, 1987)	$7,848,830	Black Hole, The (BV, 1979)	$25,437,000
Bellboy, The (Par, 1960)	$3,600,000	Black Moon Rising (NW, 1985)	$3,450,000
Bells of St. Mary's, The (RKO, 1945)	$8,000,000	Black Rain (Par, 1989)	$25,000,000
Ben-Hur (MGM, 1926)	$4,578,640	Black Robe (Goldwyn, 1991)	$4,250,000
Ben-Hur (MGM, 1959)	$36,922,090	Black Stallion, The (UA, 1979)	$17,043,685
Bend of the River (U, 1952)	$3,000,000	Black Stallion Returns, The (MGM/UA, 1983)	$4,718,810
Beneath the 12-mile Reef (Fox, 1953)	$3,200,000	Black Sunday (Par, 1977)	$14,202,600
Beneath the Planet of the Apes (Fox, 1970)	$8,600,000	Black Widow (Fox, 1987)	$11,500,000
Benji (Mulberry Square, 1974)	$16,890,000	Blackbeard's Ghost (BV, 1968)	$9,675,000
Benji: The Hunted (BV, 1987)	$9,430,000	Blackboard Jungle, The (MGM, 1955)	$5,459,000
Bermuda Triangle, The (Sunn/Taft, 1978)	$10,800,000	Blacula (AIP, 1972)	$1,980,000
Bernardine (Fox, 1957)	$3,700,000	Blade Runner (WB, 1982)	$16,650,000
Best Defense (Par, 1984)	$10,500,000	Blame It on Rio (Fox, 1984)	$9,750,000
Best Friends (WB, 1982)	$19,000,000	Blazing Saddles (WB, 1974)	$47,800,000
Best Little Whorehouse in Texas, The (U, 1982)	$47,333,927	Blind Date (TriStar, 1987)	$17,078,000
Best Years of Our Lives, The (RKO, 1946)	$11,300,000	Blood Beach (Jerry Gross, 1981)	$2,000,000
Betrayed (MGM/UA, 1988)	$11,126,475	Blood on the Sun (UA, 1945)	$3,400,000
Betsy, The (AA, 1978)	$7,850,000	Blood Simple (Circle, 1985)	$3,275,045
Beverly Hills Cop (Par,1984)	$108,000,000	Bloodfist (Concorde, 1989)	$1,000,000
Beverly Hills Cop 2 (Par, 1987)	$80,857,775	Bloodline (Par, 1979)	$5,366,000
Beyond and Back (Sunn/Taft, 1978)	$11,702,000	Bloodsport (Cannon, 1988)	$4,661,000
Beyond the Door (FVI, 1975)	$7,143,970	Blow Out (Filmways, 1981)	$8,000,000
Beyond the Valley of the Dolls (Fox, 1970)	$7,000,000	Blow-up (Premier/MGM, 1966)	$6,322,100
Bible, The (Fox, 1966)	$15,000,000	Blue Collar (U, 1978)	$3,097,091
Big (Fox, 1988)	$53,700,000	Blue Hawaii (Par, 1961)	$4,700,000
Big Bad Mama (NW, 1974)	$2,800,000	Blue Lagoon, The (Col, 1980)	$28,838,020
Big Blue, The (Col, 1988)	$1,200,000	Blue Max, The (Fox, 1966)	$7,275,000
Big Brawl, The (WB, 1980)	$3,000,000	Blue Skies (Par, 1946)	$5,700,000
Big Business (BV, 1988)	$17,849,000	Blue Thunder (Col, 1983)	$21,890,000
Big Chill, The (Col, 1983)	$24,060,000	Blue Velvet (DEG, 1986)	$4,009,855
Big Country, The (UA, 1958)	$3,500,000	Blues Brothers, The (U, 1980)	$32,098,717
Big Doll House (NW, 1971)	$3,000,000	Blume in Love (WB, 1973)	$3,000,000
Big Easy, The (Col, 1987)	$7,761,500	Boat, The {Das Boot} (Triumph/Col, 1982)	$4,500,000
Big Fisherman, The (BV, 1959)	$3,000,000	Boatniks, The (BV, 1970)	$9,150,000
Big Fix, The (U, 1978)	$6,257,000	Bob & Carol & Ted & Alice (Col, 1969)	$14,600,000
Big Jake (NGP/WB, 1971)	$7,500,000	Bobby Deerfield (Col ,1977)	$4,400,000
Big Parade, The (MGM, 1925)	$5,120,800	Body and Soul (UA, 1947)	$2,500,000
Big Sleep, The (WB, 1946)	$3,000,000	Body Double (Col, 1984)	$3,700,000
Big Top Pee-Wee (Par, 1988)	$7,000,000	Body Heat (Ladd/WB, 1981)	$11,500,000
Big Touble in Little China (Fox, (1986)	$6,000,000	Body Rock (NW, 1984)	$1,600,000
Bill & Ted's Excellent Adventure (Orion, 1989)	$16,801,525	Bodyguard, The (WB, 1992)	$58,000,000
Bill & Ted's Bogus Journey (Orion, 1991)	$17,248,530	Bolero (Cannon, 1984)	$4,512,680
Billy Jack (WB, 1971)	$32,500,000	Bon Voyage (BV, 1962)	$5,000,000
Billy Jack, The Trial of (WB, 1974)	$31,100,000	Bonnie and Clyde (WB, 1967)	$22,800,000
Biloxi Blues (U, 1988)	$19,552,890	Boogens, The (Jensen Farley, 1981)	$3,044,433
Bingo Long Traveling All-Stars (U, 1976)	$4,719,290	Boogey Man, The (Jerry Gross, 1980)	$2,100,000
Bird on a Wire (U, 1990)	$38,436,975	Boom Town (MGM, 1940)	$4,586,415
Birdman of Alcatraz (UA, 1962)	$3,100,000	Boomerang (Par, 1992)	$34,000,000
Birds, The (U, 1963)	$5,090,370	Bootleggers (Howco, 1974)	$2,800,000
Birth of a Nation, The (Epoch, 1915)	$10,000,000	Border, The (U, 1982)	$4,587,025

Title (Distributor, Year Released)	$ Rentals	Title (Distributor, Year Released)	$ Rentals
Born Free (Col, 1966)	$3,600,000	Buddy Holly Story, The (Col, 1978)	$6,470,000
Born in East LA (1987)	$7,456,920	Bugsy (TriStar, 1991)	$21,000,000
Born Losers (AIP/FWS, 1967+1974 reissue)	$12,500,000	Bull Durham (Orion, 1988)	$21,900,000
Born on the Fourth of July (U, 1989)	$36,803,148	Bullies (U, 1986)	$1,169,000
Born Yesterday (Col, 1950)	$4,115,000	Bullitt (WB, 1968)	$19,000,000
Boston Strangler, The (Fox, 1968)	$8,000,000	Burbs, The (U, 1989)	$17,315,425
Bostonians, The (Almi, 1984)	$1,750,000	Burglar (WB, 1987)	$8,100,000
Bounty, The (Orion, 1984)	$4,713,255	Bus Stop (Fox, 1956)	$4,250,000
Boxcar Bertha (AIP, 1972)	$1,100,000	Buster and Billie (Col, 1974)	$4,000,000
Boy and His Dog, A (LQ/Jaf, 1975)	$2,500,000	Bustin' Loose (U, 1981)	$15,417,626
Boy Named Charlie Brown, A (NGP/WB, 1969)	$6,000,000	Butch Cassidy and the Sundance Kid (Fox, 1969)	$45,953,000
Boy on a Dolphin (Fox, 1957)	$3,000,000	Butterfield 8 (MGM, 1960)	$7,551,650
Boy Who Could Fly, The (Fox, 1986)	$2,857,000	Butterflies Are Free (Col, 1972)	$6,329,470
Boy, Did I Get a Wrong Number (UA, 1966)	$4,304,900	Bwana Devil (UA, 1952)	$3,000,000
Boys From Brazil, The (Fox, 1978)	$8,000,000	Bye Bye Birdie (Col, 1963)	$6,200,000
Boys in Company C, The (Col, 1978)	$4,295,000	C.H.O.M.P.S. (AIP, 1979)	$1,800,000
Boys in the Band, The (NGP, 1970)	$3,500,000	Cabaret (AA, 1972)	$20,250,000
Boys Town (MGM, 1938)	$3,000,000	Cactus Flower (Col, 1969)	$11,850,000
Boys' Night Out (MGM, 1962)	$3,400,000	Caddy, The (Par, 1953)	$3,500,000
Boyz N the Hood (Col, 1991)	$26,700,000	Caddyshack (Orion/WB, 1980)	$20,500,000
Brainstorm (MGM/UA, 1983)	$4,750,840	Caddyshack II (WB, 1988)	$6,200,000
Bram Stoker's Dracula (Col, 1992)	$47,200,000	Cadence (NL, 1991)	$1,000,000
Bramble Bush, The (WB,1960)	$3,000,000	Cadillac Man (Orion, 1990)	$12,559,620
Brazil (U, 1985)	$4,468,390	Cahill—US Marshal (WB, 1973)	$4,100,000
Break and Chocolate (World Northal, 1978)	$2,000,000	Caine Mutiny, The (Col, 1954)	$8,700,000
Breaker Breaker (AIP, 1977)	$1,500,000	California (Par, 1947)	$3,900,000
Breaker Morant (NW/Quartet, 1980)	$3,500,000	California Split (Col, 1974)	$4,784,000
Breakfast at Tiffany's (Par, 1961)	$4,200,000	California Suite (Col, 1978)	$28,386,200
Breakfast Club, The (U, 1985)	$17,727,045	Caligula (Analysis/Penthouse, 1980)	$9,750,000
Breakin' (Cannon-MGM/UA, 1984)	$15,734,499	Camelot (WB/7 Arts, 1967)	$14,000,000
Breakin' 2: Electric Boogaloo (TriStar, 1985)	$7,200,000	Can't Buy Me Love (BV, 1987)	$13,313,000
Breaking Away (Fox, 1979)	$10,300,000	Can-Can (Fox, 1960)	$4,200,000
Breakout (Col, 1975)	$7,528,000	Candleshoe (BV, 1978)	$7,225,000
Breathless (Orion, 1983)	$10,063,975	Candy (CRC/Col, 1968)	$7,370,000
Brewster's Millions (U, 1985)	$19,907,490	Candy Tangerine Man (Moonstone, 1975)	$1,000,000
Bridge on the River Kwai (Col, 1957)	$17,195,000	Candyman (TriStar, 1992)	$10,000,000
Bridge Too Far, A (UA, 1977)	$20,375,410	Cannonball (NW, 1976)	$1,500,000
Bridges at Toko-Ri, The (Par, 1954)	$5,000,000	Cannonball Run, The (Fox, 1981)	$36,800,000
Bright Lights, Big City (MGM/UA, 1988)	$6,971,000	Cannonball Run II (WB, 1984)	$14,600,000
Brighton Beach Memoirs (U, 1986)	$6,313,520	Cape Fear (U, 1991)	$39,490,060
Brink's Job (U,1978)	$4,686,810	Capricorn One (WB, 1978)	$12,000,000
Broadcast News (Fox, 1987)	$24,900,000	Captain From Castile (Fox, 1948)	$3,600,000
Broadway Danny Rose (Orion, 1984)	$5,356,115	Captain Newman, M.D. (U, 1963)	$4,000,000
Broadway Melody, The (MGM, 1929)	$3,000,000	Car Wash (U, 1976)	$8,534,650
Broken Arrow (Fox, 1950)	$3,600,000	Car, The (U, 1977)	$3,066,735
Broken Lance (Fox, 1954)	$3,800,000	Carbon Copy (Avemb, 1981)	$4,208,405
Bronco Billy (WB, 1980)	$15,000,000	Cardinal, The (Col, 1963)	$5,275,000
Brother From Another Planet (Cinecom, 1985)	$3,700,000	Care Bears Movie, The (Goldwyn, 1985)	$9,435,000
Brother of the Wind (Sunn, 1972)	$12,000,000	Care Bears: Adv. in Wonderland (Cineplex, 1987)	$1,000,000
Brother, Can You Spare A Dime? (Dimen.s, 1975)	$1,400,000	Career (Par, 1959)	$3,000,000
Brubaker (Fox, 1980)	$19,300,000	Careful He Might Hear You (Fox/TLC, 1984)	$1,540,000
Buccaneer, The (Par, 1958)	$3,200,000	Carmen Baby (Audubon, 1967)	$4,200,000
Buck and the Preacher (Col, 1972)	$3,100,000	Carnal Knowledge (Avemb, 1971)	$14,075,075
Buck Rogers (U, 1979)	$10,745,750	Carousel (Fox, 1956)	$3,700,000

Title (Distributor,Year Released)	$ Rentals	Title (Distributor, Year Released)	$ Rentals
Carpetbaggers, The (Par, 1964)	$15,500,000	Chipmunk Adventure, The (Goldwyn, 1987)	$2,821,725
Carrie (UA, 1976)	$15,207,515	Chisum (WB, 1970)	$6,000,000
Casablanca (MGM/UA, 1943)	$4,750,000	Chitty Chitty Bang Bang (UA, 1968)	$7,120,217
Casey's Shadow (Col, 1978)	$4,013,000	Choirboys, The (U, 1977)	$6,849,540
Casino Royale (Col, 1967)	$10,200,000	Choose Me (Island/Alive, 1984)	$1,538,000
Cass Timberlane (MGM, 1947)	$3,983,450	Choosen, The (Fox Classics, 1983)	$2,150,000
Cassandra Crossing, The (Avemb, 1977)	$4,184,000	Chorus Line, A (Fox, 1980)	$9,828,485
Cast a Giant Shadow (UA, 1966)	$3,200,000	Christine (Col, 1983)	$9,319,800
Casual Sex (U, 1988)	$5,205,240	Christmas in Connecticut (WB, 1945)	$3,273,000
Cat & Mouse (Quartet, 1977)	$1,100,000	Christmas Story, A (MGM/UA, 1983)	$8,153,880
Cat Ballou (Col, 1965)	$9,300,000	CHUD (NW, 1984)	$2,100,000
Cat From Outer Space (BV, 1978)	$8,488,000	Cincinnati Kid, The (MGM, 1965)	$3,900,000
Cat on a Hot Tin Roof (MGM, 1958)	$8,785,160	Cinderella (RKO/BV, 1949)	$41,087,000
Cat People (U, 1982)	$5,027,605	Cinderella (Group 1, 1977)	$2,600,000
Catch-22 (Par, 1970)	$12,250,000	Cinderella Liberty (Fox, 1973)	$4,005,000
Cathy's Curse (21st Century, 1980)	$1,261,230	Cinderella 2000 (Independent/Int'l, 1977)	$1,500,000
Caveman (MGM/UA, 1981)	$5,898,650	Cinema Paradiso (Miramax, 1989)	$5,500,000
Cemetery Girls (MPM, 1979)	$1,200,000	Cinerama Holiday (CRC, 1955)	$12,000,000
Centennial Summer (Fox, 1946)	$3,000,000	Circle of Iron (Avemb, 1979)	$1,000,000
Chained Heat (Jensen Farley, 1983)	$4,000,000	City Heat (WB, 1984)	$21,000,000
Chalk Garden, The (U, 1964)	$3,200,000	City Lights (UA/Col Classics, 1931)	$3,300,000
Challenge to Be Free (PIE, 1975)	$7,729,000	City Slickers (Col, 1991)	$60,750,000
Champ, The (MGM/UA, 1979)	$12,615,300	Clash of the Titans (MGM/UA, 1981)	$17,450,467
Change of Seasons, A (Fox,1980)	$7,400,000	Class (Orion, 1983)	$10,488,780
Changeling, The (AFD, 1980)	$5,300,000	Class Action (Fox, 1991)	$13,102,000
Chapman Report, The (WB, 1962)	$3,500,000	Class of '44 (WB, 1973)	$7,000,000
Chapter Two (Col, 1980)	$14,917,709	Class of 1984 (UFD, 1982)	$2,161,720
Charade (U, 1963)	$6,362,783	Class Of Nuke 'Em High (Troma, 1986)	$1,900,000
Charge at Feather River, The (WB, 1953)	$3,700,000	Classroom Teasers (MPM, 1981)	$1,075,000
Chariots of Fire (Ladd/WB, 1981)	$30,600,000	Claudine (Fox, 1974)	$3,039,000
Chariots of the Gods (Sunn/Taft, 1973)	$12,460,000	Clean And Sober (WB, 1988)	$4,000,000
Charlie Chan:Curse of Dragon Qn. (AC, 1981)	$1,500,000	Cleopatra (Fox, 1963)	$26,000,000
Charly (CRC/Col, 1968)	$7,260,000	Cleopatra Jones (WB, 1973)	$4,100,000
Cheap Detective, The (Col, 1978)	$19,203,000	Cloak & Dagger (U, 1984)	$4,001,180
Cheaper by the Dozen (Fox, 1950)	$4,425,000	Clock, The (MGM, 1945)	$3,000,000
Cheaper to Keep Her (Amer. Cinema, 1981)	$1,400,000	Clockwork Orange, A (WB,1971)	$17,000,000
Cheech & Chong's Next Movie (U, 1980)	$21,557,620	Close Encounters of the Third Kind (Col, 1977)	$82,750,000
Cheech & Chong's Nice Dreams (Col, 1981)	$18,432,000	Club Paradise (WB, 1986)	$6,900,000
Cheech & Chong Still Smokin' (Par, 1983)	$5,904,000	Coach (Crown, 1978)	$2,500,000
Cheerleaders, The (Cinemation, 1973)	$2,500,000	Coal Miner's Daughter (U, 1980)	$35,030,225
Cherry, Harry & Raquel (Eve/RM Films, 1969)	$3,000,000	Cobra (WB, 1986)	$28,000,000
Cheyenne Autumn (WB, 1964)	$3,500,000	Cocktail (BV, 1988)	$36,474,000
Cheyenne Social Club, The (NGP/WB, 1970)	$5,250,000	Cocoon (Fox, 1985)	$40,000,000
Chicken Chronicles, The (Avemb, 1977)	$1,350,000	Cocoon: The Return (Fox, 1988)	$6,600,000
Child's Play (MGM/UA, 1988)	$14,726,000	Code of Silence (Orion, 1985)	$8,277,725
Child's Play 2 (U, 1990)	$14,077,395	Coffy (AIP, 1973)	$4,000,000
Children of a Lesser God (Par, 1986)	$12,056,608	Cold Blood, In (Col, 1967)	$6,000,000
Children of the Corn (NW, 1984)	$6,900,000	Cold Turkey (UA, 1971)	$4,986,840
Children of the Corn II (Miramax, 1993)	$2,720,000	Collector, The (Col, 1965)	$3,500,000
Children, The (Northal, 1980)	$2,100,000	Color of Money, The (BV, 1986)	$24,435,000
China Cry (Penland, 1990)	$2,500,000	Color Purple, The (WB, 1985)	$49,800,000
China Syndrome, The (Col, 1979)	$25,342,000	Colors (Orion,1988)	$21,196,860
Chinatown (Par, 1974)	$12,400,000	Coma (MGM/UA, 1978)	$14,538,860
Chinese Connection, The (Pagoda/NGP/WB, 1972)	$3,800,000	Come Back to 5 & Dime Jimmy Dean (Cc, 1982)	$1,100,000

Title (Distributor, Year Released)	$ Rentals
Come Back, Little Sheba (Par, 1952)	$3,500,000
Come Blow Your Horn (Par, 1963)	$6,000,000
Come September (U, 1961)	$5,721,515
Come to the Stable (Fox, 1949)	$3,000,000
Comes a Horseman (UA, 1978)	$4,172,175
Comin' At Ya (FWS, 1981)	$5,252,400
Coming Home (UA, 1978)	$13,470,505
Coming to America (Par, 1988)	$65,000,000
Command Decision (MGM, 1949)	$3,000,000
Commando (Fox, 1985)	$17,000,000
Company of Wolves, The (Cannon, 1985)	$2,350,225
Competition, The (Col, 1980)	$7,001,000
Compromising Positions (Par, 1985)	$5,400,000
Computer Wore Tennis Shoes, The (BV, 1970)	$6,000,000
Conan the Barbarian (U, 1982)	$21,730,000
Conan the Destroyer (U, 1984)	$14,293,015
Concrete Jungle, The (Pentagon, 1982)	$3,234,700
Coney Island (Fox, 1943)	$3,305,000
Conn. Yankee In King Arthur's Court (Par, 1949)	$3,000,000
Conqueror, The (RKO, 1956)	$4,500,000
Conquest of the Planet of the Apes (Fox, 1972)	$4,500,000
Consenting Adults (BV, 1992)	$10,000,000
Continental Divide (U, 1981)	$8,299,420
Convoy (UA, 1978)	$9,529,665
Coogan's Bluff (U, 1968)	$3,011,145
Cook,Thief, His Wife & Her Lover (Miramax, 1990)	$3,900,000
Cool Hand Luke (WB/7 Arts, 1967)	$7,300,000
Cooley High (AIP, 1975)	$2,600,000
Corvette Summer (MGM/UA, 1978)	$6,492,660
Cotton Club, The (Orion, 1984)	$12,562,910
Cotton Comes to Harlem (UA, 1970)	$5,145,075
Couch Trip, The (Orion, 1988)	$4,650,000
Country Girl, The (Par, 1954)	$6,500,000
Court-Martial of Billy Mitchell, The (WB, 1955)	$3,000,000
Cousin Cousine (Libra, 1976)	$3,700,000
Cousins (Par, 1979)	$10,000,000
Covered Wagon, The (Par, 1923)	$4,000,000
Cowboys, The (WB, 1972)	$7,500,000
Crater Lake Monster (Crown, 1977)	$1,050,000
Crazy Mama (NW, 1975)	$2,300,000
Crazy People (Par, 1990)	$5,500,000
Creepshow (WB, 1982)	$10,000,000
Creepshow 2 (NW, 1987)	$4,900,000
Cries and Whispers (NW, 1972)	$3,500,000
Crime Zone (Concorde, 1988)	$1,656,410
Crimes of Passion (NW, 1984)	$1,500,000
Crimes of the Heart (DEG, 1986)	$7,000,000
Criminal Law (Hemdale, 1989)	$3,896,500
Critical Condition (Par, 1987)	$8,890,435
Critters (NL, 1986)	$4,300,000
Critters 2 (NL, 1988)	$1,700,000
Crocodile Dundee (Par, 1986)	$70,227,000
Crocodile Dundee II (Par, 1988)	$57,300,000
Cross of Iron (Avemb, 1977)	$1,509,000

Title (Distributor, Year Released)	$ Rentals
Crossfire (RKO, 1947)	$3,000,000
Crossing Delancey (War, 1988)	$7,000,000
Cruising (UA, 1980)	$6,788,140
Cry Of The Banshee (AIP, 1970)	$1,306,000
Crying Game, The (Miramax, 1992)	$28,137,000
Cujo (WB, 1983)	$9,800,000
Curly Sue (WB, 1991)	$14,000,000
Curtains (Jensen Farley, 1983)	$2,000,000
Cutting Edge, The (MGM/UA, 1992)	$10,122,385
Cyborg (Can, 1989)	$4,100,000
D.A.R.Y.L. (Par, 1985)	$3,500,000
D.C. Cab (U, 1983)	$7,045,940
D.O.A. (BV, 1988)	$5,361,000
Dad (U, 1989)	$10,753,400
Daddy's Gone A-Hunting (NGP, 1969)	$3,000,000
Damage (NL, 1992)	$3,200,000
Damnation Alley (Fox, 1977)	$5,031,000
Dance With A Stranger (Goldwyn, 1985)	$1,125,260
Dances With Wolves (Orion, 1990)	$81,537,970
Dangerous Liaisons (WB, 1988)	$15,500,000
Darby O'Gill and the Little People (BV, 1959)	$8,336,000
Dark Crystal, The (U/AFD, 1982)	$23,887,850
Dark Eyes (Island, 1987)	$1,013,825
Dark Passage (WB, 1947)	$3,000,000
Darkman (U, 1990)	$16,158,155
Darling (Par, 1970)	$3,600,000
Date With Judy, A (MGM, 1948)	$3,700,000
David and Bathsheba (Fox, 1951)	$4,720,000
Dawn of the Dead (UFD, 1979)	$7,383,575
Day of the Dolphin, The (Avemb, 1973)	$6,230,750
Day of the Jackal, The (U, 1973)	$8,595,060
Days of Thunder (Par, 1990)	$40,000,000
Days of Wine and Roses (WB, 1962)	$4,400,000
Dead Again (Par, 1991)	$17,500,000
Dead Heat (NW, 1988)	$1,424,390
Dead Men Don't Wear Plaid (U, 1982)	$11,504,810
Dead Poets Society (BV, 1989)	$48,427,510
Dead Pool, The (WB, 1988)	$19,000,000
Dead Ringers (Fox, 1988)	$3,900,000
Dead Time Stories (Cinema Group, 1986)	$1,100,000
Dead Zone (Par, 1983)	$8,158,000
Dead, The (Vestron, 1987)	$1,653,210
Deadly Blessing (1981)	$2,882,000
Deal of The Century (WB, 1983)	$4,900,000
Dear John (Sigma 3, 1964)	$4,250,000
Dear Ruth (Par, 1947)	$3,800,000
Death Becomes Her (U, 1992)	$30,433,485
Death Before Dishonor (NW, 1987)	$1,500,000
Death on the Nile (Par, 1978)	$8,800,000
Death Race 2000 (NW, 1975)	$4,000,000
Death Ship (Avemb, 1980)	$1,750,000
Death Wish (Par, 1974)	$8,800,000
Death Wish 2 (Filmways, 1982)	$9,042,245
Death Wish 3 (Cannon, 1985)	$6,466,675

Title (Distributor, Year Released)	$ Rentals	Title (Distributor, Year Released)	$ Rentals
Death Wish 4 (Cannon, 1987)	$2,808,333	Doctor, The (BV, 1991)	$17,562,885
Deathstalker (NW, 1984)	$1,500,000	Dog Day Afternoon (WB, 1975)	$22,500,000
Deathtrap (WB, 1982)	$9,000,000	Dolemite (Dimension, 1975)	$1,100,000
Deceived (BV, 1991)	$12,255,235	Dolly Sister, The (Fox, 1945)	$3,952,000
Decline of Amer. Emp. (Cinep. Odeon, 1986)	$1,000,000	Dominick & Eugene (Orion, 1988)	$1,100,000
Deep Cover (NL, 1992)	$7,200,000	Domino Principle, The (Avemb, 1977)	$1,700,000
Deep in My Heart (MGM, 1954)	$3,500,000	Dona Flor & Her 2 Husbands (NYer, 1978)	$1,200,000
Deep Throat (Damiano Films, 1972)	$20,000,000	Don't Answer the Phone (Crown, 1980)	$2,000,000
Deep, The (Col, 1977)	$31,266,000	Don't Give Up the Ship (Par, 1959)	$4,000,000
Deer Hunter, The (U, 1978)	$27,436,325	Don't Go Into the House (FV, 1980)	$2,950,000
Defenseless (NL/7Arts, 1991)	$2,600,000	Don't Go Near the Water (MGM, 1957)	$4,473,645
Delicate Delinquent, The (Par, 1956)	$3,400,000	Don't Tell Mom the Babysitter's Dead (WB, 1991)	$10,500,000
Deliverance (WB, 1972)	$22,600,000	Donovan's Reef (Par, 1963)	$3,300,000
Delta Force, The (Cannon, 1986)	$7,000,000	Doors, The (TriStar, 1991)	$16,500,000
Demetrius and the Gladiators (Fox, 1954)	$4,250,000	Double Impact (Col, 1991)	$12,050,000
Desert Fury (Par, 1947)	$3,000,000	Down and out in Beverly Hills (BV, 1986)	$28,277,000
Desert Hearts (Goldwyn, 1986)	$1,140,740	Dr. No (UA, 1963)	$6,434,800
Desiree (Fox, 1954)	$4,500,000	Dr. Phibes (AIP, 1971)	$1,827,000
Desperately Seeking Susan (Orion, 1985)	$10,799,540	Dr. Strangelove (Col, 1964)	$5,000,000
Destination Tokyo (WB, 1944)	$3,237,000	Dracula (U, 1979)	$10,738,351
Detective, The (Fox, 1968)	$6,500,000	Dragnet (WB, 1954)	$4,750,000
Devil And Max Devlin, The (BV, 1981)	$6,133,000	Dragnet (U, 1987)	$30,234,468
Devil at 4 O'Clock, The (Col, 1961)	$3,000,000	Dragonslayer (Par, 1981)	$6,800,000
Devil in Miss Jones, The (MB Distributors, 1973)	$15,000,000	Dragonwyck (Fox, 1946)	$3,000,000
Devil's Brigade, The (UA, 1968)	$3,800,000	Dream A Little Dream (Vestron, 1989)	$2,219,275
Devil's Rain, The (Bryanston, 1975)	$1,800,000	Dream Is Alive, The (IMAX, 1985)	$17,000,000
Dial M for Murder (WB,1954)	$3,500,000	Dream Team, The (U, 1989)	$14,383,782
Diamond Head (Col, 1962)	$4,500,000	Dreamscape (Fox, 1984)	$5,700,000
Diamond Horseshoe (Fox, 1945)	$3,220,000	Dressed to Kill (FWS, 1980)	$15,000,000
Diamonds Are Forever (UA, 1971)	$19,726,830	Dressor, The (Col, 1984)	$2,548,000
Diary of a Mad Housewife (U, 1970)	$5,891,000	Drive-In (Col 1976)	$4,131,000
Dick Tracy (BV, 1990)	$60,611,145	Driving Miss Daisy (WB, 1989)	$50,500,000
Die Hard (Fox, 1988)	$36,000,000	Drop Dead Fred (NL, 1991)	$6,350,000
Die Hard 2 (Fox, 1990)	$67,512,000	Drugstore Cowboy (Ave, 1989)	$1,800,000
Dillinger (AIP, 1973)	$2,000,000	Drum Beat (WB, 1955)	$3,000,000
Diner (MGM, 1982)	$5,588,490	Duchess and the Dikrtwater Fox, The (Fox 1976)	$4,977,000
Dirt (ACR, 1979)	$4,200,000	Duel in the Sun (SRO, 1946)	$11,300,000
Dirty Dancing (Vestron, 1987)	$25,009,305	Dumbo (RKO/BV, 1941)	$3,000,000
Dirty Dozen, The (MGM, 1967)	$20,403,825	Dune (U, 1984)	$16,560,165
Dirty Harry (WB, 1971)	$18,000,000	Dungeonmaster (Empire, 1984)	$1,687,040
Dirty Mary, Crazy Larry (Fox, 1974)	$15,200,000	Dunwich Horror, The (AIP, 1970)	$1,035,000
Dirty Rotten Scoundrels (Orion, 1988)	$19,186,930	Dying Young (Fox, 1991)	$19,000,000
Disorderlies (WB, 1987)	$4,400,000	E.T. The Extra-Terrestrial (U, 1982)	$228,618,940
Distinguished Gentleman, The (BV, 1992)	$22,000,000	Eagle Has Landed, The (Col, 1977)	$4,151,000
Divorce American Style (Col, 1967)	$5,500,000	Earth Girls Are Easy (Vestron, 1989)	$1,845,910
Dixie (Par, 1943)	$3,100,000	Earthquake (U, 1974)	$35,850,000
Do Not Disturb (U, 1966)	$3,600,000	East of Eden (WB, 1955)	$5,000,000
Do the Right Thing (U, 1989)	$13,270,330	Easter Parade (MGM, 1948)	$4,190,000
Do You Love Me? (Fox, 1946)	$3,000,000	Easy Money (Orion, 1983)	$14,207,170
Doc Hollywood (WB, 1991)	$24,500,000	Easy Rider (Col, 1969)	$19,100,000
Doctor Detroit (U, 1983)	$5,548,510	Easy to Wed (MGM, 1946)	$4,028,230
Doctor Dollitle (Fox, 1967)	$6,215,000	Eat My Dust (NW, 1976)	$4,500,000
Doctor Zhivago (MGM, 1965)	$47,253,760	Eating (Rainbow, 1990)	$1,201,241
Doctor's Wives (Col, 1971)	$3,000,000	Eating Raoul (Fox Classics, 1983)	$1,600,000

Title (Distributor, Year Released)	$ Rentals	Title (Distributor, Year Released)	$ Rentals
Eddie and the Cruisers (Emb, 1983)	$1,760,000	Exit the Dragon...(Dimension, 1976)	$1,455,235
Eddy Duchin Story, The (Col, 1956)	$5,300,000	Exodus (UA, 1960)	$8,331,580
Educating Rita (Col, 1983)	$3,490,000	Exorcist, The (WB, 1973)	$89,000,000
Edward Scissorhands (Fox, 1990)	$27,500,000	Exorcist II: The Heretic (WB, 1977)	$13,900,000
Egg and I, The (U, 1947)	$5,500,000	Exorcist III, The (Fox, 1990)	$11,500,000
Egyptian, The (Fox, 1954)	$4,250,000	Explorers (Par, 1985)	$5,500,000
Eiger Sanction, The (U, 1975)	$6,736,620	Exterminator, The (Avemb, 1980)	$4,000,000
8 1/2 (Emb/Kino/Corinth, 1963)	$3,850,000	Exterminator 2 (Cannon, 1984)	$1,101,000
18 Again (NW, 1988)	$1,093,245	Extremities (Atlantic, 1986)	$5,100,000
Eight on the Lam (UA, 1967)	$3,108,000	Eye for an Eye, An (Avemb, 1981)	$6,750,775
El Cid (AA, 1961)	$12,000,000	Eye of The Needle (MGM/UA, 1981)	$6,714,020
El Dorado (Par, 1967)	$6,000,000	Eyes of Laura Mars (Col, 1978)	$9,000,000
El Norte (Island Alive/Cinecom, 1984)	$2,200,000	F.I.S.T. (UA, 1978)	$9,176,685
Electric Horseman, The (Col, 1979)	$30,282,970	F/X (Orion, 1986)	$8,169,000
Elephant Man, The (Par, 1980)	$12,010,000	Facts of Life, The (UA, 1960)	$3,200,000
Elephant Walk (Par, 1954)	$3,000,000	Fade To Black (American Cinema, 1980)	$2,800,000
Eliminators (Empire, 1986)	$1,400,000	Falcon & The Snowman, The (Orion, 1985)	$7,720,165
Elivira, Mistress of the Dark (NW, 1988)	$2,460,112	Falling Down (WB, 1993)	$16,000,000
Elmer Gantry (UA, 1960)	$4,623,860	Falling In Love (Par, 1984)	$5,799,000
Elvira Madigan (Cinema 5/Atl, 1967)	$4,350,000	Fame (MGM/UA, 1980)	$7,798,235
Emerald Forest, The (Embassy, 1985)	$10,754,555	Family Plot (U, 1976)	$6,621,950
Emmanuelle (Col, 1975)	$4,908,000	Fanny (WB, 1961)	$4,500,000
Emperor Waltz, The (Par, 1948)	$4,000,000	Fanny And Alexander (Emb, 1983)	$4,039,470
Empire Of The Ants (AIP, 1977)	$2,000,000	Fanny Hill (Cinemation, 1969)	$4,000,000
Empire of the Sun (WB, 1987)	$10,500,000	Fantasia (RKO/BV, 1940)	$41,660,000
Empire Strikes Back, The (Fox, 1980)	$141,672,000	Fantastic Voyage (Fox, 1966)	$5,500,000
Enchanted April (Miramax, 1992)	$5,500,000	Far and Away (U, 1992)	$28,910,700
Enchanted Cottage, The (RKO, 1945)	$2,000,000	Far From the Madding Crowd (MGM, 1967)	$3,500,000
Encino Man (BV, 1992)	$17,579,000	Farewell to Arms, A (Fox, 1957)	$5,000,000
End, The (UA, 1978)	$20,654,480	Farmer's Daughter, The (RKO, 1947)	$3,300,000
Endless love (U, 1981)	$16,532,810	Fast Break (Col, 1979)	$8,630,000
Enemy Mine (Fox, 1985)	$5,600,000	Fast Times at Ridgemont High (U, 1982)	$15,783,735
Enforcer, The (WB, 1976)	$24,000,000	Fatal Attraction (Par, 1987)	$70,000,000
Enter the Dragon (WB, 1973)	$11,500,000	Fatal Beauty (MGM/UA, 1987)	$4,756,275
Entity, The (Fox, 1983)	$6,500,000	Father Goose (U, 1964)	$5,455,325
Entre Nous (UA Classics, 1984)	$1,900,000	Father of the Bride (MGM, 1950)	$4,054,405
Eraserhead (Libra, 1977)	$3,000,000	Father of the Bride (BV, 1991)	$43,027,000
Ernest Goes to Camp (BV, 1987)	$9,960,000	Father's Little Dividend (MGM, 1951)	$3,100,000
Ernest Saves Christmas (BV, 1988)	$12,440,000	Fatso (Fox, 1980)	$3,750,000
Ernest Goes to Jail (BV, 1990)	$11,421,000	FBI Story, The (WB, 1959)	$3,500,000
Escape From Alcatraz (Par, 1979)	$21,500,000	Fear No Evil (Avemb, 1981)	$3,000,000
Escape From New York (Embassy, 1981)	$11,715,390	FernGully: The Last Rainforest (Fox, 1992)	$10,022,000
Escape to Witch Mountain (BV, 1975)	$9,500,000	Ferris Bueller's Day Off (Par, 1986)	$28,600,000
Europeans, The (Levitt-Pickman, 1979)	$1,220,000	Few Good Men, A (Col, 1992)	$67,000,000
Evel Knievel (Fanfare, 1971)	$2,900,000	Fiddler on the Roof (UA, 1971)	$38,260,955
Every Which Way But Loose (WB, 1978)	$51,900,000	Field Of Dreams (U, 1989)	$30,531,165
Everybody's All-American (WB, 1988)	$7,000,000	Fiendish Plot of Dr. Fu Manchu (Ori./WB, 1980)	$5,000,000
Evil Dead (NL, 1983)	$1,173,000	Fiesta (MGM, 1947)	$3,500,000
Evil Dead 2 (Rosebud, 1987)	$1,700,000	Fifth Floor, The (FVI, 1980)	$3,775,000
Evil That Men Do, The (TriStar, 1984)	$5,500,000	55 Days At Peking (AA, 1963)	$5,000,000
Evil Under the Sun (U/AFD, 1982)	$4,000,000	52 Pick-Up (Cannon, 1986)	$2,000,000
Evthg You Al. Wan. to Kw About Sex...(UA, 1972)	$8,827,925	Final Analysis (WB, 1992)	$12,700,000
Excalibur (Orion/WB, 1981)	$17,100,000	Final Conflict, The (Fox, 1981)	$10,000,000
Executive Action (NGP, 1973)	$4,500,000	Final Countdown, The (UA, 1980)	$6,702,233

Title (Distributor, Year Released)	$ Rentals	Title (Distributor, Year Released)	$ Rentals
Finders Keepers (WB, 1984)	$1,000,000	Foul Play (Par, 1978)	$27,500,000
Finian's Rainbow (WB/7 Arts, 1968)	$5,500,000	4 Horsemen of the Apocalypse (Metro, 1921)	$3,800,000
Firefox (WB, 1982)	$25,000,000	Four Musketeers, The (Fox, 1975)	$8,766,000
Firestarter (U, 1984)	$7,553,420	Four Seasons, The (U, 1981)	$27,137,478
Firewalker (Can, 1986)	$4,500,000	Fourth Protocol, The (Lorimar, 1988)	$5,500,000
First Blood (Orion, 1982)	$22,947,560	48 HRS (Par, 1982)	$30,328,000
First Deadly Sin, The (FWS, 1980)	$3,000,000	Fox and the Hound, The (BV, 1981)	$29,812,000
First Family (WB, 1980)	$8,700,000	Fox, The (WB/7 Arts, 1967)	$8,600,000
First Monday in October (Par, 1981)	$6,000,000	Foxes of Harrow,The (Fox, 1947)	$3,200,000
First Turn On, The (Troma, 1984)	$1,200,000	Francis (U, 1950)	$3,000,000
Fish Called Wanda, A (MGM/UA, 1988)	$29,766,000	Frankenstein (Bryanston/Landmark, 1974)	$5,400,000
Fisher King, The (TriStar, 1991)	$18,000,000	Frankie and Johnny (Par, 1991)	$11,000,000
Fistful of Dollars, A (UA, 1967)	$4,248,905	Frantic (WB, 1988)	$8,400,000
Fists of Fury (NGP/WB, 1973)	$3,100,000	Fraternity Vacation (NW, 1985)	$1,600,000
Five Card Stud (Par, 1968)	$4,250,000	Freaky Friday (BV, 1976)	$11,708,000
Five Easy Pieces (Col, 1970)	$8,900,000	Freebie and the Bean (WB, 1974)	$13,500,000
Five Fingers of Death (WB, 1973)	$4,600,000	French Connection, The (Fox, 1971)	$26,315,000
Five Pennies, The (Par, 1959)	$3,000,000	French Connection II (Fox, 1975)	$5,618,000
Flame and the Arrow, The (WB, 1950)	$3,000,000	French Lieutenant's Woman (MGM/UA, 1981)	$11,270,800
Flamingo Kid, The (Fox, 1984)	$11,600,000	French Line, The (RKO, 1954)	$3,000,000
Flash Gordon (U, 1980)	$14,879,250	Frenchman's Creek (Par, 1944)	$3,500,000
Flashdance (Par, 1983)	$36,180,000	Frenzy (U, 1972)	$6,384,520
Flatliners (Col, 1990)	$31,000,000	Friday the 13th (Par, 1980)	$17,113,000
Flesh Gordon (Mammoth, 1974)	$5,300,000	Friday the 13th Pt 2 (Par, 1981)	$9,500,000
Fleshburn (Crown, 1984)	$2,000,000	Friday the 13th Pt 3 (Par, 1982)	$16,500,000
Fletch (U, 1985)	$24,495,615	Friday the 13th Pt 4—Final Chapter (Par, 1984)	$16,000,000
Fletch lives (U, 1989)	$17,814,075	Friday the 13th Pt 5 — New Begin... (Par, 1985)	$10,000,000
Flight of The Navigator (BV, 1986)	$8,283,000	Friday the 13th Pt 6 (Par, 1986)	$9,400,000
Flower Drum Song (U, 1961)	$4,833,077	Friday the 13th Pt 7- New Blood (Par, 1988)	$9,100,000
Flowers In The Attic (NW, 1987)	$6,600,000	Fried Green Tomatoes (U, 1991)	$37,402,827
Fly, The (Fox, 1986)	$17,500,000	Friendly Persuasion (AA, 1956)	$5,050,000
Fog, The (Avemb, 1980)	$9,905,115	Fright Night (Col, 1985)	$10,710,000
Follow Me Boys (BV, 1966)	$7,300,000	Fright Night Pt 2 (New Century/Vista, 1989)	$1,134,255
Food of the Gods, The (AIP, 1976)	$4,005,950	Frisco Kid, The (WB, 1979)	$5,300,000
Footloose (Par, 1984)	$34,000,000	Fritz the Cat (Cinemation, 1972)	$4,700,000
For a Few Dollars More (UA, 1967)	$4,346,200	Frogs (AIP, 1972)	$1,900,000
For Keeps (TriStar, 1988)	$7,000,000	From Here to Eternity (Col, 1953)	$12,200,000
For Love of Ivy (CRC/Col, 1968)	$5,560,000	From Russia With Love (UA, 1964)	$9,924,280
For Pete's Sake (Col, 1974)	$10,662,000	From the Terrace (Fox, 1960)	$5,200,000
For the Boys (Fox, 1991)	$10,463,000	Front Page, The (U, 1974)	$7,223,845
For the Love of Benji (Mulberry Square, 1977)	$5,000,000	Front, The (Col, 1976)	$4,994,000
For Whom the Bell Tolls (Par, 1943)	$7,100,000	Frontier Fremont (Sunn/Taft, 1976)	$5,520,000
For Your Eyes Only (MGM/UA, 1981)	$26,577,735	Full Metal Jacket (WB, 1987)	$22,700,000
Force 10 From Navarone (AIP, 1978)	$3,200,000	Fuller Brush Man (Col, 1948)	$3,100,000
Force Five (ACR, 1981)	$4,200,000	Fun in Acapulco (Par, 1963)	$3,100,000
Force of One, A (ACR, 1979)	$9,980,000	Fun With Dick and Jane (Col, 1977)	$13,618,000
Forced Vengence (MGM, 1982)	$2,100,000	Funeral Home (MPM, 1982)	$1,301,700
Forever Amber (Fox, 1947)	$5,000,000	Funhouse (1981)	$3,800,000
Forever Young (WB, 1992)	$27,000,000	Funny Farm (WB, 1988)	$11,800,000
Formula, The (MGM/UA, 1980)	$3,729,725	Funny Girl (Col, 1968)	$26,325,000
Fort Apache (RKO, 1948)	$3,000,000	Funny Lady (Col, 1975)	$19,313,000
Fort Apache, the Bronx (Fox, 1981)	$3,000,000	Funny Thg Happ. on Way to Forum (UA, 1966)	$3,400,000
Fortune Cookie, The (UA, 1966)	$3,000,000	Fury, The (Fox, 1978)	$11,100,000
Fortune, The (Col, 1975)	$3,000,000	Future Kill (IFM, 1985)	$1,100,000

Title (Distributor, Year Released)	$ Rentals
Futureworld (AIP/FWS, 1976)	$4,000,000
Fuzz (UA, 1972)	$3,000,000
G.I. Blues (Par, 1960)	$4,300,000
Gable and Lombard (U, 1976)	$5,755,080
Galaxina (Crown, 1980)	$3,500,000
Galaxy Of Terror (NW, 1981)	$1,300,000
Game of Death (Col, 1979)	$4,947,000
Gandhi (Col, 1982)	$24,970,000
Garden of Evil (Fox, 1954)	$3,100,000
Gaslight (MGM, 1944)	$3,000,000
Gate, The (New Century, 1987)	$5,073,615
Gates of Hell, The (MPM, 1983)	$1,897,350
Gator (UA, 1976)	$5,377,045
Gauntlet, The (WB, 1977)	$17,700,000
Geisha Boy, The (Par, 1958)	$3,200,000
Gentleman's Agreement (Fox, 1948)	$3,900,000
Gentlemen Prefer Blondes (Fox, 1953)	$5,100,000
Georgy Girl (Col, 1966)	$7,600,000
Getaway, The (NGP/WB, 1972)	$18,000,000
Get out Your Hankerchiefs (NL, 1978)	$2,086,000
Getting Straight (Col, 1970)	$6,000,000
Ghost (Par, 1990)	$98,200,000
Ghost Story (U, 1981)	$11,136,175
Ghostbusters (Col, 1984)	$132,720,000
Ghostbusters II (Col, 1989)	$60,490,000
Ghoulies (Empire, 1985)	$4,860,405
Giant (WB, 1956)	$14,000,000
Gift, The (Goldwyn, 1983)	$1,010,000
Gigi (MGM, 1958)	$7,321,425
Gilda (Col, 1946)	$3,800,000
Girl Can't Help It, The (Fox, 1956)	$3,200,000
Girl Crazy (MGM, 1943)	$3,000,000
Girl Happy (MGM, 1965)	$3,200,000
Girls Just Want to Have Fun (NW, 1985)	$2,750,000
Girls! Girls! Girls! (Par, 1962)	$3,600,000
Give 'Em Hell, Harry (TV/Avemb, 1975)	$3,000,000
Glass Bottom Boat, The (MGM, 1966)	$4,600,000
Glengarry Glen Ross (NL, 1992)	$4,900,000
Glenn Miller Story, The (U, 1954)	$7,591,000
Gloria (Col, 1980)	$1,485,000
Glory (TriStar, 1989)	$13,000,000
Gnome-Mobile, The (BV, 1967)	$7,493,000
God is My Co-Pilot (WB, 1945)	$3,373,000
God's Little Acre (UA, 1958)	$3,500,000
Godfather, The (Par, 1972)	$86,275,000
Godfather Pt II, The (Par, 1974)	$30,673,000
Godfather Pt III, The (Par, 1990)	$38,000,000
Gods Must Be Crazy, The (Fox, 1984)	$13,000,000
Godsend, The (Cannon, 1980)	$1,650,000
Godzilla 1985 (NW, 1985)	$2,000,000
Goin' Coconuts (Osmond, 1978)	$1,234,650
Goin' South (Par, 1978)	$4,766,000
Goin' All the Way (Saturn Int'l, 1981)	$3,500,000
Going in Style (WB, 1979)	$14,200,000

Title (Distributor, Year Released)	$ Rentals
Going My Way (Par, 1944)	$6,500,000
Gold Rush, The (UA/Col Classics, 1925)	$3,500,000
Golden Child, The (Par, 1986)	$39,723,090
Golden Earrings (Par, 1947)	$3,000,000
Golden Seal, The (Goldwyn, 1983)	$2,600,000
Golden Voyage of Sinbad, The (Col, 1974)	$5,153,000
Goldfinger (UA, 1964)	$22,997,710
Gone With the Wind (MGM/UA/TEC, 1939)	$79,375,080
Gong Show Movie, The (U, 1980)	$3,209,800
Good Guys Wear Black (American Cinema, 1978)	$8,300,000
Good Morning, Vietnam (BV, 1987)	$58,083,110
Good Neighbor Sam (Col, 1964)	$4,950,000
Good Sam (RKO, 1948)	$3,000,000
Good, the Bad and the Ugly, The (UA, 1967)	$6,111,960
Goodbye Girl, The (MGM/WB, 1977)	$41,839,170
Goodbye, Charlie (Fox, 1964)	$3,700,000
Goodbye, Columbus (Par, 1969)	$10,500,000
Goodfellas (WB, 1990)	$20,500,000
Goonies, The (WB, 1985)	$29,900,000
Gorillas in the Mist (U, 1988)	$11,485,875
Gorky Park (Orion, 1983)	$7,982,550
Gotcha (U, 1985)	$4,495,990
Graduate, The (Avemb,1968)	$44,090,730
Graduation Day (IFI, 1981)	$1,150,000
Grand Canyon (Fox, 1991)	$15,077,000
Grand Canyon: The Hidden Secrets (IMAX, 1984)	$12,820,000
Grand Prix (MGM, 1966)	$9,388,684
Grand Theft Auto (NW, 1977)	$2,500,000
Grass Is Greener, The (U, 1960)	$3,000,000
Gray Lady Down (U, 1978)	$4,058,000
Grease (Par, 1978)	$96,300,000
Grease 2 (Par, 1982)	$6,500,000
Greased Lightning (WB, 1977)	$7,600,000
Great Caruso, The (MGM, 1951)	$4,531,000
Great Dictator, The (UA/Col Classics, 1940)	$3,500,000
Great Escape, The (UA, 1963)	$5,545,690
Great Gatsby, The (Par, 1974)	$14,200,000
Great Imposter, The (U, 1960)	$3,000,000
Great Lover, The (Par, 1949)	$3,300,000
Great Mouse Detective, The (BV, 1986)	$11,484,000
Great Muppet Caper, The (U/AFD, 1981)	$16,654,346
Great Outdoors, The (U, 1988)	$19,218,200
Great Race, The (WB, 1965)	$11,400,000
Great Santini, The (WB, 1980)	$3,500,000
Great Scout and Cathouse Thursday (AIP, 1976)	$3,600,000
Great Train Robbery, The (UA, 1979)	$5,136,530
Great Waldo Pepper, The (U, 1975)	$9,289,315
Great Ziegfeld, The (MGM, 1936)	$3,000,000
Greatest Show on Earth, The (Par, 1952)	$14,000,000
Greatest Story Ever Told, The (UA, 1965)	$6,962,715
Greatest, The (Col, 1977)	$3,800,000
Greek Tycoon, The (U, 1978)	$7,249,575
Green Berets, The (WB/7 Arts, 1968)	$9,750,000
Green Card (BV, 1990)	$13,782,836

Title (Distributor,Year Released)	$ Rentals
Green Dolphin Street (MGM, 1947)	$4,384,380
Green Years, The (MGM, 1946)	$4,222,030
Gregory's Girl (Goldwyn, 1982)	$1,400,000
Gremlins (WB, 1984)	$79,500,000
Gremlins 2: The New Batch (WB, 1990)	$20,800,000
Greystoke: The Legend of Tarzan (WB, 1984)	$23,200,000
Grifters, The (Miramax, 1990)	$5,100,000
Grizzly (FVI, 1976)	$7,563,405
Grizzly Adams (Sunn/Taft, 1975)	$21,895,000
Groove Tube, The (Levitt-Pickman, 1974)	$9,283,850
Group, The (UA, 1966)	$3,000,000
Guess Who's Coming to Dinner (Col, 1968)	$25,500,000
Guide for the Married Man, A (Fox, 1967)	$5,500,000
Gumball Rally, The (WB, 1976)	$7,900,000
Gums (Analysis, 1976)	$1,200,000
Gunfight at the OK Corral (Par, 1957)	$4,700,000
Gung Ho (Par, 1957)	$15,500,000
Guns of Navarone, The (Col, 1961)	$13,000,000
Gus (BV, 1976)	$9,850,000
Guy Named Joe, A (MGM, 1944)	$4,125,085
Guys and Dolls (MGM, 1955)	$6,874,675
Gypsy (WB, 1962)	$6,000,000
H.O.T.S. (Derio, 1979)	$1,400,000
Hair (UA, 1979)	$6,237,965
Hairspray (NL, 1988)	$3,200,000
Hallelujah Trial, The (UA, 1965)	$3,000,000
Halloween (Compass, 1978)	$18,500,000
Halloween II (U, 1981)	$11,919,620
Halloween III: Season of the Witch (U, 1982)	$7,239,230
Halloween IV (Galaxy, 1988)	$8,550,000
Halloween V (Galaxy Int'l, 1989)	$4,900,000
Hamburger Hill (Par, 1987)	$5,750,450
Hamlet (U, 1948)	$3,400,000
Hamlet (WB, 1964)	$3,100,000
Hand that Rocks the Cradle, The (BV, 1992)	$39,334,000
Hand, The (Orion, 1981)	$1,100,000
Handmaid's Tale, The (Cinecom, 1990)	$2,300,000
Hang 'Em High (UA, 1968)	$6,777,925
Hangar 18 (Sunn/Taft, 1980)	$5,759,930
Hanky Panky (Col, 1982)	$5,252,110
Hannah and Her Sisters (Orion, 1986)	$18,196,010
Hans Christian Andersen (RKO, 1952)	$6,000,000
Happiest Millionaire, The (BV, 1967)	$5,100,000
Happy Birthday To Me (Col, 1981)	$5,012,000
Hard Day's Night, A (UA/U, 1964)	$6,165,380
Hard Times (Col, 1975)	$5,651,000
Hard To Hold (U, 1984)	$5,042,460
Hard to Kill (WB, 1990)	$30,000,000
Hard Way, The (U, 1991)	$13,232,365
Hardbodies (Col, 1984)	$3,144,000
Hardcore (Col, 1979)	$7,021,000
Hardly Working (Fox, 1981)	$9,100,000
Harlem Nights (Par, 1989)	$31,500,000
Harlow (Par, 1965)	$3,500,000

Title (Distributor, Year Released)	$ Rentals
Harm's Way, In (Par, 1965)	$4,250,000
Harper (WB, 1966)	$6,000,000
Harper Valley P.T.A. (April Fool Films, 1978)	$8,550,000
Happily Ever After (First Nat'l, 1981)	$1,250,000
Harrad Experiment, The (CRC, 1973)	$3,000,000
Harry and the Hendersons (U, 1987)	$17,430,020
Harry and Tonto (Fox, 1974)	$4,600,000
Harry and Walter Go to New York (Col, 1976)	$4,618,000
Harum Scarum (MGM, 1965)	$3,300,000
Harvey Girls, The (MGM, 1946)	$4,134,040
Hatari (Par, 1962)	$7,000,000
Hawaii (UA, 1966)	$15,553,020
Hawmps (Mulberry Square, 1976)	$2,350,000
He Knows Your Alone (MGM, 1980)	$1,750,000
Hear My Song (Miramax, 1991)	$1,300,000
Hearse, The (Crown, 1980)	$2,500,000
Heart Condition (NL, 1990)	$2,000,000
Heart Is a Lonely Hunter, The (WB/7 Arts, 1968)	$5,900,000
Heartbreak Hotel (TriStar, 1988)	$2,000,000
Heartbreak Kid, The (Fox, 1972)	$5,530,460
Heartbreak Ridge (WB, 1986)	$21,600,000
Heartburn (Par, 1986)	$11,800,000
Heartland (Levitt-Pickman, 1981)	$1,400,000
Hearts of the World (Comstock/World, 1918)	$3,900,000
Heat (New Century/Vista, 1987)	$1,149,340
Heaven Can Wait (Par, 1978)	$49,400,000
Heaven Knows, Mr. Allison (Fox, 1957)	$4,200,000
Heavenly Kid, The (Orion, 1985)	$1,846,000
Heavy Metal (Col, 1981)	$10,753,880
Helen of Troy (WB, 1956)	$3,200,000
Hell Night (Compass Int'l, 1981)	$1,318,000
Hell's Angels (UA, 1930)	$3,500,000
Hellfighters, The (U, 1968)	$3,480,880
Hello Again (BV, 1987)	$8,965,000
Hello Dolly (Fox, 1969)	$15,200,000
Hellraiser (NW, 1987)	$5,700,000
Hellraiser II (NW, 1988)	$4,984,675
Hellraiser III (Dimension/Miramax, 1992)	$5,000,000
Hell Up in Harlem (AIP, 1974)	$1,550,000
Help (UA, 1965)	$5,430,165
Henry V (Goldwyn, 1989)	$4,900,000
Herbie, "The Love Bug" (BV, 1969)	$23,150,000
Herbie Rides Again (BV, 1974)	$17,000,000
Herbie Goes to Monte Carlo (BV, 1977)	$14,000,000
Herbie Goes Bananas (BV, 1980)	$8,000,000
Hercules (MGM/UA, 1983)	$4,090,340
Hercules (WB, 1959)	$4,700,000
Here Come the Littles (Atl, 1985)	$2,350,000
Hero and the Terror (Cannon, 1988)	$2,098,630
Hero at Large (MGM/UA, 1980)	$5,324,425
Heroes (U, 1977)	$15,061,655
Hester Street (Midwest, 1975)	$2,055,500
Hidden, The (NL, 1987)	$4,500,000
High and the Mighty, The (WB, 1954)	$6,100,000

Title (Distributor, Year Released)	$ Rentals	Title (Distributor, Year Released)	$ Rentals
High Anxiety (Fox, 1977)	$19,163,000	House Calls (U, 1978)	$14,282,330
High Noon (UA, 1952)	$3,400,000	House of Wax, The (WB/Stereovision, 1953)	$9,500,000
High Plains Drifter (U, 1973)	$7,451,435	House on Sorority Row (FVI, 1983)	$4,241,000
High Risk (American Cinema, 1981)	$1,100,000	House Party (NL, 1990)	$12,000,000
High Road to China (WB, 1983)	$15,500,000	House Party II (NL, 1991)	$9,500,000
High Society (MGM, 1956)	$5,878,365	Houseboat (Par, 1958)	$3,500,000
Highlander II (InterStar, 1991)	$5,707,377	Housesitter (U, 1992)	$30,390,625
Hindenburg, The (U, 1975)	$14,517,065	How the West Was Won (CRC/MGM, 1962)	$20,932,885
History of the World—Part 1 (Fox, 1981)	$14,400,000	How to Beat High Cost of Liv. (Filmwys, 1980)	$2,400,000
Hitcher, The (TriStar, 1986)	$2,500,000	How to Marry a Millionaire (Fox, 1953)	$7,300,000
Hitchhikers, The (EVI, 1975)	$1,425,000	How to Murder Your Wife (UA, 1965)	$5,719,000
Hitler Gang, The (Par, 1944)	$3,000,000	How to Steal a Million (Fox, 1966)	$4,400,000
Hitman, The (Cannon, 1991)	$1,600,000	How to Succeed in Business Without ... (UA, 1967)	$3,000,000
Hoffa (Fox, 1992)	$11,700,000	Howard the Duck (U, 1986)	$10,154,150
Hole in the Head, A (UA, 1959)	$4,964,715	Howards End (Sony Pictures Classics, 1992)	$12,950,000
Holiday in Mexico (MGM, 1946)	$3,766,230	Howling, The (Avemb, 1981)	$8,687,000
Holiday Inn (Par, 1942)	$3,800,000	Hucksters, The (MGM, 1947)	$3,637,510
Hollywood Canteen (WB, 1944)	$4,200,000	Hud (Par, 1963)	$5,000,000
Hollywood High (Peter Perry, 1978)	$1,251,000	Humanoids From the Deep (NW, 1980)	$2,100,000
Hollywood Knights, The (Col, 1980)	$7,103,815	Hunger, The (MGM, 1983)	$2,075,000
Hollywood or Bust (Par, 1956)	$3,300,000	Hunt for Red October, The (Par, 1990)	$58,500,000
Hollywood Shuffle (Goldwyn, 1987)	$2,354,400	Hunter, The (Par, 1980)	$8,314,000
Hombre (Fox, 1967)	$5,610,000	Hurricane, The (UA, 1937)	$3,200,000
Home Alone (Fox ,1990)	$140,099,000	Hurry Sundown (Par, 1967)	$4,050,000
Home Alone 2 (Fox, 1992)	$102,000,000	Hush, Hush, Sweet Charlotte (Fox, 1964)	$3,800,000
Home From the Hill (MGM, 1960)	$3,200,000	Hustle (Par, 1975)	$10,390,000
Homecoming (MGM, 1948)	$3,699,285	Hustler, The (Fox, 1961)	$3,100,000
Homeward Bound (BV, 1993)	$17,500,000	I Am Curious [Yellow] (Grove Press, 1969)	$8,500,000
Homework (Jensen Farley, 1982)	$4,047,995	I Never Promised You a Rose Garden (NW, 1977)	$3,200,000
Hondo (WB, 1953)	$4,100,000	I Ought To Be In Pictures (Fox, 1982)	$4,250,000
Honey, I Shrunk the Kids (BV, 1989)	$72,007,000	I Remember Mama (RKO, 1948)	$3,000,000
Honey, I Blew Up the Kid (BV, 1992)	$27,417,000	I Want to Live (UA, 1958)	$3,200,000
Honeysuckle Rose (WB, 1980)	$10,500,000	I Was A Male War Bride (Fox, 1949)	$4,100,000
Hook (TriStar, 1991)	$65,000,000	I Wonder Who's Kissing Her Now (Fox, 1947)	$3,200,000
Hooper (WB, 1978)	$34,900,000	I'll Cry Tomorrow (MGM, 1955)	$6,004,000
Hoosiers (Orion, 1986)	$11,631,140	I'll See You in My Dreams (WB, 1951)	$3,000,000
Hope And Glory (Col, 1987)	$4,292,910	I'm Gonna Get You Sucka (MGM/UA, 1988)	$1,500,000
Hopscotch (Avemb, 1980)	$6,725,100	I, a Woman (Audubon, 1966)	$4,500,000
Horror Planet (Almi, 1983)	$1,500,000	Ice Castles (Col, 1978)	$9,217,000
Horse Soldiers, The (UA, 1959)	$3,800,000	Ice Pirates (MGM/UA, 1984)	$5,881,530
Hospital, The (UA,1971)	$9,042,285	Ice Station Zebra (MGM, 1968)	$4,640,600
H.O.T.S. (Derio, 1979)	$1,400,000	If It's Tuesday, This Must Be Belgium (UA, 1969)	$3,000,000
Hot Dog the Movie (Par, 1984)	$8,100,000	If You Could See What I Hear (JF, 1982)	$5,640,924
Hot Lead, Cold Feet (BV, 1978)	$10,452,000	If You Don't Stop It You'll Go Blind (Topar, 1974)	$5,000,000
Hot Pursuit (Par, 1987)	$1,716,000	Imitation of Life (U, 1959)	$6,417,810
Hot Rock, The (Fox, 1972)	$3,500,000	Impossible Years, The (MGM, 1968)	$6,059,000
Hot Shot (IFM, 1986)	$1,250,000	Impromptu (Hemdale, 1991)	$1,392,995
Hot Shots! (Fox, 1991)	$33,761,000	Improper Channels (Crown, 1981)	$1,250,000
Hot Stuff (Col, 1979)	$8,794,040	In Cold Blood (Col, 1967)	$6,000,000
Hot to Trot (WB, 1988)	$3,000,000	In Harm's Way (Par, 1965)	$4,250,000
Hotel (WB, 1967)	$4,000,000	In Like Flint (Fox, 1967)	$5,000,000
House (NW, 1986)	$8,600,000	In Praise of Older Women (Avemb, 1979)	$1,150,000
House II (NW, 1987)	$3,300,000	In Search of Historic Jesus (Sunn/Taft, 1980)	$10,614,050
House by the Cemetary (Almi, 1984)	$1,400,000	In Search of Noah's Ark (Schick Sunn, 1976)	$23,770,000

Title (Distributor, Year Released)	$ Rentals
In Search of the Castaways (BV, 1962)	$9,975,000
In the Good Old Summertime (MGM, 1949)	$3,400,000
In the Heat of the Night (UA, 1967)	$10,974,030
In-Laws, The (WB, 1979)	$19,100,000
Incredible Journey, The (BV, 1963)	$4,500,000
Incredible Shrinking Woman, The (U, 1981)	$9,201,400
Incubus (Film Ventures, 1982)	$5,000,000
Indiscreet (WB, 1958)	$3,600,000
Infra-Man (Joseph Brenner, 1976)	$7,000,000
Inn of the Sixth Happiness (Fox, 1958)	$4,400,000
Innerspace (WB, 1987)	$13,700,000
Innocent Man, An (BV, 1989)	$10,499,000
Inside Moves (AFD, 1981)	$1,200,000
Interiors (UA, 1978)	$4,632,810
Internal Affairs (Par, 1990)	$11,000,000
Interns, The (Col, 1962)	$5,000,000
Invaders from Mars (Cannon, 1986)	$1,900,000
Invasion of the Body Snatchers (UA, 1978)	$11,132,640
Invasion USA (Cannon, 1985)	$6,923,800
Ipcress Film, The (UA, 1965)	$3,300,000
Irma La Douce (UA, 1963)	$11,921,785
Iron Eagle (TriStar, 1986)	$10,893,000
Iron Eagle II (TriStar, 1988)	$4,500,000
Iron Mistress, The (WB, 1952)	$3,000,000
Irreconcilable Differences (WB, 1984)	$6,000,000
Ishtar (Col, 1987)	$7,685,525
Island At The Top Of The World (BV, 1974)	$10,200,000
Island in the Sun (Fox, 1957)	$5,000,000
Island of Dr. Moreau, The (AIP/FWS, 1977)	$4,000,000
Island, The (U, 1980)	$9,592,095
Islands in the Stream (Par, 1977)	$4,035,000
It's a Mad, Mad, Mad World (MGM, 1963)	$20,849,785
It's a Wonderful Life (RKO, 1947)	$3,300,000
It's Alive (WB, 1977)	$7,100,000
It's My Turn (Col, 1980)	$5,855,000
Ivanhoe (MGM, 1952)	$6,258,000
Jacknife (Cineplex Odeon, 1989)	$2,200,000
Jackson County Jail (NW, 1975)	$2,300,000
Jacob's Ladder (TriStar, 1990)	$11,600,000
Jagged Edge (Col, 1985)	$16,630,000
Jailhouse Rock (MGM, 1957)	$3,900,000
Jakes Speed (NW, 1986)	$1,150,000
Jaws (U, 1975)	$129,549,325
Jaws 2 (U, 1978)	$50,431,970
Jaws 3-D (U, 1983)	$27,035,450
Jaws—The Revenge (U, 1987)	$10,850,400
Jazz Singer, The (AFD, 1980)	$13,000,000
Jean De Florette (Orion Classics, 1988)	$2,400,000
Jeanne Eagles (Col, 1957)	$3,100,000
Jennifer (AIP, 1978)	$1,000,000
Jeremiah Johnson (WB, 1972)	$21,900,000
Jerk, The (U, 1979)	$42,989,660
Jesus (WB, 1979)	$7,100,000
Jesus Christ Superstar (U, 1973)	$13,105,730

Title (Distributor, Year Released)	$ Rentals
Jewel of the Nile, The (Fox, 1985)	$36,500,000
JFK (WB, 1991)	$34,000,000
Jimmy The Kid (NW, 1982)	$2,600,000
Jo Jo Dancer, Your Life Is Calling (Col, 1986)	$8,049,425
Joan of Arc (RKO, 1948)	$4,100,000
Joe (Cannon, 1970)	$9,500,000
Joe Kidd (U, 1972)	$5,827,400
Joe Versus the Volcano (WB, 1990)	$18,900,000
John And Mary (Fox, 1969)	$4,200,000
John Goldfarb, Please Come Home (Fox, 1965)	$3,000,000
Johnny Be Good (Orion, 1988)	$7,800,000
Johnny Belinda (WB, 1948)	$4,100,000
Johnny Dangerously (Fox, 1984)	$9,100,000
Joker Is Wild, The (Par, 1957)	$3,000,000
Jolson Sings Again (Col, 1949)	$5,000,000
Jolson Story, The (Col, 1946)	$7,600,000
Journey of Natty Gann (BV, 1985)	$3,100,000
Journey to the Center of the Earth (Fox, 1959)	$4,777,000
Joy in the Morning (MGM, 1965)	$3,000,000
Joystick (Jensen Farley, 1983)	$1,256,315
Judgment at Nuremberg (UA, 1961)	$3,900,000
Julia (Fox, 1977)	$13,055,000
Jumpin' Jack Flash (Fox, 1986)	$11,000,000
Jumping Jacks (Par, 1952)	$4,000,000
Jungle Book, The (BV, 1967)	$60,964,000
Jungle Fever (U, 1991)	$15,718,217
Just for You (Par, 1952)	$3,000,000
Just One Of The Guys (Col, 1985)	$4,886,935
Just You and Me Kid (Col, 1979)	$3,850,000
K-9 (U, 1989)	$18,598,415
Kansas (TWE, 1988)	$1,000,000
Karamoja (Hallmark /Modern Film Dist., 1958)	$3,000,000
Karate Kid, The (Col, 1984)	$43,120,000
Karate Kid Pt II, The (Col, 1986)	$58,310,000
Karate Kid Pt III, The (Col, 1989)	$19,030,000
Kelly's Heroes (MGM, 1970)	$5,239,645
Kentucky Fried Movie, The (UFD, 1977)	$7,110,000
Key Largo (WB, 1948)	$3,300,000
Kickboxer (Cannon, 1989)	$6,500,000
Kid From Brooklyn, The (RKO, 1946)	$4,000,000
Kids Are Alright, The (NW, 1979)	$1,500,000
Kill and Kill Again (FVI, 1981)	$4,300,000
Kill Or Be Killed (FVI, 1980)	$6,800,000
Killer Elite, The (UA, 1975)	$4,129,735
Killer Force (AIP, 1975)	$1,400,000
Killing Fields, The (WB, 1984)	$15,900,000
Killpoint (Crown, 1984)	$1,600,000
Kim (MGM, 1950)	$3,000,000
Kindergarten Cop (U, 1990)	$47,365,485
Kindred, The (F/M Entertainment, 1987)	$1,100,000
King and I, The (Fox, 1956)	$8,500,000
King Kong (RKOJanus/Kino/TEC/Par, 1933)	$4,000,000
King Kong (Par, 1976)	$36,915,000
King of Kings (MGM, 1961)	$6,520,000

Title (Distributor,Year Released)	$ Rentals
King of New York (NL/7 Arts, 1990)	$1,150,000
King of the Gypsies (Par, 1978)	$4,010,000
King Ralph (U, 1991)	$15,252,480
King Solomon's Mines (MGM, 1950)	$5,586,000
King Solomon's Mines (Cannon, 1985)	$6,000,000
Kinjite (Cannon, 1987)	$1,353,940
Kiss Me Goodbye (Fox, 1982)	$7,600,000
Kiss of the Spider Woman (Island/Alive, 1985)	$6,387,000
Kissin' Cousins (MGM, 1964)	$3,000,000
Kitty (Par, 1946)	$3,500,000
Klute (WB, 1971)	$8,000,000
Knights of the Round Table (MGM, 1953)	$4,864,000
Knock on Wood (Par, 1954)	$3,800,000
Koyaanisqatsi (Island Alive, 1983)	$1,624,196
Krakatoa, East of Java (Cinerama, 1969)	$3,700,000
Kramer Vs. Kramer (Col, 1979)	$59,986,335
Krull (Col, 1983)	$8,743,860
Krush Groove (WB, 1985)	$5,100,000
L.A. Story (TriStar, 1991)	$12,400,000
La Bamba (Col, 1987)	$24,320,000
La Cage aux Folles (UA, 1979)	$8,064,670
La Dolce Vita (Pathe/Astor/Landau/AIP/FWS, 1961)	$8,000,000
La Femme Nikita (Goldwyn, 1991)	$3,290,000
Labyrinth (TriStar, 1986)	$5,300,000
Lady and the Tramp (BV, 1955)	$40,249,000
Lady Sings the Blues (Par, 1972)	$9,666,000
Ladyhawke (WB, 1985)	$7,900,000
Land Before Time, The (U, 1988)	$22,912,846
Land That Time Forgot, The (AIP, 1975)	$2,500,000
Lassiter (WB, 1984)	$9,000,000
Last American Virgin, The (Cannon, 1982)	$3,665,000
Last Boy Scout, The (WB, 1991)	$27,600,000
Last Detail, The (Col, 1973)	$4,745,000
Last Dragon, The, (TriStar,1985)	$11,500,000
Last Emperor, The (Col, 1987)	$18,880,000
Last Flight of Noah's Ark, The (BV, 1980)	$4,272,000
Last House On The Left, The (AIP, 1972)	$2,273,000
Last Married Couple in America, The (U, 1980)	$7,078,265
Last of the Mohicans, The (Fox, 1992)	$31,491,000
Last Picture Show, The (Col, 1972)	$13,110,000
Last Remake of Beau Geste, The (U, 1977)	$6,616,125
Last Starfighter, The (U, 1984)	$13,148,455
Last Summer (AA, 1969)	$4,100,000
Last Sunset, The (U, 1961)	$3,000,000
Last Tango in Paris (UA, 1973)	$16,711,350
Last Unicorn, The (Jensen Farley, 1982)	$3,436,055
Late Great Planet Earth, The (PIE, 1977)	$8,850,000
Law and Disorder (Col, 1974)	$3,000,000
Lawnmower Man, The (New Line, 1992)	$13,600,000
Lawrence of Arabia (Col, 1962)	$20,310,000
Le Mans (CCF/NGP, 1971)	$5,500,000
League of Their Own, A (Col, 1992)	$53,100,000
Lean on Me (WB, 1989)	$14,400,000
Leap of Faith (Par, 1992)	$10,700,000

Title (Distributor, Year Released)	$ Rentals
Leave Her to Heaven (Fox, 1945)	$5,505,000
Left Hand of God, The (Fox, 1955)	$4,000,000
Legacy, The (U, 1979)	$5,103,888
Legal Eagles (U, 1986)	$27,244,590
Legend (U, 1986)	$6,188,185
Legend of Billy Jean (TriStar, 1985)	$1,300,000
Legend of Boggy Creek, The (Howco, 1972)	$3,000,000
Legend of Nigger Charley, The (Par, 1972)	$3,000,000
Legend Of The Lone Ranger, The (U/AFD, 1981)	$6,739,785
Lenny (UA, 1974)	$11,622,370
Leprechaun (Trimark, 1993)	$3,400,000
Less Than Zero (Fox, 1987)	$4,500,000
Let's Do It Again (WB, 1975)	$11,800,000
Let's Make Love (Fox, 1960)	$3,000,000
Let's Spend the Night Together (Emb, 1983)	$1,504,175
Lethal Weapon (WB, 1987)	$29,500,000
Lethal Weapon 2 (WB, 1989)	$79,500,000
Lethal Weapon 3 (WB, 1992)	$80,000,000
Li'l Abner (Par, 1959)	$3,200,000
Licence to Kill (MGM/UA, 1989)	$17,964,000
License To Drive (Fox, 1988)	$9,330,000
Lt. Robin Crusoe, U.S.N. (BV, 1966)	$10,164,000
Life & Times of Grizzly Adams, The(Sunn, 1975)	$21,895,000
Life and Times of Judge Roy Bean (NGP/WB, 1972)	$8,100,000
Life With Father (WB, 1947)	$5,057,000
Lifeforce (TriStar, 1985)	$5,000,000
Light Of Day (TriStar, 1987)	$4,000,000
Like Father Like Son (TriStar, 1987)	$15,777,000
Lincoln Conspiracy, The (Sunn/Taft, 1977)	$5,614,000
Lion in Winter, The (Avemb, 1968)	$10,005,710
Lion of the Desert (UFD, 1981)	$1,500,000
Lionheart (U, 1991)	$10,550,000
Lipstick (Par, 1976)	$4,615,000
Liquid Sky (Cinevista, 1983)	$1,164,205
Little Big Man (NGP/WB, 1970)	$15,000,000
Little Boy Lost (Par, 1953)	$3,000,000
Little Darlings (Par, 1980)	$16,700,000
Little Fauss and Big Halsy (Par, 1970)	$3,100,000
Little Man Tate (Orion, 1991)	$10,223,000
Little Mermaid, The (BV, 1989)	$40,227,000
Little Miss Marker (U, 1980)	$3,275,150
Little Romance, A (Orion/WB, 1979)	$4,000,000
Little Sex, A (U, 1982)	$2,500,000
Little Shop of Horrors (Geffen/WB, 1986)	$19,300,000
Little Women (MGM, 1949)	$3,600,000
Live and Let Die (UA, 1973)	$15,925,285
Livin' Large (Goldwyn, 1991)	$2,935,000
Living Daylights, The (MGM/UA, 1987)	$27,878,805
Living It Up (Par, 1954)	$4,250,000
Local Hero (WB, 1983)	$2,800,000
Logan's Run (MGM/UA, 1976)	$9,426,000
Lolita (MGM, 1962)	$3,700,000
Lollipop Girls in 'Hard Candy', The (Parli., 1977)	$3,500,000
Lone Wolf McQuade (Orion, 1983)	$7,000,000

Title (Distributor, Year Released)	$ Rentals
Long Gray Line, The (Col, 1955)	$3,900,000
Long Hot Summer, The (Fox, 1958)	$3,500,000
Long Riders, The (UA, 1980)	$6,081,560
Long, Long Trailer, The (MGM, 1954)	$4,291,000
Long Walk Home (Miramax, 1990)	$1,700,000
Longest Day, The (Fox, 1962)	$17,600,000
Longest Yard, The (Par, 1974)	$23,017,000
Longtime Companion (Goldwyn, 1990)	$2,200,000
Look Who's Talking (TriStar, 1989)	$68,872,000
Look Who's Talking Too (TriStar, 1990)	$21,600,000
Looker (WB, 1981)	$2,000,000
Looking for Mr. Goodbar (Par, 1977)	$16,900,000
Lord Jim (Col, 1965)	$3,300,000
Lord of the Rings, The (UA, 1978)	$14,122,590
Lords of Discipline (Par, 1983)	$5,201,000
Lords of Flatbush (Col, 1974)	$4,265,000
Lost Boys, The (WB, 1987)	$14,100,000
Lost Horizon (Col, 1937)	$3,500,000
Lost Horizon (Col, 1973)	$3,800,000
Lost In America (Geffen/WB, 1985)	$4,300,000
Lost Weekend, The (Par, 1945)	$4,300,000
Love and Death (UA, 1975)	$7,374,470
Love at First Bite (AIP/FWS, 1979)	$20,600,000
Love Finds Andy Hardy (MGM, 1938)	$3,000,000
Love Is a Many Splendored Thing (Fox, 1955)	$4,000,000
Love Letters (Par, 1945)	$3,000,000
Love Machine, The (Col, 1971)	$4,600,000
Love Me Or Leave Me (MGM, 1955)	$4,153,000
Love Me Tender (Fox, 1956)	$4,200,000
Love Story (Par, 1970)	$48,700,000
Love with the Proper Stranger (Par, 1963)	$3,600,000
Lover Come Back (U, 1961)	$7,624,790
Lovers and Other Strangers (CRC/Col, 1970)	$6,750,000
Lovesick (Ladd/WB, 1983)	$5,100,000
Loving You (Par, 1957)	$3,700,000
Lucas (Fox, 1986)	$3,300,000
Lucky Lady (Fox, 1975)	$12,697,000
Lunch Wagon (Borde, 1981)	$1,170,000
M*A*S*H (Fox, 1970)	$36,720,000
MacArthur (U, 1977)	$8,298,270
Mack, The (CRC/AIP/Blossom, 1973)	$4,300,000
MacKenna's Gold (Col, 1969)	$3,100,000
Macon County Line (AIP/FWS, 1974)	$9,100,000
Mad Max (Filmways, 1980)	$3,500,000
Mad Max 2, "The Road Warrior" (WB, 1982)	$11,300,000
Mad Max Beyond Thunderdome (WB, 1985)	$17,900,000
Madame Curie (MGM, 1943)	$3,500,000
Madame Rosa (Atl, 1978)	$2,600,000
Made In Heaven (Lorimar, 1987)	$2,200,000
Madman (Jensen Farley, 1982)	$1,347,115
Magic (UA, 1978)	$13,268,000
Magnificent Obsession (U, 1954)	$5,200,000
Magnum Force (WB, 1973)	$20,100,000
Mahogany (Par, 1975)	$6,917,775

Title (Distributor, Year Released)	$ Rentals
Maid to Order (New Century, 1987)	$3,967,290
Main Event, The (WB, 1979)	$26,400,000
Major League (Par, 1989)	$21,500,000
Making Love (Fox, 1982)	$6,100,000
Making the Grade (Cannon, 1984)	$1,650,000
Malcolm X (WB, 1992)	$24,000,000
Mame (WB, 1974)	$6,500,000
Man and a Woman, A (AA, 1966)	$6,300,000
Man and Wife (Aquarius/Maurer, 1969)	$4,000,000
Man Called Horse, A (NGP/WB, 1970)	$6,500,000
Man Called Peter, A (Fox, 1955)	$4,777,000
Man for All Seasons, A (Col, 1966)	$12,750,000
Man From Laramie, The (Col, 1955)	$3,300,000
Man From Snowy River, The (Fox, 1982)	$9,250,000
Man in the Gray Flannel Suit, The (Fox, 1956)	$4,350,000
Man Who Fell to Earth, The (C5, 1976)	$3,000,000
Man Who Knew Too Much (Par/U Classics, 1956)	$5,100,000
Man Who Loved Cat Dancing, The (MGM, 1973)	$3,600,000
Man Who Loved Women, The (Col, 1983)	$4,828,485
Man Who Shot Liberty Valance, The (Par, 1962)	$3,200,000
Man Who Would Be King, The (AA, 1975)	$11,000,000
Man With One Red Shoe, The (Fox, 1985)	$4,300,000
Man With the Golden Arm, The (UA/AA, 1955)	$4,079,780
Man With the Golden Gun, The (UA, 1974)	$9,440,865
Man With Two Brains, The (WB, 1983)	$4,600,000
Man's Favorite Sport? (U, 1964)	$3,000,000
Manchurian Candidate (MGM/UA Classics, 1962)	$4,180,630
Mandingo (Par, 1975)	$8,600,000
Manhattan (UA, 1979)	$17,582,660
Manhunter (DEG, 1986)	$4,010,000
Maniac (Analysis, 1981)	$5,100,000
Manitou, The (Avemb, 1978)	$1,500,000
Mannequin (Fox, 1987)	$18,000,000
Manon of the Spring (Orion Classics, 1988)	$2,000,000
Map of the Human Heart (Miramax, 1993)	$1,150,000
Marathon Man (Par, 1976)	$16,575,000
Margie (Fox, 1946)	$4,100,000
Marie Antoinette (MGM, 1938)	$3,000,000
Marjorie Morningstar (WB, 1958)	$3,000,000
Marked for Death (Fox, 1990)	$20,000,000
Marnie (U, 1964)	$3,300,000
Marooned (Col, 1969)	$4,350,000
Marriage on the Rocks (WB, 1965)	$3,000,000
Marriage, Italian Style (Avemb, 1964)	$4,100,000
Married To The Mob (Orion, 1988)	$9,000,000
Mary Poppins (BV, 1964)	$45,000,000
Mary, Queen of Scots (U, 1972)	$3,600,000
Mask (U, 1985)	$20,478,605
Masquerade (MGM/UA, 1988)	$6,834,000
Master Gunfighter (Taylor-Laughlin, 1975)	$1,800,000
Masters Of The Universe (Cannon, 1987)	$7,683,000
Matewan (Cinecom, 1987)	$1,000,000
Matter of Time, A (AIP, 1976)	$2,500,000
Maurice (Cinecom, 1987)	$1,100,000

Title (Distributor, Year Released)	$ Rentals
Mausoleum (MPM, 1983)	$1,342,900
Max Dugan Returns (Fox, 1983)	$8,800,000
Maytime (MGM, 1937)	$3,400,000
McCabe and Mrs. Miller (WB, 1971)	$4,100,000
McConnell Story, The (WB, 1955)	$3,500,000
McLintock (UA, 1963)	$4,523,500
McQ (WB, 1974)	$4,100,000
Meatballs (Par, 1979)	$21,200,000
Medicine Man (BV, 1992)	$20,909,000
Mediterraneo (Miramax, 1992)	$2,000,000
Meet Me in St. Louis (MGM/UA/TEC, 1944)	$5,132,200
Melvin & Howard (U, 1981)	$2,000,000
Memories Within Miss Aggie (Inish Kae, 1974)	$3,000,000
Memphis Belle (WB, 1990)	$11,700,000
Menace II Society (NL, 1993)	$11,750,000
Mephisto (Analysis, 1982)	$1,600,000
Mermaids (Orion, 1990)	$15,116,875
Messenger of Death (Cannon, 1988)	$1,157,205
Metalstorm (U, 1983)	$2,758,000
Meteor (AIP/FWS, 1979)	$6,000,000
Metropolitan (NL, 1990)	$1,350,000
Micki & Maude (Col, 1984)	$12,330,000
Middle Age Crazy (Fox, 1980)	$6,000,000
Midnight Cowboy (UA, 1969)	$20,499,285
Midnight Express (Col, 1978)	$15,065,000
Midnight Lace (U, 1960)	$3,500,000
Midnight Run (U, 1988)	$18,413,645
Midsummer Night's Sex Comedy (Orion/WB, 1982)	$4,500,000
Midway (U, 1976)	$21,610,435
Mighty Ducks, The (BV, 1992)	$22,700,000
Milagro Beanfield War, The (U, 1988)	$5,732,755
Mildred Pierce (WB, 1945)	$3,483,000
Million Dollar Duck (BV, 1971)	$5,250,000
Miracle of Our Lady of Fatima (WB, 1952)	$3,000,000
Miracle on 34th St. (Fox, 1946)	$3,100,000
Mirror Crack'd, The (AFD, 1980)	$5,500,000
Misadventures of Merlin Jones, The (BV, 1964)	$4,000,000
Mischief (Fox, 1985)	$4,100,000
Misery (Col, 1990)	$26,880,000
Misfits,The (UA, 1961)	$3,900,000
Miss Sadie Thompson (Col, 1953)	$3,000,000
Missing (U, 1982)	$7,883,695
Missing in Action (Cannon, 1984)	$10,000,000
Missing in Action 2 (Cannon, 1985)	$4,217,310
Missing in Action 3 (Cannon, 1988)	$2,425,140
Mission, The (WB, 1986)	$8,300,000
Mississipi Burning (Orion, 1988)	$14,716,130
Mississippi Gambler, The (U, 1953)	$3,000,000
Mississippi Masala (Goldwyn, 1992)	$3,500,000
Missouri Breaks, The (UA, 1976)	$7,009,940
Mister Roberts (WB, 1955)	$8,500,000
Mo' Money (Col, 1992)	$19,200,000
Moby Dick (WB, 1956)	$4,788,055
Modern Problems (Fox, 1981)	$14,800,000

Title (Distributor, Year Released)	$ Rentals
Modern Romance (Col, 1981)	$1,333,000
Modern Times (UA/Col Classics, 1936)	$3,000,000
Moderns, The (Alive, 1988)	$1,000,000
Mogambo (MGM, 1953)	$4,688,000
Mom and Dad (Modern Film Distribs, 1944)	$16,000,000
Moment by Moment (U, 1978)	$7,119,830
Mommie Dearest (Par, 1981)	$8,600,000
Mon Oncle D'Amerique (NW, 1980)	$1,000,000
Mona Lisa (Island, 1986)	$2,534,000
Money From Home (Par, 1953)	$3,500,000
Money Pit, The (BV, 1986)	$16,712,770
Monkey Shines (Orion, 1988)	$2,100,000
Monkey's Uncle, The (BV, 1965)	$4,300,000
Monkeys, Go Home (BV, 1967)	$3,000,000
Monsieur Beaucaire (Par, 1946)	$3,500,000
Monsignor (Fox, 1982)	$6,500,000
Montenegro (Atl, 1981)	$1,000,000
Monty Python and the Holy Grail (C5, 1975)	$5,170,000
Monty Python's Life of Brian (Orion/WB, 1979)	$10,500,000
Monty Python's The Meaning of Life (U, 1983)	$7,260,675
Moon Is Blue, The (UA, 1953)	$4,088,120
Moon Over Parador (U, 1988)	$5,384,130
Moon Pilot (BV, 1962)	$3,500,000
Moon-Spinners, The (BV, 1964)	$3,500,000
Moonraker (UA, 1979)	$33,924,010
Moonstruck (MGM/UA, 1987)	$34,393,000
More American Graffiti (U, 1979)	$8,416,185
Morning After, The (Fox, 1986)	$12,000,000
Mortuary (Film Ventures, 1983)	$2,027,493
Moscow Does Not Believe in Tears (IFE, 1980)	$1,300,000
Moscow on the Hudson (Col, 1984)	$12,210,000
Mosquito Coast, The (WB, 1986)	$7,700,000
Motel Hell (UA, 1980)	$1,440,000
Mother Wore Tights (Fox, 1947)	$4,100,000
Mother's Day (UFD, 1980)	$4,000,000
Mother, Jugs & Speed (Fox, 1976)	$7,631,000
Moulin Rouge (UA, 1952)	$4,251,915
Mountain Family Robinson (PIE, 1979)	$6,520,000
Mountain Men, The (Col, 1980)	$3,283,000
Move Over, Darling (Fox, 1963)	$6,000,000
Moving (WB, 1988)	$5,000,000
Moving Violations (Fox, 1985)	$4,900,000
Mr. & Mrs. Bridge (Miramax, 1990)	$3,400,000
Mr. Belvedere Goes to College (Fox, 1949)	$3,700,000
Mr. Hobbs Takes a Vacation (Fox, 1962)	$4,000,000
Mr. Majestyk (UA, 1974)	$3,500,000
Mr. Mom (Fox, 1983)	$32,000,000
Mr. Smith Goes to Washington (Col, 1939)	$3,500,000
Mrs. Miniver (MGM, 1942)	$5,390,010
Mrs. Parkington (MGM, 1944)	$3,000,000
Muppet Movie, The (AFD, 1979)	$32,000,000
Muppets Take Manhattan, The (TriStar, 1984)	$13,000,000
Muppet Christmas Carol, The (BV, 1992)	$12,500,000
Murder by Death (Col, 1976)	$19,106,000

Title (Distributor,Year Released)	$ Rentals
Murder by Decree (Avemb, 1979)	$3,100,000
Murder on the Orient Express (Par, 1974)	$19,124,000
Murderers' Row (Col, 1966)	$6,350,000
Murphy's Law (Cannon, 1986)	$3,500,000
Murphy's Romance (Col, 1985)	$13,620,000
Music Man, The (WB, 1962)	$8,100,000
Mutiny on the Bounty (MGM, 1962)	$7,409,785
My Beautiful Laundrette (Orion Classics, 1986)	$2,000,000
My Bloody Valentine (1981)	$2,657,000
My Blue Heaven (WB, 1990)	$10,800,000
My Bodyguard (Fox, 1980)	$10,700,000
My Brilliant Career (Analysis, 1980)	$2,750,000
My Chauffeur (Crown, 1986)	$1,500,000
My Cousin Vinny (Fox, 1992)	$25,565,000
My Demon Lover (NL, 1987)	$1,520,000
My Dinner With Andre (New Yorker, 1981)	$1,900,000
My Fair Lady (WB, 1964)	$34,000,000
My Favorite Brunette (Par, 1947)	$3,100,000
My Favorite Year (MGM/UA, 1982)	$7,113,795
My Girl (Col, 1991)	$27,700,000
My Heroes H. Al. B. Cowboys (Gldwn, 1991)	$1,670,000
My Left Foot (Miramax, 1989)	$7,000,000
My Life as a Dog (Skouras, 1987)	$4,102,670
My Own Private Idaho (FL, 1991)	$2,900,000
My Reputation (WB, 1946)	$3,000,000
My Science Project (BV, 1985)	$1,100,000
My Stepmother Is an Alien (Col, 1988)	$5,300,000
My Tutor (Crown, 1983)	$7,000,000
My Wild Irish Rose (WB, 1948)	$3,400,000
Myra Breckinridge (Fox, 1970)	$4,300,000
Mysterious Monsters (Sunn/Taft, 1975)	$10,960,000
Mystic Pizza (Goldwyn, 1988)	$6,547,330
Naked Gun, The (Par, 1988)	$34,400,000
Naked Gun 2 1/2, The (Par, 1991)	$44,200,000
Napoleon (Zoetrope, 1981 re)	$2,500,000
Nashville (Par, 1975)	$8,744,000
Nasty Girl, The (Miramax, 1990)	$1,000,000
National Lampoon's Animal House (WB, 1985)	$70,826,000
Nat'l Lampoon's Class Reunion (Fox, 1982)	$5,000,000
National Lampoon's Vacation (WB, 1983)	$30,400,000
Nat'l Lampoon's European Vacation (WB, 1985)	$25,600,000
Nat'l Lampoon's Christmas Vacation (WB, 1989)	$34,800,000
Nat'l Lampoon's Loaded Weapon 1 (NL, 1993)	$12,500,000
National Velvet (MGM, 1945)	$4,244,340
Natural, The (TriStar, 1984)	$25,000,000
Navy Seals (Orion, 1990)	$11,306,765
Near Dark (DEG, 1987)	$1,335,000
Necessary Roughness (Par, 1991)	$12,500,000
Neighbors (Col, 1981)	$17,127,210
Neptune's Daughter (MGM, 1949)	$3,500,000
Network (MGM/UA, 1976)	$13,921,740
Nevada Smith (Par, 1966)	$5,500,000
Never a Dull Moment (BV, 1968)	$6,510,000
Never Cry Wolf (BV, 1983)	$14,674,000

Title (Distributor, Year Released)	$ Rentals
Never on Sunday (Lopert/UA, 1960)	$3,500,000
Never Say Never Again (WB, 1983)	$28,200,000
Never So Few (MGM, 1959)	$3,000,000
Neverending Story, The (WB, 1984)	$10,100,000
New Centurions, The (Col, 1972)	$7,113,000
New Jack City (WB, 1991)	$22,000,000
New Leaf, A (Par, 1971)	$5,000,000
New York, New York (UA, 1977)	$6,553,413
Next Man, The (AA, 1976)	$3,500,000
Nicholas and Alexandra (Col, 1971)	$6,990,000
Nickelodeon (Col, 1976)	$5,561,000
Niagara -IMAX (Destination Cinema, 1987)	$4,195,000
Night and Day (WB, 1946)	$4,000,000
Night of the Comet (Atlantic, 1984)	$5,800,000
Night of the Demons (IFM/Paragon, 1988)	$1,009,655
Night of the Iguana (MGM, 1964)	$4,324,950
Night of the Living Dead (Continental, 1968)	$3,000,000
Night Patrol (NW, 1984)	$3,500,000
Night Shift (WB, 1982)	$8,000,000
Night the Lights Went out in Georgia (Emb, 1981)	$7,053,460
Night They Raided Minsky's, The (UA, 1969)	$3,000,000
Nightfall (Concorde, 1988)	$1,600,000
Nighthawks (U, 1981)	$7,257,575
Nightmare (21st Century, 1982)	$4,300,000
Nightmare on Elm Street, A (NL, 1984)	$9,337,942
Nightmare on Elm Street Pt 2, A (NL, 1985)	$13,500,000
Nightmare on Elm Street Pt 3, A (NL, 1987)	$21,345,000
Nightmare on Elm Street Pt 4, A (NL, 1988)	$22,000,000
Nightmare on Elm Street Pt 5, A (NL, 1989)	$10,000,000
Freddy's Dead: Final Nightmare (NL, 1991)	$17,700,000
Nightmares (U, 1983)	$3,123,000
Nightwing (Col, 1979)	$3,750,000
9 Deaths of the Ninja (Crown, 1985)	$3,000,000
Nine Lives of Fritz the Cat, The (AIP, 1974)	$3,000,000
976-EVIL (NL, 1989)	$1,200,000
9 to 5 (Fox, 1980)	$59,068,000
1984 (Atl, 1984)	$4,375,000
1941 (U, 1979)	$23,254,390
1990: The Bronx Warriors (UFD, 1983)	$1,158,000
1969 (Atlantic, 1988)	$2,000,000
No Deposit, No Return (BV, 1976)	$10,578,000
No Holds Barred (NL, 1989)	$7,000,000
No Mercy (TriStar, 1986)	$7,000,000
No Retreat, No Surrender (NW, 1986)	$1,800,000
No Time for Sergeants (WB, 1958)	$7,500,000
No Way Out (Orion, 1987)	$15,805,310
No Way to Treat a Lady (Par, 1968)	$3,100,000
Nob Hill (Fox, 1945)	$3,104,000
Nomads (Atl, 1986)	$1,110,000
Norma Rae (Fox, 1979)	$10,000,000
North Avenue Irregulars (BV, 1979)	$9,944,000
North by Northwest (MGM, 1959)	$6,702,530
North Dallas 40 (Par, 1979)	$16,100,000
North to Alaska (Fox, 1960)	$5,000,000

Title (Distributor, Year Released)	$ Rentals	Title (Distributor, Year Released)	$ Rentals
Not A Love Story (Quartet Inc, 1982)	$1,040,000	Only the Lonely (Fox, 1991)	$11,748,000
Not As a Stranger (UA, 1955)	$6,176,150	Only When I Laugh (Col, 1981)	$12,507,140
Nothing in Common (TriStar, 1986)	$13,529,000	Opening of Misty Beethoven, The (Catalyst, 1976)	$3,000,000
Notorious (RKO, 1946)	$4,800,000	Operation Crossbow (MGM, 1965)	$3,700,000
Now You See Him, Now You Don't (BV, 1972)	$4,610,000	Operation Petticoat (U, 1959)	$9,321,555
Nowhere to Run (Col, 1993)	$10,000,000	Orca (Par, 1977)	$9,430,000
Nude Bomb, The (U, 1980)	$8,170,000	Ordinary People (Par, 1980)	$23,123,000
Nun's Story, The (WB, 1959)	$5,750,000	Oscar (BV, 1991)	$10,161,000
Nuts (WB, 1987)	$14,100,000	Other People's Money (WB, 1991)	$12,300,000
Nutty Professor, The (Par, 1963)	$4,000,000	Other Side of Midnight, The (Fox, 1977)	$18,408,000
Object of Beauty, The (Avenue, 1991)	$2,302,465	Other Side of the Mountain, The (U, 1975)	$18,011,525
Obsession (Col, 1976)	$4,468,000	Other Side of the Mountain Pt 2, The (U, 1978)	$6,234,685
Ocean's Eleven (WB, 1960)	$5,650,000	Other, The (Fox, 1972)	$3,500,000
Octagon, The (American Cinema, 1980)	$5,500,000	Our Man Flint (Fox, 1966)	$7,200,000
Octopussy (MGM/UA, 1983)	$34,031,200	Our Vines Have Tender Grapes (MGM, 1945)	$3,000,000
Odd Couple, The (Par, 1968)	$20,000,000	Out for Justice (WB, 1991)	$18,500,000
Ode to Billy Joe (WB, 1976)	$11,600,000	Out of Africa (U, 1985)	$43,448,255
Odessa File, The (Col, 1974)	$5,654,000	Out-of-Towners, The (Par, 1970)	$7,250,000
Officer and a Gentleman, An (Par, 1982)	$55,223,000	Outland (Ladd/WB, 1981)	$10,000,000
Official Story, The (Almi, 1985)	$1,400,000	Outlaw Blues (WB, 1977)	$4,300,000
Oh, God! (WB, 1977)	$31,500,000	Outlaw Josey Wales, The (WB, 1976)	$13,500,000
Oh, God! Book II (WB, 1980)	$9,700,000	Outlaw, The (UA/RKO, 1943)	$5,075,000
Oh, God! You Devil (WB, 1984)	$11,000,000	Outrageous Fortune (BV, 1987)	$22,678,000
Oh, Heavenly Dog! (Fox, 1980)	$3,750,000	Outsiders, The (WB, 1983)	$12,400,000
Oklahoma! (Goldwyn, 1955)	$7,100,000	Over The Top (WB, 1987)	$8,300,000
Old Yeller (BV, 1957)	$10,050,000	Overboard (MGM/UA, 1987)	$12,793,000
Oliver & Company (BV, 1988)	$25,268,000	Owl and the Pussycat, The (Col, 1970)	$11,645,000
Oliver! (Col, 1968)	$16,800,000	Oxford Blues (MGM, 1984)	$3,000,000
Oliver's Story (Par, 1978)	$8,458,000	Pacific Heights (Fox, 1990)	$14,000,000
Omega Man, The (WB, 1971)	$4,000,000	Paint Your Wagon (Par, 1969)	$14,500,000
Omen, The (Fox, 1976)	$28,544,000	Pal Joey (Col, 1957)	$4,700,000
Omen II: Damien (Fox, 1978)	$12,100,000	Pale Rider (WB, 1985)	$20,800,000
On a Clear Day You Can See Forever (Par, 1970)	$5,350,000	Paleface, The (Par, 1948)	$4,500,000
On an Island With You (MGM, 1948)	$3,200,000	Paper Chase, The (Fox, 1973)	$4,000,000
On Golden Pond (U/AFD, 1981)	$61,175,030	Paper Moon (Par, 1973)	$16,559,000
On Her Majesty's Secret Service (UA, 1969)	$9,117,167	Papillion (AA, 1973)	$22,500,000
On the Beach (UA, 1959)	$4,802,900	Paradise (Emb, 1982)	$2,355,145
On The Right Track (Fox, 1981)	$5,900,000	Paradise Alley (U, 1978)	$4,213,255
On the Town (MGM, 1949)	$3,000,000	Paradise—Hawaiian Style (Par, 1966)	$3,200,000
On the Waterfront (Col, 1954)	$4,200,000	Parasite (Avemb, 1981)	$1,500,000
Once Bitten (Goldwyn, 1985)	$4,415,285	Pardners (Par, 1956)	$3,600,000
Once Is Not Enough (Par, 1975)	$8,870,435	Parent Trap, The (BV, 1961)	$11,322,000
One and Only, The (Par, 1978)	$12,189,000	Parenthood (U, 1989)	$50,004,367
One Crazy Summer (WB, 1986)	$5,800,000	Paris Is Burning (Off White/Prestige, 1991)	$1,750,000
One Dark Night (Comworld, 1983)	$3,700,000	Parrish (WB, 1961)	$4,200,000
One Down Two to Go (Almi, 1982)	$1,150,000	Party Animal, The (IFM, 1985)	$1,900,000
One Flew Over the Cuckoo's Nest (UA, 1975)	$59,939,700	Party, The (UA, 1968)	$3,000,000
100 Rifles (Fox, 1969)	$3,500,000	Passage To India, A (Col, 1984)	$13,853,920
101 Dalmatians (BV, 1961)	$68,648,000	Passenger 57 (WB, 1992)	$21,700,000
One Magic Christmas (BV, 1985)	$7,000,000	Patch of Blue, A (MGM, 1966)	$6,792,000
One of Our Dinosaurs Is Missing (BV, 1975)	$4,775,000	Paternity (Par, 1981)	$8,500,000
One-Eyed Jacks (Par, 1961)	$4,300,000	Patriot Games (Par, 1992)	$37,500,000
One-on One (WB, 1977)	$13,100,000	Patton (Fox, 1970)	$28,100,000
Onion Field, The (Avemb, 1979)	$4,317,615	Paul J. Rainey's African Hunt (Laemmle, 1912)	$3,000,000

Title (Distributor, Year Released)	$ Rentals
Pee-Wee's Big Adventure (WB, 1985)	$18,100,000
Peggy Sue Got Married (TriStar, 1986)	$16,844,000
Pelle The Conqueror (Miramax, 1988)	$1,000,000
Penelope (MGM, 1966)	$3,000,000
Penitentiary (Jerry Gross, 1980)	$4,000,000
People That Time Forgot, The (AIP, 1977)	$2,000,000
Pepe (Col, 1960)	$4,800,000
Perfect (Col, 1985)	$6,112,555
Perils Of Gwendoline, The (Goldwyn, 1985)	$1,173,365
Perils of Pauline (Par, 1947)	$3,800,000
Personals, The (NW, 1983)	$2,000,000
Pet Sematary (Par, 1989)	$26,400,000
Pete 'n' Tillie (U, 1972)	$7,350,090
Pete Kelly's Blues (WB, 1955)	$5,000,000
Pete's Dragon (BV, 1977)	$18,400,000
Peter Pan (RKO/BV, 1953)	$37,584,000
Peyton Place (Fox, 1957)	$11,500,000
Phantasm (Avemb, 1979)	$6,800,000
Phantom Of The Opera (21st Century, 1989)	$3,952,160
Philadelphia Experiment, The (NW, 1984)	$3,100,000
Pick Up Artist, The (Fox, 1987)	$6,000,000
Pick Up Summer (Film Ventures, 1981)	$1,240,000
Picnic (Col, 1955)	$6,350,000
Picture of Dorian Gray, The (MGM, 1944)	$3,000,000
Piece of the Action, A (WB, 1977)	$6,700,000
Pieces (Film Ventures, 1983)	$1,173,475
Pillow Talk (U, 1959)	$7,669,715
Pink Flamingos (NL, 1972)	$1,900,000
Pink Floyd (April Fools, 1974)	$1,100,000
Pink Floyd—The Wall (MGM/UA, 1982)	$9,123,580
Pink Panther, The (UA, 1964)	$5,934,515
Pink Panther Strikes Again, The (UA, 1976)	$19,882,530
Pinky (Fox, 1949)	$3,800,000
Pinocchio (RKO/BV, 1940)	$40,442,000
Piranha (NW, 1978)	$2,900,000
Pirate Movie, The (Fox, 1982)	$4,000,000
Place in the Sun, A (Par, 1951)	$3,500,000
Places in the Heart (TriStar, 1984)	$16,000,000
Planes, Trains & Automobiles (Par, 1987)	$22,100,000
Planet of the Apes (Fox, 1968)	$15,000,000
Planet of the Apes, Beneath The (Fox, 1970)	$8,600,000
Planet of the Apes, Escape From the (Fox, 1971)	$5,560,000
Platoon (Orion, 1986)	$69,937,100
Playboys (Goldwyn, 1992)	$2,400,000
Player, The (FL, 1992)	$9,100,000
Play It Again, Sam (Par, 1972)	$5,757,000
Play Misty for Me (U, 1971)	$5,048,645
Plaza Suite (Par, 1971)	$4,000,000
Please Don't Eat the Daisies (MGM, 1960)	$5,368,770
Pleasure of His Company, The (Par, 1961)	$3,100,000
Plymouth Adventure (MGM, 1952)	$3,000,000
Point Blank (MGM, 1967)	$3,200,000
Point Break (Fox, 1991)	$19,791,000
Police Academy (Ladd/WB, 1984)	$38,500,000

Title (Distributor, Year Released)	$ Rentals
Police Academy 2—First Assignment (WB, 1985)	$27,200,000
Police Academy 3: Back in Training (WB, 1986)	$21,000,000
Police Academy 4: Citizens on Patrol (WB, 1987)	$14,000,000
Police Academy 5: Assign. Miami B. (WB, 1988)	$9,100,000
Poltergeist (MGM/UA, 1982)	$38,248,765
Poltergeist II (MGM/UA, 1986)	$20,482,580
Poltergeist III (MGM/UA, 1988)	$5,899,000
Polyester (NL, 1981)	$1,120,000
Pom Pom Girls, The (Crown, 1976)	$7,425,000
Poor White Trash (UA/Cinema Distribs, 1957)	$6,000,000
Poor White Trash Pt 2 (Ripps Rel/Aquarius, 1976)	$3,014,610
Popcorn (Studio Three, 1991)	$2,043,179
Popeye (Par, 1980)	$24,568,540
Porky's (Fox, 1982)	$55,559,000
Porky's II: The Next Day (Fox, 1983)	$17,200,000
Porky's Revenge (Fox, 1985)	$10,200,000
Portnoy's Complaint (WB, 1972)	$3,100,000
Portrait in Black (U, 1960)	$3,500,000
Poseidon Adventure, The (Fox, 1972)	$42,000,000
Posse (Gramercy, 1993)	$8,555,000
Postcards From the Edge (Col, 1990)	$17,240,000
Postman Always Rings Twice, The (MGM, 1946)	$3,785,350
Postman Always Rings Twice, The (Par, 1981)	$6,070,000
Predator (Fox, 1987)	$31,000,000
Predator 2 (Fox, 1990)	$15,700,000
Presidio, The (Par, 1988)	$9,600,000
Presumed Innocent (WB, 1990)	$43,800,000
Pretty Baby (Par, 1978)	$4,197,000
Pretty In Pink (Par, 1986)	$16,600,000
Pretty Woman (BV, 1990)	$81,905,530
Pride and the Passion, The (UA, 1957)	$3,500,000
Pride of the Yankees, The (RKO, 1942)	$3,671,000
Prime Cut (NGP, 1972)	$3,200,000
Prince Of Darkness (U, 1987)	$5,891,130
Prince Of The City (Orion/WB, 1981)	$4,500,000
Prince of Tides, The (Col, 1991)	$36,100,000
Princess and the Pirate, The (RKO, 1944)	$2,823,000
Princess Bride, The (Fox, 1987)	$13,300,000
Principal, The (TriStar, 1987)	$9,000,000
Prisoner of Zenda, The (U, 1979)	$3,670,225
Private Benjamin (WB, 1980)	$34,400,000
Private Eyes, The (NW, 1980)	$4,000,000
Private Function, A (Island, 1985)	$1,047,000
Private Lessons (JFP, 1981)	$12,503,610
Private School (U, 1983)	$6,641,000
Prize Fighter, The (NW, 1979)	$3,000,000
Prize, The (MGM, 1963)	$3,500,000
Prizzi's Honor (Fox, 1985)	$13,000,000
Problem Child (U, 1990)	$25,134,780
Problem Child 2 (U, 1991)	$11,748,265
Professionals, The (Col, 1966)	$8,800,000
Project X (Fox, 1987)	$7,700,000
Prom Night (Avemb, 1980)	$6,126,380
Prom Night II: Hello Mary Lou (Goldwyn, 1987)	$1,100,000

Title (Distributor, Year Released)	$ Rentals	Title (Distributor, Year Released)	$ Rentals
Promise, The (U, 1978)	$5,574,820	Red Heat (TriStar, 1988)	$16,000,000
Prophecy (Par, 1979)	$10,499,000	Red River (UA, 1948)	$4,506,825
Protocol (WB, 1984)	$14,200,000	Red Scorpion (Shapiro Glickenhaus, 1989)	$2,000,000
Proud and the Profane, The (Par, 1956)	$3,900,000	Red Shoes, The (Eagle/Lion, 1948)	$5,000,000
Prudence and the Pill (Fox, 1968)	$4,500,000	Reds (Par, 1981)	$21,000,000
Psycho (Par/U, 1960)	$11,200,000	Reefer Madness (NL, reissue, 1970)	$1,443,000
Psycho II (U, 1983)	$15,908,435	Regarding Henry (Par, 1991)	$20,000,000
Psycho III (U, 1986)	$6,475,055	Reincar. of Peter Proud (CRC/AIP/FWS, 1975)	$5,000,000
PT 109 (WB, 1963)	$3,500,000	Reivers, The (NGP/WB, 1970)	$8,500,000
Pumpkinhead (MGM/UA, 1988)	$1,000,000	Relentless (NL, 1989)	$3,000,000
Pump Up the Volume (NL, 1990)	$4,000,000	Rescuers, The (BV, 1977)	$30,090,000
Punchline (Col, 1988)	$10,200,000	Rescurers Down Under, The (BV, 1990)	$13,575,889
Purple Rain (WB, 1984)	$31,700,000	Return From Witch Mountain (BV, 1978)	$7,398,000
Purple Rose Of Cairo, The (Orion, 1985)	$5,075,015	Return of Martin Guerre (European Int'l, 1982)	$1,730,000
Pursued (WB, 1947)	$3,000,000	Return of the Dragon (Bryanston, 1974)	$5,200,000
Putney Swope (C5, 1969)	$3,000,000	Return of the Jedi (Fox, 1983)	$169,193,000
Quadrophenia (World Northal, 1979)	$1,050,000	Return of the Living Dead (Fox, 1985)	$6,011,000
Quest for Fire (Fox, 1982)	$12,250,000	Return of the Living Dead II (Lorimar, 1988)	$3,200,000
Quiet Earth, The (Skouras, 1985)	$1,110,605	Return of the Pink Panther, The (UA, 1975)	$20,170,225
Quiet Man, The (Republic, 1952)	$3,800,000	Return To Macon County (AIP, 1975)	$3,500,000
Quo Vadis (MGM, 1951)	$11,901,660	Return To Oz (BV, 1985)	$4,634,000
Rabbit Test (Avemb, 1978)	$4,289,655	Return to Peyton Place (Fox, 1961)	$4,500,000
Rabid (NW, 1977)	$2,200,000	Return To Snowy River Pt 2 (BV, 1988)	$5,759,000
Race With the Devil (Fox, 1975)	$5,821,000	Revenge of the Nerds (Fox, 1984)	$19,500,000
Rachel, Rachel (WB, 1968)	$6,100,000	Revenge of the Nerds II (Fox, 1987)	$14,200,000
Radio Days (Orion, 1987)	$6,442,260	Revenge Of The Ninja (MGM/UA, 1983)	$5,027,580
Rage in Harlem, A (Miramax, 1991)	$4,200,000	Revenge of the Pink Panther (UA, 1978)	$25,406,180
Raging Bull (UA, 1980)	$10,111,080	Rhapsody in Blue (WB, 1945)	$3,342,000
Ragtime (Par, 1981)	$10,000,000	Rhinestone (Fox, 1984)	$12,250,000
Raiders of the Lost Ark (Par, 1981)	$115,598,000	Rich And Famous (MGM/UA, 1981)	$5,461,285
Indiana Jones and the Temple of Doom (Par, 1984)	$109,000,000	Richard Pryor Live in Concert (Emerson, 1979)	$6,000,000
Indiana Jones and the Last Crusade (Par, 1989)	$115,500,000	Richard Pryor Live on Sunset Strip (Col, 1982)	$18,280,000
Rain Man (MGM/uA, 1988)	$86,813,000	Richard Pryor—Here And Now (Col, 1983)	$7,238,850
Raintree County (MGM, 1957)	$5,962,840	Ricochet (WB, 1991)	$10,400,000
Raise the Titanic (AFD, 1980)	$6,800,000	Right Stuff, The (Ladd/WB, 1983)	$10,400,000
Raising Arizona (Fox, 1987)	$10,000,000	Rio Bravo (WB, 1959)	$5,750,000
Rally 'Round the Flag, Boys (Fox, 1959)	$3,400,000	Rio Lobo (CCF/NGP/WB, 1970)	$4,250,000
Rambling Rose (NL/7 Arts, 1991)	$3,000,000	Risky Business (Geffen/WB, 1983)	$30,400,000
Rambo: First Blood (Orion, 1982)	$22,947,560	River of No Return (Fox, 1954)	$3,800,000
Rambo: First Blood Pt II (TriStar, 1985)	$78,919,250	River Runs Through It, A (Col, 1992)	$19,000,000
Rambo III (TriStar, 1988)	$28,509,000	River's Edge (Hemdale/Island, 1986)	$1,700,000
Random Harvest (MGM, 1942)	$4,665,500	River, The (U, 1984)	$5,105,300
Rappin' (Cannon, 1985)	$1,247,495	Road House (MGM/UA, 1989)	$12,616,000
Rat Race, The (Par, 1960)	$3,400,000	Road to Bali (Par, 1953)	$3,000,000
Raw (Par, 1987)	$24,800,000	Road to Morocco (Par, 1942)	$3,800,000
Raw Deal (DEG, 1986)	$7,890,570	Road to Rio (Par, 1947)	$4,500,000
Razor's Edge, The (Fox, 1946)	$5,000,000	Road to Utopia (Par, 1945)	$4,500,000
Re-Animator (Empire, 1985)	$1,628,000	Road Warrior, The [Mad Max 2] (WB, 1982)	$11,300,000
Real Genius (TriStar, 1985)	$5,800,000	Roadie (UA, 1980)	$1,458,000
Reap the Wild Wind (Par, 1942)	$4,000,000	Robe, The (Fox, 1953)	$17,500,000
Rear Window (Par/U Classics, 1954)	$9,812,270	Robin and Marian (Col, 1976)	$4,000,000
Rebecca (UA/Kino, 1940)	$3,000,000	Robin and the Seven Hoods (WB, 1964)	$4,500,000
Rebel Without a Cause (WB, 1955)	$4,600,000	Robin Hood (BV, 1973)	$17,160,000
Red Dawn (MGM/UA, 1984)	$17,938,435	Robin Hood: Prince of Thieves (WB, 1991)	$86,000,000

Title (Distributor,Year Released)	$ Rentals	Title (Distributor, Year Released)	$ Rentals
Robocop (Orion, 1987)	$24,036,727	Santa Claus (TriStar, 1985)	$13,000,000
Robocop 2 (Orion, 1990)	$22,505,560	Saratoga Trunk (WB, 1946)	$4,250,000
Rock-a-Bye Baby (Par, 1958)	$3,100,000	Sgt. Pepper's Lonely Hearts Club Band (U, 1978)	$11,414,535
Rock-a-Doodle (Goldwyn, 1992)	$5,600,000	Satan's Playthings (MPM, 1980)	$1,060,000
Rocketeer, The (BV, 1991)	$23,178,970	Satisfaction (Fox, 1988)	$3,300,000
Rocky Horror Picture Show, The (Fox, 1975)	$38,096,000	Saturday Night Fever (Par, 1977)	$74,100,000
Rocky (UA, 1976)	$56,524,970	Saturday the 14th (NW, 1981)	$2,200,000
Rocky II (UA, 1979)	$42,169,390	Saturn 3 (AFD, 1980)	$4,900,000
Rocky III (MGM/UA, 1982)	$66,262,800	Savage Sam (BV, 1963)	$3,000,000
Rocky IV (MGM/UA, 1985)	$76,023,250	Savannah Smiles (Emb, 1982)	$4,632,480
Rocky V (MGM/UA, 1990)	$20,000,000	Save the Tiger (Par, 1973)	$3,000,000
Roller Boogie (UA, 1979)	$4,929,540	Say One for Me (Fox, 1959)	$3,900,000
Rollerball (UA, 1975)	$9,055,280	Sayonara (WB, 1957)	$10,500,000
Rollercoaster (U, 1977)	$8,694,770	Scandal (Miramax, 1989)	$3,500,000
Rollover (Orion/WB, 1981)	$6,700,000	Scanners (Avemb, 1981)	$6,568,775
Roman Holiday (Par, 1953)	$3,000,000	Scarecrow (WB, 1973)	$4,300,000
Romancing the Stone (Fox, 1984)	$36,000,000	Scared Stiff (Par, 1953)	$3,500,000
Romeo and Juliet (Par, 1968)	$17,473,000	Scarface (U, 1983)	$23,333,440
Rookie, The (WB, 1990)	$10,000,000	Scavenger Hunt (Fox, 1979)	$3,800,000
Room With a View, A (Cinecom/Norstar, 1986)	$12,000,000	Scenes From a Marriage (Cinema 5, 1974)	$3,100,000
Rooster Cogburn (U, 1975)	$7,010,410	Scent of a Woman (U, 1992)	$26,000,000
Roots of Heaven, The (Fox, 1958)	$3,000,000	School Daze (Columbia, 1988)	$6,105,000
Rose Tatoo, The (Par, 1955)	$4,200,000	Scream and Scream Again (AIP, 1970)	$1,217,000
Rose, The (Fox, 1979)	$19,100,000	Scream, Blacula, Scream (AIP, 1973)	$1,000,000
Rosemary's Baby (Par, 1968)	$15,000,000	Screwballs (NW, 1983)	$1,350,000
Rough Cut (Par, 1980)	$10,000,000	Scrooge (NGP, 1970)	$3,000,000
Roustabout (Par, 1965)	$3,300,000	Scrooged (Par, 1988)	$31,500,000
Roxanne (Col, 1987)	$18,040,000	Sea Chase, The (WB, 1955)	$6,000,000
Ruby (Dimension, 1977)	$2,233,128	Sea of Grass, The (MGM, 1947)	$3,600,000
Rumble Fish (U, 1983)	$1,282,000	Sea of Love (U, 1989)	$28,623,525
Runaway Train (Cannon, 1985)	$3,000,000	Searchers, The (WB, 1956)	$4,900,000
Running (U, 1979)	$3,364,480	Secret Ceremony (U, 1969)	$3,000,000
Running Man, The (TriStar, 1987)	$16,335,000	Secret Heart, The (MGM, 1947)	$3,000,000
Running Scared (MGM/UA, 1986)	$17,129,005	Secret Life of an American Wife, The (Fox, 1968)	$3,000,000
Russia House, The (MGM/UA, 1990)	$10,200,000	Secret Life of Walter Mitty, The (RKO, 1947)	$3,400,000
Russians Are Coming..., The (UA, 1966)	$9,771,270	Secret of my Success, The (U, 1987)	$29,855,540
Ruthless People (BV, 1986)	$31,443,000	Secret Of NIMH, The (MGM/UA, 1982)	$5,276,065
Ryan's Daughter (MGM, 1970)	$14,661,420	Secret of the Sword, The (Atl, 1985)	$2,650,000
S*P*Y*S (Fox, 1974)	$5,205,000	Secret Policeman's Other Ball (Miramax, 1982)	$1,800,000
S.O.B. (Par, 1981)	$6,200,000	Secret War of Harry Frigg, The (U, 1968)	$3,500,000
Sabrina (Par, 1954)	$4,000,000	Seduction of Joe Tynan, The (U, 1970)	$9,485,685
Sad Sack, The (Par, 1957)	$3,500,000	Seduction, The (Emb, 1982)	$5,429,935
Sailor Beware (Par, 1951)	$4,300,000	See No Evil, Hear No Evil (TriStar, 1989)	$20,390,000
Sailor Who Fell From Grace..., The (Avemb, 1976)	$4,236,810	Seems Like Old Times (Col, 1980)	$21,558,000
Sallam Bombay (Cinecom, 1988)	$1,000,000	Semi-Tough (UA, 1977)	$22,940,810
Salome (Col, 1953)	$4,750,000	Send Me No Flowers (U, 1964)	$4,108,160
Salsa (Cannon, 1988)	$3,266,935	Sentimental Journey (Fox, 1946)	$3,000,000
Same Time, Next Year (U, 1978)	$11,361,770	Sentinel, The (U, 1977)	$4,382,680
Samson and Delilah (Par, 1949)	$11,500,000	Separate Tables (UA, 1958)	$3,100,000
San Antonio (WB, 1945)	$3,553,000	Sergeant York (WB, 1941)	$6,135,710
San Francisco (MGM, 1936)	$3,785,870	Sergeants Three (UA, 1962)	$4,315,590
Sand Pebbles, The (Fox, 1967)	$13,500,000	Serial (Par, 1980)	$5,600,000
Sandpiper, The (MGM, 1965)	$6,160,960	Serpent & the Rainbow (U, 1988)	$8,563,000
Sands of Iwo Jima (Republic, 1949)	$5,000,000	Serpico (Par, 1974)	$14,600,000

Title (Distributor, Year Released)	$ Rentals
Sesame Street: Follow That Bird (WB, 1985)	$5,500,000
Seven Brides for Seven Brothers (MGM, 1954)	$6,298,000
Seven Days in May (Par, 1964)	$3,700,000
Seven Little Foys, The (Par, 1955)	$4,000,000
Seven Per-Cent Solution, The (U, 1976)	$4,804,860
Seven Wonders of the World (CRC, 1956)	$12,500,000
Seven Year Itch, The (Fox, 1955)	$6,000,000
Seven-Ups, The (Fox, 1973)	$4,500,000
Seventh Cross, The (MGM, 1944)	$3,000,000
Seventh Sign, The (TriStar, 1988)	$7,500,000
Seventh Voyage of Sinbad, The (Col, 1958)	$6,500,000
Sex Education (MPM, 1979)	$1,100,000
Sex, and the Single Girl (WB, 1964)	$4,250,000
sex, lies, and videotape (Miramax, 1989)	$10,600,000
Sexual Freedom in Denmark (Art Films Intl., 1970)	$7,000,000
Shaft (MGM/UA, 1971)	$7,067,825
Shaft's Big Score (MGM, 1972)	$3,675,000
Shag (Hemdale, 1989)	$2,701,000
Shaggy D.A., The (BV, 1976)	$10,550,000
Shaggy Dog, The (BV, 1959)	$12,317,000
Shakedown (U, 1988)	$4,309,785
Shampoo (Col, 1975)	$23,822,000
Shamus (Col, 1972)	$3,300,000
Shane (Par, 1953)	$9,000,000
Sharky's Machine (Orion/WB, 1981)	$18,400,000
She's Gotta Have It (Island, 1986)	$3,100,000
She's Having A Baby (Par, 1988)	$6,800,000
Shenandoah (U, 1965)	$7,771,032
Shining Through (Fox, 1992)	$11,552,000
Shining, The (WB, 1980)	$30,900,000
Shoah (NY, 1985)	$1,100,000
Shock To The System, A (Corsair, 1990)	$1,500,000
Shoot the Moon (MGM/UA, 1982)	$3,562,000
Shoot to Kill (BV, 1988)	$12,498,000
Shootist, The (Par, 1976)	$5,987,000
Short Circuit (TriStar, 1986)	$17,878,000
Short Circuit 2 (TriStar, 1988)	$8,500,000
Shot in the Dark, A (UA, 1964)	$6,748,225
Shout At The Devil (AIP, 1977)	$2,800,000
Show Boat (MGM, 1951)	$5,533,000
Sid and Nancy (Goldwyn, 1986)	$1,288,990
Sign O' The Times (Cineplex, 1987)	$1,000,000
Silence of the Lambs, The (Orion, 1991)	$59,882,870
Silencers, The (Col, 1966)	$7,350,000
Silent Movie (Fox, 1976)	$21,242,000
Silent Night, Deadly Night (TriStar, 1984)	$1,500,000
Silent Rage (Col, 1982)	$4,923,280
Silent Scream (ACR, 1979)	$7,900,000
Silkwood (Fox, 1983)	$17,825,000
Silver Bullet (Par, 1985)	$5,400,000
Silver Chalice, The (WB, 1954)	$3,200,000
Silver Streak (Fox, 1976)	$30,018,000
Silverado (Col, 1985)	$17,010,000
Sinbad and the Eye of the Tiger (Col, 1977)	$7,935,000

Title (Distributor, Year Released)	$ Rentals
Since You Went Away (UA, 1945)	$4,924,755
Singin' in the Rain (MGM/UA/TEC, 1952)	$4,220,605
Singing Fool, The (WB, 1928)	$3,821,000
Singing Nun, The (MGM, 1966)	$3,700,000
Single White Female (Col, 1992)	$21,100,000
Sink the Bismarck (Fox, 1960)	$3,000,000
Sister Act (BV, 1992)	$62,420,000
Sisters (AIP, 1973)	$1,000,000
Sitting Pretty (Fox, 1948)	$3,600,000
Six Pack (Fox, 1982)	$10,700,000
Six Weeks (U, 1982)	$5,227,880
Sixteen Candles (U, 1984)	$9,557,000
Skyjacked (MGM/UA, 1972)	$6,648,530
Slap Shot (U, 1977)	$13,594,900
Slaughter (AIP, 1972)	$2,500,000
Slaughterhouse-Five (U, 1972)	$3,777,140
Sleeper (UA, 1973)	$8,253,605
Sleeping Beauty (BV, 1959)	$21,998,000
Sleeping With the Enemy (Fox, 1991)	$46,629,000
Sleepwalkers (Col, 1992)	$13,200,000
Sleuth (Fox, 1972)	$5,607,000
Small Change (NW, 1976)	$1,250,000
Smokey and the Bandit (U, 1977)	$58,949,940
Smokey and the Bandit II (U, 1980)	$38,911,475
Smoky (Fox, 1946)	$4,000,000
Smurfs and the Magic Flute, The (Atlantic, 1983)	$9,488,805
Snake Pit, The (Fox, 1948)	$4,100,000
Snakefist Vs. The Dragon (21st Century, 1980)	$1,400,000
Sneakers (U, 1992)	$23,417,960
Snow White and Seven Dwarfs (RKO/BV, 1937)***	$84,960,000
Snowball Express (BV, 1972)	$7,100,000
Snows of Kilimanjaro (Fox, 1952)	$6,500,000
So Fine (WB, 1981)	$4,900,000
So Proudly We Hail (Par, 1943)	$3,000,000
Soapdish (Par, 1991)	$15,700,000
Soldier Blue (Avemb, 1970)	$1,200,000
Soldier's Story, A (Col, 1984)	$10,120,000
Soldier, The (Emb, 1982)	$2,169,075
Soloman and Sheba (UA, 1959)	$5,186,170
Some Came Running (MGM, 1958)	$4,441,980
Some Kind of Hero (Par, 1982)	$11,000,000
Some Kind Of Wonderful (Par, 1987)	$7,250,860
Some Like It Hot (UA, 1959)	$8,127,835
Someone To Watch Over Me (Col, 1987)	$4,467,888
Sometimes a Great Notion (U, 1971)	$3,751,775
Somewhere I'll Find You (MGM, 1942)	$3,000,000
Somewhere in Time (U, 1980)	$4,444,715
Sommersby (WB, 1993)	$21,000,000
Son of Flubber (BV, 1963)	$10,450,000
Son of Paleface (Par, 1952)	$3,400,000
Song of Bernadette (Fox, 1943)	$4,701,000
Song of Love (MGM, 1947)	$3,100,000
Song of Norway (CRC/Col, 1970)	$4,450,000
Song of the South (RKO/BV, 1946)	$29,228,720

Title (Distributor, Year Released)	$ Rentals
Song Remains the Same, The (WB, 1976)	$5,700,000
Sons of Katie Elder, The (Par, 1965)	$6,000,000
Sophie's Choice (U/AFD, 1982)	$14,218,635
Sorcerer (U/Par, 1977)	$5,942,175
Sorceress (NW, 1982)	$1,500,000
Sorrowful Jones (Par, 1949)	$3,400,000
Soul Man (New World, 1986)	$13,500,000
Sound of Music, The (Fox, 1965)	$79,975,000
Sounder (Fox, 1972)	$8,726,000
South Pacific (Fox, 1958)	$17,500,000
Soylent Green (MGM, 1973)	$3,600,000
Spaceballs (MGM/UA, 1987)	$19,027,000
SpaceCamp (Fox, 1986)	$5,000,000
Spacehunter: Adv.s in Forbidden Zone (Col, 1983)	$8,136,790
Spanish Main, The (RKO, 1945)	$3,185,000
Spartacus (U, 1960)	$11,100,000
Speedway (MGM, 1968)	$3,000,000
Spellbound (UA, 1945)	$4,970,585
Special Day, A (Cinema V, 1978)	$1,050,000
Spencer's Mountain (WB, 1963)	$4,750,000
Spies Like Us (WB, 1985)	$30,500,000
Spinout (MGM, 1966)	$3,000,000
Splash (BV, 1984)	$34,103,000
Splendor in the Grass (WB, 1961)	$4,250,000
Split Second (InterStar, 1992)	$2,080,930
Spring Break (Col, 1983)	$11,190,000
Spring Fever (Comworld, 1983)	$2,900,000
Spy Who Came in From the Cold, The (Par, 1965)	$3,500,000
Spy Who Loved Me, The (UA, 1977)	$24,364,500
Spys (Fox, 1974)	$5,205,000
Squeeze Play (Troma, 1980)	$3,000,000
St. Elmo's Fire (Col, 1985)	$16,850,000
Stage Door Canteen (UA, 1943)	$4,339,535
Stagecoach (Fox, 1966)	$4,000,000
Stakeout (BV, 1987)	$28,215,000
Stalag 17 (Par, 1953)	$3,300,000
Stand & Deliver (WB, 1988)	$5,759,000
Stand by Me (Col, 1986)	$22,050,000
Star (Fox, 1968)	$4,200,000
Star Is Born, A (WB, 1954)	$6,100,000
Star Is Born, A (WB, 1976)	$37,100,000
Star Spangled Rhythm (Par, 1943)	$3,900,000
Star Trek (Par, 1979)	$56,000,000
Star Trek II: Wrath of Khan (Par, 1982)	$40,000,000
Star Trek III: Search for Spock (Par, 1984)	$39,000,000
Star Trek IV: Voyage Home (Par, 1986)	$56,820,070
Star Trek V: Final Frontier (Par, 1989)	$27,100,000
Star Trek VI: Undiscovered Country (Par, 1991)	$36,000,000
Star Wars (Fox, 1977)	$193,777,000
Star Wars 2: "Empire Strikes Back" (Fox, 1980)	$141,672,000
Star Wars 3: "Return of the Jedi" (Fox, 1983)	$169,193,000
Star! (Fox, 1968)	$4,200,000
Starchaser: Legend of Orin (Atl, 1985)	$1,014,083
Starcrash (NW, 1979)	$2,250,000

Title (Distributor, Year Released)	$ Rentals
Stardust Memories (UA, 1980)	$4,103,345
Starman (Col, 1984)	$13,730,000
Stars and Stripes Forever (Fox, 1952)	$3,000,000
Starting Over (Par, 1979)	$19,100,000
State Fair (Fox, 1945)	$4,018,000
State Fair (Fox, 1962)	$3,400,000
State of the Union (MGM, 1948)	$3,500,000
Staying Alive (Par, 1983)	$33,650,000
Staying Together (Hemdale, 1989)	$1,506,000
Steel Magnolias (TriStar, 1989)	$40,000,000
Stella (BV, 1990)	$10,341,000
Stepford Wives, The (Col, 1975)	$4,000,000
Sterile Cuckoo, The (Par, 1969)	$6,400,000
Stewardesses, The (Sherpix, 1970)	$6,878,450
Sting, The (U, 1973)	$78,212,000
Stir Crazy (Col, 1980)	$58,364,420
Stolen Life, A (WB, 1946)	$3,000,000
Stooge, The (Par, 1952)	$3,500,000
Stop Making Sense (Island Alive/Cinecom, 1985)	$2,200,000
Stop! or My Mom Will Shoot (U, 1992)	$12,650,455
Stork Club, The (Par, 1946)	$3,200,000
Story of Adele H. (NW, 1975)	$1,100,000
Story of G.I. Joe, The (UA, 1945)	$3,000,000
Story of Joanna, The (Blueberry Hill, 1975)	$4,000,000
Story of O (AA/Lorimar, 1975)	$4,700,000
Straight Time (WB, 1978)	$4,200,000
Straight out of Brooklyn (Goldwyn, 1991)	$1,200,000
Strange Love of Martha Ivers (Par, 1946)	$3,300,000
Stranger Than Paradise (Goldwyn, 1984)	$1,253,295
Strangers When We Meet (Col, 1960)	$3,200,000
Strategic Air Command (Par, 1955)	$6,000,000
Stratton Story, The (MGM, 1949)	$4,025,035
Straw Dogs (CRC/AIP, 1971)	$4,000,000
Streets Of Fire (U, 1984)	$4,429,845
Streetcar Named Desire, A (WB/UA, 1951)	$4,800,000
Stripes (Col, 1981)	$40,886,590
Stroker Ace (U, 1983)	$8,939,630
Strongest Man in the World, The (BV, 1975)	$6,875,000
Stuck On You (Troma, 1982)	$1,105,000
Student Bodies (Par, 1982)	$3,761,000
Suburban Commando (NL, 1991)	$3,200,000
Sudden Impact (WB, 1983)	$34,800,000
Suddenly Last Summer (Col, 1959)	$6,375,000
Sugarland Express (U, 1974)	$3,169,300
Summer Camp (Borde, 1979)	$1,465,000
Summer Magic (BV, 1963)	$4,000,000
Summer of '42 (WB, 1971)	$20,500,000
Summer Place, A (WB, 1959)	$4,700,000
Summer Rental (Par, 1985)	$10,000,000
Summer School (Paramount, 1987)	$15,748,560
Sun Also Rises, The (Fox, 1957)	$3,000,000
Sundowners, The (WB, 1960)	$3,800,000
Sunshine Boys, The (MGM/UA, 1975)	$6,969,370
Super Fuzz (Emb, 1981)	$1,000,000

Title (Distributor, Year Released)	$ Rentals	Title (Distributor, Year Released)	$ Rentals
Superdad (BV, 1974)	$6,275,000	Tender Trap, The (MGM, 1955)	$3,000,000
Superfly (WB, 1972)	$6,400,000	Tentacles (AIP, 1977)	$2,000,000
Supergirl (TriStar, 1984)	$6,000,000	Tequila Sunrise (WB, 1988)	$19,100,000
Superman (WB, 1978)	$82,800,000	Terminator, The (Orion, 1984)	$16,822,345
Superman II (WB, 1981)	$65,100,000	Terminator 2 (TriStar, 1991)	$112,500,000
Superman III (WB, 1983)	$37,200,000	Terms of Endearment (Par, 1983)	$50,250,000
Supervixens (RM Films, 1975)	$4,000,000	Terror In The Aisles (U, 1984)	$4,015,895
Support Your Local Sheriff (UA, 1969)	$5,190,070	Terror Train (Fox, 1980)	$3,500,000
Sure Thing, The (Embassy, 1985)	$7,943,335	Terror Within, The (Concorde, 1989)	$1,888,255
Survive (Par, 1976)	$6,975,000	Tess (Col, 1980)	$9,869,000
Survivors, The (Col, 1983)	$6,986,820	Testament (Par, 1983)	$1,040,000
Susan Slade (WB, 1961)	$3,000,000	Tex (1982)	$3,500,000
Suspect (TriStar, 1987)	$8,000,000	Texas Across the River (U, 1966)	$4,190,625
Swamp Thing (Emb, 1982)	$2,125,000	Texas Chain Saw Massacre (NL/Castle Hill, 1974)	$14,421,000
Swarm, The (WB, 1978)	$7,700,000	Texas Chainsaw Massacre 2, The (Cannon, 1986)	$2,500,000
Swashbuckler (U, 1976)	$30,000,000	Texas Chainsaw Mass. 3: Leatherface (NL, 1990)	$2,600,000
Sweet Charity (U, 1969)	$4,036,800	Thank God It's Friday (Col, 1978)	$7,800,000
Sweet Dreams (TriStar, 1985)	$4,200,000	That Darn Cat (BV, 1965)	$12,628,000
Sweet Liberty (U, 1986)	$7,642,005	That Touch of Mink (U, 1962)	$7,942,020
Sweet Sweetback's Badass Song (CM, 1971)	$4,100,000	That's Entertainment (MGM/UA, 1974)	$12,083,620
Sweethearts (MGM, 1938)	$3,000,000	That's Entertainment, Pt 2 (MGM/UA, 1976)	$3,000,000
Swimming to Cambodia (Cinecom, 1987)	$1,100,000	That's My Boy (Par, 1951)	$3,800,000
Swing Shift (WB, 1984)	$4,600,000	The Boatniks (BV, 1970)	$9,150,000
Swiss Family Robinson (BV, 1960)	$20,178,000	The Incredible Journey (BV, 1963)	$4,500,000
Sword and the Sorcerer, The (Group 1, 1982)	$11,000,000	Thelma & Louise (MGM/Pathe, 1991)	$20,000,000
Sword in the Stone (BV, 1963)	$10,475,000	There's a Girl in My Soup (Col, 1970)	$4,500,000
Take Her, She's Mine (Fox, 1963)	$3,400,000	There's No Business like Show Bus. (Fox, 1954)	$5,000,000
Take Me Out to the Ball Game (MGM, 1949)	$3,400,000	Therese and Isabelle (Audubon, 1968)	$3,000,000
Take the Money and Run (CRC, 1969)	$3,000,000	They Call Me Bruce (Film Ventures, 1982)	$4,000,000
Take This Job and Shove It (Avemb, 1981)	$8,082,100	They Call Me Trinity (Avemb, 1971)	$1,208,000
Taking of Pelham One Two Three, The (UA, 1974)	$3,800,000	They Shoot Horses Don't They (CRC/AIP, 1969)	$5,980,000
Tall Men, The (Fox, 1955)	$5,000,000	They Were Expendable (MGM, 1945)	$3,200,000
Taming of the Shrew, The (Col, 1967)	$3,600,000	Thief (MGM/UA, 1981)	$4,340,545
Tammy and the Bachelor (U, 1957)	$3,000,000	Thief of Bagdad, The (UA/Kino, 1924)	$3,000,000
Tango & Cash (WB, 1989)	$30,100,000	Thief Of Hearts (Par, 1984)	$5,000,000
Tank (U, 1984)	$7,005,255	Thing, The (U, 1982)	$9,814,580
Taps (Fox, 1981)	$20,500,000	Things Are Tough All Over (Col, 1982)	$9,597,060
Taras Bulba (UA, 1962)	$3,400,000	Thirty Seconds Over Tokyo (MGM, 1944)	$4,471,080
Tarzan, the Ape Man (MGM/UA, 1981)	$15,896,780	This Earth is Mine (U, 1959)	$3,400,000
Taxi Driver (Col, 1976)	$12,569,000	This Is Cinerama (CRC, 1952)	$15,400,000
Teacher, The (Crown, 1974)	$1,400,000	This is Spinal Tap (Emb, 1984)	$2,000,000
Teachers (MGM/UA, 1984)	$11,746,010	This Is The Army (WB, 1943)	$8,500,000
Teahouse of the August Moon (MGM, 1956)	$5,712,000	This Time for Keeps (MGM, 1947)	$3,600,000
Teen Wolf (Atlantic, 1985)	$12,950,000	Thomas Crown Affair, The (UA, 1968)	$6,271,480
Teen Wolf Too (Atl, 1987)	$3,200,000	Thoroughly Modern Millie (U, 1967)	$15,455,260
Teenage Mutant Ninja Turtles (New Line, 1990)	$67,650,000	Those Calloways (BV, 1965)	$3,500,000
Teenage Mutant Ninja Turtles II (New Line, 1991)	$41,900,000	Those Magnifi. Men in Their Flying... (Fox, 1965)	$14,000,000
Teenage Mutant Ninja Turtles III (New Line, 1993)	$21,150,000	Thousands Cheer (MGM, 1944)	$3,500,000
Telefon (MGM/UA, 1977)	$4,278,700	Three Amigos (Orion, 1986)	$19,396,165
Tempest (Col, 1982)	$2,169,000	Three Coins in the Fountain (Fox, 1954)	$5,000,000
10 (Orion/WB, 1979)	$37,000,000	Three Days of the Condor (Par, 1975)	$20,014,000
Ten Commandments, The (Par, 1923)	$4,100,000	Three Fugitives (BV, 1989)	$18,565,530
Ten Commandments, The (Par, 1956)	$43,000,000	Three in the Attic (AiP/FWS, 1968)	$6,000,000
Tender Mercies (U, 1983)	$2,571,000	Three Little Girls in Blue (Fox, 1946)	$3,000,000

Title (Distributor,Year Released)	$ Rentals
Three Men and a Baby (BV, 1987)	$81,313,000
Three Men and a Cradle (Goldwyn, 1986)	$1,041,000
Three Men and a little Lady (BV, 1990)	$37,757,380
Three Musketeers, The (MGM/UA, 1948)	$4,306,875
Three Musketeers, The (Fox, 1974)	$11,434,000
3 Ninjas (BV, 1992)	$11,861,000
Three Ring Circus (Par, 1954)	$3,900,000
Three the Hard Way (AA, 1974)	$3,500,000
Thrill of a Romance (MGM, 1945)	$4,338,460
Thrill of It All, The (U, 1963)	$5,300,590
Throw Momma From the Train (Orion, 1987)	$27,758,310
Thunder and Lightning (Fox, 1977)	$3,100,000
Thunder Road (UA, 1958)	$3,000,000
Thunderball (UA, 1965)	$28,621,435
Thunderbolt and Lightfoot (UA, 1974)	$9,202,170
Tickle Me (AA, 1965)	$3,400,000
Tidal Wave (NW, 1976)	$3,700,000
Tie Me Up! Tie Me Down! (Miramax, 1990)	$1,900,000
Tightrope (WB, 1984)	$22,500,000
Till the Clouds Roll By (MGM, 1946)	$4,761,653
Time After Time (Orion/WB, 1979)	$6,500,000
Time Bandits (Embassy, 1981)	$20,533,500
Time, the Place and the Girl, The (WB, 1947)	$3,400,000
Timerider (Jensen Farley, 1983)	$3,643,510
Timewalker (NW, 1982)	$1,800,000
Tin Drum, The (NW, 1980)	$2,000,000
Tin Men (BV, 1987)	$11,306,000
TNT Jackson (NW, 1975)	$1,300,000
To Be Or Not To Be (Fox, 1983)	$6,000,000
To Catch a Thief (Par, 1955)	$4,500,000
To Each His Own (Par, 1946)	$3,600,000
To Fly (IMAX, 1976)	$20,000,000
To Have and Have Not (WB, 1945)	$3,652,000
To Hell and Back (U, 1955)	$5,799,850
To Kill a Mockingbird (U, 1962)	$7,112,370
To Live And Die In L.A. (MGM/UA, 1985)	$6,593,340
To Sir With Love (Col, 1967)	$19,100,000
Toby Tyler (BV, 1960)	$3,000,000
Tom Horn (WB, 1980)	$4,400,000
Tom Jones (UA/Goldwyn, 1963)	$17,070,000
Tom Sawyer (UA, 1973)	$5,122,220
Tomboy (Crown, 1984)	$2,000,000
Tommy (Col, 1975)	$17,793,000
Tomorrow Is Forever (RKO, 1946)	$3,200,000
Tony Rome (Fox, 1967)	$3,800,000
Tootsie (Col, 1982)	$94,910,000
Top Gun (Par, 1986)	$79,400,000
Top Secret (Par, 1984)	$10,000,000
Topaz (U, 1969)	$3,017,400
Topkapi (UA, 1964)	$3,500,000
Tora! Tora! Tora! (Fox, 1970)	$14,530,000
Torch Song Trilogy (NL, 1988)	$2,500,000
Torchlight (IFM, 1985)	$1,300,000
Torn Curtain (U, 1966)	$6,549,840

Title (Distributor, Year Released)	$ Rentals
Total Recall (TriStar, 1990)	$63,511,050
Touch of Class, A (Avemb, 1973)	$7,795,640
Tough Guys (BV, 1986)	$9,030,000
Tougher Than Leather (NL, 1988)	$1,500,000
Tous les Matins du Monde (Oct Films,1992)	$1,413,000
Towering Inferno, The (Fox/WB, 1974)	$48,838,000
Town That Dreaded Sundown (AIP/FWS, 1976)	$3,500,000
Toxic Avenger, The (Troma, 1985)	$2,500,000
Toy, The (Col, 1982)	$24,440,000
Toys (Fox, 1992)	$10,800,000
Traces of Red (Goldwyn, 1992)	$1,500,000
Trading Places (Par, 1983)	$40,600,000
Train, The (UA, 1964)	$3,500,000
Transylvania 6-5000 (NW, 1986)	$4,550,000
Trapeze (UA, 1956)	$7,269,464
Treasure of Matecumbe (BV, 1976)	$4,713,000
Treasure of the Four Crowns (Cannon, 1983)	$4,450,000
Tree Grows in Brooklyn, A (Fox, 1945)	$3,468,000
Tribute (Fox, 1980)	$4,450,000
Trick or Treat (DEG, 1986)	$3,036,000
Trip to Bountiful (Island, 1986)	$2,900,000
Trip, The (AIP/FWS, 1967)	$5,500,000
Troll (Empire, 1986)	$2,400,000
Tron (BV, 1982)	$16,704,000
Trouble With Angels,The (Col, 1966)	$4,200,000
True Confessions (MGM/UA, 1981)	$5,088,455
True Grit (Par, 1969)	$14,250,000
Truth or Dare (Miramax, 1991)	$5,100,000
Tucker: The Man And His Dreams (Par, 1988)	$8,900,000
Tuff Turf (NW, 1985)	$3,700,000
Tunnelvision (World Wide, 1976)	$4,350,000
Turner & Hooch (BV, 1989)	$35,260,000
Turning Point, The (Fox, 1977)	$17,060,000
Twelve Chairs, The (UMC/UA Classics, 1970)	$3,000,000
Twelve O'Clock High (Fox, 1950)	$3,300,000
20,000 Leagues Under the Sea (BV, 1954)	$11,267,000
Twice in a Lifetime (Yorkin Co, 1985)	$2,000,000
Twilight Zone—The Movie (WB, 1983)	$16,400,000
Twilight's Last Gleaming (AA, 1977)	$4,500,000
Twin Peaks (NL, 1992)	$1,760,000
Twins (U, 1988)	$57,715,130
Two for the Road (Fox, 1967)	$3,000,000
Two Girls and a Sailor (MGM, 1944)	$3,500,000
Two Minute Warning (U, 1976)	$8,394,960
Two Mules for Sister Sara (U, 1970)	$4,638,735
Two of a Kind (Fox, 1983)	$12,000,000
Two Sisters From Boston (MGM, 1946)	$3,600,000
2001: A Space Odyssey (MGM/UA, 1968)	$25,521,920
2010 (MGM/UA, 1984)	$20,186,660
Two Women (Embassy, 1961)	$3,000,000
Two Years Before the Mast (Par, 1946)	$4,400,000
U2 Rattle And Hum (Par, 1988)	$4,100,000
Ugly American, The (U, 1963)	$3,500,000
Ugly Dachshund, The (BV, 1966)	$6,000,000

Title (Distributor, Year Released)	$ Rentals
Unbearabel Lightness of Being (1988)	$4,300,000
Uncle Buck (U, 1989)	$30,335,175
Uncle Tom's Cablin (Indep.-Intl., 1969)	$4,000,000
Uncommon Valor (Par, 1983)	$13,000,000
Unconquered (Par, 1947)	$5,250,000
Undefeated, The (Fox, 1969)	$4,000,000
Under Siege (WB, 1992)	$40,000,000
Under The Cherry Moon (WB, 1986)	$5,800,000
Under The Rainbow (Orion/WB, 1981)	$8,400,000
Under the Yum Yum Tree (Col, 1963)	$5,000,000
Undercurrent (MGM, 1946)	$3,200,000
Unfaithfully Yours (Fox, 1984)	$10,000,000
Unforgiven, The (UA, 1960)	$3,100,000
Unholy, The (Vestron, 1987)	$2,281,415
Unidentified Flying Oddball (BV, 1979)	$4,475,000
Universal Soldier (TriStar, 1992)	$16,000,000
Unlawful Entry (Fox, 1992)	$26,357,000
Unmarried Woman, An (Fox, 1978)	$12,000,000
Unsinkable Molly Brown, The (MGM, 1964)	$6,039,610
Untouchables, The (Par, 1987)	$36,866,530
Up in Arms (RKO, 1944)	$3,344,000
Up in Smoke (Par, 1978)	$28,300,000
Up the Academy (WB, 1980)	$5,100,000
Up the Creek (Orion, 1984)	$4,670,000
Up the Down Staircase (WB/7 Arts, 1967)	$6,250,000
Up the Sandbox (NGP, 1972)	$3,500,000
Uptown Saturday Night (NGP/WB, 1974)	$7,400,000
Urban Cowboy (Par, 1980)	$23,810,000
Used Cars (Col, 1980)	$5,652,000
V.I.P.s, The (MGM, 1963)	$4,681,480
Valachi Papers, The (Col, 1972)	$8,381,540
Valdez Is Coming (UA, 1971)	$3,000,000
Valley Girl (Atlantic, 1983)	$6,400,000
Valley of Decision (MGM, 1945)	$4,566,755
Valley of the Dolls (Fox, 1967)	$20,000,000
Valley of the Dolls, Beyond the (Fox, 1970)	$7,000,000
Vamp (NW, 1986)	$2,100,000
Vampire Playgirls (Compass, 1980)	$1,320,000
Van Nuys Blvd. (Crown, 1979)	$1,750,000
Van, The (Crown, 1977)	$5,000,000
Vanishing Point (Fox, 1971)	$5,004,000
Vanishing Wilderness (PIE, 1973)	$7,395,540
Variety Girl (Par, 1947)	$3,600,000
Venom (Par, 1982)	$2,000,000
Vera Cruz (UA, 1954)	$4,566,755
Verdict, The (Fox, 1982)	$26,650,000
Vertigo (Par/U Classics, 1958)	$5,306,082
Vice Squad (Avemb, 1982)	$5,935,675
Vice Versa (Col, 1988)	$5,771,920
Victor/Victoria (MGM/UA, 1982)	$10,490,315
Victory (Par, 1981)	$4,200,000
Videodrome (U, 1983)	$1,309,000
View to a Kill, A (MGM/UA, 1985)	$25,316,185
Vigilante (FV, 1983)	$2,584,015

Title (Distributor, Year Released)	$ Rentals
Vikings, The (UA, 1958)	$5,282,800
Villain, The (Col, 1979)	$9,883,885
Vincent & Theo (Hemdale, 1990)	$1,032,321
Virginian, The (Par, 1946)	$3,400,000
Vision Quest (WB, 1985)	$5,200,000
Visit to a Small Planet (Par, 1960)	$3,200,000
Visiting Hours (Fox, 1982)	$6,500,000
Viva Las Vegas (MGM, 1964)	$5,152,000
Vixen (RM Films, 1968)	$5,000,000
Volunteers (TriStar, 1985)	$8,900,000
Von Ryan's Express (Fox, 1965)	$7,700,000
Voyage of the Damned (Avemb, 1976)	$1,750,000
W.W. and the Dixie Dance Kings (Fox, 1975)	$7,791,000
Wackiest Ship in the Army, The (Col, 1960)	$3,400,000
Wait Until Dark (WB/7 Arts, 1967)	$7,900,000
Waitress! (Troma, 1982)	$2,500,000
Wake Island (Par, 1942)	$3,500,000
Walk on the Wild Side (Col, 1962)	$3,000,000
Walk, Don't Run (Col, 1966)	$4,000,000
Walking Tall (CRC/AIP/FWS, 1973)	$10,000,000
Walking Tall, Pt 2 (CRC/AIP/FWS, 1975)	$9,400,000
Walking Tall, Final Chapter (AIP, 1977)	$6,350,000
Wall Street (Fox, 1987)	$20,200,000
Wanted: Dead or Alive (NW, 1987)	$2,500,000
War and Peace (Par, 1956)	$6,250,000
War Between Men and Women, The (NGP, 1972)	$3,800,000
War of the Roses, The (Fox, 1989)	$41,400,000
War Wagon, The (U, 1967)	$5,932,520
WarGames (MGM/UA, 1983)	$38,519,835
Warlock (Trimark, 1991)	$4,275,000
Warlords of the 21st Century (NW, 1982)	$1,300,000
Warriors, The (Par, 1979)	$14,500,000
Watership Down (Avemb, 1978)	$3,500,000
Way Down East (UA, 1921)	$3,900,000
Way We Were, The (Col, 1973)	$22,457,000
Wayne's World (Par, 1992)	$54,000,000
We're No Angels (Par, 1955)	$3,000,000
Wedding, A (Fox, 1978)	$3,600,000
Weekend at Bernie's (Fox, 1989)	$14,000,000
Weekend at the Waldorf (MGM, 1945)	$4,366,050
Weekend Pass (Crown, 1984)	$3,750,000
Weird Science (U, 1985)	$10,005,830
Welcome Stranger (Par, 1947)	$6,100,000
West Side Story (UA, 1961)	$19,645,570
Westworld (MGM/UA, 1973)	$7,283,245
What A Way to Go (Fox, 1967)	$6,100,000
What About Bob? (BV, 1991)	$29,282,225
What Do You Say to a Naked Lady? (UA, 1970)	$5,122,620
What Price Glory? (Fox, 1926)	$4,000,000
What's New Pussycat? (UA, 1965)	$8,468,710
What's Up, Doc? (WB, 1972)	$28,000,000
Whatever Happened to Baby Jane (WB, 1962)	$4,050,000
Wheeler Dealers, The (MGM, 1963)	$3,000,000
When a Stranger Calls (Col, 1979)	$10,828,455

Title (Distributor,Year Released)	$ Rentals
When Harry Met Sally... (Col, 1989)	$41,790,000
When My Baby Smiles at Me (Fox, 1948)	$3,400,000
Where Eagles Dare (MGM/UA, 1968)	$7,131,430
Where Love Has Gone (Par, 1964)	$3,500,000
Where The Boys Are (MGM, 1960)	$3,500,000
Where the Buffalo Roam (U, 1980)	$4,189,645
Where There's Life (Par, 1947)	$3,000,000
Where Were You When the Lights ...? (U, 1968)	$3,500,000
Which Way Is Up? (U, 1977)	$8,668,370
White Christmas (Par, 1954)	$12,000,000
White Cliffs of Dover (MGM, 1944)	$4,045,250
White Fang (BV, 1991)	$15,208,000
White Lightning (UA, 1973)	$6,127,400
White Line Fever (Col, 1975)	$7,032,000
White Men Can't Jump (Fox, 1992)	$34,115,000
White Nights (Col, 1985)	$21,130,000
Who Framed Roger Rabbit (BV, 1988)	$81,244,000
Who Is Killing Great Chefs of Eur.? (WB, 1978)	$6,000,000
Who Was That Lady? (Col, 1960)	$3,100,000
Who's Afraid of Virginia Woolf? (WB, 1966)	$14,500,000
Who's That Man? (NL, 1993)	$4,950,000
Wholly Moses (Par, 1980)	$7,692,000
Wifemistress (Quartet, 1979)	$1,300,000
Wild Angels, The (AIP/FWS, 1966)	$7,000,000
Wild at Heart (Goldwyn, 1990)	$6,300,000
Wild Bunch, The (WB, 1969)	$5,300,000
Wild Country, The (BV, 1971)	$4,000,000
Wild Geese, The (AA, 1978)	$3,500,000
Wild in the Streets (AIP/FWS, 1968)	$5,500,000
Wild Life, The (U, 1984)	$4,581,265
Wildcats (WB, 1986)	$13,600,000
Wilderness Family Pt 2, The (PIE, 1978)	$6,723,000
Willard (CRC/AIP/FWS, 1971)	$9,300,000
Willow (MGM/UA, 1988)	$27,835,000
Wilson (Fox, 1944)	$3,103,000
Wind and the Lion, The (MGM/UA, 1975)	$4,858,485
Windwalker (PIE, 1980)	$9,059,655
Wings (Par, 1927)	$3,800,000
Wings of Desire (Orion Classics, 1988)	$1,500,000
Winning (U, 1969)	$6,703,450
Wisdom (1987)	$1,400,000
Wish You Were Here (Atl, 1987)	$1,750,000
Witchboard (Cinema Group, 1987)	$3,211,000
Witches of Eastwick, The (WB, 1987)	$31,800,000
With a Song in My Heart (Fox, 1952)	$3,300,000
With Six You Get Egg Roll (CCF/NGP/WB, 1968)	$4,500,000
Without a Stitch (Harris, 1970)	$3,000,000
Without A Trace (Fox, 1983)	$4,300,000
Without Love (MGM, 1945)	$3,000,000
Without Reservations (RKO, 1946)	$3,000,000
Witness (Par, 1985)	$28,500,000
Witness for the Prosecution (UA, 1957)	$3,800,000
Wiz, The (U, 1978)	$12,264,750
Wizard of Oz, The (MGM/UA/TEC, 1939)	$4,759,890

Title (Distributor, Year Released)	$ Rentals
Wizards (Fox, 1977)	$4,659,000
Wolfen (Orion/WB, 1981)	$4,500,000
Woman in Red, The (Orion, 1984)	$10,976,780
Woman Under the Influence, A (Faces/CH, 1974)	$6,117,815
Woman's World (Fox, 1954)	$3,000,000
Women in Love (UA, 1970)	$3,000,000
Wonder of It All, The (PIE, 1974)	$4,321,000
Wonderful World of Bro.s Grimm (MGM/UA, 1962)	$4,832,040
Woodstock (WB, 1970)	$16,400,000
Words and Music (MGM, 1949)	$3,500,000
Working Girl (Fox, 1988)	$28,600,000
World According to Garp, The (WB, 1982)	$14,700,000
World Apart, A (Atl, 1988)	$1,050,000
World in His Arms, The (U, 1952)	$3,000,000
World of Suzie Wong, The (Par, 1960)	$7,500,000
World's Greatest Athlete, The (BV, 1973)	$12,089,000
World's Greatest Lover, The (Fox, 1977)	$10,645,000
Wraith, The (New Century, 1986)	$1,171,780
Written on the Wind (U, 1956)	$4,282,235
Wuthering Heights (AIP, 1971)	$2,200,000
Xanadu (U, 1980)	$10,942,035
XTRO (NL, 1983)	$1,208,000
Yankee Doodle Dandy (WB, 1942)	$4,719,680
Year Of The Dragon (MGM/UA, 1985)	$7,331,890
Yearling, The (MGM, 1946)	$5,567,820
Yellow Rolls-Royce, The (MGM, 1965)	$4,646,645
Yellow Submarine (UA, 1969)	$3,700,000
Yentl (MGM/UA, 1983)	$19,680,130
Yesterday, Today and Tomorrow (Avemb, 1964)	$4,100,000
You Light Up My Life (Col, 1977)	$8,386,000
You Only Live Twice (UA, 1967)	$19,388,690
You're Never Too Young (Par, 1955)	$3,400,000
Young Doctors in Love (Fox, 1982)	$15,200,000
Young Frankenstein (Fox, 1975)	$38,823,000
Young Guns (Fox, 1988)	$19,960,000
Young Guns II (Fox, 1990)	$19,700,000
Young Lions, The (Fox, 1958)	$4,480,000
Young Sherlock Holmes (Par, 1985)	$8,700,000
Youngblood (AIP, 1978)	$1,000,000
Yours, Mine and Ours (UA, 1968)	$11,639,245
Z (C5, 1969)	$7,100,000
Zapped (Embassy, 1982)	$7,255,675
Zelig (WB/Orion, 1983)	$6,800,000
Ziegfeld Follies (MGM, 1946)	$3,599,300
Zombie (Jerry Gross, 1980)	$1,925,000
Zorba the Greek (Fox, 1964)	$4,400,000
Zorro, The Gay Blade (Fox, 1981)	$5,100,000

Abbreviations used for Film Distributors

AA: Allied Artists
AC or ACR: American Cinema Releasing
AFD: Associated Film Distribution
Almi: Almi Pictures
AIP: American International Pictures
Anal: Analysis
Atl: Atlantic Releasing
Ave: Avenue Pictures
Avemb: Avco Embassy
BV: Buena Vista
Can: Cannon
CI: Compass International
C 5 or Cine V: Cinema Five
Cinem.: Cinemation
CG: Cinema Group
CRC: Cinerama Releasing Corporation
Col: Columbia Pictures
Crw: Crown International Pictures
DEG: De Laurentiis Entertainment
    Group

Dimen: Dimension
Emb: Embassy
FL: Fine Line
Fox: Twentieth Century Fox
FV: Film Ventures International
FWS: Filmworld Studios
Gldwyn: Samuel Goldwyn Company
IFI: IFI Releasing
IFM: International Film Marketing
Isl: Island
JF or JFP: Jensen Farley Pictures
JG: Jerry Gross
MB: Marvin Distribution
MGM: Metro Goldwyn Mayer
Mira: Miramax International
MPM: MPM Pictures
NC: New Century
NGP: National General Corporation
NYer: New Yorker
NL: New Line Cinema
NW: New World International

Oct Fm: October Films
Parli: Parliament Releasing
PIE: Pacific International Entertainment
Par: Paramount Pictures
Pres: Prestige
RKO: RKO Radio
RM: RM Films International
Shap/Glick: Shapiro/Glickenhaus
    Entertainment
Tri: Trimark Pictures
TWE: Trans World Entertainment
U: Universal Pictures
UA: United Artists
UFD: United Film Distribution
Ves: Vestron
WB : Warner Brothers

How Film Rentals Relate to Box Office Gross

Film rentals are the portion of the film's box office gross that the exhibitors (theater owners) pay to the film's distributor for renting the film for viewing in their theaters. The rental figure does not include taxes and is the amount paid after the theater owner takes several deductions which include his percentage and his house nut (house operating expenses).

Many first time producers are surprised to find out that the average rental figure a distributor receives is an amount equal to less than 50% of the gross. This amount can vary from 40% to 65% according to the contract. An eagerly anticipated film with huge stars and strong box office potential or a sequel to an immense blockbuster can leverage a much better contract hence a larger percentage of the gross. A movie that has no stars from a small distributor with little box office potential gravitates to the low end of the percentage spectrum.

An example of this can be seen in how the original *Home Alone* compares with *Empire Strikes Back* (See Section 1: Top 150 Blockbusters). The original *Home Alone* comedy had a little known star in Macaulay Culkin and was made for a very modest budget (by studio standards). If you compare its reported box office gross with its reported rental figure ($281,493,907 to $140,099,000) you'll see it retained only 49% of it's gross. Now compare *Empire Strikes Back*, ($223,000,000 to $141,672,000) a high budgeted sequel following an established blockbuster, eargerly anticipated by the public and you'll see it retained 63.5% of its gross. Twentieth Century Fox was able to leverage a much better deal because it had a very valuable commodity and every theater owner competing for its use knew it.

If you find *Home Alone II,* and notice its numbers you will find it retained 59% of its gross ($172,667,450 to $102,000,000) the next time around because it was a sequel to a proven product with a known audience.

Another reason why large blockbuster movies have a higher rental to gross average is because the house nut is a constant figure not varying. The larger the audience and more gross per week, translates to a larger sum for the theater owners and distributors to split up after the house nut is deducted. And the split always favors the distributors (by sometimes as much as a 90/10 split) over the exhibitors. This also applies if the exhibitor first takes his percentage out and then deducts the nut.

Industry Statistics

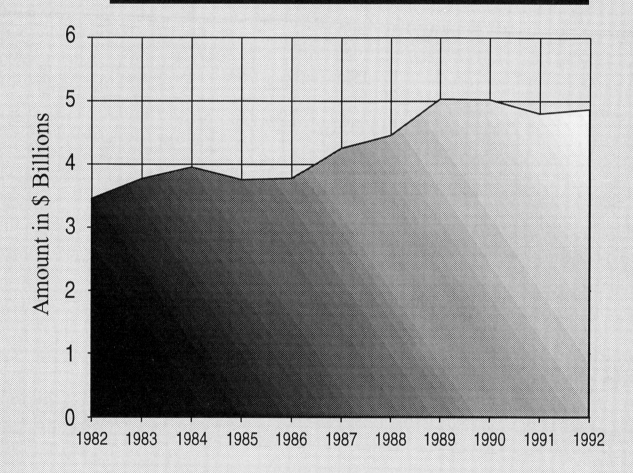

Domestic Box Office Gross

Amount in $ Billions

1982 1983 1984 1985 1986 1987 1988 1989 1990 1991 1992

*United States and Canada

1992 Gross: $4,871,000,000
+ 1.4% from 1991
+ 41.1% since 1982

Movie Attendance

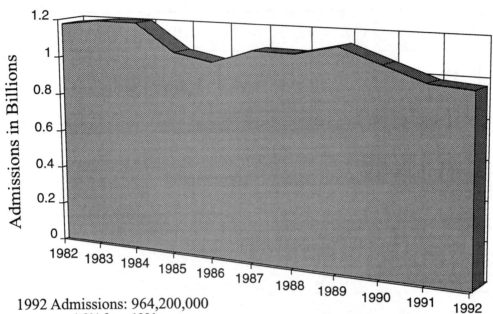

1992 Admissions: 964,200,000
-1.8% from 1991
-18% since 1982.

Average Admission Price

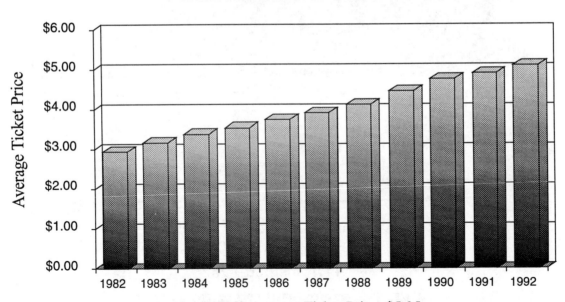

1992 Average Ticket Price: $5.05
+3.3% from 1991
+72% since 1982

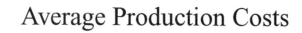

Average Production Costs

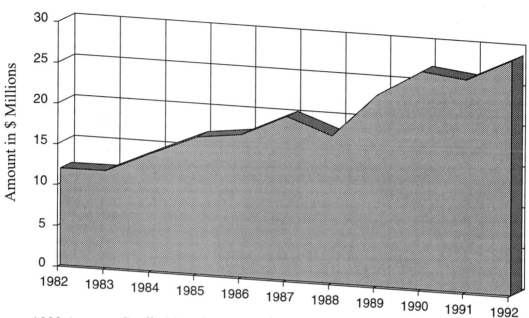

1992 Average Studio Negative Costs: $28,858,300
+10.4% from 1991
+143.5% since 1982

Average Prints and Advertising Costs

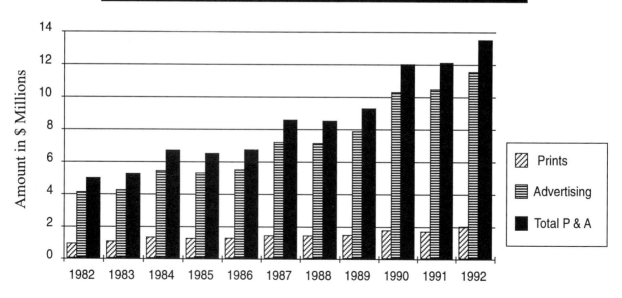

1992 Average Studio P&A Costs: $13,456,000
+11.5% from 1991
+172.6% since 1982

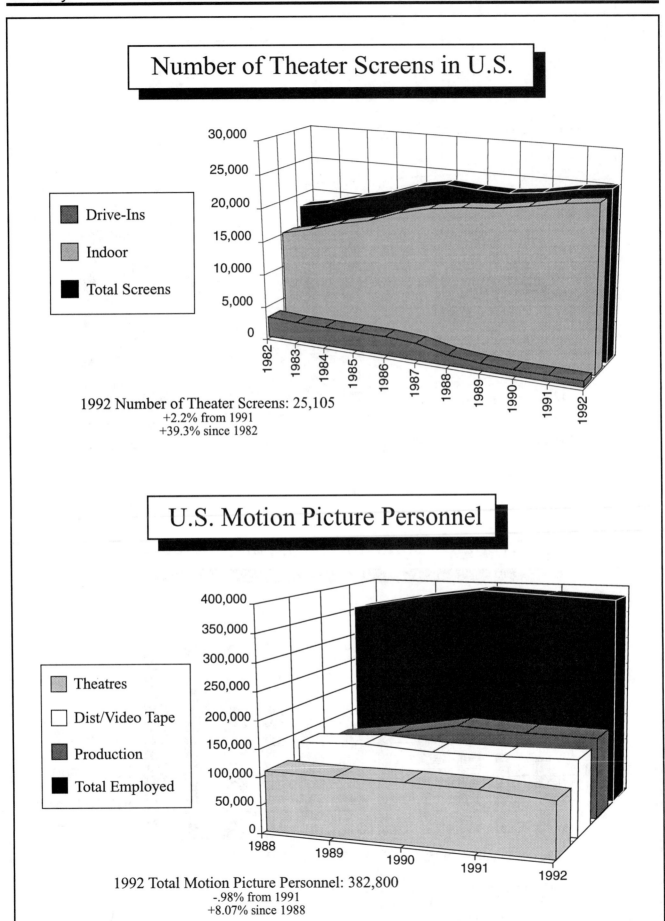

Number of Theater Screens in U.S.

Drive-Ins

Indoor

Total Screens

30,000
25,000
20,000
15,000
10,000
5,000
0

1982 1983 1984 1985 1986 1987 1988 1989 1990 1991 1992

1992 Number of Theater Screens: 25,105
+2.2% from 1991
+39.3% since 1982

U.S. Motion Picture Personnel

Theatres

Dist/Video Tape

Production

Total Employed

400,000
350,000
300,000
250,000
200,000
150,000
100,000
50,000
0

1988 1989 1990 1991 1992

1992 Total Motion Picture Personnel: 382,800
-.98% from 1991
+8.07% since 1988

     This five year study consists of films released from 6/1/88 through 6/30/93 and uses reported domestic (United States and Canada) box office figures through 10/4/93. The additional three months added to the release window was used to give films released in June of 1993 time to amass the greatest portion of their box office potential. In this manner a truer sense of averages used in this section can be obtained.

     Although there were many more films released than the 1,385 films used in this survey, it is estimated that 91% or more of the box office gross attributed to this time frame is accounted for by these films. The unaccounted 9% is a conservative estimate attributed to films not tracked (such as pornography) or films that had such a limited release or earned such an insignificant gross that they did not report.

     The total reporting gross for films used in this study is $22,020,756,906.

Qualifications for

Top Directors: Only live-action directed features were considered (no animation).

Top Actors: Must have acted in two or more films in the five year period; must have been considered a starring lead in at least one of the movies they appeared in; no voice-over or animation films are considered as part of their totals which include every movie they've appeared in except for minor cameo roles (such as in "The Player").

Top Actresses: Must have acted in two or more films in the five year period; must have been considered a starring lead in at least one of the movies they appeared in; no voice-over or animation films are considered as part of their totals which include every movie they've appeared in except for minor cameo roles (such as in "The Player").

"Average Per Movie Rank" is limited to comparing only those already on the list.

Top 50 Films

*** Still in release

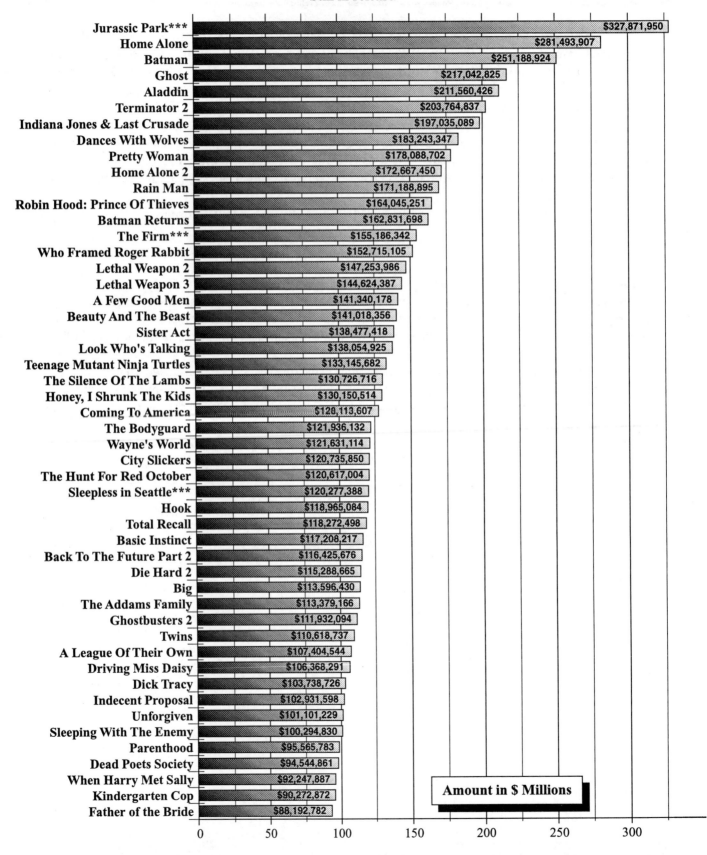

Film	Amount
Jurassic Park***	$327,871,950
Home Alone	$281,493,907
Batman	$251,188,924
Ghost	$217,042,825
Aladdin	$211,560,426
Terminator 2	$203,764,837
Indiana Jones & Last Crusade	$197,035,089
Dances With Wolves	$183,243,347
Pretty Woman	$178,088,702
Home Alone 2	$172,667,450
Rain Man	$171,188,895
Robin Hood: Prince Of Thieves	$164,045,251
Batman Returns	$162,831,698
The Firm***	$155,186,342
Who Framed Roger Rabbit	$152,715,105
Lethal Weapon 2	$147,253,986
Lethal Weapon 3	$144,624,387
A Few Good Men	$141,340,178
Beauty And The Beast	$141,018,356
Sister Act	$138,477,418
Look Who's Talking	$138,054,925
Teenage Mutant Ninja Turtles	$133,145,682
The Silence Of The Lambs	$130,726,716
Honey, I Shrunk The Kids	$130,150,514
Coming To America	$128,113,607
The Bodyguard	$121,936,132
Wayne's World	$121,631,114
City Slickers	$120,735,850
The Hunt For Red October	$120,617,004
Sleepless in Seattle***	$120,277,388
Hook	$118,965,084
Total Recall	$118,272,498
Basic Instinct	$117,208,217
Back To The Future Part 2	$116,425,676
Die Hard 2	$115,288,665
Big	$113,596,430
The Addams Family	$113,379,166
Ghostbusters 2	$111,932,094
Twins	$110,618,737
A League Of Their Own	$107,404,544
Driving Miss Daisy	$106,368,291
Dick Tracy	$103,738,726
Indecent Proposal	$102,931,598
Unforgiven	$101,101,229
Sleeping With The Enemy	$100,294,830
Parenthood	$95,565,783
Dead Poets Society	$94,544,861
When Harry Met Sally	$92,247,887
Kindergarten Cop	$90,272,872
Father of the Bride	$88,192,782

Amount in $ Millions

0   50   100   150   200   250   300

Distributors

Box Office Rank	Distributor	Total Box Office Gross	Box Office Share	Average Per Movie	Average Per Movie Rank	Total Films Released	G	PG	PG-13	R	NC-17	NR
1	Buena Vista	$3,471,293,277	15.76%	$35,786,529	2	97	16	31	24	24	0	2
2	Warner Bros.	$3,324,124,253	15.09%	$27,025,400	6	123	1	28	34	60	0	0
3	Universal	$2,982,918,295	13.54%	$32,074,390	3	93	3	23	26	39	1	1
4	Paramount	$2,807,686,302	12.75%	$36,463,458	1	77	1	9	29	36	0	2
5	20th Century Fox	$2,445,237,077	11.10%	$29,109,965	5	84	2	7	24	50	0	1
6	TriStar	$1,798,099,435	8.16%	$30,476,262	4	59	0	10	13	36	0	0
7	Columbia	$1,772,028,544	8.04%	$21,876,896	8	81	3	17	22	38	0	1
8	Orion	$936,325,108	4.25%	$19,108,676	9	49	1	10	14	24	0	0
9	New Line	$671,430,759	3.04%	$10,829,528	11	62	1	11	8	41	0	1
10	UA	$377,772,753	1.71%	$26,983,768	7	14	1	1	4	8	0	0
11	MGM	$360,566,948	1.63%	$8,584,927	13	42	0	5	10	25	0	2
12	Miramax	$279,777,259	1.27%	$4,440,909	16	63	0	9	5	28	0	21
13	Goldwyn	$138,323,521	0.62%	$4,068,339	17	34	1	3	2	16	0	12
14	Triumph	$82,807,285	0.37%	$3,600,317	18	23	0	6	4	13	0	0
15	Cannon	$47,003,349	0.21%	$2,043,624	20	23	1	1	3	17	0	1
16	Orion Classics	$45,951,589	0.20%	$1,584,538	22	29	1	10	5	11	0	2
17	Fine Line	$33,949,418	0.15%	$1,476,062	23	23	0	1	1	16	1	4
18	Hemdale	$33,583,420	0.15%	$1,158,049	25	29	1	2	6	19	0	1
19	Sony Classics	$31,809,896	0.14%	$5,301,649	15	6	0	3	2	1	0	0
20	MGM/UA	$30,680,096	0.13%	$1,614,742	21	19	0	0	1	15	0	3
21	Galaxy	$29,411,011	0.13%	$14,705,506	10	2	0	0	0	2	0	0
22	Trimark	$21,094,092	0.09%	$2,109,409	19	10	0	1	1	6	1	1
23	Interstar	$21,034,159	0.09%	$7,011,386	14	3	0	0	0	3	0	0
24	Avenue	$20,469,409	0.09%	$1,462,101	24	14	0	2	5	7	0	0
25	Dimension	$19,515,947	0.08%	$9,757,974	12	2	0	0	0	2	0	0
	All Others Dist.	$237,863,704	1.08%	$734,147		324	1	21	35	140	3	124
Totals		$22,020,756,906	100.00%			1385	34	211	278	677	6	179

NR (Not Rated) movies are almost all reissues of older movies (before the code) by the major studios. Some smaller distributors released movies that did not report box office and therefore their totals may be slightly higher.

	Majors	**Mini-Majors**	**Independents**
	8% or more share of marketplace; Buena Vista, Warner Bros., Universal, Paramount, 20th Century Fox, TriStar and Columbia.	1%-8% share of the Marketplace; Orion, MGM/UA (MGM, UA and MGM/UA), New Line, Miramax.	Less than 1% share of the martketplace; all others.
Number of Movies Released	614	249	522
Average Gross Per Release	$30,295,419	$10,668,887	$1,524,553
% which grossed under $1 million	9.77%	31.73%	68.39%
% which grossed under $5 Million	23.29%	61/04%	92.15%
% which grossed under $10 Million	36.64%	72.29%	95.98%
% which grossed under $20 Million	57%	83.53%	99.23%
% which grossed over $50 Million	19.38%	3.21%	0%
% which grossed over $75 Million	10.59%	2%	0%
% which grossed over $100 Million	6.68%	1.6%	0%
% which grossed over $125 Million	3.42%	1.6%	0%
% which grossed over $150 Million	2.12%	.8%	0%
% which grossed over $200 Million	.98%	0%	0%

Top Directors

Box Office Rank	Director	Total Box Office Gross	# of Movies Released	Average Per Movie	Average Per Movie Rank	Last Film Released in Study
1	Steven Spielberg	$683,578,478	4	$170,894,620	3	Jurassic Park
2	Chris Columbus	$479,459,387	4	$119,864,847	6	Home Alone 2
3	Tim Burton	$468,176,193	3	$156,058,731	4	Batman Returns
4	Robert Zemeckis	$414,047,092	4	$103,511,773	9	Death Becomes Her
5	Richard Donner	$356,351,714	4	$89,087,929	13	Radio Flyer
6	Ivan Reitman	$320,530,572	4	$80,132,643	20	Dave
7	John McTiernan	$296,372,568	4	$74,093,142	24	Last Action Hero
8	Rob Reiner	$295,221,813	3	$98,407,271	10	A Few Good Men
9	Penny Marshall	$272,571,487	3	$90,857,162	12	A League of their Own
10	Renny Harlin	$268,573,453	4	$67,143,363	30	Cliffhanger
11	James Cameron	$258,028,924	2	$129,014,462	5	Terminator 2
12	Barry Levinson	$257,305,739	4	$64,326,435	32	Toys
13	Garry Marshall	$256,535,048	3	$85,511,683	16	Frankie & Johnny
14	Paul Verhoeven	$235,480,715	2	$117,740,358	7	Basic Instinct
15	Ron Howard	$231,996,561	3	$77,332,187	21	Far and Away
16	Emile Ardolino	$225,898,519	3	$75,299,506	23	Sister Act
17	Jerry Zucker	$216,818,693	1	$216,818,693	1	Ghost
18	Amy Heckerling	$184,657,201	2	$92,328,601	11	Look Who's Talking Too
19	Kevin Costner	$183,243,347	1	$183,243,347	2	Dances with Wolves
20	Oliver Stone	$177,733,804	4	$44,433,451	58	JFK
21	Joe Johnston	$176,702,370	2	$88,351,185	14	The Rocketeer
22	Francis Ford Coppola	$168,677,193	3	$56,225,731	39	Bram Stroker's Dracula
23	David Zucker	$164,762,967	2	$82,381,484	17	The Naked Gun 2 1/2
24	Kevin Reynolds	$164,153,497	2	$82,076,749	18	Robin Hood: Prince of Theives
25	Sydney Pollack	$163,734,389	2	$81,867,195	19	The Firm
26	Frank Oz	$163,429,414	3	$54,476,471	43	Housesitter
27	Tony Scott	$157,126,316	3	$52,375,439	45	Last Boy Scout
28	John Landis	$156,590,441	3	$52,196,814	47	Innocent Blood
29	Joel Schumacher	$156,174,217	4	$39,043,554	64	Falling Down
30	Jim Abrahams	$152,162,873	4	$38,040,718	66	Hot Shots! Part Deux
31	Jonathan Demme	$152,033,192	2	$76,016,596	22	The Silence of the Lambs
32	Mick Jackson	$150,805,929	3	$50,268,643	48	The Bodyguard
33	Mike Nichols	$142,642,651	3	$47,547,550	51	Regarding Henry
34	Ron Shelton	$141,799,608	3	$47,266,536	53	White Men Can't Jump
35	Steve Barron	$139,739,639	2	$69,869,820	28	Teenage Mutant Ninja Turtles
36	Ron Underwood	$136,210,915	2	$68,105,458	29	City Slickers
37	Bruce Beresford	$135,124,317	5	$27,024,863	85	Rich In Love
38	Walter Hill	$134,994,972	4	$33,748,743	72	Trespass
39	Martin Scorsese	$132,165,067	3	$44,055,022	59	Cape Fear
40	Adrian Lyne	$131,908,756	2	$65,954,378	31	Indecent Proposal
41	Phillip Noyce	$128,248,795	5	$25,649,759	87	Sliver
42	Roger Spottiswoode	$127,590,077	3	$42,530,026	60	Stop! Or My Mom Will Shoot
43	Clint Eastwood	$126,003,186	4	$31,500,797	75	Unforgiven
44	John Badham	$124,790,189	3	$41,596,730	63	Point of No Return
45	Peter Weir	$124,299,030	2	$62,149,515	33	Green Card
46	Nora Ephron	$122,118,958	2	$61,059,479	34	Sleepless in Seattle
47	Penelope Spheeris	$122,004,857	2	$61,002,429	35	Wayne's World
48	Spike Lee	$121,765,387	4	$30,441,347	76	Malcolm X
49	Stephen Herek	$115,765,342	3	$38,588,447	65	The Mighty Ducks
50	Roger Donaldson	$113,481,052	3	$37,827,017	67	White Sands

Box Office Rank	Director	Total Box Office Gross	# of Movies Released	Average Per Movie	Average Per Movie Rank	Last Film Released in Study
51	Barry Sonnenfield	$113,379,166	1	$113,379,166	8	The Addams Family
52	Phil Alden Robinson	$112,756,051	2	$56,378,026	38	Sneakers
53	Alan J. Pakula	$112,200,808	3	$37,400,269	68	Consenting Adults
54	John G. Avildsen	$111,548,842	4	$27,887,211	83	Power of One
55	Randal Kleiser	$109,297,983	4	$27,324,496	84	Honey, I Blew Up the Kid
56	Joseph Ruben	$109,008,538	2	$54,504,269	42	Sleeping With the Enemy
57	Jonathan Lynn	$107,566,449	3	$35,855,483	70	My Cousin Vinny
58	Danny DeVito	$107,395,953	2	$53,697,977	44	Hoffa
59	Herbert Ross	$104,973,763	3	$34,991,254	71	True Colors
60	Martin Brest	$100,287,060	2	$50,143,530	49	Scent of a Woman
61	Curtis Hanson	$100,138,852	2	$50,069,426	50	Hand That Rocks the Cradle
62	Ridley Scott	$96,336,924	3	$32,112,308	73	1492: Conquest of Paradise
63	Richard Benjamin	$95,131,178	4	$23,782,795	90	Made in America
64	Jeremiah Chechik	$94,589,796	2	$47,294,898	52	Benny & Joon
65	John Hughes	$93,848,629	2	$46,924,315	54	Curly Sue
66	Andrew Davis	$93,827,355	2	$46,913,678	55	Under Siege
67	Reginald Hudlin	$93,045,005	2	$46,522,503	56	Boomerang
68	Jonathan Kaplan	$91,370,646	4	$22,842,662	91	Unlawful Entry
69	Frank Marshall	$89,493,814	2	$44,746,907	57	Alive
70	Charles Shyer	$88,192,752	1	$88,192,752	15	Father of the Bride
71	Joe Dante	$85,761,258	3	$28,587,086	81	Matinee
72	Howard A. Zieff	$84,989,211	2	$42,494,606	61	My Girl
73	David S. Ward	$83,305,789	2	$41,652,895	62	King Ralph
74	Neil Jordan	$82,411,350	4	$20,602,838	94	The Crying Game
75	Lawrence Kasdan	$78,162,587	3	$26,054,196	86	Grand Canyon
76	Mary Lambert	$74,560,595	2	$37,280,298	69	Pet Sematary Two
77	Kenneth Branagh	$72,826,895	4	$18,206,724	96	Much Ado About Nothing
78	Barbra Streisand	$72,705,397	1	$72,705,397	25	The Prince of Tides
79	Michael Mann	$72,155,275	1	$72,155,275	26	The Last of the Mohicans
80	Steve Miner	$71,729,653	3	$23,909,884	89	Forever Young
81	Harold Ramis	$70,835,374	1	$70,835,374	27	Groundhog Day
82	Michael Apted	$69,966,670	5	$13,993,334	99	Thunderheart
83	Stephen Frears	$64,636,825	3	$21,545,608	92	Hero
84	Andrei Konchalovsky	$63,999,671	3	$21,333,224	93	The Inner Circle
85	Barbet Schroeder	$63,459,168	2	$31,729,584	74	Single White Female
86	Eddie Murphy	$60,857,262	1	$60,857,262	36	Harlem Nights
87	Sidney Lumet	$60,488,018	5	$12,097,604	100	Guilty As Sin
88	Nick Castle	$60,370,165	2	$30,185,083	77	Dennis the Menace
89	John Flynn	$59,691,874	3	$19,897,291	95	Watch It
90	Christopher Cain	$58,502,281	2	$29,251,141	78	Pure Country
91	Harold Becker	$57,415,695	2	$28,707,848	79	Sea of Love
92	Geoff Murphy	$57,291,562	2	$28,645,781	80	Freejack
93	Brian Lebant	$56,970,868	1	$56,970,868	37	Beethoven
94	Andrew Bergman	$56,476,021	2	$28,238,011	82	Honeymoon in Vegas
95	John Singleton	$56,128,283	1	$56,128,283	40	Boyz N the Hood
96	David Fincher	$54,780,116	1	$54,780,116	41	Alien 3
97	Jon Amiel	$53,084,251	3	$17,694,750	97	Sommersby
98	William Shatner	$52,206,498	1	$52,206,498	46	Star Trek 5
99	Tom Holland	$51,471,649	3	$17,157,216	98	The Temp
100	Terry Gilliam	$49,904,529	2	$24,952,265	88	The Fisher King

Top Actors

Box Office Rank	Actor	Total Box Office Gross	# of Movies Released	Average Per Movie	Average Per Movie Rank	Last Film Released in Study
1	Joe Pesci	$782,989,236	8	$97,873,655	2	The Public Eye
2	Tom Cruise	$755,871,628	7	$107,981,661	1	The Firm
3	John Heard	$752,814,155	12	$62,734,513	19	Home Alone 2
4	Kevin Costner	$667,916,489	7	$95,416,641	3	The Bodyguard
5	Christopher Lloyd	$578,038,530	11	$52,548,957	32	Dennis the Menace
6	Arnold Schwarzenegger	$552,342,581	6	$92,057,097	5	Last Action Hero
7	John Candy	$526,533,137	12	$43,877,761	43	Once Upon A Crime
8	Tom Hanks	$526,189,873	9	$58,465,541	23	Sleepless in Seattle
9	Mel Gibson	$508,452,006	7	$72,636,001	14	Lethal Weapon 3
10	Michael Keaton	$488,856,393	6	$81,476,066	7	Batman Returns
11	Sam Neill	$474,112,781	6	$79,018,797	8	Jurassic Park
12	Harrison Ford	$470,830,571	5	$94,166,114	4	Patriot Games
13	Morgan Freeman	$465,576,975	10	$46,557,698	40	Unforgiven
14	Rick Moranis	$451,871,872	7	$64,553,125	18	Splitting Heirs
15	Dustin Hoffman	$440,741,778	6	$73,456,963	13	Hero
16	Sean Connery	$435,152,785	8	$54,394,098	29	Medicine Man
17	Jack Nicholson	$429,314,709	5	$85,862,942	6	A Few Good Men
18	Dan Aykroyd	$414,037,383	11	$37,639,762	55	Chaplin
19	Danny Glover	$400,330,029	8	$50,041,254	35	Lethal Weapon 3
20	Steve Martin	$390,632,764	8	$48,829,096	37	Leap of Faith
21	Gene Hackman	$384,760,159	13	$29,596,935	69	The Firm
22	Bruce Willis	$383,154,262	9	$42,572,696	48	Death Becomes Her
23	Eddie Murphy	$382,903,536	5	$76,580,707	10	The Distinguished Gentleman
24	Keanu Reeves	$373,958,537	10	$37,395,854	56	Much Ado About Nothing
25	Danny DeVito	$354,534,783	6	$59,089,131	22	Jack the Bear
26	Jeff Goldblum	$347,790,857	7	$49,684,408	36	Jurassic Park
27	Bob Hoskins	$347,274,950	9	$38,586,106	53	Super Mario Bros.
28	Christian Slater	$346,927,548	12	$28,910,629	70	Untamed Heart
29	Robin Williams	$340,774,271	6	$56,795,712	25	Toys
30	Robert De Niro	$339,959,716	14	$24,282,837	80	Mad Dog and Glory
31	Bill Murray	$332,466,570	6	$55,411,095	26	Mad Dog and Glory
32	Al Pacino	$322,810,317	6	$53,801,720	30	Scent of a Woman
33	Patrick Swayze	$314,843,222	6	$52,473,870	33	City of Joy
34	Michael J. Fox	$312,849,612	6	$52,141,602	34	Life with Mikey
35	Michael Douglas	$308,765,311	5	$61,753,062	21	Falling Down
36	Harvey Keitel	$306,541,509	11	$27,867,410	72	Point of No Return
37	Nick Nolte	$302,985,737	9	$33,665,082	63	Lorenzo's Oil
38	John Goodman	$288,275,770	11	$26,206,888	78	Matinee
39	Richard Geer	$284,149,126	6	$47,358,188	39	Sommersby
40	Macaulay Culkin	$276,468,319	4	$69,117,080	15	Home Alone 2
41	Alan Rickman	$275,640,026	8	$34,455,003	61	Bob Roberts
42	Wesley Snipes	$274,876,347	9	$30,541,816	65	Boiling Point
43	Alec Baldwin	$270,376,164	10	$27,037,616	75	Glengarry Glen Ross
44	Charlie Sheen	$270,319,243	10	$27,031,924	76	Hot Shots! Part Deux
45	Kurt Russell	$260,928,653	6	$43,488,109	44	Unlawful Entry
46	Sylvester Stallone	$258,902,690	6	$43,150,448	45	Cliffhanger
47	Anthony Hopkins	$258,713,113	6	$43,118,852	46	Bram Stroker's Dracula
48	Kevin Kline	$242,796,174	8	$30,349,522	67	Dave
49	Kevin Bacon	$237,641,576	7	$33,948,797	62	A Few Good Men
50	Woody Harrelson	$232,611,649	3	$77,537,216	9	Indecent Proposal

Box Office Rank	Actor	Total Box Office Gross	# of Movies Released	Average Per Movie	Average Per Movie Rank	Last Film Released in Study
51	Billy Crystal	$229,938,466	4	$57,484,617	24	Mr. Saturday Night
52	Lloyd Bridges	$228,427,917	6	$38,071,320	54	Hot Shots! Part Deux
53	Ed Harris	$223,423,523	6	$37,237,254	57	The Firm
54	River Phoenix	$222,062,570	5	$44,412,514	41	My Own Private Idaho
55	Edward Furlong	$221,182,510	3	$73,727,503	12	American Heart
56	Bill Pullman	$220,513,755	8	$27,564,219	74	Sommersby
57	Steven Seagal	$211,919,286	4	$52,979,822	31	Under Siege
58	Chevy Chase	$210,977,384	8	$26,372,173	77	Memoirs of An Invisible Man
59	William Baldwin	$208,191,172	5	$41,638,234	49	Sliver
60	Andy Garcia	$207,580,462	7	$29,654,352	68	Jennifer Eight
61	Emillio Estevez	$195,533,750	6	$32,588,958	64	Nat'l Lamp. Loaded Weapon 1
62	Gary Elwes	$191,098,712	4	$47,774,678	38	The Crush
63	John Travolta	$188,105,986	3	$62,701,995	20	Shout
64	Kiefer Sutherland	$187,287,478	10	$18,728,748	92	The Vanishing
65	Randy Quaid	$183,991,593	9	$20,443,510	90	Texasville
66	Richard Dreyfuss	$182,418,707	8	$22,802,338	84	Lost in Yonkers
67	James Belushi	$181,194,712	10	$18,119,471	95	Traces of Red
68	Tommy Lee Jones	$179,078,095	5	$35,815,619	58	House of Cards
69	Charles Grodin	$176,897,166	4	$44,224,292	42	Dave
70	Clint Eastwood	$173,735,015	5	$34,747,003	59	Unforgiven
71	Laurence Fishburne	$173,514,000	7	$24,787,714	79	What's Love Got to Do W/It
72	William Defoe	$173,446,650	10	$17,344,665	96	Body of Evidence
73	Martin Short	$172,760,814	5	$34,552,163	60	Captain Ron
74	Ray Liotta	$171,019,498	4	$42,754,875	47	Unlawful Entry
75	Christopher Walken	$169,775,794	6	$28,295,966	71	Mistress
76	Leslie Nielsen	$166,139,028	3	$55,379,676	27	The Naked Gun 2 1/2
77	Robert Redford	$165,675,437	3	$55,225,146	28	Indecent Proposal
78	Gary Oldman	$165,086,299	8	$20,635,787	89	Bram Stoker's Dracula
79	Chris O'Donnell	$164,442,240	4	$41,110,560	50	School Ties
80	Tom Selleck	$162,775,439	7	$23,253,634	81	Mr. Baseball
81	Danny Aiello	$158,121,115	11	$14,374,647	99	The Pickle
82	Ted Danson	$157,831,363	4	$39,457,841	51	Made in America
83	Gary Busey	$155,981,516	4	$38,995,379	52	Under Siege
84	John Lithgow	$154,153,751	7	$22,021,964	86	Cliffhanger
85	Liam Neeson	$152,902,618	11	$13,900,238	100	Ethan Frome
86	Warren Beatty	$152,830,288	2	$76,415,144	11	Bugsy
87	Jean-Claude Van Damme	$149,779,351	7	$21,397,050	87	Nowhere to Run
88	Denzel Washington	$145,630,239	8	$18,203,780	94	Much Ado About Nothing
89	Tom Berenger	$143,043,659	7	$20,434,808	91	Sniper
90	James Caan	$139,208,051	5	$27,841,610	73	Honeymoon in Vegas
91	Robert Duvall	$137,613,590	6	$22,935,598	82	Falling Down
92	Anthony Quinn	$137,050,996	6	$22,841,833	83	Last Action Hero
93	Alan Arkin	$135,827,974	6	$22,637,996	85	Indian Summer
94	Rob Lowe	$134,257,157	2	$67,128,579	16	Wayne's World
95	Tim Robbins	$133,641,094	8	$16,705,137	98	Bob Roberts
96	Dana Carvey	$132,156,619	2	$66,078,310	17	Wayne's World
97	Joe Mantegna	$129,312,529	7	$18,473,218	93	Queens Logic
98	Bryan Brown	$124,340,625	6	$20,723,438	88	Blame it on the Bellboy
99	Spike Lee	$121,765,387	4	$30,441,347	66	Malcolm X
100	Fred Ward	$119,883,878	7	$17,126,268	97	Equinoz

Top Actresses

Box Office Rank	Actress	Total Box Office Gross	# of Movies Released	Average Per Movie	Average Per Movie Rank	Last Film Released in Study
1	Julia Roberts	$584,725,463	7	$83,532,209	3	Hook
2	Demi Moore	$510,544,491	7	$72,934,927	4	Indecent Proposal
3	Whoopi Goldberg	$503,385,874	10	$50,338,587	12	Made in America
4	Laura Dern	$350,094,307	5	$70,018,861	5	Jurassic Park
5	Meg Ryan	$324,475,315	6	$54,079,219	8	Sleepless in Seattle
6	Sigourney Weaver	$321,865,353	6	$53,644,226	9	Dave
7	Michelle Pfeiffer	$319,233,887	8	$39,904,236	28	Love Field
8	Kim Basinger	$318,175,800	5	$63,635,160	7	Final Analysis
9	Valeria Golino	$294,474,160	7	$42,067,737	21	Hot Shot! Part Deux
10	Mary Eliza. Mastrantonia	$277,143,259	7	$39,591,894	29	Consenting Adults
11	Jeannie Tripplehorn	$273,570,566	3	$91,190,189	2	The Night We Never Met
12	Mary McDonnell	$266,528,413	4	$66,632,103	6	Sneakers
13	Jodie Foster	$245,148,450	6	$40,858,075	24	Sommersby
14	Madonna	$242,368,216	6	$40,394,703	26	Body of Evidence
15	Laura San Giacomo	$238,692,469	7	$34,098,924	33	Where the Day Takes You
16	Rene Russo	$237,851,391	5	$47,570,278	15	Lethal Weapon 3
17	Bridget Fonda	$233,716,178	11	$21,246,925	66	Point of No Return
18	Anabella Sciorra	$227,159,802	9	$25,239,978	50	The Night We Never Met
19	Kathy Bates	$220,375,724	9	$24,486,192	54	Used People
20	Geena Davis	$219,294,685	6	$36,549,114	32	Hero
21	Linda Hamilton	$219,120,150	2	$109,560,075	1	Terminator 2
22	Goldie Hawn	$218,540,631	5	$43,708,126	19	Death Becomes Her
23	Penelope Ann Miller	$218,487,453	9	$24,276,384	55	Gun in Betty Lou's Handbag
24	Holly Hunter	$212,563,881	5	$42,512,776	20	The Firm
25	Lea Thompson	$209,291,957	4	$52,322,989	10	Article 99
26	Bette Midler	$196,187,701	6	$32,697,950	35	For the Boys
27	Elizabeth Perkins	$195,461,887	6	$32,576,981	36	Indian Summer
28	Mary Steenburgen	$193,174,228	4	$48,293,557	13	The Butcher's Wife
29	Winona Ryder	$192,156,086	6	$32,026,014	37	Bram Stroker's Dracula
30	Rebecca DeMornay	$191,701,135	5	$38,340,227	30	Hand that Rocks the Cradle
31	Rachel Ticotin	$191,464,683	4	$47,866,171	14	Falling Down
32	Annette Bening	$190,860,853	7	$27,265,836	46	Regarding Henry
33	Nancy Travis	$187,456,582	7	$26,779,512	48	The Vanishing
34	Laura Flynn Boyle	$183,141,765	9	$20,349,085	67	The Temp
35	Jamie Lee Curtis	$180,984,600	4	$45,246,150	16	Forever Young
36	Melanie Griffith	$174,579,804	7	$24,939,972	52	Born Yesterday
37	Nicholle Kidman	$166,426,933	5	$33,285,387	34	Flirting
38	Anjelica Huston	$165,044,121	7	$23,577,732	59	The Addams Family
39	Sharon Stone	$164,095,231	4	$41,023,808	22	Sliver
40	Glenne Headly	$163,562,087	4	$40,890,522	23	Mortal Thoughts
41	Diane Keaton	$162,828,662	4	$40,707,166	25	Father of the Bride
42	Madeleine Stowe	$157,449,810	6	$26,241,635	49	The Last of the Mohicans
43	Sally Field	$152,430,815	4	$38,107,704	31	Soapdish
44	Patsy Kensit	$150,643,193	5	$30,128,639	40	Blame iton the Bellboy
45	Andie MacDowell	$147,595,380	5	$29,519,076	43	Groundhog Day
46	Kelly Lynch	$147,133,266	6	$24,522,211	53	Three of Hearts
47	Jennifer Jason Leigh	$143,738,115	8	$17,967,264	71	Single White Female
48	Lorraine Bracco	$143,332,052	8	$17,916,507	73	Traces of Red
49	Shirley MacLaine	$140,095,166	5	$28,019,033	44	Used People
50	Mary Stuart Masterson	$136,327,179	6	$22,721,197	62	Benny & Joon

Box Office Rank	Actress	Total Box Office Gross	# of Movies Released	Average Per Movie	Average Per Movie Rank	Last Film Released in Study
51	Amy Madigan	$135,678,476	3	$45,226,159	17	The Dark Half
52	Daryl Hannah	$135,362,486	6	$22,560,414	63	Memoirs of an Invisible Man
53	Meryl Streep	$134,466,380	5	$26,893,276	47	Death Becomes Her
54	Susan Sarandon	$130,336,543	8	$16,292,068	77	Lorenzo's Oil
55	Barbara Hershey	$127,456,326	9	$14,161,814	83	Splitting Heirs
56	Kathleen Turner	$125,793,230	4	$31,448,308	39	House of Cards
57	Greta Scacchi	$119,786,888	5	$23,957,378	56	The Player
58	Rosie Perez	$118,746,878	4	$29,686,720	42	Untamed Heart
59	Mercedes Reuhl	$117,087,627	6	$19,514,605	70	Last Action Hero
60	Jessica Lange	$107,690,059	6	$17,948,343	72	Night and the City
61	Beverly DeAngelo	$105,282,921	6	$17,547,154	74	Man Trouble
62	Dolly Parton	$101,129,804	2	$50,564,902	11	Straight Talk
63	Emma Thompson	$99,180,893	6	$16,530,149	76	Much Ado About Nothing
64	Diane Ladd	$98,131,642	5	$19,626,328	69	Carnosaur
65	Kim Cattrall	$95,614,512	4	$23,903,628	57	Split Second
66	Anne Archer	$94,688,570	4	$23,672,143	58	Patriot Games
67	Uma Thurman	$94,244,940	6	$15,707,490	78	Mad Dog and Glory
68	Karen Allen	$92,355,471	4	$23,088,868	61	The Sandlot
69	Janine Turner	$88,695,191	2	$44,347,596	18	Cliffhanger
70	Kristie Alley	$88,639,790	4	$22,159,948	64	Sibling Rivalry
71	Kristy Swanson	$86,645,137	4	$21,661,284	65	Buffy the Vampire Slayer
72	Ellen Barkin	$85,995,422	6	$14,332,570	82	This Boy's Life
73	Miranda Richardson	$83,244,962	3	$27,748,321	45	Damage
74	Isabella Rossellini	$80,114,586	2	$40,057,293	27	Death Becomes Her
75	Lolita Davidovich	$78,197,644	6	$13,032,941	85	Boiling Point
76	Sissy Spacek	$75,144,684	3	$25,048,228	51	Hard Promises
77	Marisa Tomei	$70,057,689	3	$23,352,563	60	Untamed Heart
78	Sarah Jessica Parker	$64,047,234	2	$32,023,617	38	Honeymoon in Vegas
79	Phoebe Cates	$63,719,177	5	$12,743,835	86	Bodies, Rest & Motion
80	Sean Young	$62,793,141	6	$10,465,524	92	Once Upon a Crime
81	Christine Lahti	$61,792,087	5	$12,358,417	90	Leaving Normal
82	Kelly Preston	$60,111,856	4	$15,027,964	79	Run
83	Jennifer Tilly	$59,689,508	4	$14,922,377	80	Made in America
84	Dana Delaney	$59,527,699	2	$29,763,850	41	Light Sleeper
85	Jennifer Connelly	$59,090,288	4	$14,772,572	81	The Rocketeer
86	Mimi Rodgers	$51,004,430	6	$8,500,738	95	White Sands
87	Kate Capshaw	$50,702,845	3	$16,900,948	75	My Heroes Have Al. Been Cow.
88	Debra Winger	$50,541,934	4	$12,635,484	88	Leap of Faith
89	Rosanne Arquette	$49,799,733	4	$12,449,933	89	Nowhere to Run
90	Mia Farrow	$49,341,069	6	$8,223,512	97	Husbands and Wives
91	Joanne Whalley-Kilmer	$44,738,704	7	$6,391,243	100	Storyville
92	Ally Sheedy	$40,764,763	3	$13,588,254	84	Only the Lonely
93	Lily Tomlin	$40,185,628	2	$20,092,814	68	Search for Intelli. Signs of Life
94	Ellen Burstyn	$38,030,827	3	$12,676,942	87	The Cemetary Club
95	Courteney Cox	$34,874,400	3	$11,624,800	91	The Opposite Sex
96	Maria Conchito Alonso	$29,238,317	3	$9,746,106	93	McBain
97	Samatha Mathis	$23,832,214	3	$7,944,071	98	Super Mario Bros.
98	Lesley Ann Warren	$22,513,027	3	$7,504,342	99	Pure Country
99	Sandra Bernhard	$18,406,255	2	$9,203,128	94	Hudson Hawk
100	Lena Olin	$16,994,032	2	$8,497,016	96	Havana

Average Number of Releases per Month

January 16.8	April 24.2	July 19	October 27.8
February 21.6	May 24.2	August 25.6	November 25.6
March 27	June 15.3	September 24.8	December 22

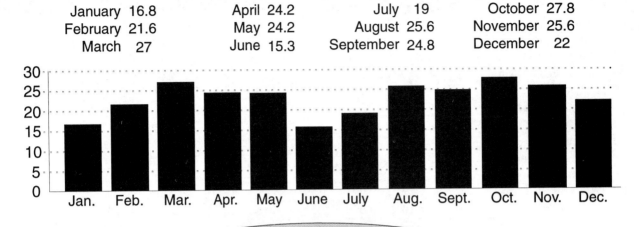

Tracking the Film Ratings

Ratings	# of Movies Released	% of Total Released	Total Box Office Gross	% of Box Office Gross	Average per Movie		Average Days in Release
G	34	2.45%	$1,020,782,277	4.63%	$30,023,008	1	109.62
PG	211	15.23%	$5,385,356,363	24.45%	$25,523,016	2	95.75
PG-13	278	20.07%	$5,787,206,284	26.28%	$20,817,289	3	75.56
R	677	48.88%	$9,587,231,969	43.53%	$14,161,347	4	70.44
NC-17	6	0.43%	$15,944,990	0.07%	$2,657,498	5	82.83
NR	179	12.92%	$224,235,023	1.01%	$1,252,710	6	98.29
Totals	1385		$22,020,756,906	100.00%	Average per Film Rank		

G: General Audiences; All Ages Admitted.

PG: Parental Guidance Suggested; Some Material May Not Be Suitable For Children.

PG-13: Parents Strongly Cautioned; Some Material May be inappropriate for Children Under 13.

R: Restricted; Under 17 Requires Accompanying Parent or Adult Guardian.

NC-17: No Children Under 17 Admitted.

NR: A movie not rated by the MPAA (Motion Picture Association of America)

Releases by Genre

Drama 33.07%

Comedy 25.78%

Action 13.86%

Mys/Sus/Thriller 7%

Horror 6.57%

Sci-Fi/Fantasy 4.12%

Animated 2.89%

Documentary 2.53%

Musicals 1.81%

Family 1.59%

Westerns .51%

All Others .27%

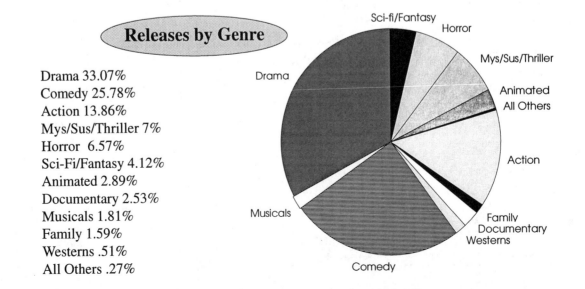

Many observers consider "Premiere Magazine" to be "*the*" magazine in the motion picture industry. Since 1990 in their May issue they have published an annual power list of those in control of the magic in Hollywood. The following represents the 1993 rankings as well as positions from the previous years. Viewing the listing as a whole one can see how some power mongers are seated firmly, others steadily climbing or how many others are but mere flickers in the insatiable flame. ****Indicates not listed in that year.

Rank	92	91	90	Person	Job Description
1	3	6	8 & 55	**Bob Daly/ Terry Semel**	Charman/CEO and President/ COO, Warner Bros.
2	2	2	3	**Michael Eisner**	Chairman/CEO, Walt Disney Company.
3	1	1	1	**Michael Ovitz**	CAA Shogun; King of pop (Creative Artists Agency)
4	5	10	11	**Peter Guber**	Chairman/CEO, Sony Pictures Entertainment.
5	4	****	****	**Rupert Murdoch**	Chairman/CEO, News Corporation.
6	8	9	42	**Stanley Jaffe**	President/COO, Paramount Communications.
7	17	14	87	**Kevin Costner**	Actor/Producer/Director/Dreamboat.
8	10	13	20	**Arnold Schwarzenegger**	Master of the Universe.
9	9	5	7	**Jeffrey Katzenberg**	Chairman, Walt Disney Studios.
10	13	****	****	**Mark Canton**	Chairman, Columbia Pictures.
11	83	73	42	**Sherry Lansing**	Chairman, Paramount Pictures.
12	11	7	9	**Tom Pollock**	Chairman, MCA Motion Picture Group.
13	16	12	12	**Steven Spielberg**	Wunderkind.
14	18	26	66	**Rob Reiner**	King of Castle Rock.
15	25	15	41	**John Hughes**	Writer/Director/Producer.
16	20	17	22	**Jeff Berg**	Chariman/CEO, ICM (International Creative Mgmt.)
17	21	19	23	**Ron Meyer**	Number two man, CAA.
18	23	16	15	**Tom Cruise**	Matinee idol.
19	12	8	16	**Joe Roth**	Producer? Studio Chief ? (Disney)
20	27	34	69	**Tim Burton**	Director from another planet.
21	29	90	****	**James Cameron**	Fully Funded Visionary.
22	22	25	31	**Ron Howard**	Director/Producer/Nice Guy.
23	37	40	46	**Mel Gibson**	Hunk.
24	26	32	35	**Oliver Stone**	Provocateur.
25	30	31	33	**Joel Silver**	Demolition Man. (producer)
26	49	****	****	**Scott Rudin**	Packager-producer supreme.
27	82	****	****	**Jonathan Dolgen**	President motion picture group, Sony Pictures Ent.
28	14	18	19	**Mike Medavoy**	Chairman, TriStar.
29	****	****	****	**Peter Chernin**	Chairman, Twentieth Century Fox Film Corp.
30	19	11	28	**David Geffen**	Self-made billionaire gossip.
31	28	29	18	**Larry Gordon**	Producer-san.
32	50	****	****	**Paul Verhoeven**	Auteur of sex and violence. (director)
33	72	93	****	**Penny Marshall**	Director.
34	52	****	****	**Jodie Foster**	Triple threat.
35	36	39	52	**Robin Williams**	Chameleon.
36	51	****	****	**Robert Zemeckis**	Back-to-the-Futurist writer-director.
37	80	92	****	**John McTiernan**	Action director whether he likes it or not.
38	44	49	36	**Jack Nicholson**	Best supporting actor.
39	32	38	****	**Julia Roberts**	Troubled princess.

Rank	92	91	90	Person	Job Description
40	56	74	****	**Arnon Milchan**	Owner of Regency Enterprises.
41	34	37	53	**Harrison Ford**	Carpenter-star.
42	****	99	88	**Clint Eastwood**	Vindicated director-star.
43	75	60	40	**Robert Redford**	Actor, Director, film-festival sponsor.
44	45	77	89	**Barbra Streisand**	Diva, Inc.
45	47	71	****	**Martin Scorsese**	Auteur (Director).
46	48	24	26	**James L. Brooks**	Producer-director.
47	76	88	****	**Richard Donner**	Director-producer.
48	53	100	****	**Kit Culkin/Macaulay**	Big Mack Daddy. (father of Macaulay Culkin)
49	31	27	44	**Michael Douglas**	Enduring Star.
50	****	86	96	**Steven Seagal**	Actor/would-be director.
51	33	23	24	**Jake Bloom**	Attorney-adviser to the (male, muscled) stars.
52	****	****	****	**Sean Connery**	Superstar emeritus for hire.
53	54	33	37	**Ivan Reitman**	Popmeister (director/producer).
54	****	****	****	**Sharon Stone**	Instant star.
55	62	****	****	**Francis Ford Coppola**	Cooperative former genius.
56	46	35	39	**Barry Levinson**	Heartbroken would-be visionary. (director/producer)
57	35	41	43	**Danny DeVito**	Actor-director-producer.
58	24	22	17	**Eddie Murphy**	Former Comedian?
59	41	36	25	**Jack Rapke**	Directors agent; cohead of picture division, CAA.
60	59	61	61	**Ed Limato**	Last of the old-time agents. (ICM)
61	77	43	34	**Sylvester Stallone**	Star, rewriter.
62	61	83	93	**Robert Shaye**	CEO, New Line Cinema.
63	****	****	86	**Kathleen Kennedy/Frank Marshall**	Producing team, with directing sideline.
64	66	56	27	**Barry Hirsch**	Shrink-attorney.
65	40	44	45	**Warren Beatty**	Auteur-hubby.
66	60	58	47	**Bert Fields**	Litigator-pulp novelist (under the name D. Kincaid).
67	****	****	****	**Wesley Snipes**	Great black hope.
68	67	62	****	**Marty Bauer**	President, United Talent Agency.
69	96	20	21	**Mario Kassar**	Carolco boss.
70	43	54	70	**James Robinson**	Morgan Creek mogul.
71	****	****	****	**Lowell Ganz/Babaloo Mandel**	Screenwriters.
72	57	****	****	**David and Jerry Zucker**	Producers-directors-brothers.
73	74	78	****	**Andy Vajna**	Cinergi mogul.
74	86	95	****	**Jim Wiatt**	President, ICM.
75	39	55	56	**Robert W. Cort**	Producer. (President, Interscope Communications)
76	63	63	62	**Rick Nicita**	Cohead of motion picture division, CAA.
77	73	51	32	**Sydney Pollack**	Director-producer-actor.
78	79	42	****	**Bruce Willis**	Self-enchanted actor.
79	69	79	29	**Ray Stark**	Hollywood's Cardinal Richelieu.
80	****	66	71	**Alan Ladd, Jr.**	Cochairman and CEO, MGM, such as it is.
81	71	67	82	**Spike Lee**	Auteur-troublemaker.
82	****	****	****	**Adrian Lyne**	Slick director.
83	****	****	****	**Joe Eszterhas**	Spec-script king.
84	****	****	****	**Harvey and Bob Weinstein**	The Miramax brothers.
85	55	****	****	**Brian Grazer**	Cheerleader-producer.
86	88	47	59	**David Hoberman**	Touchstone boss.
87	****	****	****	**Michael Kuhn**	CEO, PolyGram film division.
88	68	68	91	**Mike Nichols**	Director.
89	90	****	****	**Bruce Berman**	President of production, Warner Bros.
90	87	84	****	**Jay Moloney and The Young Turks**	CAA's next generation.
91	****	****	****	**Ismail Merchant/James Ivory**	Producer and director, respectively.
92	****	****	****	**Whoopi Goldberg**	Actress.

Rank	92	91	90	Person	Job Description
93	97	97	79	**Arnold Rifkin**	Head of motion picture division, William Morris.
94	****	****	****	**Michael Crichton**	Novelist, screenwriter, reformed director.
95	94	98	85	**The Media**	Pests and sycophants.
96	****	****	****	**Larry Estes**	Sr. VP of equity acquisitions, Col.\ TriStar Home Video.
97	****	****	****	**Stephen King**	Uber-novelist.
98	92	****	****	**Billy Crystal**	Comic actor.
99	****	****	****	**Lorne Michaels**	Sketch-comedy alchemist, producer.
100	****	****	****	**Whitney Houston**	Diva-in-development.
****	6	3	4	**Barry Diller**	Entrepeneur-in-Waiting.
****	7	4	6	**Sid Sheinberg**	President/COO, MCA Inc.
****	15	****	****	**Brandon Tartikoff**	Paramount Pictures head.
****	38	52	38	**Ted Field**	Owner, Interscope Communications
****	42	45	49	**Peter Dekom**	Lawyer.
****	58	57	50	**Dustin Hoffman**	Difficult actor.
****	64	30	13	**Jon Peters**	Lone wolf. (producer)
****	65	****	****	**Skip Brittenham**	Lawyer.
****	70	69	67	**Steve Martin**	Writer, actor.
****	78	65	65	**Bruce Ramer**	Lawyer.
****	81	91	83	**Woody Allen**	Writer, director, actor.
	84	64	95	**Rosalie Swedlin**	Agent (CAA) turned independent producer.
****	85	81	84	**Sam Cohn**	Vice chairman, ICM.
****	89	48	58	**Ricardo Mestres**	President, Hollywood Pictures.
****	91	46	57	**Casey Silver**	Production president, Universal Pictures.
****	93	82	80	**Bill Block**	Founding partner, InterTalent.
****	95	53	14	**Don Simpson/Jerry Buckheimer**	Producers.
****	98	****	****	**Francois Gille**	Deputy General Manager, Credit Lyonnais.
****	99	****	****	**John Singleton**	Writer, director.
****	100	****	****	**Stanley Kubrick**	Auteur in exile.
****	****	21	78	**Frank Price**	Chairman, Columbia Pictures.
****	****	28	10	**Frank Mancuso**	Chairman, Paramount.
****	****	50	****	**David Kirkpatrick**	Copresident, Paramount Pictures.
****	****	59	51	**Tom Hanks**	Actor, nice guy.
****	****	70	****	**Bill Bernstein**	Executive vice president, Orion.
****	****	72	72	**George Lucas**	Mogul in absentia.
****	****	75	74	**Cher**	Being Cher.
****	****	76	****	**Robert De Niro**	Actor, producer, role model.
****	****	80	****	**Harvey Weinstein**	Cochairman, Miramax Films.
****	****	85	60	**Richard D. And Lili Fini Zanuck**	Producers.
****	****	87	****	**Garry Marshall**	Director.
****	****	89	76	**Bette Midler**	Disney diva.
****	****	94	****	**Michelle Pfeiffer**	Actress, producer, fantasy woman.
****	****	96	****	**Meryl Streep**	Brilliant, unbankable actress; industry gadfly.
****	****	****	2	**Lew Wasserman**	CEO, MCA
****	****	****	5	**Steve Ross**	Chairman, Time Warner.
****	****	****	30	**Ken Liffren**	Lawyer.
****	****	****	48	**Bill Murray**	Actor.
****	****	****	54	**Sid Ganis**	Marketing, Paramount.
****	****	****	63	**Paula Wagner**	Agent.
****	****	****	64	**Peter Benedek**	Agency head, Bauer Benedek.
****	****	****	68	**Dan Melnick**	Producer.
****	****	****	73	**Michael Keaton**	Actor.
****	****	****	75	**Morton Franklow**	Literary agent.
****	****	****	77	**Lawrence Kasdan**	Screenwriter, director, producer.

Rank	92	91	90	Person	Job Description
****	****	****	81	Jerry Weintraub	Entertainment Group.
****	****	****	90	Barry Gordon	President, SAG
****	****	****	92	Chevy Chase	Actor.
****	****	****	94	Larry Brezner	Agent.
****	****	****	97	Alex the Madam	Hollywood prostitution ring.
****	****	****	98	Swifty Lazar	Literary agent/ Oscar party.
****	****	****	99	Jack Valenti	Head of MPAA (Motion Picture Assoc. of America)
****	****	****	100	Screenwriter du jour	Brief power.

Job descriptions are from the latest year ranked.

About the Awards

Academy Awards

Award: Statuette, "The Oscar".

Who Votes: the members of the Academy of Motion Picture Arts and Sciences (approximately 4,610).

When & how they vote: first nominating ballots are sent out the second week in January. Each branch within the Academy nominates its own members. They are sent a ballot listing films that are eligible for nomination and they select 5 choices in order of preference for each category. Nominations are then tallied and announced the second week in February. The final ballot listing all categories is voted on by the entire membership and is sent out the third week in February. The final ballot is due the week before the awards ceremony.

Winners are announced: at the awards ceremony.

The awards ceremony: traditionally a Monday night either the third or fourth week in March. It has been held the last few years at either the Dorothy Chandler Pavilion or the Shrine Auditorium in Los Angeles.

Cannes Film Festival

Award: Best Film receives an actual golden palm, "Palme d'Or".

Who votes: the festival is held during the last days of May and a jury is selected by the director of the festival and his advisors. The jury consists of 7-10 members normally famous persons inside the film industry. They vote on movies entered in the festival and decide the major award winners.

Winners are announced: the last night of the festival.

The awards ceremony: traditionally on a Monday, the twelfth day and last night of the festival. Held at the Palias des Festivale in Cannes, France. The "best picture" winner is screened afterwards.

Directors Guild of America

Award: Gold Medallion with DGA emblem.

Who Votes: Members of the Directors Guild of America (approximately 9,960).

When & how they vote: first ballots are mailed to the membership the first week in January (they nominate five in each category). The five nominees for each category are announced the last Monday in January. The final ballot is immediately mailed and is due by the end of February (the week before the ceremony).

Winners are announced: at the awards ceremony.

The awards ceremony: traditionally the first or second week in March (generally two award ceremonies are held concurrently; one in Los Angeles at Beverly Hilton Hotel and one at the World Trade Center in New York).

Golden Globe Awards

Award: Golden Statuette, "Golden Globe".

Who votes: Members of the Hollywood Press Corps (approximately 90).

When & how they vote: nominating ballots are sent out to the membership the second week in December. Nominations are announced the fourth week in December. Final Ballots are sent out the first week in January and due the 18th of January.

Winners are announced: at the awards ceremony.

The awards ceremony: traditionally held at the Beverly Hilton Hotel on the third Saturday night in January.

Independent Feature Project /West

Award: Statuette, "Spirit Award".

Who votes: The members of the Independent Feature Project/West (approximately 5,000).

When & how they vote: A nomination committee (chosen by the board of directors by membership suggestion) of eleven nominates five choices in each category. A ballot is mailed out at the end of February and the members vote for one choice from each category. A win is determined by simple majority vote.

Winners are announced: at the awards ceremony.

The awards ceremony: the weekend before the Academy Awards. Locations change regularly (in 1993 it was held in a pavilion on Santa Monica Beach).

Los Angeles Film Critics Association

Award: plaque (brass on wood)

Who votes: its members who are the top film critics in the Los Angeles area (approximately 35).

When & how they vote: a meeting of all members occurs the second week in December and at that time they nominate categories by weighted rounds of casting points (3pt, 2pt, 1pt for first, second or third respectively in each category). Then the points are tallied and a vote by show of hands on the top two contenders in each category decides the winners.

Winners are announced: immediately after their meeting (second week in December).

The awards ceremony: is held on the third Tuesday in January.

National Society of Film Critics

Award: certificate (mailed to the winners).

Who votes: approximately 36 top film critics across the United States.

When & how they vote: ballots are sent out mid December and a membership meeting is held on the first Saturday or Sunday in January after the New Year's Weekend. Mail-in ballots are tabulated in with the attending members' vote on the first round of voting only. Each round requires members to pick their top three choices in a weighted ballot system (top choice gets three points, second gets two points, third gets one point). After the tabulation of both the mail-in vote and the attending members vote then another open ballot is cast by the attending members. Winners must appear on a plurality of ballots.

Winners are announced: after the meeting to the press.

The awards ceremony: none is held but the meeting is traditionally held at the Algonquin Hotel in New York.

New York Film Critics Circle

Who votes: approximately 25 film critics from New York Daily Newspapers, the weekly Village Voice, the national newsweeklies and other major New York publications.

When & how they vote: a membership meeting is held at the Newspaper Guild in New York on the third Thursday in December.

Winners are announced: after the meeting to the press.

Writers Guild of America

Award: plaque (brass on wood)

Who votes: the members of the Writers Guild of America (approximately 7,000).

When & how they vote: during the third week in January the first round nominating ballots are sent out to the membership. They nominate five choices for each category and their nominations are announced at the beginning of February Final ballots are sent out the third week in February and members vote for one choice in each category.

Winners are announced: at the awards ceremony.

The awards ceremony: traditionally held at the Beverly Hilton Hotel in Los Angeles on the twentieth of March.

Academy Awards Quick List

Year	Best Picture	Best Director
1993	Unforgiven	Clint Eastwood "Unforgiven"
1992	The Silence of the Lambs	Jonathan Demme "The Silence of the Lambs"
1991	Dances With Wolves	Kevin Costner "Dances With Wolves"
1990	Driving Miss Daisy	Oliver Stone "Born on the Fourth of July"
1989	Rain Man	Barry Levinson "Rain Man"
1988	The Last Emperor	Bernardo Bertolucci "The Last Emperor"
1987	Platoon	Oliver Stone "Platoon"
1986	Out of Africa	Sydney Pollack "Out of Africa"
1985	Amadeus	Milos Forman "Amadeus"
1984	Terms of Endearment	James L. Brooks "Terms of Endearment"
1983	Gandhi	Richard Attenborough "Gandhi"
1982	Chariots of Fire	Warren Beatty "Reds"
1981	Ordinary People	Robert Redford "Ordinary People"
1980	Kramer vs. Kramer	Robert Benton "Kramer vs. Kramer"
1979	The Deer Hunter	Michael Cimino "The Deer Hunter"
1978	Annie Hall	Woody Allen "Annie Hall"
1977	Rocky	John G. Avildsen "Rocky"
1976	One Flew Over the Cuckoo's Nest	Milos Forman "One Flew Over the Cuckoo's Nest"
1975	The Godfather, Part II	Francis Ford Coppola "The Godfather, Part II"
1974	The Sting	George Roy Hill "The Sting"
1973	The Godfather	Bob Fosse "Cabaret"
1972	The French Connection	William Friedkin "The French Connection"
1971	Patton	Franklin J. Shaffner "Patton"
1970	Midnight Cowboy	John Schlesinger "Midnight Cowboy"
1969	Oliver!	Carol Reed "Oliver!"
1968	In the Heat of the Night	Mike Nichols "The Graduate"
1967	A Man for All Seasons	Fred Zinnemann "A Man for All Seasons"
1966	The Sound of Music	Robert Wise "The Sound of Music"
1965	My Fair Lady	George Cukor "My Fair Lady"
1964	Tom Jones	Tony Richardson "Tom Jones"
1963	Lawrence of Arabia	David Lean "Lawrence of Arabia"
1962	West Side Story	Robert Wise & Jerome Robbins "West Side Story"
1961	The Apartment	Billy Wilder "The Apartment"
1960	Ben-Hur	William Wyler "Ben-Hur"
1959	Gigi	Vincente Minnelli "Gigi"
1958	The Bridge on the River Kwai	David Lean "The Bridge on the River Kwai"
1957	Around the World in 80 Days	George Stevens "Giant"
1956	Marty	Delbert Mann "Marty"
1955	On the Waterfront	Elia Kazan "On the Waterfront"
1954	From Here to Eternity	Fred Zinnemann "From Here to Eternity"
1953	The Greatest Show on Earth	John Ford "High Noon"
1952	An American in Paris	George Stevens "A Place in the Sun"
1951	All About Eve	Joseph L. Mankiewicz "All About Eve"
1950	All the King's Men	Joseph L. Mankiewicz "A Letter to Three Wives"
1949	Hamlet	John Huston "Treasure of Sierra Madre"
1948	Gentleman's Agreement	Elia Kazan "Gentleman's Agreement"
1947	The Best Years of Our Lives	William Wyler "The Best Years of Our Lives"
1946	The Lost Weekend	Billy Wilder "The Lost Weekend"
1945	Going My Way	Leo McCarey "Going My Way"

Academy Awards Quick List

Year	Best Picture	Best Director
1944	Casablanca	Michael Curtiz "Casablanca"
1943	Mrs. Miniver	William Wyler "Mrs. Miniver"
1942	How Green Was My Valley	John Ford "How Green Was My Valley"
1941	Rebecca	John Ford "The Grapes of Wrath"
1940	Gone With the Wind	Victor Fleming "Gone With the Wind"
1939	You Can't Take It with You	Frank Capra "You Can't Take It with You"
1938	The Life of Emile Zola	Leo McCarey "The Awful Truth"
1937	The Great Ziegfeld	Frank Capra "Mr. Deeds Goes to Town"
1936	Mutiny on the Bounty	John Ford "The Informer"
1935	It Happened One Night	Frank Capra "It Happened One Night"
1934	Cavalcade	Frank Lloyd "Cavalcade"
1933	Grand Hotel	Frank Borzage "Bad Girl"
1932	Cimarron	Norman Taurog "Skippy"
1931	All Quiet on the Western Front	Lewis Milestone "All Quiet on the Western Front"
1930	The Broadway Melody	Frank Lloyd "The Divine Lady"
1929	Wings	Frank Borzage "Seventh Heaven"

Year	Best Actor	Best Actress
1993	Al Pacino "Scent of a Woman"	Susan Sarandon "Lorenzo's Oil"
1992	Anthony Hopkins "The Silence of the Lambs"	Jodie Foster "The Silence of the Lambs"
1991	Jeremy Irons "Reversal of Fortune"	Kathy Bates "Misery"
1990	Daniel Day-Lewis "My Left Foot"	Jessica Tandy "Driving Miss Daisy"
1989	Dustin Hoffman "Rain Man"	Jodie Foster "The Accused"
1988	Michael Douglas "Wall Street"	Cher "Moonstruck"
1987	Paul Newman "The Color of Money"	Marlee Matlin "Children of a Lesser God"
1986	William Hurt "Kiss of the Spider Woman"	Geraldine Page "The Trip to Bountiful"
1985	F. Murray Abraham "Amadeus"	Sally Field "Places in the Heart"
1984	Robert Duvall "Tender Mercies"	Shirley MacLaine "Terms of Endearment"
1983	Ben Kingsley "Gandhi"	Meryl Streep "Sophie's Choice"
1982	Henry Fonda "On Golden Pond"	Katharine Hepburn "On Golden Pond"
1981	Robert De Niro "Raging Bull"	Sissy Spacek "Coal Miner's Daughter"
1980	Dustin Hoffman "Kramer vs. Kramer"	Sally Field "Norma Rae"
1979	Jon Voight "Coming Home"	Jane Fonda "Coming Home"
1978	Richard Dreyfuss "The Goodbye Girl"	Diane Keaton "Annie Hall"
1977	Peter Finch "Network"	Faye Dunaway "Network"
1976	Jack Nicholson "One Flew Over the Cuckoo's Nest"	Louise Fletcher "One Flew Over the Cuckoo's Nest"
1975	Art Carney "Harry and Tonto"	Ellen Burstyn "Alice Doesn't Live Here Anymore"
1974	Jack Lemmon "Save the Tiger"	Glenda Jackson "A Touch of Class"
1973	Marlon Brando "The Godfather"	Liza Minnelli "Cabaret"
1972	Gene Hackman "The French Connection"	Jane Fonda "Klute"
1971	George C. Scott "Patton" (award declined)	Glenda Jackson "Women in Love"
1970	John Wayne "True Grit"	Maggie Smith "The Prime of Miss Jean Brodie"
1969	Cliff Robertson "Charly"	Katharine Hepburn "The Lion in Winter"
1968	Rod Steiger "In the Heat of the Night"	Katharine Hepburn "Guess Who's Coming to Dinner?"
1967	Paul Scofield "A Man for All Seasons"	Elizabeth Taylor "Who's Afraid of Virginia Woolf?"
1966	Lee Marvin "Cat Ballou"	Julie Christie "Darling"
1965	Rex Harrison "My Fair Lady"	Julie Andrews "Mary Poppins"
1964	Sidney Poitier "Lilies of the Field"	Patricia Neal "Hud"

Academy Awards Quick List

Year	Best Actor	Best Actress
1963	**Gregory Peck** "To Kill a Mockingbird"	**Anne Bancroft** "The Miracle Worker"
1962	**Maximilian Schell** "Judgment at Nuremberg"	**Sophia Loren** "Two Women"
1961	**Burt Lancaster** "Elmer Gantry"	**Elizabeth Taylor** "Butterfield 8"
1960	**Charlton Heston** "Ben-Hur"	**Simone Signoret** "Room at the Top"
1959	**David Niven** "Separate Tables"	**Susan Hayward** "I Want to Live!"
1958	**Alec Guinness** "The Bridge on the River Kwai"	**Joanne Woodward** "The Three Faces of Eve"
1957	**Yul Brynner** "The King and I"	**Ingrid Bergman** "Anastasia"
1956	**Ernest Borgnine** "Marty"	**Anna Magnani** "The Rose Tattoo"
1955	**Marlon Brando** "On the Waterfront"	**Grace Kelly** "The Country Girl"
1954	**William Holden** "Stalag 17"	**Audrey Hepburn** "Roman Holiday"
1953	**Gary Cooper** "High Noon"	**Shirley Booth** "Come Back, Little Sheba"
1952	**Humphrey Bogart** "The African Queen"	**Vivien Leigh** "A Streetcar Named Desire"
1951	**Jose Ferrer** "Cyrano de Bergerac"	**Judy Holliday** "Born Yesterday"
1950	**Broderick Crawford** "All the King's Men"	**Olivia de Havilland** "The Heiress"
1949	**Laurence Olivier** "Hamlet"	**Jane Wyman** "Johnny Belinda"
1948	**Ronald Colman** "A Double Life"	**Loretta Young** "The Farmer's Daughter"
1947	**Fredric March** "The Best Years of Our Lives"	**Olivia de Havilland** "To Each His Own"
1946	**Ray Milland** "The Lost Weekend"	**Joan Crawford** "Mildred Pierce"
1945	**Bing Crosby** "Going My Way"	**Ingrid Bergman** "Gaslight"
1944	**Paul Lukas** "Watch on the Rhine"	**Jennifer Jones** "The Song of Bernadette"
1943	**James Cagney** "Yankee Doodle Dandy"	**Greer Garson** "Mrs. Miniver"
1942	**Gary Cooper** "Sergeant York"	**Joan Fontaine** "Suspicion"
1941	**James Stewart** "The Philadelphia Story"	**Ginger Rogers** "Kitty Foyle"
1940	**Robert Donat** "Goodbye, Mr. Chips"	**Vivien Leigh** "Gone With the Wind"
1939	**Spencer Tracy** "Boys Town"	**Bette Davis** "Jezebel"
1938	**Spencer Tracy** "Captains Courageous"	**Luise Rainer** "The Good Earth"
1937	**Paul Muni** "The Story of Louis Pasteur"	**Luise Rainer** "The Great Ziegfeld"
1936	**Victor McLaglen** "The Informer"	**Bette Davis** "Dangerous"
1935	**Clark Gable** "It Happened One Night"	**Claudette Colbert** "It Happened One Night"
1934	**Charles Laughton** "The Private Life of Henry VIII"	**Katharine Hepburn** "Morning Glory"
1933	**Wallace Beery** "The Champ"	**Helen Hayes** "The Sin of Madelon Claudet"
1932	**Lionel Barrymore** "A Free Soul"	**Marie Dressler** "Min and Bill"
1931	**George Arliss** "Disraeli"	**Norma Shearer** "The Divorcee"
1930	**Warner Baxter** "In Old Arizona"	**Mary Pickford** "Coquette"
1929	**Emil Jannings** "The Last Command" & "The Way of All Flesh"	**Janet Gaynor** "Seventh Heaven" "Street Angel" & Sunrise"

Correction
Emma Thompson was the winner of the
1993 Best Actress category for the Academy.
Also note this revision on Page 98.

1993

65th Annual Academy Awards
(Oscars given for pictures released in 1992)

Best Picture: "Unforgiven," Warner Brothers Production; Clint Eastwood, Producer.
Others Nominated:
"The Crying Game," Palace Pictures production, Miramax; Stephen Woolley, producer.
"A Few Good Men," Castle Rock Entertainment production, Columbia; David Brown, Rob Reiner, Andrew Scheinman, producers.
"Howards End," Merchant Ivory production, Sony Pictures Classics; Ismail Merchant, producer.
"Scent of a Woman," Universal Pictures production, Universal; Martin Brest, producer.

Best Director: Clint Eastwood, "Unforgiven."
Others Nominated: Neil Jordan, "The Crying Game"; James Ivory, "Howards End"; Robert Altman, "The Player"; Martin Brest, "Scent of a Woman."

Best Actor: Al Pacino, "Scent of a Woman."
Others Nominated: Robert Downey Jr., "Chaplin"; Clint Eastwood, "Unforgiven"; Stephen Rea, "The Crying Game"; Denzel Washington, "Malcolm X."

Best Actress: Susan Sarandon, "Lorenzo's Oil."
Others Nominated: Catherine Deneuve, "Indochine"; Mary McDonnell, "Passion Fish"; Michelle Pfeiffer, "Love Field"; Emma Thompson, "Howards End."

Best Supporting Actor: Gene Hackman, "Unforgiven."
Others Nominated: Jaye Davidson, "The Crying Game"; Jack Nicholson, "A Few Good Men"; Al Pacino, "Glengarry Glen Ross"; David Paymer, "Mr. Saturday Night."

Best Supporting Actress: Marisa Tomei, "My Cousin Vinny."
Others Nominated: Judy Davis, "Husbands and Wives"; Joan Plowright, "Enchanted April"; Vanessa Redgrave, "Howards End"; Miranda Richardson, "Damage."

Original Screenplay: Neil Jordan, "The Crying Game."
Others Nominated: Woody Allen, "Husbands and Wives"; George Miller & Nick Enright, "Lorenzo's Oil"; John Sayles, "Passion Fish"; David Webb Peoples, "Unforgiven."

Screenplay Adaptation: Richard Friedenberg, "A River Runs Through It."
Others Nominated: Peter Barnes, "Enchanted April"; Ruth Prawer Jhabvala, "Howards End"; Michael Tolkin, "The Player"; Bo Goldman, "Scent of a Woman."

Directors Guild Of America

1992 Best Director: Clint Eastwood, "Unforgiven."

Writers Guild Of America
(Awards given for pictures released in 1992)

Best Screenplay Written Directly for the Screen: Neil Jordan, "The Crying Game."
Best Screenplay Based On Material Previously Produced or Published: Michael Tolkin, "The Player." Based on his novel.

Golden Globe Awards
(For 1991 Releases)

Best Picture-Drama: "Scent of a Woman."
Best Picture-Musical/Comedy: "The Player."
Best Director: Clint Eastwood, "Unforgiven."
Best Actress-Drama: Emma Thompson, "Howards End."
Best Actor-Drama: Al Pacino, "Scent of a Woman."
Best Actress-Musical/Comedy: Miranda Richardson, "Enchanted April."
Best Actor-Musical/Comedy: Tim Robbins, "The Player."
Best Supporting Actress: Joan Plowright, "Enchanted April."
Best Supporting Actor: Gene Hackman, "Unforgiven."
Best Screenplay: Bo Goldman, "Scent of a Woman."

National Society Of Film Critics
(Awards for films released in 1992)

Best Picture: "Unforgiven."
Best Director: Clint Eastwood, "Unforgiven."
Best Actor: Stephen Rea, "The Crying Game."
Best Actress: Emma Thompson, "Howards End."
Best Supporting Actor: Gene Hackman, "Unforgiven."
Best Supporting Actress: Judy Davis, "Husbands."
Best Screenplay: David Webb Peoples, "Unforgiven."

New York Film Critics
(Awards for 1992 Releases)

Best Picture: "The Player."
Best Director: Robert Altman, "The Player."
Best Actor: Denzel Washington, "Malcolm X."
Best Actress: Emma Thompson, "Howards End."
Best Supporting Actor: Gene Hackman, "Unforgiven."
Best Supporting Actress: Miranda Richardson, "Crying Game", "Enchanted April" & "Damage."
Best Screenplay: Neil Jordan, "The Crying Game."

Los Angeles Film Critics
(Awards for films released in 1982)

Best Picture: "Unforgiven"
Best Director: Clint Eastwood, "Unforgiven."
Best Actor: Clint Eastwood, "Unforgiven."
Best Actress: Emma Thompson, "Howards End."
Best Supporting Actor: Gene Hackman, "Unforgiven."
Best Supporting Actress: Judy Davis, "Husbands and Wives."
Best Screenplay: David Webb Peoples, "Unforgiven."

46th Cannes Film Festival
(May 1993)

Best Picture (Palme d'Or): (tie)
   "The Piano" & "Farewell to My Concubine."
Best Director: Mike Leigh, "Naked."
Best Actor: David Thewlis, "Naked."
Best Actress: Holly Hunter, "The Piano."
International Critics Prize (for competed film):
   "Farewell to My Concubine."

Independent Spirit Awards
(Awards for films released in 1992)

Best Picture: "The Player."
Best Director: Carl Franklin, "One False Move."
Best Actor: Harvey Keitel, "Bad Lieutenant."
Best Actress: Fairuza Balk, "Gas, Food, Lodging."
Best Supporting Actor: Steve Buscemi, "Reservoir Dogs."
Best Supporting Actress: Alfre Woodard, "Passion Fish."
Best Screenplay: Neal Jimenez, "The Waterdance."
Best Foreign Film: "The Crying Game."

1993

1992

64th Annual Academy Awards
(Oscars given for pictures released in 1991)

Best Picture: "The Silence of the Lambs," Strong Heart/Demme Productions, Orion; Edward Saxon, Kenneth Utt and Ron Bozman, producers.

Others Nominated:
"Beauty and the Beast," Walt Disney Pictures production, Buena Vista; Don Hahn, producer.
"Bugsy," TriStar; Mark Johnson, Barry Levinson and Warren Beatty, producers.
"JFK," Camelot production, Warner Bros.; A. Kitman Ho and Oliver Stone, producers.
"The Prince of Tides," Barwood/Longfellow production, Columbia; Barbra Streisand and Andrew Karsch.

Best Director: Jonathan Demme, "The Silence of the Lambs."

Others Nominated: John Singleton, "Boyz N the Hood"; Barry Levinson, "Bugsy"; Oliver Stone, "JFK"; Ridley Scott, "Thelma & Louise."

Best Actor: Anthony Hopkins, "The Silence of the Lambs."

Others Nominated: Warren Beatty, "Bugsy"; Robert De Niro, "Cape Fear"; Nick Nolte, "The Prince of Tides"; Robin Williams, "The Fisher King."

Best Actress: Jodie Foster, "The Silence of the Lambs."

Others Nominated: Geena Davis, "Thelma & Louise"; Laura Dern, "Rambling Rose"; Bette Midler, "For the Boys"; Susan Sarandon, "Thelma & Louise."

Best Supporting Actor: Jack Palance, "City Slickers."

Others Nominated: Tommy Lee Jones, "JFK"; Harvey Keitel, "Bugsy"; Ben Kingsley, "Bugsy"; Michael Lerner, "Barton Fink."

Best Supporting Actress: Mercedes Ruehl, "The Fisher King."

Others Nominated: Diane Ladd, "Rambling Rose"; Juliette Lewis, "Cape Fear"; Kate Nelligan, "The Prince of Tides"; Jessica Tandy, "Fried Green Tomatoes."

Original Screenplay: Callie Khouri, "Thelma & Louise."

Others Nominated: John Singleton, "Boyz N the Hood"; James Toback, "Bugsy"; Richard LaGravenese, "The Fisher King"; Lawrence Kasdan & Meg Kasdan, "Grand Canyon."

Screenplay Adaptation: Ted Tally, "The Silence of the Lambs."

Others Nominated: Agnieszka Holland, "Europa, Europa"; Fannie Flagg & Carol Sobieski, "Fried Green Tomatoes"; Oliver Stone & Zachary Sklar, "JFK"; Pat Conroy & Becky Johnston, "The Prince of Tides."

Directors Guild Of America

1991 Best Director: Jonathan Demme, "The Silence of the Lambs."

Writers Guild Of America
(Awards given for pictures released in 1991)

Best Screenplay Written Directly for the Screen: Callie Khouri, "Thelma & Louise."

Best Screenplay Based on Material from Another Medium: Ted Tally, "The Silence of the Lambs." Based on the novel by Thomas Harris.

Golden Globe Awards
(For 1991 Releases)

Best Picture-Drama: "Bugsy."

Best Picture-Musical/Comedy: "Beauty and the Beast."

Best Director: Oliver Stone, "JFK."

Best Actress-Drama: Jodie Foster, "The Silence of the Lambs."

Best Actor-Drama: Nick Nolte, "The Prince of Tides."

Best Actress-Musical/Comedy: Bette Midler, "For the Boys."

Best Actor-Musical/Comedy: Robin Williams, "The Fisher King."

Best Supporting Actress: Mercedes Ruehl, "The Fisher King."

Best Supporting Actor: Jack Palance, "City Slickers."

Best Screenplay: Callie Khouri, "Thelma & Louise."

National Society Of Film Critics
(Awards for films released in 1991)

Best Picture: "Life is Sweet."

Best Director: David Cronenberg, "Naked Lunch."

Best Actor: River Phoenix, "My Own Private Idaho."

Best Actress: Alison Steadman, "Life is Sweet."

Best Supporting Actor: Harvey Keitel, "Bugsy," "Mortal Thoughts," and "Thelma & Louise."

Best Supporting Actress: Jane Horrocks, "Life is Sweet."

Best Screenplay: David Cronenberg, "Naked Lunch."

New York Film Critics
(Awards for 1991 Releases)

Best Picture: "The Silence of the Lambs."

Best Director: Jonathan Demme, "The Silence of the Lambs."

Best Actor: Anthony Hopkins, "The Silence of the Lambs."

Best Actress: Jodie Foster, "The Silence of the Lambs."

Best Supporting Actor: Samuel L. Jackson, "Jungle Fever."

Best Supporting Actress: Judy Davis, "Naked Lunch" & "Barton Fink."

Best Screenplay: David Cronenberg, "Naked Lunch."

Los Angeles Film Critics
(Awards for films released in 1991)

Best Picture: "Bugsy."

Best Director: Barry Levinson, "Bugsy."

Best Actor: Nick Nolte, "Prince of Tides."

Best Actress: Mercedes Ruehl, "The Fisher King."

Best Supporting Actor: Michael Lerner, "Barton Fink."

Best Supporting Actress: Jane Horrocks, "Life is Sweet."

Best Screenplay: James Toback, "Bugsy."

45th Cannes Film Festival
(May 1992)

Best Picture (Palme d'Or): "The Best Intentions"

Best Director: Robert Altman, "The Player."

Best Actor: Tim Robbins, "The Player."

Best Actress: Pernilla August, "The Best Intentions."

Independent Spirit Awards
(Awards for films released in 1991)

Best Picture: "Rambling Rose."

Best Director: Martha Coolidge, "Rambling Rose."

Best Actor: River Phoenix, "My Own Private Idaho."

Best Actress: Judy Davis, "Impromptu."

Best Supporting Actor: David Strathairn, "City of Hope."

Best Supporting Actress: Diane Ladd, "Rambling Rose."

Best Screenplay: Gus Van Sant, "My Own Private Idaho."

Best Foreign Film: "An Angel at my Table."

1992

1991

63rd Annual Academy Awards
(Oscars given for pictures released in 1990)

Best Picture:"Dances With Wolves,"Tig production, Orion; Jim Wilson and Kevin Costner, producers.
   Others Nominated:
      "Awakenings," Columbia; Walter F. Parkes and Lawrence Lasker, producers.
      "Ghost," Howard W. Koch production, Paramount; Lisa Weinstein, producer.
      "The Godfather, Part III," Zoetrope Studios, Paramount; Francis Ford Coppola, producer.
      "Goodfellas," Warner Bros.; Irwin Winkler, producer.
Best Director: Kevin Costner, "Dances With Wolves."
   Others Nominated: Francis Ford Coppola, "The Godfather, Part III"; Stephen Frears, "The Grifters"; Barbet
      Schroeder, "Reversal of Fortune"; Martin Scorsese, "Goodfellas."
Best Actor: Jeremy Irons, "Reversal of Fortune."
   Others Nominated: Kevin Costner, "Dances With Wolves"; Robert De Niro, "Awakenings"; Gerard
      Depardieu, "Cyrano de Bergerac"; Richard Harris, "The Field."
Best Actress: Kathy Bates, "Misery."
   Others Nominated: Anjelica Huston, "The Grifters"; Julia Roberts, "Pretty Woman"; Meryl Streep,
      "Postcards from the Edge"; Joanne Woodward, "Mr. & Mrs. Bridge."
Best Supporting Actor: Joe Pesci, "Goodfellas."
   Others Nominated: Bruce Davison, "Longtime Companion"; Andy Garcia, "The Godfather,Part III";
      Graham Greene, "Dances With Wolves"; Al Pacino, "Dick Tracy."
Best Supporting Actress: Whoopi Goldberg, "Ghost."
   Others Nominated: Annette Bening, "The Grifters"; Lorraine Bracco, "Goodfellas"; Diane Ladd, "Wild at
      Heart"; Mary McDonnell, "Dances With Wolves."
Original Screenplay: Bruce Joel Rubin, "Ghost."
   Others Nominated: Woody Allen, "Alice"; Barry Levinson, "Avalon"; Whit Stillman, "Metropolitan"; Peter
      Weir, "Green Card."
Screenplay Adaptation: Michael Blake, "Dances With Wolves."
   Others Nominated: Nicholas Kazan, "Reversal of Fortune"; Nicholas Pileggi & Martin Scorsese,
      "Goodfellas"; Donald E. Westlake, "The Grifters"; Steven Zaillian, "Awakenings."

Directors Guild Of America

1990 Best Director: Kevin Costner, "Dances With Wolves."

Writers Guild Of America
(Awards given for pictures released in 1990)

Best Screenplay Written Directly for the Screen: Barry Levinson, "Avalon."
Best Screenplay Based on Material From Another Medium: Michael Blake, "Dances With
   Wolves." Based on his novel.

Golden Globe Awards
(For 1990 Releases)

Best Picture-Drama: "Dances With Wolves"
Best Picture-Musical/Comedy: "Green Card."
Best Director: Kevin Costner, "Dances With Wolves."
Best Actress-Drama: Kathy Bates, "Misery."
Best Actor-Drama: Jeremy Irons, "Reversal of Fortune."
Best Actress-Musical/Comedy: Julia Roberts, "Pretty Woman."
Best Actor-Musical/Comedy: Gerard Depardieu, "Green Card."
Best Supporting Actress: Whoopi Goldberg, "Ghost."
Best Supporting Actor: Bruce Davison, "Longtime Companion."
Best Screenplay: Michael Blake, "Dances With Wolves."

National Society Of Film Critics
(Awards for films released in 1990)

Best Picture: "Goodfellas."
Best Director: Martin Scorsese, "Goodfellas."
Best Actor: Jeremy Irons, "Reversal of Fortune."
Best Actress: Anjelica Huston, "The Grifters."
Best Supporting Actor: Bruce Davison, "Longtime Companion."
Best Supporting Actress: Annette Bening, "The Grifters."
Best Screenplay: Charles Burnett, "To Sleep with Anger."

New York Film Critics
(Awards for 1990 Releases)

Best Picture: "Goodfellas."
Best Director: Martin Scorsese, "Goodfellas."
Best Actor: Robert De Niro, "Awakenings" & "Goodfellas."
Best Actress: Joanne Woodward, "Mr. & Mrs. Bridge."
Best Supporting Actor: Bruce Davison, "Longtime Companion."
Best Supporting Actress: Jennifer Jason Leigh, "Miami Blues" & "Last Exit to Brooklyn."
Best Screenplay: Ruth Prawer Jhabvala, "Mr. & Mrs. Bridge."

Los Angeles Film Critics
(Awards for films released in 1990)

Best Picture: "Goodfellas."
Best Director: Martin Scorsese, "Goodfellas."
Best Actor: Jeremy Irons, "Reversal of Fortune."
Best Actress: Anjelica Huston, "The Grifters" & "The Witches."
Best Supporting Actor: Joe Pesci, "Goodfellas."
Best Supporting Actress: Lorraine Bracco, "Goodfellas."
Best Screenplay: Nicholas Kazan, "Reversal of Fortune."

44th Cannes Film Festival
(1991)

Best Picture (Golden Palm): "Barton Fink."
Best Director: Joel & Ethan Coen, "Barton Fink."
Best Actor: John Turturro, "Barton Fink."
Best Actress: Irene Jacob, "The Double Life of Veronique."
Best Supporting Actor (special): Samuel L. Jackson, "Jungle Fever."

Independent Spirit Awards
(Awards for films released in 1990)

Best Picture: "The Grifters."
Best Director: Charles Burnett, "To Sleep with Anger."
Best Actor: Danny Glover, "To Sleep with Anger."
Best Actress: Anjelica Huston, "The Grifters."
Best Supporting Actor: Bruce Davison, "Longtime Companion."
Best Supporting Actress: Sheryl Lee Ralph, "To Sleep with Anger."
Best Screenplay: Charles Burnett, "To Sleep with Anger."
Best Foreign Film: "Sweetie."

1991

1990

62nd Annual Academy Awards
(Oscars given for pictures released in 1989)

Best Picture: "Driving Miss Daisy," Zanuck Co., Warner Bros.; Richard D. & Lili Fini Zanuck.
"Born on the Fourth of July," A. Kitman Ho & Ixtlan Production, Universal; A. Kitman Ho & Oliver Stone producers.
"Dead Poets Society," Touchstone Pictures with Silver Screen Partners IV, Buena Vista; Steven Haft, Paul Junger Witt & Tony Thomas, producers.
"Field of Dreams," Gordon Co. production, Universal; Lawrence Gordon & Charles Gordon, producers.
"My Left Foot," Ferndale Films production, Miramax; Noel Pearson, producer.

Best Director: Oliver Stone, "Born on the Fourth of July."
Others Nominated: Woody Allen, "Crimes and Misdemeanors"; Kenneth Branagh, "Henry V"; Jim Sheridan, "My Left Foot"; Peter Weir, "Dead Poets Society."

Best Actor: Daniel Day-Lewis, "My Left Foot."
Others Nominated: Kenneth Branagh, "Henry V"; Tom Cruise, "Born on the Fourth of July"; Morgan Freeman, "Driving Miss Daisy"; Robin Williams, "Dead Poets Society."

Best Actress: Jessica Tandy, "Driving Miss Daisy."
Others Nominated: Isabelle Adjani, "Camille Claudel"; Pauline Collins, "Shirley Valentine"; Jessica Lange, "The Music Box"; Michelle Pfeiffer, "The Fabulous Baker Boys."

Best Supporting Actor: Denzel Washington, "Glory."
Others Nominated: Danny Aiello, "Do the Right Thing"; Dan Aykroyd, "Driving Miss Daisy"; Marlon Brando, "A Dry White Season"; Martin Landau, "Crimes and Misdemeanors."

Best Supporting Actress: Brenda Fricker, "My Left Foot."
Others Nominated: Anjelica Huston, "Enemies, A Love Story"; Lena Olin, "Enemies, A Love Story"; Julia Roberts, "Steel Magnolias"; Dianne Wiest, "Parenthood."

Original Screenplay: Tom Schulman, "Dead Poets Society."
Others Nominated: Woody Allen, "Crimes and Misdemeanors"; Nora Ephron, "When Harry Met Sally..."; Spike Lee, "Do the Right Thing"; Steven Soderbergh, "sex, lies, and videotape."

Screenplay Adaptation: Phil Alden Robinson, "Field of Dreams."
Others Nominated: Jim Sheridan & Shane Connaughton, "My Left Foot"; Roger L. Simon & Paul Mazursky, "Enemies, A Love Story"; Oliver Stone & Ron Kovic, "Born on the Fourth of July"; Alfred Uhry, "Driving Miss Daisy."

Directors Guild Of America

1989 Best Director: Oliver Stone, "Born on the Fourth of July."

Writers Guild Of America
(Awards given for pictures released in 1989)

Best Screenplay Written Directly for the Screen: Woody Allen, "Crimes and Misdemeanors."
Best Screenplay Based on Material From Another Medium: Alfred Uhry, "Driving Miss Daisy." Based on his play, "Driving Miss Daisy."

Golden Globe Awards
(For 1989 Releases)

Best Picture-Drama: "Born on the Fourth of July."
Best Picture-Musical/Comedy: "Driving Miss Daisy."
Best Director: Oliver Stone, "Born on the Fourth of July."
Best Actress-Drama: Michelle Pfeiffer, "The Fabulous Baker Boys."
Best Actor-Drama: Tom Cruise, "Born on the Fourth of July."
Best Actress-Musical/Comedy: Jessica Tandy, "Driving Miss Daisy."
Best Actor-Musical/Comedy: Morgan Freeman, "Driving Miss Daisy."
Best Supporting Actress: Julia Roberts, "Steel Magnolias."
Best Supporting Actor: Denzel Washington, "Glory."
Best Screenplay: Oliver Stone & Ron Kovic, "Born on the Fourth of July."

National Society Of Film Critics
(Awards for films released in 1989)

Best Picture: "Drugstore Cowboy."
Best Director: Gus Van Sant, "Drugstore Cowboy."
Best Actor: Daniel Day-Lewis, "My Left Foot."
Best Actress: Michelle Pfeiffer, "The Fabulous Baker Boys."
Best Supporting Actor: Beau Bridges, "The Fabulous Baker Boys."
Best Supporting Actress: Anjelica Huston, "Enemies, A Love Story."
Best Screenplay: Gus Van Sant & Daniel Yost, "Drugstore Cowboy."

New York Film Critics
(Awards for 1989 Releases)

Best Picture: "My Left Foot."
Best Director: Paul Mazursky, "Enemies, A Love Story."
Best Actor: Daniel Day-Lewis, "My Left Foot."
Best Actress: Michelle Pfeiffer, "The Fabulous Baker Boys."
Best Supporting Actor: Alan Alda, "Crimes and Misdemeanors."
Best Supporting Actress: Lena Olin, "Enemies, A Love Story."
Best Screenplay: Gus Van Sant & Daniel Yost, "Drugstore Cowboy."

Los Angeles Film Critics
(Awards for films released in 1989)

Best Picture: "Do the Right Thing"
Best Director: Spike Lee, "Do the Right Thing."
Best Actor: Daniel Day-Lewis, "My Left Foot."
Best Actress: (tie)
  Michelle Pfeiffer, "The Fabulous Baker Boys"
  Andie MacDowell, "sex, lies, and Videotape."
Best Supporting Actor: Danny Aiello, "Do the Right Thing."
Best Supporting Actress: Brenda Fricker, "My Left Foot."
Best Screenplay: Gus Van Sant & Daniel Yost, "Drugstore Cowboy."

43rd Cannes Film Festival
(1990)

Best Picture (Golden Palm): "Wild at Heart"
Best Director: Pavei Lungin, "Taxi Blues."
Best Actor: Gerard Depardieu, "Cyrano de Bergerac."
Best Actress: Krystyna Janda, "The Interrogation."

Independent Spirit Awards
(Awards for films released in 1989)

Best Picture: "sex, lies, and videotape."
Best Director: Steven Soderbergh, "sex, lies, and videotape."
Best Actor: Matt Dillon, "Drugstore Cowboy."
Best Actress: Andie McDowell, "sex, lies, and videotape."
Best Supporting Actor: Max Perlich, "Drugstore Cowboy."
Best Supporting Actress: Laura San Giacomo, "sex, lies, and videotape."
Best Screenplay: Gus Van Sant & Daniel Yost, "Drugstore Cowboy."
Best Foreign Film: "My Left Foot."

1990

1989

61st Annual Academy Awards
(Oscars given for pictures released in 1988)

Best Picture: "Rain Man," Guber-Peters Co., United Artists; Mark Johnson, producer.
Others Nominated:
"The Accidental Tourist," Warner Bros; Lawrence Kasdan, Charles Okun & Michael Grillo, producers.
"Dangerous Liaisons," NFH Limited Production from Lorimar Film Entertainment/Warner Bros.;
Norma Heyman & Hank Moonjean, producers.
"Mississippi Burning," Frederick Zollo/Orion; Frederick Zollo, Robert F. Colesberry, producers.
"Working Girl," 20th Century Fox; Douglas Wick, producer.

Best Director: Barry Levinson, "Rain Man."
Others Nominated: Charles Crichton, "A Fish Called Wanda"; Mike Nichols, "Working Girl"; Alan Parker,
"Mississippi Burning"; Martin Scorsese, "The Last Temptation of Christ."

Best Actor: Dustin Hoffman, "Rain Man."
Others Nominated: Gene Hackman, "Mississippi Burning"; Tom Hanks, "Big"; Edward James Olmos,
"Stand and Deliver"; Max Von Sydow, "Pelle the Conqueror."

Best Actress: Jodie Foster, "The Accused."
Others Nominated: Glenn Close, "Dangerous Liaisons"; Melanie Griffith, "Working Girl"; Meryl Streep,
"A Cry in the Dark"; Sigourney Weaver, "Gorillas in the Mist."

Best Supporting Actor: Kevin Kline, "A Fish Called Wanda."
Others Nominated: Alec Guinness, "Little Dorrit"; Martin Landau, "Tucker: The Man and His Dream";
River Phoenix, "Running on Empty"; Dean Stockwell, "Married to the Mob."

Best Supporting Actress: Geena Davis, "The Accidental Tourist."
Others Nominated: Joan Cusack, "Working Girl"; Frances McDormand, "Mississippi Burning"; Michelle
Pfeiffer, "Dangerous Liaisons"; Sigourney Weaver, "Working Girl."

Original Screenplay: Ronald Bass, Barry Morrow (SP) Barry Morrow (S), "Rain Man."
Others Nominated: Gary Ross & Anne Spielberg, "Big"; Ron Shelton, "Bull Durham"; John Cleese (SP),
John Cleese, Charles Crichton (S), "A Fish Called Wanda"; Naomi Foner, "Running on Empty."

Screenplay Adaptation: Frank Galati & Lawrence Kasdan, "The Accidental Tourist."
Others Nominated: Christopher Hampton, "Dangerous Liaisons"; Anna Hamilton Phelan (SP), Anna
Hamilton Phelan & Tab Murphy (S), "Gorillas in the Mist"; Christine Edzard, "Little Dorrit"; Jean-
Claude Carriere & Philip Kaufman, "The Unbearable Lightness of Being."

Directors Guild Of America

1988 Best Director: Barry Levinson, "Rain Man."

Writers Guild Of America
(Awards given for pictures released in 1988)

Best Screenplay Written Directly for the Screen: Ron Shelton, "Bull Durham."
Best Screenplay Based on Material From Another Medium: Christopher Hampton,
"Dangerous Liaisons." Based on the novel "Les Liaisons Dangereuses" by Choderlos De Laclos.

Golden Globe Awards
(For 1988 Releases)

Best Picture-Drama: "Rain Man."
Best Picture-Musical/Comedy: "Working Girl."
Best Director: Clint Eastwood, "Bird."
Best Actress-Drama: (3-way tie)
   Jodie Foster, "The Accused."
   Shirley MacLaine, "Madame Sousatzka"
   Sigourney Weaver, "Gorillas in the Mist."
Best Actor-Drama: Dustin Hoffman, "Rain Man."
Best Actress-Musical/Comedy: Melanie Griffith, "Working Girl."
Best Actor-Musical/Comedy: Tom Hanks, "Big."
Best Supporting Actress: Sigourney Weaver, "Working Girl."
Best Supporting Actor: Martin Landau, "Tucker: The Man and His Dream."
Best Screenplay: Naomi Foner, "Running on Empty."

National Society Of Film Critics
(Awards for films released in 1988)

Best Picture: "The Unbearable Lightness of Being."
Best Director: Philip Kaufman, "The Unbearable Lightness of Being."
Best Actor: Michael Keaton, "Beetlejuice" & "Clean and Sober."
Best Actress: Judy Davis, "High Tide."
Best Supporting Actor: Dean Stockwell, "Married to the Mob."
Best Supporting Actress: Mercedes Ruehl, "Married to the Mob."
Best Screenplay: Ron Shelton, "Bull Durham."

New York Film Critics
(Awards for 1988 Releases)

Best Picture: "The Accidental Tourist."
Best Director: Chris Menges, "A World Apart."
Best Actor: Jeremy Irons, "Dead Ringers."
Best Actress: Meryl Streep, "A Cry in the Dark."
Best Supporting Actor: Dean Stockwell, "Tucker: The Man and His Dream" & "Married to the Mob."
Best Supporting Actress: Diane Venora, "Bird."
Best Screenplay: Ron Shelton, "Bull Durham."

Los Angeles Film Critics
(Awards for films released in 1988)

Best Picture: "Little Dorrit."
Best Director: David Cronenberg, "Dead Ringers."
Best Actor: Tom Hanks, "Big" & "Punchline."
Best Actress: Christine Lahti, "Running on Empty."
Best Supporting Actor: Alec Guinness, "Little Dorrit."
Best Supporting Actress: Genevieve Bujold, "The Moderns" & "Dead Ringers."
Best Screenplay: Ron Shelton, "Bull Durham."

42nd Cannes Film Festival
(1989)

Best Picture (Palme d'Or): "sex, lies, and video-tape."
Best Director: Emir Kusturica, "Time of the Gypsies."
Best Actor: James Spader, "sex, lies, and videotape."
Best Actress: Meryl Streep, "A Cry in the Dark."

Independent Spirit Awards
(Awards for films released in 1988)

Best Picture: "Stand and Deliver."
Best Director: Ramon Menendez, "Stand And Deliver."
Best Actor: Edward James Olmos, "Stand and Deliver."
Best Actress: Jodie Foster, "Five Corners."
Best Supporting Actor: Lou Diamond Phillips, "Stand and Deliver."
Best Supporting Actress: Rosanna De Soto, "Stand And Deliver."
Best Screenplay: Ramon Menendez, "Stand and Deliver."
Best Foreign Film: "Wings of Desire."

1989

1988

60th Annual Academy Awards
(Oscars given for pictures released in 1987)

Best Picture: "The Last Emperor," Hemdale Film, Columbia; Jeremy Thomas, producer.
Others Nominated:
"Broadcast News," 20th Century Fox; James L. Brooks, producer.
"Fatal Attraction," Jaffe/Lansing, Paramount; Stanley R. Jaffe & Sherry Lansing, producers.
"Hope and Glory," Davros Production Services, Columbia; John Boorman, producer.
"Moonstruck," Patrick Palmer & Norman Jewison, MGM; Patrick Palmer & Norman Jewison, producers.

Best Director: Bernardo Bertolucci, "The Last Emperor."
Others Nominated: Adrian Lyne, "Fatal Attraction"; John Boorman, "Hope and Glory"; Norman Jewison, "Moonstruck"; Lasse Hallstrom, "My Life as a Dog."

Best Actor: Michael Douglas, "Wall Street."
Others Nominated: William Hurt, "Broadcast News"; Marcello Mastroianni, "Dark Eyes"; Jack Nicholson, "Ironweed"; Robin Williams, "Good Morning, Vietnam."

Best Actress: Cher, "Moonstruck."
Others Nominated: Glenn Close, "Fatal Attraction"; Holly Hunter, "Broadcast News"; Sally Kirkland, "Anna"; Meryl Streep, "Ironweed."

Best Supporting Actor: Sean Connery, "The Untouchables."
Others Nominated: Albert Brooks, "Broadcast News"; Morgan Freeman, "Street Smart"; Vincent Gardenia, "Moonstruck"; Denzel Washington, "Cry Freedom."

Best Supporting Actress: Olympia Dukakis, "Moonstruck."
Others Nominated: Norma Aleandro, "Gaby-A True Story"; Anne Archer, "Fatal Attraction"; Anne Ramsey, "Throw Momma from the Train"; Ann Sothern, "The Whales of August."

Original Screenplay: John Patrick Shanley, "Moonstruck."
Others Nominated: Louis Malle, "Au Revoir Les Enfants"; James L. Brooks, "Broadcast News"; John Boorman, "Hope and Glory"; Woody Allen, "Radio Days."

Screenplay Adaptation: Mark Peploe & Bernardo Bertolucci, "The Last Emperor."
Others Nominated: Tony Huston, "The Dead"; James Dearden, "Fatal Attraction"; Stanley Kubrick, Michael Herr & Gustav Hasford, "Full Metal Jacket."

Directors Guild Of America

1987 Best Director: Bernardo Bertolucci ,"The Last Emperor."

Writers Guild Of America
(Awards given for pictures released in 1987)

Best Screenplay Written Directly for the Screen: John Patrick Shanley, "Moonstruck."
Best Written Screenplay Based on Material From Another Medium: Steve Martin, "Roxanne." Based on "Cyrano de Bergerac" by Edmund Rostand.

Golden Globe Awards
(For 1987 Releases)

Best Picture-Drama: "The Last Emperor."
Best Picture-Musical/Comedy: "Hope and Glory."
Best Director: Bernardo Bertolucci, "The Last Emperor."
Best Actress-Drama: Sally Kirkland, "Anna."
Best Actor-Drama: Michael Douglas, "Wall Street."
Best Actress-Musical/Comedy: Cher, "Moonstruck."
Best Actor-Musical/Comedy: Robin Williams, "Good Morning, Vietnam."
Best Supporting Actress: Olympia Dukakis, "Moonstruck."
Best Supporting Actor: Sean Connery, "The Untouchables."
Best Screenplay: Mark Peploe & Bernardo Bertolucci, "The Last Emperor."

National Society Of Film Critics
(Awards for films released in 1987)

Best Picture: "The Dead."
Best Director: John Boorman, "Hope and Glory."
Best Actor: Steve Martin, "Roxanne."
Best Actress: Emily Lloyd, "Wish You Were Here."
Best Supporting Actor: Morgan Freeman, "Street Smart."
Best Supporting Actress: Kathy Baker, "Street Smart."
Best Screenplay: John Boorman, "Hope and Glory."

New York Film Critics
(Awards for 1987 Releases)

Best Picture: "Broadcast News."
Best Director: James L. Brooks, "Broadcast News."
Best Actor: Jack Nicholson, "Broadcast News", "Ironweed" & "The Witches of Eastwick."
Best Actress: Holly Hunter, "Broadcast News."
Best Supporting Actor: Morgan Freeman, "Street Smart."
Best Supporting Actress: Vanessa Redgrave, "Prick Up Your Ears."
Best Screenplay: James L. Brooks, "Broadcast News."

Los Angeles Film Critics
(Awards for films released in 1987)

Best Picture: "Hope and Glory"
Best Director: John Boorman, "Hope and Glory."
Best Actor: (tie) Steve Martin, "Roxanne" & **Jack Nicholson,** "Ironweed", "The Witches of Eastwick."
Best Actress: (tie) Holly Hunter, "Broadcast News" & **Sally Kirkland,** "Anna."
Best Supporting Actor: Morgan Freeman, "Street Smart."
Best Supporting Actress: Olympia Dukakis, "Moonstruck."
Best Screenplay: John Boorman, "Hope and Glory."

41st Cannes Film Festival
(May 1988)

Best Picture (Palme d'Or): "Pelle the Conqueror"
Best Director: Fernando Solanas, "The South."
Best Actor: Forest Whitaker, "Bird."
Best Actress: (shared) Barbara Hershey, Jodhi May & Linda Myuse for "A World Apart."
International Critics Prize (shared): "Thou Shalt Not Kill" & "Hotel Terminus."

Independent Spirit Awards
(Awards for films released in 1987)

Best Picture: "River's Edge."
Best Director: John Huston, "The Dead."
Best Actor: Dennis Quaid, "The Big Easy."
Best Actress: Sally Kirkland, "Anna."
Best Supporting Actor: Morgan Freeman, "Street Smart."
Best Supporting Actress: Anjelica Huston, "The Dead."
Best Screenplay: Neal Jimenez, "River's Edge."
Best Foreign Film: "My Life as a Dog."

1988

1987

59th Annual Academy Awards
(Oscars given for pictures released in 1986)

Best Picture: "Platoon," Hemdale, Orion; Arnold Kopelson, producer.
Others Nominated:
   "Children of a Lesser God," Sugarman, Paramount; Burt Sugarman & Patrick Palmer, producers.
   "Hannah and Her Sisters," Rollins and Joffee, Orion; Robert Greenhut, producers.
   "The Mission," Warner Bros; Fernando Ghia & David Puttnam, producers.
   "A Room with a View," Merchant Ivory, Cinecom; Ismail Merchant, producer.

Best Director: Oliver Stone, "Platoon."
Others Nominated: David Lynch, "Blue Velvet"; Woody Allen, "Hannah and Her Sisters"; Roland Joffe, "The Mission"; James Ivory, "A Room with a View."

Best Actor: Paul Newman, "The Color of Money."
Others Nominated: Dexter Gordon, "Round Midnight"; Bob Hoskins, "Mona Lisa"; William Hurt, "Children of a Lesser God"; James Woods, "Salvador."

Best Actress: Marlee Matlin, "Children of a Lesser God."
Others Nominated: Jane Fonda, "The Morning After"; Sissy Spacek, "Crimes of the Heart"; Kathleen Turner, "Peggy Sue Got Married"; Sigourney Weaver, "Aliens."

Best Supporting Actor: Michael Caine, "Hannah and Her Sisters."
Others Nominated: Tom Berenger, "Platoon"; Willem Dafoe, "Platoon"; Denholm Elliott, "A Room with a View"; Dennis Hopper, "Hoosiers."

Best Supporting Actress: Dianne Wiest, "Hannah and Her Sisters."
Others Nominated: Tess Harper, "Crimes of the Heart"; Piper Laurie, "Children of a Lesser God"; Mary Elizabeth Mastrantonio, 'The Color of Money'; Maggie Smith, "A Room with a View."

Original Screenplay: Woody Allen, "Hannah and Her Sisters."
Others Nominated: Paul Hogan, Ken Shadie & John Cornell, "Crocodile Dundee"; Hanif Kureishi, "My Beautiful Laundrette"; Oliver Stone, "Platoon"; Oliver Stone & Richard Boyle, "Salvador."

Screenplay Adaptation: Ruth Prawer Jhabvala, "A Room with a View."
Others Nominated: Hesper Anderson & Mark Medoff, "Children of a Lesser God"; Richard Price, "Crimes of the Heart"; Raynold Gideon & Bruce A. Evans, "Stand By Me."

Directors Guild Of America

1986 Best Director: Oliver Stone, "Platoon."

Writers Guild Of America
(Awards given for pictures released in 1986)

Best Screenplay Written Directly for the Screen: Woody Allen, "Hannah and Her Sisters."
Best Screenplay Based on Material From Another Medium: Ruth Prawer Jhabvala, "A Room With a View." Based on the Novel by E.M. Forster.

Golden Globe Awards
(For 1986 Releases)

Best Picture-Drama: "Platoon."
Best Picture-Musical/Comedy: "Hannah and Her Sisters."
Best Director: Oliver Stone, "Platoon."
Best Actress-Drama: Marlee Martin, "Children of a Lesser God."
Best Actor-Drama: Bob Hoskins, "Mona Lisa."
Best Actress-Musical/Comedy: Sissy Spacek, "Crimes of the Heart."
Best Actor-Musical/Comedy: Paul Hogan, "Crocodile Dundee."
Best Supporting Actress: Maggie Smith, "A Room with a View"
Best Supporting Actor: Tom Berenger, "Platoon."
Best Screenplay: Robert Bolt, "The Mission."

National Society Of Film Critics
(Awards for films released in 1986)

Best Picture: "Blue Velvet."
Best Director: David Lynch, "Blue Velvet."
Best Actor: Bob Hoskins, "Mona Lisa."
Best Actress: Chloe Webb, "Sid and Nancy."
Best Supporting Actor: Dennis Hopper, "Blue Velvet."
Best Supporting Actress: Dianne Wiest, "Hannah and Her Sisters."
Best Screenplay: Hanif Kureishi, "My Beautiful Laundrette."

New York Film Critics
(Awards for 1986 Releases)

Best Picture: "Hannah and Her Sisters."
Best Director: Woody Allen, "Hannah and Her Sisters."
Best Actor: Bob Hoskins, "Mona Lisa."
Best Actress: Sissy Spacek, "Crimes of the Heart."
Best Supporting Actor: Daniel Day-Lewis, "My Beautiful Laundrette" & "A Room with a View."
Best Supporting Actress: Dianne Wiest, "Hannah and Her Sisters."
Best Screenplay: Hanif Kureishi, "My Beautiful Laundrette."

Los Angeles Film Critics
(Awards for films released in 1986)

Best Picture: "Hannah and Her Sisters."
Best Director: David Lynch, "Blue Velvet."
Best Actor: Bob Hoskins, "Mona Lisa."
Best Actress: Sandrine Bonnaire, "Vagabond."
Best Supporting Actor: Dennis Hopper, "Blue Velvet" & "Hoosiers."
Best Supporting Actress:
 Dianne Wiest, "Hannah and Her Sisters."
 Cathy Tyson, "Mona Lisa."
Best Screenplay: Woody Allen, "Hannah and Her Sisters."

40th Cannes Film Festival
(May 1987)

Best Picture (Palme d'Or): "Under the Sun of Satan"
Best Director: Wim Wenders, "Wings of Desire."
Best Actor: Marcello Mastroianni, "Black Eyes."
Best Actress: Barbara Hershey, "Shy People."
International Critics Prize (for competed film): "Repentance."

Independent Spirit Awards
(Awards for films released in 1986)

Best Picture: "Blue Velvet."
Best Director: Oliver Stone, "Platoon."
Best Actor: James Woods, "Salvador."
Best Actress: Isabella Rossellini, "Blue Velvet."
Best Supporting Actor: (Not awarded)
Best Supporting Actress: (Not awarded)
Best Screenplay: Oliver Stone, "Platoon."
Best Foreign Film: "A Room with a View."

1987

1986

58th Annual Academy Awards
(Oscars given for pictures released in 1985)

Best Picture: "Out of Africa," Universal; Sydney Pollack, producer.

Others Nominated:
"Back to the Future," Universal; Steven Spielberg, Kathleen Kennedy, Frank Marshall & Quincy Jones.
"Kiss of the Spider Woman," Island Alive; David Weisman, producer.
"Prizzi's Honor," ABC, 20th Century-Fox; John Foreman, producer.
"Witness," Feldman, Paramount; Edward S. Feldman, producer.

Best Director: Sydney Pollack, "Out of Africa."

Others Nominated: Hector Babenco, "Kiss of the Spider Woman"; John Huston, "Prizzi's Honor"; Akira Kurosawa, "Ran"; Peter Weir, "Witness."

Best Actor: William Hurt, "Kiss of the Spider Woman."

Others Nominated: Harrison Ford, "Witness"; James Garner, "Murphy's Romance"; Jack Nicholson, "Prizzi's Honor"; Jon Voight, "Runaway Train."

Best Actress: Geraldine Page, "The Trip to Bountiful."

Others Nominated: Anne Bancroft, "Agnes of God"; Whoopi Goldberg, "The Color Purple"; Jessica Lange, "Sweet Dreams"; Meryl Streep, "Out of Africa."

Best Supporting Actor: Don Ameche, "Cocoon."

Others Nominated: Klaus Maria Brandauer, "Out of Africa"; William Hickey, "Prizzi's Honor"; Robert Loggia, "Jagged Edge"; Eric Roberts, "Runaway Train."

Best Supporting Actress: Anjelica Huston, "Prizzi's Honor."

Others Nominated: Margaret Avery, "The Color Purple"; Amy Madigan, "Twice in a Lifetime"; Meg Tilly, "Agnes of God"; Oprah Winfrey, "The Color Purple."

Original Screenplay: William Kelley, Pamela Wallace & Earl W. Wallace, "Witness."

Others Nominated: Robert Zemeckis & Bob Gale, "Back to the Future"; Terry Gilliam, Tom Stoppard & Charles McKeown, "Brazil"; Luis Puenzo & Aida Bortnik, "The Official Story"; Woody Allen, "The Purple Rose of Cairo";

Screenplay Adaptation: Kurt Luedtke, "Out of Africa."

Others Nominated: Menno Mayjes, "The Color Purple"; Leonard Schrader, "Kiss of the Spider Woman"; Richard Condon & Janet Roach, "Prizzi's Honor"; Horton Foote, "The Trip to Bountiful."

Directors Guild Of America

1985 Best Director: Steven Spielberg, "The Color Purple."

Writers Guild Of America
(Awards given for pictures released in 1985)

Best Screenplay Written Directly for the Screen: Earl W. Wallace & William Kelley, "Witness", story by **William Kelley, Pamela Wallace & Earl Wallace.**

Best Screenplay Based on Material From Another Medium: Richard Condon & Janet Roach, "Prizzi's Honor." Based on the novel by Richard Condon.

Golden Globe Awards
(For 1985 Releases)

Best Picture-Drama: "Out of Africa."
Best Picture-Musical/Comedy: "Prizzi's Honor."
Best Director: John Huston, "Prizzi's Honor."
Best Actress-Drama: Whoopi Goldberg, "The Color Purple."
Best Actor-Drama: Jon Voight, "Runaway Train."
Best Actress-Musical/Comedy: Kathleen Turner, "Prizzi's Honor."
Best Actor-Musical/Comedy: Jack Nicholson, "Prizzi's Honor."
Best Supporting Actress: Meg Tilly, "Agnes of God."
Best Supporting Actor: Klaus Maria Brandauer, "Out of Africa."
Best Screenplay: Woody Allen, "The Purple Rose of Cairo."

National Society Of Film Critics
(Awards for films released in 1985)

Best Picture: "Ran."
Best Director: John Huston, "Prizzi's Honor."
Best Actor: Jack Nicholson, "Prizzi's Honor."
Best Actress: Vanessa Redgrave, "Wetherby."
Best Supporting Actor: John Gielgud,"The Shooting Party/Plenty."
Best Supporting Actress: Anjelica Huston, "Prizzi's Honor."
Best Screenplay: Albert Brooks and Monica Johnson, "Lost in America."

New York Film Critics
(Awards for 1985 Releases)

Best Picture: "Prizzi's Honor."
Best Director: John Huston, "Prizzi's Honor."
Best Actor: Jack Nicholson, "Prizzi's Honor."
Best Actress: Norma Aleandro, "The Official Version."
Best Supporting Actor: Klaus Maria Brandauer, "Out of Africa."
Best Supporting Actress: Anjelica Huston, "Prizzi's Honor."
Best Screenplay: Woody Allen, "The Purple Rose of Cairo."

Los Angeles Film Critics
(Awards for films released in 1985)

Best Picture: "Brazil."
Best Director: Terry Gilliam, "Brazil."
Best Actor: William Hurt, "Kiss of the Spider Woman."
Best Actress: Meryl Streep, "Out of Africa."
Best Supporting Actor: John Gielgud, "Plenty" and "The Shooting Party."
Best Supporting Actress: Anjelica Huston, "Prizzi's Honor."
Best Screenplay: Terry Gilliam, Tom Stoppard, and Charles McKeown, "Brazil."

Cannes Film Festival
(May 1986)

Best Picture (Palme d'Or): "The Mission"
Best Director: Martin Scorsese, "After Hours."
Best Actor: Bob Hoskins, "Mona Lisa."
Best Actress: (tie)
    Barbara Sukowa, "Rosa Luxembourg"
    Fernanda Torres, "Love Me Forever or Never."
International Critics Prize (for competed film): "The Sacrifice."

Independent Spirit Awards
(Awards for films released in 1985)

Best Picture: "After Hours."
Best Director: (tie)
    Martin Scorsese, "After Hours."
    Joel Coen, "Blood Simple
Best Actor: E. Emmit Walsh, "Blood Simple."
Best Actress: Geraldine Page, "Trip to Bountiful."
Best Supporting Actor: (Not awarded)
Best Supporting Actress: (Not awarded)
Best Screenplay: Horton Foote, "The Trip to Bountiful."
Best Foreign Film: "Kiss of the Spider Woman."

1986

1985

57th Annual Academy Awards
(Oscars given for pictures released in 1984)

Best Picture: "Amadeus," Zaentz, Orion; Saul Zaentz, producer.

Others Nominated:

"The Killing Fields," Enigma, Warner Bros.; David Puttnam, producer.

"A Passage to India," G.W. Films, Columbia; John Brabourne and Richard Goodwin, producers.

"Places in the Heart," TriStar; Arlene Donovan, producer.

"A Soldier's Story," Caldix, Columbia; Norman Jewison, Ronald L. Schwary & Patrick Palmer, producers.

Best Director: Milos Forman, "Amadeus."

Others Nominated: Woody Allen, "Broadway Danny Rose"; Roland Joffe, "The Killing Fields"; David Lean, "A Passage to India"; Robert Benton, "Places in the Heart."

Best Actor: F. Murray Abraham, "Amadeus."

Others Nominated: Jeff Bridges, "Starman"; Albert Finney, "Under the Volcano"; Tom Hulce, "Amadeus"; Sam Waterston, "The Killing Fields."

Best Actress: Sally Field, "Places in the Heart."

Others Nominated: Judy Davis, "A Passage to India"; Jessica Lange, "Country"; Vanessa Redgrave, "The Bostonians"; Sissy Spacek, "The River."

Best Supporting Actor: Dr. Haing S. Ngor, "The Killing Field."

Others Nominated: Adolph Caesar, "A Soldier's Story"; John Malkovich, "Places in the Heart"; Noriyuki Pat Morita, "The Karate Kid."

Best Supporting Actress: Peggy Ashcroft, "A Passage to India."

Others Nominated: Glenn Close, "The Natural"; Lindsay Crouse, "Places in the Heart"; Christine Lahti, "Swing Shift"; Geraldine Page, "The Pope of Greenwich Village."

Original Screenplay: Robert Benton, "Places in the Heart."

Others Nominated: Daniel Petrie, Jr. & Danilo Bach, "Beverly Hills Cop"; Woody Allen, "Broadway Danny Rose"; Gregory Nava & Anna Thomas, "El Norte"; Lowell Ganz, Babaloo Mandel, Bruce Jay Friedman & Brian Grazer, "Splash."

Screenplay Adaptation: Peter Schaffer, "Amadeus."

Others Nominated: P.H. Vazak & Michael Austin, "Greystoke: The Legend of Tarzan, Lord of the Apes"; Bruce Robinson, "The Killing Fields"; David Lean, "A Passage to India"; Charles Fuller, "A Soldier's Story."

Directors Guild Of America

1984 Best Director: Milos Forman, "Amadeus."

Writers Guild Of America
(Awards given for pictures released in 1984)

Best Written Comedy Written Directly for the Screen: Woody Allen, "Broadway Danny Rose."

Best Written Drama Adapted from Another Medium: Bruce Robinson, "The Killing Fields."

Based on Sydney Schanberg's "*N.Y. Times*" magazine article.

Golden Globe Awards
(For 1984 Releases)

Best Picture-Drama: "Amadeus."
Best Picture-Musical/Comedy: "Romancing the Stone."
Best Director: Milos Forman, "Amadeus."
Best Actress-Drama: Sally Field, "Places in the Heart."
Best Actor-Drama: F. Murray Abraham, "Amadeus."
Best Actress-Musical/Comedy: Kathleen Turner, "Romancing the Stone."
Best Actor-Musical/Comedy: Dudley Moore, "Arthur."
Best Supporting Actress: Peggy Ashcroft, "A Passage to India."
Best Supporting Actor: Dr. Haing S. Ngor, "The Killing Fields."
Best Screenplay: Peter Shaffer, "Amadeus."

National Society Of Film Critics
(Awards for films released in 1984)

Best Picture: "Stranger Than Paradise."
Best Director: Robert Bresson, "L'Argent."
Best Actor: Steve Martin, "All of Me."
Best Actress: Vanessa Redgrave, "The Bostonians."
Best Supporting Actor: John Malkovich, "Places in the Heart."
Best Supporting Actress: Melanie Griffith, "Body Double."
Best Screenplay: Babaloo Mandel, Lowell Ganz, & Bruce Jay Friedman, "Splash."

New York Film Critics
(Awards for 1984 Releases)

Best Picture: "A Passage to India."
Best Director: David Lean, "A Passage to India."
Best Actor: Steve Martin, "All of Me."
Best Actress: Peggy Ashcroft, "A Passage to India."
Best Supporting Actor: Ralph Richardson, "Greystoke: The Legend of Tarzan, Lord of the Apes" & "Give My Regards to Broad Street."
Best Supporting Actress: Christine Lahti, "Swing Shift."
Best Screenplay: Robert Benton, "Places in the Heart."

Los Angeles Film Critics
(Awards for films released in 1984)

Best Picture: "Amadeus."
Best Director: Milos Forman, "Amadeus."
Best Actor:
    F. Murray Abraham, "Amadeus."
    Albert Finney, "Under the Volcano."
Best Actress: Kathleen Turner, "Crimes of Passion" & "Romancing the Stone."
Best Supporting Actor: Adolph Caesar, "A Soldier's Story."
Best Supporting Actress: Peggy Ashcroft, "A Passage to India."
Best Screenplay: Peter Shaffer, "Amadeus."

Cannes Film Festival
(May 1985)

Best Picture (Palme d'Or): "Fathers on a Business Trip."
Best Director: Andre Techine, "Rendezvous."
Best Actor: William Hurt, "Kiss of the Spider Woman."
Best Actress: (tie)
    Norma Aleandro, "Official Version"
    Cher, "Mask."
International Critics Prize (for competed film): "Purple Rose of Cairo."

Independent Spirit Awards
(First presented in 1986)

1985

1984

56th Annual Academy Awards
(Oscars given for pictures released in 1983)

Best Picture: "Terms of Endearment," Brooks, paramount; James L. Brooks, producer.
Others Nominated:
"The Big Chill," Carson, Columbia; Michael Shamberg, producer.
"The Dresser," Goldcrest, Columbia; Peter Yates, producer.
"The Right Stuff," Chartoff-Winkler, The Ladd Company through Warner Bros.; Irwin Winkler & Robert Chartoff, producers.
"Tender Mercies," EMI, Universal/AFD; Philip S. Hobel, producer.

Best Director: James L. Brooks, "Terms of Endearment."
Others Nominated: Peter Yates, "The Dresser"; Ingmar Bergman, "Fanny and Alexander"; Mike Nichols, "Silkwood"; Bruce Beresford, "Tender Mercies."

Best Actor: Robert Duvall, "Tender Mercies."
Others Nominated: Michael Caine, "Educating Rita"; Tom Conti, "Reuben, Reuben"; Tom Courtenay, "The Dresser"; Albert Finney, "The Dresser."

Best Actress: Shirley MacLaine, "Terms of Endearment."
Others Nominated: Jane Alexander, "Testament"; Meryl Streep, "Silkwood"; Julie Walters, "Educating Rita"; Debra Winger, "Terms of Endearment."

Best Supporting Actor: Jack Nicholson, "Terms of Endearment"
Others Nominated: Charles Durning, "To Be or Not to Be"; John Lithgow, "Terms of Endearment"; Sam Shepard, "The Right Stuff"; Rip Torn, "Cross Creek."

Best Supporting Actress: Linda Hunt, "The Year of Living Dangerously."
Others Nominated: Cher, "Silkwood"; Glenn Close, "The Big Chill"; Amy Irving, "Yentl"; Alfre Woodard, "Cross Creek."

Original Screenplay: Horton Foote, "Tender Mercies."
Others Nominated: Lawrence Kasdan & Barbara Benedek, "The Big Chill"; Ingmar Bergman, "Fanny and Alexander"; Nora Ephron & Alice Arlen, "Silkwood"; Lawrence Lasker & Walter F. Parkes, "Wargames."

Screenplay Adaptation: James L. Brooks, "Terms of Endearment."
Others Nominated: Harold Pinter, "Betrayal"; Ronald Harwood, "The Dresser"; Willy Russell, "Educating Rita"; Julius J. Epstein, "Reuben, Reuben."

Directors Guild Of America

1983 Best Director: James L. Brooks, "Terms of Endearment."

Writers Guild Of America
(Awards given for pictures released in 1983)

Best Written Comedy Written Directly for the Screen: Lawrence Kasdan & Barbara Benedek, "The Big Chill."

Best Written Comedy Adapted from Another Medium: James L. Brooks, "Terms of Endearment." Based on the novel by Larry McMurtry.

Best Written Drama Written Directly for the Screen: Horton Foote, "Tender Mercies."

Best Written Drama Adapted from Another Medium: Julius J. Epstein, "Reuben, Reuben." Based on the novel by Peter DeVries and the play "Spofford" by Herman Shumlin.

Golden Globe Awards
(For 1983 Releases)

Best Picture-Drama: "Terms of Endearment."
Best Picture-Musical/Comedy: "Yentl."
Best Director: Barbra Streisand, "Yentl."
Best Actress-Drama: Shirley MacLaine, "Terms of Endearment."
Best Actor-Drama: (tie) Tom Courtenay, "The Dresser" & Robert Duvall, "Tender Mercies."
Best Actress-Musical/Comedy: Julie Walters, "Educating Rita."
Best Actor-Musical/Comedy: Michael Caine, "Educating Rita."
Best Supporting Actress: Cher, "Silkwood."
Best Supporting Actor: Jack Nicholson, "Terms of Endearment."
Best Screenplay: James L. Brooks, "Terms of Endearment."

National Society Of Film Critics
(Awards for films released in 1983)

Best Picture: "The Night of the Shooting Stars."
Best Director: Paolo and Vittorio Taviani, "The Night of the Shooting Stars."
Best Actor: Gerard Depardieu, "The Return of Martin Guerre."
Best Actress: Debra Winger, "Terms of Endearment."
Best Supporting Actor: Jack Nicholson, "Terms of Endearment."
Best Supporting Actress: Sandra Bernhard, "The King of Comedy."
Best Screenplay: Bill Forsyth, "Local Hero."

New York Film Critics
(Awards for 1983 Releases)

Best Picture: "Terms of Endearment."
Best Director: Ingmar Bergman, "Fanny and Alexander."
Best Actor: Robert Duvall, "Tender Mercies."
Best Actress: Shirley MacLaine, "Terms of Endearment."
Best Supporting Actor: Jack Nicholson, "Terms of Endearment."
Best Supporting Actress: Linda Hunt, "The Year of Living Dangerously."
Best Screenplay: Bill Forsyth, "Local Hero."

Los Angeles Film Critics
(Awards for films released in 1983)

Best Picture: "Terms of Endearment."
Best Director: James L. Brooks, "Terms of Endearment."
Best Actor: Robert Duvall, "Tender Mercies."
Best Actress: Shirley MacLaine, "Terms of Endearment."
Best Supporting Actor: Jack Nicholson, "Terms of Endearment."
Best Supporting Actress: Linda Hunt, "The Year of Living Dangerously."
Best Screenplay: James L. Brooks, "Terms of Endearment."

Cannes Film Festival
(May 1984)

Best Picture (Palme d'Or): "Paris, Texas"
Best Director: Bertrand Tavernier, "A Sunday in the Country."
Best Actor: (shared) Alfredo Landa & Francisco Rabal, "Los Santos Inocentes."
Best Actress: Helen Mirren, "Cal."
Original Screenplay: Tonino Guerra, "Voyage to Cythera."
International Critics Prize (for competed film): "Paris, Texas."

Independent Spirit Awards
(First presented in 1986)

1984

1983

55th Annual Academy Awards
(Oscars given for pictures released in 1982)

Best Picture: "Gandhi," Columbia; Richard Attenborough, producer.
  Others Nominated:
    "E.T. The Extra-Terrestrial," Universal; Steven Spielberg and Kathleen Kennedy, producer.
    "Missing," Lewis, Universal; Edward Lewis and Mildred Lewis, producers.
    "Tootsie," Mirage/Punch, Columbia; Sydney Pollack and Dick Richards, producers.
    "The Verdict," Zanuck/Brown, 20th Century-Fox; Richard D. Zanuck and David Brown, producers.
Best Director: Richard Attenborough, "Gandhi."
  Others Nominated: Wolfgang Petersen, "Das Boot"; Steven Spielberg, "E.T. The Extra-Terrestrial";
    Sydney Pollack, "Tootsie"; Sydney Lumet, "The Verdict."
Best Actor: Ben Kingsley, "Gandhi."
  Others Nominated: Dustin Hoffman, "Tootsie"; Jack Lemmon, "Missing"; Paul Newman, "The Verdict";
    Peter O'Toole, "My Favorite Year."
Best Actress: Meryl Streep, "Sophie's Choice."
  Others Nominated: Julie Andrews, "Victor/Victoria"; Jessica Lange, "Frances"; Sissy Spacek, "Missing";
    Debra Winger, "An Officer and a Gentleman."
Best Supporting Actor: Louis Gossett, Jr., "An Officer and a Gentleman."
  Others Nominated: Charles Durning, "The Best Little Whorehouse in Texas"; John Lithgow, "The World
    According to Garp"; James Mason, "The Verdict"; Robert Preston, "Victor/Victoria."
Best Supporting Actress: Jessica Lange, "Tootsie."
  Others Nominated: Glenn Close, "The World According to Garp"; Teri Garr, "Tootsie"; Kim Stanley,
    "Frances"; Lesley Ann Warren, "Victor/Victoria."
Original Screenplay: John Briley, "Gandhi."
  Others Nominated: Barry Levinson, "Diner"; Melissa Mathison, "E.T. The Extra-Terrestrial"; Douglas Day
    Stewart, "An Officer and a Gentleman"; Larry Gelbart, Murray Schisgal & Don McGuire, "Tootsie."
Screenplay Adaptation: Constantine Costa-Gavras & Donald E. Stewart, "Missing."
  Others Nominated: Wolfgang Petersen, "Das Boot"; Alan J. Pakula, "Sophie's Choice"; David Mamet,
    "The Verdict"; Blake Edwards, "Victor/Victoria."

Directors Guild Of America

1982 Best Director: Richard Attenborough, "Gandhi."

Writers Guild Of America
(Awards given for pictures released in 1982)

Best Written Comedy Written Directly for the Screen: Larry Gelbart & Murray Schisgal,
  "Tootsie", story by Don McGuire & Larry Gelbart.
Best Written Comedy Adapted from Another Medium: Blake Edwards, "Victor/Victor."
  Based on the 1933 film "Viktor Und Viktoria."
Best Written Drama Written Directly for the Screen: Melissa Mathison, "E.T. The Extra-
  Terrestrial."
**Best Written Drama Adapted from Another Medium: Constantine Costa-Gavras &
  Donald E. Stewart**, "Missing." Based on Thomas Hauser's "The Execution of Charles Horman."

Golden Globe Awards
(For 1982 Releases)

Best Picture-Drama: "E.T. The Extra Terrestrial."
Best Picture-Musical/Comedy: "Tootsie."
Best Director: Richard Attenborough, "Gandhi."
Best Actress-Drama: Meryl Streep, "Sophie's Choice."
Best Actor-Drama: Ben Kingsley, "Gandhi."
Best Actress-Musical/Comedy: Julie Andrews, "Victor/Victoria."
Best Actor-Musical/Comedy: Dustin Hoffman, "Tootsie."
Best Supporting Actress: Jessica Lange, "Tootsie."
Best Supporting Actor: Louis Gosset Jr., "An Officer and a Gentleman."
Best Screenplay: John Briley, "Gandhi."

National Society Of Film Critics
(Awards for films released in 1982)

Best Picture: "Tootsie."
Best Director: Steven Spielberg, "E.T. The Extra-Terrestrial."
Best Actor: Dustin Hoffman, "Tootsie."
Best Actress: Meryl Streep, "Sophie's Choice."
Best Supporting Actor: Mickey Rourke, "Diner."
Best Supporting Actress: Jessica Lange, "Tootsie."
Best Screenplay: Larry Gelbart & Murray Schisgal, "Tootsie."

New York Film Critics
(Awards for 1982 Releases)

Best Picture: "Gandhi."
Best Director: Sydney Pollack, "Tootsie."
Best Actor: Ben Kingsley, "Gandhi."
Best Actress: Meryl Streep, "Sophie's Choice."
Best Supporting Actor: John Lithgow, "The World According to Garp."
Best Supporting Actress: Jessica Lange, "Tootsie."
Best Screenplay: Larry Gelbart & Murray Schisgal, "Tootsie."

Los Angeles Film Critics
(Awards for films released in 1978)

Best Picture: "E.T. The Extra Terrestrial."
Best Director: Steven Spielberg, "E.T. The Extra-Terrestrial."
Best Actor: Ben Kingsley, "Gandhi."
Best Actress: Meryl Streep, "Sophie's Choice."
Best Supporting Actor: John Lithgow, "The World According to Garp."
Best Supporting Actress: Glenn Close, "The World According to Garp."
Best Screenplay: Larry Gelbart & Murray Schisgal, "Tootsie."

Cannes Film Festival
(May 1983)

Best Picture (Palme d'Or): "The Ballad of Narayama"
Best Director: (no award)
Best Actor: Gian Maria Volonte, "La Mort De Mario Ricci."
Best Actress: Hanna Schygulla, "Storia Di Piera."
International Critics Prize (for competed film): "Nostalgia."

Independent Spirit Awards
(First presented in 1986)

1983

1982

54th Annual Academy Awards
(Oscars given for pictures released in 1981)

Best Picture: "Chariots of Fire," Enigma, The Ladd Company/Warner Bros.; David Puttnam, producer.

Others Nominated:
   "Atlantic City," ICC, Paramount; Dennis Heroux and John Kemeny, producers.
   "On Golden Pond," ITC/IPC, Universal; Bruce Gilbert, producer.
   "Raiders of the Lost Ark," Lucasfilm, Paramount; Frank Marshall, producer.
   "Reds," J.R.S., Paramount; Warren Beatty, producer.

Best Director: Warren Beatty, "Reds."

Others Nominated: Louis Malle, "Atlantic City"; Hugh Hudson, "Chariots of Fire"; Mark Rydell, "On Golden Pond"; Steven Spielberg, "Raiders of the Lost Ark."

Best Actor: Henry Fonda, "On Golden Pond."

Others Nominated: Warren Beatty, "Reds"; Burt Lancaster, "Atlantic City"; Dudley Moore, "Arthur"; Paul Newman, "Absence of Malice."

Best Actress: Katharine Hepburn, "On Golden Pond."

Others Nominated: Diane Keaton, "Reds"; Marsha Mason, "Only When I Laugh"; Susan Sarandon, "Atlantic City"; Meryl Streep, "The French Lieutenant's Woman."

Best Supporting Actor: John Gielgud, "Arthur."

Others Nominated: James Coco, "Only When I Laugh"; Ian Holm, "Chariots of Fire"; Jack Nicholson, "Reds"; Howard E. Rollins Jr. , "Ragtime."

Best Supporting Actress: Maureen Stapleton, "Reds."

Others Nominated: Melinda Dillon, "Absence of Malice"; Jane Fonda, "On Golden Pond"; Joan Hackett, "Only When I Laugh"; Elizabeth McGovern, "Ragtime."

Original Screenplay: Colin Welland, "Chariots of Fire."

Others Nominated: Kurt Luedtke, "Absence of Malice"; Steve Gordon, "Arthur"; John Guare, "Atlantic City"; Warren Beatty & Trevor Griffiths, "Reds."

Screenplay Adaptation: Ernest Thompson, "On Golden Pond."

Others Nominated: Harold Pinter, "The French Lieutenant's Woman"; Dennis Potter, "Pennies from Heaven"; Jay Presson Allen & Sidney Lumet, "Prince of the City"; Michael Weller, "Ragtime."

Directors Guild Of America

1981 Best Director: Warren Beatty, "Reds."

Writers Guild Of America
(Awards given for pictures released in 1981)

Best Written Comedy Written Directly for the Screen: Steve Gordon, "Arthur."

Best Written Comedy Adapted from Another Medium: Gerald Ayres, "Rich and Famous."
   Based on the play by John Van Druten's.

Best Written Drama Written Directly for the Screen: Warren Beatty & Trevor Griffiths, "Reds."

Best Written Drama Adapted From Another Medium: Ernest Thompson, "On Golden Pond."
   Based on his play.

Golden Globe Awards
(For 1981 Releases)

Best Picture-Drama: "On Golden Pond."
Best Picture-Musical/Comedy: "Arthur."
Best Director: Warren Beatty, "Reds."
Best Actress-Drama: Meryl Streep, "The French Lieutenant's Woman."
Best Actor-Drama: Henry Fonda, "On Golden Pond."
Best Actress-Musical/Comedy: Bernadette Peters, "Pennies from Heaven."
Best Actor-Musical/Comedy: Dudley Moore, "Arthur."
Best Supporting Actress: Joan Hackett, "Only When I Laugh."
Best Supporting Actor: John Gielgud, "Arthur."
Best Screenplay: Ernest Thompson, "On Golden Pond."

National Society Of Film Critics
(Awards for films released in 1981)

Best Picture: "Atlantic City."
Best Director: Louis Malle, "Atlantic City."
Best Actor: Burt Lancaster, "Atlantic City."
Best Actress: Marilia Pera, "Pixote."
Best Supporting Actor: Robert Preston, "S.O.B."
Best Supporting Actress: Maureen Stapleton, "Reds."
Best Screenplay: John Guare, "Atlantic City."

New York Film Critics
(Awards for 1981 Releases)

Best Picture: "Reds."
Best Director: Sidney Lumet, "Prince of the City."
Best Actor: Burt Lancaster, "Atlantic City."
Best Actress: Glenda Jackson, "Stevie."
Best Supporting Actor: John Gielgud, "Arthur."
Best Supporting Actress: Mona Washbourne, "Stevie."
Best Screenplay: John Guare, "Atlantic City."

Los Angeles Film Critics
(Awards for films released in 1981)

Best Picture: "Atlantic City."
Best Director: Warren Beatty, "Reds."
Best Actor: Burt Lancaster, "Atlantic City."
Best Actress: Meryl Streep, "The French Lieutenant's Woman."
Best Supporting Actor: John Gielgud, "Arthur."
Best Supporting Actress: Maureen Stapleton, "Stevie."
Best Screenplay: John Guare, "Atlantic City."

Cannes Film Festival
(May 1982)

Best Picture (Palme d'Or): (tie) "Missing" &"Yol."
Best Director: Werner Herzog, "Fitcarraldo."
Best Actor: Jack Lemmon, "Missing."
Best Actress: Edwiga Jankowska, "Another Way."
Best Screenplay: Jerry Skolimowksi, "Moonlighting."
International Critics Prize: (no award)

Independent Spirit Awards
(First presented in 1986)

1982

1981

53rd Annual Academy Awards
(Oscars given for pictures released in 1980)

Best Picture: "Ordinary People," Wildwood, Paramount; Ronald L. Schwary, producer.
Others Nominated:
"Coal Miner's Daughter," Schwartz, Universal; Bernard Schwartz, producer.
"The Elephant Man," Brooksfilms, Paramount; Jonathan Sanger, producer.
"Raging Bull," Chartoff-Winkler, UA; Irwin Winkler and Robert Chartoff, producers.
"Tess," Renn-Burrill, Columbia; Calude Berri, producer. Co-produced by Timothy Burrill.

Best Director: Robert Redford, "Ordinary People."
Others Nominated: David Lynch, "The Elephant Man"; Martin Scorsese, "Raging Bull"; Richard Rush , "The Stunt Man"; Roman Polanski, "Tess."

Best Actor: Robert De Niro, "Raging Bull."
Others Nominated: Robert Duvall, "The Great Santini"; John Hurt, "The Elephant Man"; Jack Lemmon, "Tribute"; Peter O'Toole, "The Stunt Man."

Best Actress: Sissy Spacek, "Coal Miner's Daughter."
Others Nominated: Ellen Burstyn, "Resurrection"; Goldie Hawn, "Private Benjamin"; Mary Tyler Moore, "Ordinary People"; Gena Rowlands, "Gloria."

Best Supporting Actor: Timothy Hutton, "Ordinary People."
Others Nominated: Judd Hirsch, "Ordinary People"; Michael O'Keefe, "The Great Santini"; Joe Pesci, "Raging Bull"; Jason Robards, "Melvin and Howard."

Best Supporting Actress: Mary Steenburgen, "Melvin and Howard."
Others Nominated: Eileen Brennan, "Private Benjamin"; Eva Le Gallienne, "Resurrection"; Cathy Moriarty, "Raging Bull"; Diana Scarwid, "Inside Moves."

Original Screenplay: Bo Goldman, "Melvin and Howard."
Others Nominated: W.D. Richter and Arthur Ross, "Brubaker"; Christopher Gore, "Fame"; Jean Gruault, "Mon Oncle D'Amerique"; Nancy Meyers, Charles Shyer & Harvey Miller, "Private Benjamin."

Screenplay Adaptation: Alvin Sargent, "Ordinary People."
Others Nominated: Jonathan Hardy, David Stevens & Bruce Beresford, "Breaker Morant"; Tom Rickman, "Coal Miner's Daughter"; Christopher DeVore, Eric Bergren & David Lynch, "The Elephant Man"; Lawrence B. Marcus & Richard Rush, "The Stunt Man."

Directors Guild Of America

1980 Best Director: Robert Redford, "Ordinary People."

Writers Guild Of America
(Awards given for pictures released in 1980)

Best Written Comedy Written Directly for the Screen: Nancy Meyers, Charles Shyer & Harvey Miller, "Private Benjamin."

Best Written Comedy Adapted from Another Medium: Jim Abrahams, David Zucker & Jerry Zucker, "Airplane."

Best Written Drama Written Directly for the Screen: Bo Goldman, "Melvin and Howard."

Best Written Drama Adapted From Another Medium: Alvin Sargent, "Ordinary People."
Based on the novel by Judith Guest.

Golden Globe Awards
(For 1980 Releases)

Best Picture-Drama: "Ordinary People."
Best Picture-Musical/Comedy: "Coal Miner's Daughter."
Best Director: Robert Redford, "Ordinary People."
Best Actress-Drama: Mary Tyler Moore, "Ordinary People."
Best Actor-Drama: Robert De Niro, "Raging Bull."
Best Actress-Musical/Comedy: Sissy Spacek, "Coal Miner's Daughter."
Best Actor-Musical/Comedy: Ray Sharkey, "The Idolmaker."
Best Supporting Actress: Mary Steenburgen, "Melvin & Howard."
Best Supporting Actor: Timothy Hutton, "Ordinary People."
Best Screenplay: William Peter Blatty, "Twinkle, Twinkle, Killer Kane."

National Society Of Film Critics
(Awards for films released in 1980)

Best Picture: "Melvin and Howard."
Best Director: Martin Scorsese, "Raging Bull."
Best Actor: Peter O'Toole, "The Stunt Man."
Best Actress: Sissy Spacek, "Coal Miner's Daughter."
Best Supporting Actor: Joe Pesci, "Raging Bull."
Best Supporting Actress: Mary Steenburgen, "Melvin and Howard."
Best Screenplay: Bo Goldman, "Melvin and Howard."

New York Film Critics
(Awards for 1980 Releases)

Best Picture: "Ordinary People."
Best Director: Jonathan Demme, "Melvin and Howard."
Best Actor: Robert De Niro, "Raging Bull."
Best Actress: Sissy Spacek, "Coal Miner's Daughter."
Best Supporting Actor: Joe Pesci, "Raging Bull."
Best Supporting Actress: Mary Steenburgen, "Melvin and Howard."
Best Screenplay: Bo Goldman, "Melvin and Howard."

Los Angeles Film Critics
(Awards for films released in 1980)

Best Picture: "Raging Bull."
Best Director: Roman Polanski, "Tess."
Best Actor: Robert De Niro, "Raging Bull."
Best Actress: Sissy Spacek, "Coal Miner's Daughter."
Best Supporting Actor: Timothy Hutton, "Ordinary People."
Best Supporting Actress: Mary Steenburgen, "Melvin and Howard."
Best Screenplay: John Sayles, "Return of the Secaucus Seven."

Cannes Film Festival
(May 1981)

Best Picture (Palme d'Or): "Man of Iron"
Best Director: Andrzej Wajda, "Man of Iron."
Best Actor: Ugo Tognazzi, "Tragedy of a Ridiculous Man."
Best Actress: Isabelle Adjani, "Quartet" & "Possession."
Best Supporting Actor: Ian Holm, "Chariots of Fire."
Best Supporting Actress: Elean Solevei, "The Fact."
Best Screenplay: Istuan Szabo & Peter Dobai, "Mephisto."
International Critics Prize (for competed film): "Mephisto."

Independent Spirit Awards
(First presented in 1986)

1981

1980

52nd Annual Academy Awards
(Oscars given for pictures released in 1979)

Best Picture: "Kramer vs. Kramer," Columbia.
Others Nominated:
  "All That Jazz," Columbia/20th Century Fox.
  "Apocalypse Now," United Artists.
  "Breaking Away," 20th Century Fox.
  "Norma Rae," 20th Century Fox.

Best Director: Robert Benton, "Kramer vs. Kramer."
Others Nominated: Bob Fosse, "All That Jazz"; Peter Yates, "Breaking Away"; Francis Ford Coppola, "Apocalypse Now"; Edouard Molinaro, "La Cage aux Folles."

Best Actor: Dustin Hoffman, "Kramer vs. Kramer."
Others Nominated: Jack Lemmon, "The China Syndrome"; Al Pacino, "And Justice For All"; Roy Scheider, "All That Jazz"; Peter Sellers, "Being There."

Best Actress: Sally Field, "Norma Rae."
Others Nominated: Jill Clayburgh, "Starting Over"; Jane Fonda, "The China Syndrome"; Marsha Mason, "Chapter Two"; Bette Midler, "The Rose."

Best Supporting Actor: Melvyn Douglas, "Being There."
Others Nominated: Robert Duvall, "Apocalypse Now"; Frederic Forrest, "The Rose"; Justin Henry, "Kramer vs. Kramer"; Mickey Rooney, "The Black Stallion."

Best Supporting Actress: Meryl Streep, "Kramer vs Kramer."
Others Nominated: Barbara Barrie, "Breaking Away"; Candice Bergen, "Starting Over"; Mariel Hemingway, "Manhattan"; Jane Alexander, "Kramer vs. Kramer."

Original Screenplay: Steve Tesich, "Breaking Away."
Others Nominated: Robert Alan Arthur & Bob Fosse, "All That Jazz"; Valerie Curtin & Barry Levinson, "And Justice For All"; Mike Gray, T.S. Cook & James Bridges, "The China Syndrome."

Screenplay Adaptation: Robert Benton, "Kramer vs. Kramer."
Others Nominated: John Milius & Francis Ford Coppola, "Apocalypse Now"; Francis Veber, Edouard Molinaro, Marcello Danon & Jean Poiret, "La Cage aux Folles."

Directors Guild Of America

1979 Best Director: Robert Benton, "Kramer vs. Kramer."

Writers Guild Of America
(Awards given for pictures released in 1979)

Best Written Comedy Written Directly for the Screen: Steve Tesich, "Breaking Away."

Best Written Comedy Adapted from Another Medium: Jerry Kosinski, "Being There." Based on his novel.

Best Written Drama Written Directly for the Screen: Mike Gray, T.S. Cook & James Bridges, "The China Syndrome."

Best Written Drama Adapted from Another Medium: Robert Benton, "Kramer vs. Kramer." Based on the novel by Avery Corman.

Golden Globe Awards
(For 1979 Releases)

Best Picture-Drama: "Kramer vs. Kramer."
Best Picture-Musical/Comedy: "Breaking Away."
Best Director: Francis Ford Coppola, "Apocalypse Now."
Best Actress-Drama: Sally Field, "Norma Rae."
Best Actor-Drama: Dustin Hoffman, "Kramer vs. Kramer."
Best Actress-Musical/Comedy: Bette Midler, "The Rose."
Best Actor-Musical/Comedy: Peter Sellers, "Being There."
Best Supporting Actress: Meryl Streep, "Kramer vs. Kramer."
Best Supporting Actor: (tie)
  Robert Duvall, "Apocalypse Now"
  Melvyn Douglass, "Being There."
Best Screenplay: Robert Benton, "Kramer vs. Kramer."

National Society Of Film Critics
(Awards for films released in 1979)

Best Picture: "Breaking Away."
Best Director: (tie)
  Robert Benton, "Kramer vs. Kramer"
  Woody Allen, "Manhattan."
Best Actor: Dustin Hoffman, "Kramer vs. Kramer"; "Agatha."
Best Actress: Sally Field, "Norma Rae."
Best Supporting Actor: Frederic Forrest, "The Rose", "Apocalypse Now."
Best Supporting Actress: Meryl Streep, "Kramer vs. Kramer"; "Manhattan."
Best Screenplay: Steve Tesich, "Breaking Away."

New York Film Critics
(Awards for 1979 Releases)

Best Picture: "Kramer vs. Kramer"
Best Director: Woody Allen, "Manhattan."
Best Actor: Dustin Hoffman, "Kramer vs. Kramer."
Best Actress: Sally Field, "Norma Rae."
Best Supporting Actor: Melvyn Douglas, "Being There."
Best Supporting Actress: Meryl Streep, "Kramer vs. Kramer"; "Manhattan."
Best Screenplay: Steve Tesich, "Breaking Away."

Los Angeles Film Critics
(Awards for films released in 1979)

Best Picture: "Kramer vs. Kramer"
Best Director: Robert Benton, "Kramer vs. Kramer."
Best Actor: Dustin Hoffman, "Kramer vs. Kramer."
Best Actress: Sally Field, "Norma Rae."
Best Supporting Actor: Melvyn Douglas, "Being There"; "Seduction Of Joe Tynan."
Best Supporting Actress: Meryl Streep, "Kramer vs. Kramer"; "Manhattan"; "Seduction of Tynan."
Best Screenplay: Robert Benton, "Kramer vs. Kramer."

Cannes Film Festival
(May 1980)

Best Picture (Palme d'Or): (tie)
  "All That Jazz"
  "Kagemusha"
Best Director: Akira Kurosawa, "Kagemusha."
Best Actor: Michel Piccoli, "Salto Nel Uvoto."
Best Actress: Anouk Aimee, "Salto Nel Uvoto."
Best Supporting Actor: Jack Thompson, "Breaker Morant."
Best Supporting Actress: (tie)
  Carla Gravina, "La Terrazza"
  Milena Dravic, "Poseban Tretman."
Best Screenplay: Ettore Scola, "La Terrazza."
International Critics Prize: (no award)

Independent Spirit Awards
(First presented in 1986)

1980

1979

51st Annual Academy Awards
(Oscars given for pictures released in 1978)

Best Picture: "The Deer Hunter," EMI/ Cimino, Universal.

Others Nominated:
"Coming Home," Hellman, United Artists.
"Heaven Can Wait," Paramount.
"Midnight Express," Columbia.
"An Unmarried Woman," 20th Century Fox.

Best Director: Michael Cimino, "The Dear Hunter."

Others Nominated: Woody Allen, "Interiors"; Hal Ashby, "Coming Home"; Warren Beatty & Buck Henry, "Heaven Can Wait"; Alan Parker, "Midnight Express."

Best Actor: Jon Voight, "Coming Home."

Others Nominated: Warren Beatty, "Heaven Can Wait"; Gary Busey, "The Buddy Holly Story"; Robert De Niro, "The Deer Hunter"; Laurence Olivier, "The Boys From Brazil."

Best Actress: Jane Fonda, "Coming Home."

Others Nominated: Ingrid Bergman, "Autumn Sonata"; Ellen Burstyn, "Same Time Next Year"; Jill Clayburgh, "An Unmarried Woman"; Geraldine Page, "Interiors."

Best Supporting Actor: Christopher Walken, "The Deer Hunter."

Others Nominated: Bruce Dern, "Coming Home"; Richard Farnsworth, "Comes A Horseman"; John Hurt, "Midnight Express"; Jack Warden, "Heaven Can Wait."

Best Supporting Actress: Maggie Smith, "California Suite."

Others Nominated: Dyan Cannon, "Heaven Can Wait"; Penelope Milford, "Coming Home"; Maureen Stapleton, "Interiors"; Meryl Streep, "The Deer Hunter."

Original Screenplay: Waldo Salt, Robert C. Jones (SP)**, Nancy Dowd** (S) "Coming Home."

Others Nominated: Robert Alan Arthur & Bob Fosse, "All That Jazz"; Valerie Curtin & Barry Levinson, "And Justice For All"; Mike Gray, T.S. Cook & James Bridges, "The China Syndrome."

Screenplay Adaptation: Oliver Stone, "Midnight Express."

Others Nominated: Elaine May & Warren Beatty, "Heaven Can Wait"; Walter Newman, "Bloodbrothers"; Neil Simon, "California Suite"; Bernard Slade, "Same Time Next Year."

Directors Guild Of America

1978 Best Director: Michael Cimino, "The Deer Hunter."

Writers Guild Of America
(Awards given for pictures released in 1978)

Best Written Comedy Written Directly for the Screen: Larry Gelbart & Sheldon Keller, "Movie, Movie."

Best Written Comedy Adapted from Another Medium: Elaine May & Warren Beatty, "Heaven Can Wait."

Best Written Drama Written Directly for the Screen: Waldo Salt, Robert C. Jones, "Coming Home", story by **Nancy Dowd.**

Best Written Drama Adapted From Another Medium: Oliver Stone, "Midnight Express."

Golden Globe Awards
(For 1978 Releases)

Best Picture-Drama: "Midnight Express."
Best Picture-Musical/Comedy: "Heaven Can Wait."
Best Director: Michael Cimino, "The Deer Hunter."
Best Actress-Drama: Jane Fonda, "Coming Home."
Best Actor-Drama: Jon Voight, "Coming Home."
Best Actress-Musical/Comedy: Maggie Smith, "California Suite."
Best Actor-Musical/Comedy: Warren Beatty, "Heaven Can Wait."
Best Supporting Actress: Dyan Cannon, "Heaven Can Wait."
Best Supporting Actor: John Hurt, "Midnight Express."
Best Screenplay: Oliver Stone, "Midnight Express."

National Society Of Film Critics
(Awards for films released in 1978)

Best Picture: "Get Out Your Handkerchiefs."
Best Director: Terrence Malick, "Days of Heaven."
Best Actor: Gary Busey, "The Buddy Holly Story."
Best Actress: Ingrid Bergman, "Autumn Sonata."
Best Supporting Actor: Richard Farnsworth, "Comes A Horseman."
Best Supporting Actress: Meryl Streep, "The Deer Hunter."
Best Screenplay: Paul Mazursky, "An Unmarried Woman."

New York Film Critics
(Awards for 1978 Releases)

Best Picture: "The Deer Hunter."
Best Director: Terrence Malick, "Days of Heaven."
Best Actor: Jon Voight, "Coming Home."
Best Actress: Ingrid Bergman, "Autumn Sonata."
Best Supporting Actor: Christopher Walken, "The Deer Hunter."
Best Supporting Actress: Colleen Dewhurst, "Interiors."
Best Screenplay: Paul Mazursky, "An Unmarried Woman."

Los Angeles Film Critics
(Awards for films released in 1978)

Best Picture: "Coming Home"
Best Director: Michael Cimino, "The Deer Hunter."
Best Actor: Jon Voight, "Coming Home."
Best Actress: Jane Fonda, "Coming Home."
Best Supporting Actor: Robert Morley, "Who Is Killing the Great Chefs Of Europe."
Best Supporting Actress:
    Maureen Stapleton, "Interiors"
    Mona Washbourne, "Stevie."
Best Screenplay: Paul Mazursky, "An Unmarried Woman."

Cannes Film Festival
(June 1979)

Best Picture: "Apocalypse Now"
Best Director: Terrence Malick, "Days Of Heaven."
Best Actor: Jack Lemmon, "The China Syndrome."
Best Actress: Sally Field, "Norma Rae."
Best Supporting Actor: Stefano Madia, "Caro Papa."
Best Supporting Actress: Eva Mattes, "Woyzeck."
International Critics Prize (for competed film): "Apocalypse Now."

Independent Spirit Awards
(First presented in 1986)

1979

1978

50th Annual Academy Awards
(Oscars given for pictures released in 1977)

Best Picture: "Annie Hall," Rollins-Joffee, United Artists.
Others Nominated:
"The Goodbye Girl," MGM-Warner Bros.
"Julia," 20th Century-Fox.
"Star Wars," 20th Century-Fox.
"The Turning Point," 20th Century Fox.

Best Director: Woody Allen, "Annie Hall."
Others Nominated: George Lucas, "Star Wars"; Herbert Ross, "The Turning Point"; Steven Spielberg, "Close Encounters of the Third Kind"; Fred Zinnemann, "Julia."

Best Actor: Richard Dreyfuss, "The Goodbye Girl."
Others Nominated: Woody Allen, "Annie Hall"; Richard Burton, "Equus"; Marcello Mastroianni, "A Special Day"; John Travolta, "Saturday Night Fever."

Best Actress: Diane Keaton, "Annie Hall."
Others Nominated: Anne Bancroft, "The Turning Point"; Jane Fonda, "Julia"; Shirley MacLaine, "The Turning Point"; Marsha Mason, "The Goodbye Girl."

Best Supporting Actor: Jason Robards, "Julia."
Others Nominated: Mikhail Baryshnikov, "The Turning Point"; Peter Firth, "Equus"; Alec Guinness, "Star Wars"; Maximilian Schell, "Julia."

Best Supporting Actress: Vanessa Redgrave, "Julia."
Others Nominated: Leslie Browne, "The Turning Point"; Quinn Cummings, "The Goodbye Girl"; Melinda Dillon, "Close Encounters of the Third Kind"; Tuesday Weld, "Looking for Mr. Goodbar."

Original Screenplay: Woody Allen & Marshall Brickman, "Annie Hall."
Others Nominated: Neil Simon, "The Goodbye Girl"; Robert Benton, "The Late Show"; George Lucas, "Star Wars"; Arthur Laurents, "The Turning Point."

Screenplay Adaptation: Alvin Sargent, "Julia."
Others Nominated: Peter Shaffer, "Equus"; Gavin Lambert & Lewis John Carlino, "I Never Promised You a Rose Garden", Larry Gelbart, "Oh God"; Luis Bunuel & Jean-Claude Carriere, "That Obscure Object of Desire."

Directors Guild Of America

1977 Best Director: Woody Allen, "Annie Hall."

Writers Guild Of America
(Awards given for pictures released in 1977)

Best Written Comedy Written Directly for the Screen: Woody Allen & Marshall Brickman, "Annie Hall."

Best Written Comedy Adapted from Another Medium: Larry Gelbart, "Oh God."

Best Written Drama Written Directly for the Screen: Avery Corman & Arthur Laurents, "The Turning Point."

Best Written Drama Adapted from Another Medium: Alvin Sargent, "Julia."

Golden Globe Awards
(For 1977 Releases)

Best Picture-Drama: "The Turning Point."
Best Picture-Musical/Comedy: "The Goodbye Girl."
Best Director: Herbert Ross, "The Turning Point."
Best Actress-Drama: Jane Fonda, "Julia."
Best Actor-Drama: Richard Burton, "Equus."
Best Actress-Musical/Comedy:
   Marsha Mason, "The Goodbye Girl."
   Diane Keaton, "Annie Hall."
Best Actor-Musical/Comedy: Richard Dreyfuss, "The Goodbye Girl."
Best Supporting Actress: Vanessa Redgrave, "Julia."
Best Supporting Actor: Peter Firth, "Equus."
Best Screenplay: Neil Simon, "The Goodbye Girl."

National Society Of Film Critics
(Awards for films released in 1977)

Best Picture: "Annie Hall."
Best Director: Luis Brunuel, "That Obscure Object of Desire."
Best Actor: Art Carney, "The Late Show."
Best Actress: Diane Keaton, "Annie Hall."
Best Supporting Actor: Edward Fox, "A Bridge Too Far"
Best Supporting Actress: Anne Wedgeworth, "Handle with Care."
Best Screenplay: Woody Allen & Marshall Brickman, "Annie Hall."

New York Film Critics
(Awards for 1977 Releases)

Best Picture: "Annie Hall."
Best Director: Woody Allen, "Annie Hall."
Best Actor: John Gielgud, "Providence."
Best Actress: Diane Keaton, "Annie Hall."
Best Supporting Actor: Maximilian Schell, "Julia."
Best Supporting Actress: Sissy Spacek, "Three Women."
Best Screenplay: Woody Allen & Marshall Brickman, "Annie Hall."

Los Angeles Film Critics
(Awards for films released in 1977)

Best Picture: "Star Wars"
Best Director: Herbert Ross, "The Turning Point."
Best Actor: Richard Dreyfuss, "The Goodbye Girl."
Best Actress: Shelley Duvall, "Three Women."
Best Supporting Actor: Jason Robards, "Julia."
Best Supporting Actress: Vanessa Redgrave, "Julia."
Best Screenplay: Woody Allen & Marshall Brickman, "Annie Hall."

Cannes Film Festival
(June of 1978)

Best Picture: "The Tree Of Wooden Clogs"
Best Director: Nagisa Oshima, "Empire of Passion."
Best Actor: Jon Voight, "Coming Home."
Best Actress: Jill Clayburgh, "An Unmarried Woman."
International Critics Prize : "Man of Marble", Andrzej Wajda, Poland.
(No awards for "Best Supporting" categories until 1979)

Independent Spirit Awards
(First presented in 1986)

1978

1977

49th Annual Academy Awards
(Oscars given for pictures released in 1976)

Best Picture: "Rocky," Chartoff-Winkler, United Artists.

Others Nominated:
"All the President's Men" Wildwood-Warner.
"Bound for Glory," United Artists.
"Network," MGM-United Artists.
"Taxi Driver," Columbia.

Best Director: John G. Avildsen, "Rocky."

Others Nominated: Alan J. Pakula, "All the President's Men"; Ingmar Bergman, "Face to Face"; Sidney Lumet, "Network"; Lina Wertmuller, "Seven Beauties."

Best Actor: Peter Finch, "Network."

Others Nominated: Robert De Niro, "Taxi Driver"; Giancarlo Giannini, "Seven Beauties"; William Holden, "Network"; Sylvester Stallone, "Rocky."

Best Actress: Faye Dunaway, "Network."

Others Nominated: Marie-Christine Barrault, "Cousin, Cousine"; Talia Shire, "Rocky"; Sissy Spacek, "Carrie"; Liv Ullmann, "Face to Face."

Best Supporting Actor: Jason Robards, "All the President's Men."

Others Nominated: Ned Beatty, "Network"; Burgess Meredith, "Rocky"; Laurence Olivier, "Marathon Man"; Burt Young, "Rocky."

Best Supporting Actress: Beatrice Straight, "Network."

Others Nominated: Jane Alexander, "All the President's Men"; Jodie Foster, "Taxi Driver"; Lee Grant, "Voyage of the Damned"; Piper Laurie, "Carrie."

Original Screenplay: Paddy Chayefsky, "Network."

Others Nominated: Jean-Charles Tacchella & Daniele Thompson, "Cousin, Cousine"; Walter Bernstein, "The Front"; Sylvester Stallone, "Rocky"; Lina Wertmuller, "Seven Beauties."

Screenplay Adaptation: William Goldman, "All the President's Men."

Others Nominated: Robert Getchell, "Bound for Glory"; Federico Fellini & Bernardino Zapponi, "Casanova"; Nicholas Meyer, "The Seven-Per-Cent Solution"; Steve Shagan & David Butler, "Voyage of the Damned."

Directors Guild Of America

1976 Best Director: John G. Avildsen, "Rocky."

Writers Guild Of America
(Awards given for pictures released in 1976)

Best Written Comedy Written Directly for the Screen: Bill Lancaster, "The Bad News Bears"

Best Written Comedy Adapted from Another Medium: Frank Waldman & Blake Edwards, "The Pink Panther Strikes Again."

Best Written Drama Written Directly for the Screen: Paddy Chayefsky, "Network."

Best Written Drama Adapted from Another Medium: William Goldman, "All the President's Men."

Golden Globe Awards
(For 1976 Releases)

Best Picture-Drama: **"Rocky."**
Best Picture-Musical/Comedy: **"A Star Is Born."**
Best Director: **Sidney Lumet,** "Network."
Best Actress-Drama: **Faye Dunaway,** "Network."
Best Actor-Drama: **Peter Finch,** "Network."
Best Actress-Musical/Comedy: **Barbra Streisand,** "A Star Is Born."
Best Actor-Musical/Comedy: **Kris Kristofferson,** "A Star Is Born."
Best Supporting Actress: **Katharine Ross,** "Voyage of the Damned."
Best Supporting Actor: **Laurence Olivier,** "Marathon Man."
Best Screenplay: **Paddy Chayefsky,** "Network."

National Society Of Film Critics
(Awards for films released in 1976)

Best Picture: **"All the President's Men."**
Best Director: **Martin Scorsese,** "Taxi Driver."
Best Actor: **Robert De Niro,** "Taxi Driver."
Best Actress: **Sissy Spacek,** "Carrie."
Best Supporting Actor: **Jason Robards,** "All the President's Men."
Best Supporting Actress: **Jodie Foster,** "Taxi Driver."
Best Screenplay: **Alain Tanner & John Berger,** "Jonah, Who Will be 25 in the Year 2000."

New York Film Critics
(Awards for 1976 Releases)

Best Picture: **"All the President's Men."**
Best Director: **Alan J. Pakula,** "All the President's Men."
Best Actor: **Robert De Niro,** "Taxi Driver."
Best Actress: **Liv Ullmann,** "Face to Face."
Best Supporting Actor: **Jason Robards,** "All the President's Men."
Best Supporting Actress: **Talia Shire,** "Rocky."
Best Screenplay: **Paddy Chayefsky,** "Network."

Los Angeles Film Critics
(Awards for films released in 1976)

Best Picture: **"Network" & "Rocky"**
Best Director: **Sidney Lumet,** "Network."
Best Actor: **Robert De Niro,** "Taxi Driver."
Best Actress: **Liv Ullmann,** "Face to Face."
Best Screenplay: **Woody Allen & Marshall Brickman,** "Annie Hall."
(No awards for "Best Supporting" categories until 1979)

Cannes Film Festival
(May of 1977)

Best Picture: **"Padre Padrone"**
Best Director: **(Not awarded)**
Best Actor: **Fernando Rey,** "Elisa My Love."
Best Actress:
  Shelley Duvall, "Three Women."
  Monique Mercure, J.A. Martin, "Photographer."
No Voting on Best Supporting Categories until 1979.
International Critics Prize : "Padre Padrone", Paolo and Vittorio Taviani, Italy.

Independent Spirit Awards
(First presented in 1986)

1977

1976

48th Annual Academy Awards

(Oscars given for pictures released in 1975)

Best Picture: "One Flew Over the Cuckoo's Nest," Fantasy-United Artists.

Others Nominated:
"Barry Lyndon," Warner Bros.
"Dog Day Afternoon," Warner Bros.
"Jaws," Universal.
"Nashville," ABC-Paramount.

Best Director: Milos Forman, "One Flew Over the Cuckoo's Nest."

Others Nominated: Robert Altman, "Nashville"; Federico Fellini, "Amarcord"; Stanley Kubrick, "Barry Lyndon"; Sidney Lumet, "Dog Day Afternoon."

Best Actor: Jack Nicholson, "One Flew Over the Cuckoo's Nest."

Others Nominated: Walter Matthau, "The Sunshine Boys"; Al Pacino, "Dog Day Afternoon"; Maximilian Schell, "The Man in the Glass Booth"; James Whitmore, "Give 'em Hell, Harry!"

Best Actress: Louise Fletcher, "One Flew Over the Cuckoo's Nest."

Others Nominated: Isabelle Adjani, "The Story of Adele H."; Ann-Margret, "Tommy"; Glenda Jackson, "Hedda"; Carol Kane, "Hester Street."

Best Supporting Actor: George Burns, "The Sunshine Boys."

Others Nominated: Brad Dourif, "One Flew Over the Cuckoo's Nest"; Burgess Meredith, "The Day of the Locust"; Chris Sarandon, "Dog Day Afternoon"; Jack Warden, "Shampoo."

Best Supporting Actress: Lee Grant, "Shampoo."

Others Nominated: Ronee Blakley, "Nashville"; Sylvia Miles, "Farewell, My Lovely"; Lily Tomlin, "Nashville"; Brenda Vaccaro, "Once is not Enough."

Best Screenplay adapted from another medium: Laurence Hauben & Bo Goldman, "One Flew Over the Cuckoo's Nest."

Others Nominated: Stanley Kubrick, "Barry Lyndon"; John Huston, "Gladys Hill"; "The Man Who Would Be King"; Ruggero Maccari & Dino Risi, "Scent of a Woman"; Neil Simon, "The Sunshine Boys."

Best Original Screenplay: Frank R. Pierson, "Dog Day Afternoon" and **Federico Fellini & Tonino Guerra**, "Amarcord".

Others Nominated: Claude Lelouch & Pierre Uytterhoeven, "And Now My Love"; Ted Allan, "Lies My Father Told Me"; Robert Towne & Warren Beatty, "Shampoo."

Directors Guild Of America

1975 Best Director: Milos Forman, "One Flew Over the Cuckoo's Nest."

Writers Guild Of America

(Awards given for pictures released in 1975)

Best Written Comedy Written Directly for the Screen: Robert Towne & Warren Beatty, "Shampoo."

Best Written Comedy Adapted from Another Medium: Neil Simon, "The Sunshine Boys."

Best Written Drama Written Directly for the Screen: Frank R. Pierson, "Dog Day Afternoon."

Best Written Drama Adapted from Another Medium: Laurence Hauben & Bo Goldman, "One Flew Over the Cuckoo's Nest."

Golden Globe Awards
(For 1975 Releases)

Best Picture-Drama: "One Flew Over the Cuckoo's Nest."

Best Picture-Musical/Comedy: "The Sunshine Boys."

Best Director: Milos Forman, "One Flew Over the Cuckoo's Nest."

Best Actress-Drama: Louise Fletcher, "One Flew Over the Cuckoo's Nest."

Best Actor-Drama: Jack Nicholson, "One Flew Over the Cuckoo's Nest"

Best Actress-Musical/Comedy: Ann-Margret, "Tommy."

Best Actor-Musical/Comedy: Walter Matthau, "The Sunshine Boys."

Best Supporting Actress: Brenda Vaccaro, "Once is not Enough."

Best Supporting Actor: Richard Benjamin, "The Sunshine Boys."

Best Screenplay: Laurence Hauben & Bo Goldman, "One Flew Over the Cuckoo's Nest."

National Society Of Film Critics
(Awards for films released in 1975)

Best Picture: "Nashville."

Best Director: Robert Altman, "Nashville."

Best Actor: Jack Nicholson, "One Flew Over the Cuckoo's Nest."

Best Actress: Isabelle Adjani, "The Story of Adele H."

Best Supporting Actor: Henry Gibson, "Nashville."

Best Supporting Actress: Lily Tomlin, "Nashville."

Best Screenplay: Robert Towne & Warren Beatty, "Shampoo."

New York Film Critics
(Awards for 1975 Releases)

Best Picture: "Nashville."

Best Director: Robert Altman, "Nashville."

Best Actor: Jack Nicholson, "One Flew Over the Cuckoo's Nest."

Best Actress: Isabelle Adjani, "The Story of Adele H."

Best Supporting Actor: Alan Arkin, "Hearts of the West."

Best Supporting Actress: Lily Tomlin, "Nashville."

Best Screenplay: Francois Truffaut, Jean Gruault & Suzanne Schiffman, "The Story of Adele H."

Cannes Film Festival
(May of 1976)

Best Picture: "Taxi Driver"

Best Director: Ettore Scola, "Brutti, Sporchi, Cattivi."

Best Actor: Jose-Luis Gomez, "La Familia de Pascual Duarte."

Best Actress:
  Mari Torocsik, "Deryne, Hol Van."
  Dominique Sanda, "L'Eredita Ferramonti"

International Critics Prize:
  "Ferdinand the Strongman", Kluge, W. Germany
  "Kings of the Road" Wim Wenders, W. Germany.

(No awards for "Best Supporting" categories until 1979)

Los Angeles Film Critics
(First awards presented in 1977)

Independent Spirit Awards
(First presented in 1986)

1976

1975

Best Picture: "The Godfather, Part II," Paramount.

Others Nominated:
"Chinatown," Paramount.
"The Conversation," Paramount.
"Lenny," United Artists.
"The Towering Inferno," 20th Century-Fox-Warner Bros.

Best Director: Francis Ford Coppola, "The Godfather, Part II"

Others Nominated: John Cassavetes, "A Woman Under the Influence"; Bob Fosse, "Lenny"; Roman Polanski, "Chinatown"; Francois Truffaut, "Day for Night."

Best Actor: Art Carney, "Harry and Tonto."

Others Nominated: Albert Finney, "Murder on the Orient Express"; Dustin Hoffman, "Lenny"; Jack Nicholson, "Chinatown"; Al Pacino, "The Godfather, Part II."

Best Actress: Ellen Burstyn, "Alice Doesn't Live Here Anymore."

Others Nominated: Diahann Carroll, "Claudine"; Faye Dunaway, "Chinatown"; Valerie Perrine, "Lenny"; Gena Rowlands, "A Woman Under the Influence."

Best Supporting Actor: Robert De Niro, "The Godfather, Part II."

Others Nominated: Fred Astaire, "The Towering Inferno"; Jeff Bridges, "Thunderbolt and Lightfoot"; Michael V. Gasso, "The Godfather, Part II"; Lee Strasberg, "The Godfather, Part II."

Best Supporting Actress: Ingrid Bergman, "Murder on the Orient Express."

Others Nominated: Valentina Cortese, "Day for Night"; Madeline Kahn, "Blazing Saddles"; Diane Ladd, "Alice Doesn't Live Here Anymore"; Talia Shire, "The Godfather, Part II."

Best Screenplay adapted from another medium: Francis Ford Coppola & Mario Puzo, "The Godfather, Part II."

Others Nominated: Mordecai Richler & Lionel Chetwynd, "The Apprenticeship of Duddy Kravitz"; Julian Barry, "Lenny"; Paul Dehn, "Murder on the Orient Express"; Gene Wilder & Mel Brooks, "Young Frankenstein."

Best Original Screenplay: Robert Towne, "Chinatown."

Others Nominated: Robert Getchell, "Alice Doesn't Live Here Anymore"; Francis Ford Coppola, "The Conversation"; Francois Truffaut, Jean-Louis Richard & Suzanne Schiffman, "Day for Night"; Paul Mazursky & Josh Greenfeld, "Harry and Tonto."

Directors Guild Of America

1974 Best Director: Francis Ford Coppola, "The Godfather, Part II."

Writers Guild Of America
(Awards given for pictures released in 1974)

Best Written Comedy Written Directly for the Screen: Mel Brooks, Norman Steinberg, Andrew Bergman, Richard Pryor & Alan Uger, "Blazing Saddles."

Best Written Comedy Adapted from Another Medium: Mordecai Richler, Lionel Chetwynd, "The Apprenticeship of Duddy Kravitz."

Best Written Drama Written Directly for the Screen: Robert Towne, "Chinatown."

Best Written Drama Adapted from Another Medium: Mario Puzo & Francis Ford Coppola, "The Godfather, Part II."

Golden Globe Awards
(For 1974 Releases)

Best Picture-Drama: "Chinatown."
Best Picture-Musical/Comedy: "The Longest Yard."
Best Director: Roman Polanski, "Chinatown."
Best Actress-Drama: Gena Rowlands, "A Woman Under the Influence."
Best Actor-Drama: Jack Nicholson, "Chinatown."
Best Actress-Musical/Comedy: Raquel Welch, "The Three Musketeers."
Best Actor-Musical/Comedy: Art Carney, "Harry and Tonto."
Best Supporting Actress: Karen Black, "The Great Gatsby."
Best Supporting Actor: Fred Astaire, "The Towering Inferno."
Best Screenplay: Robert Towne, "Chinatown."

National Society Of Film Critics
(Awards for films released in 1974)

Best Picture: "Scenes from a Marriage."
Best Director: Francis Ford Coppola, "The Conversation" & "The Godfather, Part II."
Best Actor: Jack Nicholson, "The Last Detail" & "Chinatown."
Best Actress: Liv Ullmann, "Scenes from a Marriage."
Best Supporting Actor: Holger Lowenadler, "Lacombe, Lucien."
Best Supporting Actress: Bibi Andersson, "Scenes from a Marriage."
Best Screenplay: Ingmar Bergman, "Scenes from a Marriage."

New York Film Critics
(Awards for 1974 Releases)

Best Picture: "Amarcord."
Best Director: Federico Fellini, "Amarcord."
Best Actor: Jack Nicholson, "Chinatown" & "The Last Detail."
Best Actress: Liv Ullmann, "Scenes from a Marriage."
Best Supporting Actor: Charles Boyer, "Stavisky."
Best Supporting Actress: Valerie Perrine, "Lenny."
Best Screenplay: Ingmar Bergman, "Scenes from a Marriage."

Cannes Film Festival
(May of 1975)

Best Picture: "Chronicle Of the Burning Years"
Best Director: (tie)
    Constantine Costa-Gavras, "Section Speciale"
    Michel Brault, "Les Ordes"
Best Actor: Vittoria Gassman, "Scent of a Woman."
Best Actress: Valerie Perrine, "Lenny."
International Critics Prize : "Every Man for Himself...", Werner Herzog, Germany.
(No awards for "Best Supporting" categories until 1979)

Los Angeles Film Critics
(First awards presented in 1977)
Independent Spirit Awards
(First presented in 1986)

1975

1974

46th Annual Academy Awards
(Oscars given for pictures released in 1973)

Best Picture: "The Sting," Zanuck-Brown, Universal.

Others Nominated:
"American Graffiti," Universal.
"Cries and Whispers," New World.
"The Exorcist," Warner Bros.
"A Touch of Class," Brut-Avco Embassy.

Best Director: George Roy Hill, "The Sting."

Others Nominated: Ingmar Bergman, "Cries and Whispers"; Bernardo Bertolucci, "Last Tango in Paris"; William Friedkin, "The Exorcist"; George Lucas, "American Graffiti."

Best Actor: Jack Lemmon, "Save the Tiger."

Others Nominated: Marlon Brando, "Last Tango in Paris"; Jack Nicholson, "The Last Detail"; Al Pacino, "Serpico"; Robert Redford, "The Sting."

Best Actress: Glenda Jackson, "A Touch of Class."

Others Nominated: Ellen Burstyn, "The Exorcist"; Marsha Mason, "Cinderella Liberty"; Barbra Streisand, "The Way We Were"; Joanne Woodward, "Summer Wishes, Winter Dreams."

Best Supporting Actor: John Houseman, "The Paper Chase."

Others Nominated: Vincent Gardenia, "Bang the Drum Slowly"; Jack Gilford, "Save the Tiger"; Jason Miller, "The Exorcist"; Randy Quaid, "The Last Detail"."

Best Supporting Actress: Tatum O'Neal, "Paper Moon."

Others Nominated: Linda Blair, "The Exorcist", Candy Clark, "American Graffiti"; Madeline Kahn, "Paper Moon"; Sylvia Sidney, "Summer Wishes, Winter Dreams."

Best Screenplay adapted from another medium: William Peter Blatty, "The Exorcist."

Others Nominated: Robert Towne, "The Last Detail"; James Bridges, "The Paper Chase"; Alvin Sargent, "Paper Moon", Waldo Salt & Norman Wesler, "Serpico."

Best Original Screenplay: David S. Ward, "The Sting."

Others Nominated: George Lucas, Gloria Katz & William Huyck, "American Graffiti"; Ingmar Bergman, "Cries and Whispers"; Steve Shagan, "Save the Tiger"; Melvin Frank & Jack Rose, "A Touch of Class."

Directors Guild Of America

1973 Best Director: George Roy Hill, "The Sting."

Writers Guild Of America
(Awards given for pictures released in 1973)

Best Written Comedy Written Directly for the Screen: Melvin Frank & Jack Rose, "A Touch of Class."

Best Written Comedy Adapted from Another Medium: Alvin Sargent, "Paper Moon."

Best Written Drama Written Directly for the Screen: Steve Shagan, "Save the Tiger."

Best Written Drama Adapted from Another Medium: Waldo Salt & Norman Wexler, "Serpico.

Golden Globe Awards
(For 1973 Releases)

Best Picture-Drama: "The Exorcist."
Best Picture-Musical/Comedy: "American Graffiti."
Best Director: William Friedkin, "The Exorcist."
Best Actress-Drama: Marsha Mason, "Cinderella Liberty."
Best Actor-Drama: Al Pacino, "Serpico."
Best Actress-Musical/Comedy: Glenda Jackson, "A Touch of Class."
Best Actor-Musical/Comedy: George Segal, "A Touch of Class."
Best Supporting Actress: Linda Blair, "The Exorcist."
Best Supporting Actor: John Houseman, "The Paper Chase."
Best Screenplay: William Peter Blatty, "The Exorcist."

National Society Of Film Critics
(Awards for films released in 1973)

Best Picture: "Day for Night."
Best Director: Francois Truffaut, "Day for Night."
Best Actor: Marlon Brando, "Last Tango in Paris."
Best Actress: Liv Ullmann, "The New Land."
Best Supporting Actor: Robert De Niro, "Mean Streets."
Best Supporting Actress: Valentina Cortese, "Day for Night."
Best Screenplay: George Lucas, Gloria Katzand & William Huyck, "American Graffiti."

New York Film Critics
(Awards for 1973 Releases)

Best Picture: "Day for Night."
Best Director: Francois Truffaut, "Day for Night."
Best Actor: Marlon Brando, "Last Tango in Paris."
Best Actress: Joanne Woodward, "Summer Wishes, Winter Dreams."
Best Supporting Actor: Robert De Niro, "Bang the Drum Slowly."
Best Supporting Actress: Valentina Cortese, "Day for Night."
Best Screenplay: George Lucas, Gloria Katz & William Huyck, "American Graffiti."

Cannes Film Festival
(May of 1974)

Best Picture: "The Conversation"
Best Director: (Not awarded)
Best Actor: Jack Nicholson, "The Last Detail."
Best Actress: Marie-Jose Nat, "Les Violins du Bal."
Best Screenplay: Hal Barwood & Matthew Robbins, "Sugarland Express."
International Critics Prize :
   "Lancelot du Lac", Robert Bresson
   "Fear Eats the Soul", Rainer Werner Fassbinder.
(No awards for "Best Supporting" categories until 1979)

Los Angeles Film Critics
(First awards presented in 1977)
Independent Spirit Awards
(First presented in 1986)

1974

1973

45th Annual Academy Awards
(Oscars given for pictures released in 1972)

Best Picture: "The Godfather," Paramount.
Others Nominated:
"Cabaret," ABC Pictures, Allied Artists.
"Deliverance," Warner Bros.
"The Emigrants," Warner Bros.
"Sounder," Radnitz, Mattel, 20th Century-Fox.

Best Director: Bob Fosse, "Cabaret."
Others Nominated: John Boorman, "Deliverance"; Francis Ford Coppola, "The Godfather"; Joseph L. Mankiewicz, "Sleuth"; Jan Troell, "The Emigrants."

Best Actor: Marlon Brando, "The Godfather."
Others Nominated: Michael Caine, "Sleuth"; Laurence Olivier, "Sleuth"; Peter O'Toole, "The Ruling Class"; Paul Winfield, "Sounder."

Best Actress: Liza Minnelli, "Cabaret."
Others Nominated: Diana Ross, "Lady Sings the Blues"; Maggie Smith, "Travels with My Aunt"; Cicely Tyson, "Sounder"; Liv Ullmann, "The Emigrants."

Best Supporting Actor: Joel Grey, "Cabaret."
Others Nominated: Eddie Albert, "The Heartbreak Kid"; James Caan, "The Godfather"; Robert Duvall, "The Godfather"; Al Pacino, "The Godfather."

Best Supporting Actress: Eileen Heckart, "Butterflies Are Free."
Others Nominated: Jeannie Berlin, "The Heartbreak Kid"; Geraldine Page, "Pete 'n' Tillie"; Susan Tyrrell, "Fat City"; Shelley Winters, "The Poseidon Adventure."

Best Screenplay adapted from another medium: Mario Puzo, Francis Ford Coppola, "The Godfather."
Others Nominated: Jan Troell & Bengt Forslund, "The Emigrants"; Jay Presson Allen, "Cabaret"; Julius J. Epstein, "Pete 'n' Tillie"; Lonne Elder III, "Sounder."

Best Original Screenplay: Jeremy Larner, "The Candidate."
Others Nominated: Luis Bunuel, "The Discreet Charm of the Bourgeoisie"; Terence McCloy, Chris Clark & Suzanne de Passe, "Lady Sings the Blues"; Louis Malle, "Mumur of the Heart"; Carl Foreman, "Young Winston."

Directors Guild Of America

1972 Best Director: Francis Ford Coppola, "The Godfather."

Writers Guild Of America
(Awards given for pictures released in 1972)

Best Written Comedy Written Directly for the Screen: Buck Henry, David Newman & Robert Benton, "What's Up Doc."
Best Written Comedy Adapted from Another Medium: Jay Presson Allen, "Cabaret."
Best Written Drama Written Directly for the Screen: Jeremy Larner, "The Candidate."
Best Written Drama Adapted from Another Medium: Mario Puzo & Francis Ford Coppola, "The Godfather."

Golden Globe Awards
(For 1972 Releases)

Best Picture-Drama: "The Godfather."
Best Picture-Musical/Comedy: "Cabaret."
Best Director: Francis Ford Coppola, "The Godfather
Best Actress-Drama: Liv Ullmann, "The Emigrants."
Best Actor-Drama: Marlon Brando, "The Godfather."
Best Actress-Musical/Comedy: Liza Minnelli, "Cabaret."
Best Actor-Musical/Comedy: Jack Lemmon, "Avanti."
Best Supporting Actress: Shelley Winters, "The Poseidon Adventure."
Best Supporting Actor: Joel Grey, "Cabaret."
Best Screenplay: Francis Ford Coppola & Mario Puzo, "The Godfather."

National Society Of Film Critics
(Awards for films released in 1972)

Best Picture: "The Discreet Charm of the Bourgeoisie."
Best Director: Luis Bunuel, "The Discreet Charm of the Bourgeoisie."
Best Actor: Al Pacino, "The Godfather."
Best Actress: Cicely Tyson, "Sounder."
Best Supporting Actor:
  Joel Grey, "Cabaret"
  Eddie Albert, "Heartbreak Kid."
Best Supporting Actress: Jeannie Berlin, "The Heartbreak Kid."
Best Screenplay: Ingmar Bergman, "Crys and Whispers."

New York Film Critics
(Awards for 1972 Releases)

Best Picture: "Cries and Whispers."
Best Director: Ingmar Bergman, "Cries and Whispers."
Best Actor: Laurence Olivier, "Sleuth."
Best Actress: Liv Ullmann, "Cries and Whispers."
Best Supporting Actor: Robert Duvall, "The Godfather."
Best Supporting Actress: Jeannie Berlin, "The Heartbreak Kid."
Best Screenplay: Ingmar Bergman, "Cries and Whispers."

Cannes Film Festival
(May of 1973)

Best Picture: "Scarecrow" & "The Hireling"
Best Director: (Not awarded)
Best Actor: Giancarlo Giannini, "Love And Anarchy."
Best Actress: Joanne Woodward, "The Effect of Gamma Rays..."
Best Screenplay: (Not awarded)
International Critics Prize: (Not awarded)
(No awards for "Best Supporting" categories until 1979)

Los Angeles Film Critics
(First awards presented in 1977)
Independent Spirit Awards
(First presented in 1986)

1973

1972

44th Annual Academy Awards
(Oscars given for pictures released in 1971)

Best Picture: "The French Connection," 20th Century-Fox.
Others Nominated:
   "A Clockwork Orange," Warner Bros.
   "Fiddler on the Roof," Mirisch, United Artists.
   "The Last Picture Show," BBS, Columbia.
   "Nicholas and Alexandra," Horizon, Columbia.

Best Director: William Friedkin, "The French Connection."
Others Nominated: Peter Bogdanovich, "The Last Picture Show"; Norman Jewison, "Fiddler on the Roof"; Stanley Kubrick, "A Clockwork Orange"; John Schlesinger, "Sunday Bloody Sunday."

Best Actor: Gene Hackman, "The French Connection."
Others Nominated: Peter Finch, "Sunday Bloody Sunday"; Walter Matthau, "Kotch"; George C. Scott, "The Hospital"; Topol, "Fiddler on the Roof."

Best Actress: Jane Fonda, "Klute."
Others Nominated: Julie Christie, "McCabe & Mrs. Miller"; "Glenda Jackson, "Sunday Bloody Sunday"; Vanessa Redgrave, "Mary Queen of Scots"; Janet Suzman, "Nicholas and Alexandra."

Best Supporting Actor: Ben Johnson, "The Last Picture Show."
Others Nominated: Jeff Bridges, "The Last Picture Show"; Leonard Frey, "Fiddler on the Roof"; Richard Jaeckel, "Sometimes a Great Notion"; Roy Scheider, "The French Connection."

Best Supporting Actress: Cloris Leachman, "The Last Picture Show."
Others Nominated: Ellen Burstyn, "The Last Picture Show"; Barbara Harris, "Who Is Harry Kellerman and Why is He Saying All Those Terrible Things About Me?; Margaret Leighton, "The Go-Between"; Ann-Margret, "Carnal Knowledge."

Best Screenplay adapted from another medium: Ernest Tidyman, "The French Connection."
Others Nominated: Stanley Kubrick, "A Clockwork Orange"; Bernardo Bertolucci, "The Conformist"; Ugo Pirro & Vittorio Bonicelli, "The Garden of the Finzi-Continis"; Larry McMurtry & Peter Bogdanovich, "The Last Picture Show."

Best Original Screenplay: Paddy Chayefsky, "The Hospital."
Others Nominated: Elio Petri & Ugo Pirro, "Investigation of a Citizen Above Suspicion"; Dave Lewis, "Klute"; Herman Raucher, "Summer of '42"; Penelope Gilliatt, "Sunday Bloody Sunday."

Directors Guild Of America

1971 Best Director: William Friedkin, "The French Connection."

Writers Guild Of America
(Awards given for pictures released in 1971)

Best Written Comedy Written Directly for the Screen: Paddy Chayefsky, "The Hospital."
Best Written Comedy Adapted from Another Medium: John Paxton, "Kotch."
Best Written Drama Written Directly for the Screen: Penelope Gilliatt, "Sunday Bloody Sunday"
Best Written Drama Adapted from Another Medium: Ernest Tidyman, "The French Connection."

Golden Globe Awards
(For 1971 Releases)

Best Picture-Drama: "The French Connection."
Best Picture-Musical/Comedy: "Fiddler on the Roof."
Best Director: William Friedkin, "The French Connection."
Best Actress-Drama: Jane Fonda, "Klute."
Best Actor-Drama: Gene Hackman, "The French Connection."
Best Actress-Musical/Comedy: Twiggy, "The Boy Friend."
Best Actor-Musical/Comedy: Topol, "Fiddler on the Roof."
Best Supporting Actress: Ann-Margret, "Carnal Knowledge."
Best Supporting Actor: Ben Johnson, "The Last Picture Show."
Best Screenplay: Paddy Chayefsky, "The Hospital."

National Society Of Film Critics
(Awards for films released in 1971)

Best Picture: "Claire's Knee."
Best Director: Bernardo Bertolucci, "The Conformist."
Best Actor: Peter Finch, "Sunday Bloody Sunday."
Best Actress: Jane Fonda, "Klute."
Best Supporting Actor: Bruce Dern, "Drive He Said."
Best Supporting Actress: Ellen Burstyn, "The Last Picture Show."
Best Screenplay: Penelope Gilliatt, "Sunday Bloody Sunday."

New York Film Critics
(Awards for 1971 Releases)

Best Picture: "A Clockwork Orange."
Best Director: Stanley Kubrick, "A Clockwork Orange."
Best Actor: Gene Hackman, "The French Connection."
Best Actress: Jane Fonda, "Klute."
Best Supporting Actor: Ben Johnson, "The Last Picture Show."
Best Supporting Actress: Ellen Burstyn, "The Last Picture Show."
Best Screenplay: (tie) Peter Bogdanovich & Larry McMurtry, "The Last Picture Show"; **Penelope Gilliatt**, "Sunday Bloody Sunday."

Cannes Film Festival
(May of 1972)

Best Picture: "The Working Class Goes To Paradise" & "The Mattei Affair."
Best Director: Miklos Jancso, "The Red Psalm."
Best Actor: Jean Yanne, "We Will Not Grow Old Together."
Best Actress: Susannah York, "Images."
Best Screenplay: (Not awarded)
International Critics Prize: (Not awarded)
(No awards for "Best Supporting" categories until 1979)

Los Angeles Film Critics
(First awards presented in 1977)
Independent Spirit Awards
(First presented in 1986)

1972

1971

43rd Annual Academy Awards
(Oscars given for pictures released in 1970)

Best Picture: "Patton," 20th Century-Fox.
Others Nominated:
"Airport," Hunter, Universal.
"Five Easy Pieces," BBS, Columbia.
"Love Story," Paramount.
"M*A*S*H," 20th Century-Fox.

Best Director: Franklin J. Schaffner, "Patton."
Others Nominated: Robert Altman, "M*A*S*H"; Federico Fellini, "Satyricon"; Arthur Hiller, "Love Story"; Ken Russell, "Women in Love."

Best Actor: George C. Scott, "Patton." (award declined)
Others Nominated: Melvyn Douglas, "I Never Sang for My Father"; James Earl Jones, "The Great White Hope"; Jack Nicholson, "Five Easy Pieces"; Ryan O'Neal, "Love Story."

Best Actress: Glenda Jackson, "Women in Love."
Others Nominated: Carrie Snodgress, "Diary of a Mad Housewife"; Jane Alexander, "The Great White Hope"; Ali MacGraw, "Love Story"; Sarah Miles, "Ryan's Daughter."

Best Supporting Actor: John Mills, "Ryan's Daughter."
Others Nominated: Richard Castellano, "Lovers and Other Strangers"; Chief Dan George, "Little Big Man"; Gene Hackman, "I Never Sang for My Father"; John Marley, "Love Story."

Best Supporting Actress: Helen Hayes, "Airport."
Others Nominated: Karen Black, "Five Easy Pieces"; Lee Grant, "The Landlord"; Sally Kellerman, "M*A*S*H"; Maureen Stapleton, "Airport."

Best Screenplay adapted from another medium: Ring Lardner, Jr., "M*A*S*H."
Others Nominated: George Seaton, "Airport"; Robert Anderson, "I Never Sang for My Father"; Renee Taylor, Joseph Bologna, & David Zelag Goodman, "Lovers and Other Strangers"; Larry Kramer, "Women in Love."

Best Original Screenplay: Francis Ford Coppola & Edmund H. North, "Patton."
Others Nominated: Bob Rafelson & Adrien Joyce, "Five Easy Pieces"; Norman Wexler & Joe Erich Segal, "Love Story"; Eric Rohmer, My Night at Maud's."

Directors Guild Of America

1970 Best Director: Franklin Schaffner, "Patton."

Writers Guild Of America
(Awards given for pictures released in 1970)

Best Written Comedy Written Directly for the Screen: Neil Simon, "The Out-of-Towners."
Best Written Comedy Adapted from Another Medium: Ring Lardner, Jr., "M*A*S*H."
Best Written Drama Written Directly for the Screen: Francis Ford Coppola & Edmund H. North, "Patton."
Best Written Drama Adapted from Another Medium: Robert Anderson, "I Never Sang for My Father."

Golden Globe Awards
(For 1970 Releases)

Best Picture-Drama: "Love Story."
Best Picture-Musical/Comedy: "M*A*S*H."
Best Director: Arthur Hiller, "Love Story."
Best Actress-Drama: Ali MacGraw, "Love Story."
Best Actor-Drama: George C. Scott, "Patton."
Best Actress-Musical/Comedy: Carrie Snodgress, "Diary of a Mad Housewife."
Best Actor-Musical/Comedy: Albert Finney, "Scrooge."
Best Supporting Actress: (tie)
   Karen Black, "Five Easy Pieces."
   Maureen Stapleton, "Airport."
Best Supporting Actor: John Mills, "Ryan's Daughter."
Best Screenplay: Norman Wexler & Erich Segal, "Love Story."

National Society Of Film Critics
(Awards for films released in 1970)

Best Picture: "M*A*S*H."
Best Director: Ingmar Bergman, "The Passion of Anna."
Best Actor: George C. Scott, "Patton."
Best Actress: Glenda Jackson, "Women in Love."
Best Supporting Actor: Chief Dan George, "Little Big Man."
Best Supporting Actress: Lois Smith, "Five Easy Pieces."
Best Screenplay: Eric Rohmer, "My Night at Maud's."

New York Film Critics
(Awards for 1970 Releases)

Best Picture: "Five Easy Pieces."
Best Director: Bob Rafelson, "Five Easy Pieces."
Best Actor: George C. Scott, "Patton."
Best Actress: Glenda Jackson, "Women in Love."
Best Supporting Actor: Chief Dan George, "Little Big Man."
Best Supporting Actress: Karen Black, "Five Easy Pieces."
Best Screenplay: Eric Rohmer, "My Night at Maud's."

Cannes Film Festival
(May of 1971)

Best Picture: "The Go-Between".
Best Director: (Not awarded)
Best Actor: Ricardo Cucciola, "Sacco and Vanzetti."
Best Actress: Kitty Winn, "Panic in Needle Park."
Best Screenplay: (Not awarded)
International Critics Prize: (Not awarded)
(No awards for "Best Supporting" categories until 1979)

Los Angeles Film Critics
(First awards presented in 1977)
Independent Spirit Awards
(First presented in 1986)

1971

1970

Best Picture: "Midnight Cowboy," United Artists.

Others Nominated:
"Anne of the Thousand Days," Wallis, Universal.
"Butch Cassidy and the Sundance Kid," 20th Century-Fox.
"Hello, Dolly!," Chenault, 20th Century-Fox.
"Z," Cinema V.

Best Director: John Schlesinger, "Midnight Cowboy."

Others Nominated: Constantine Costa-Gavras, "Z"; Arthur Penn, "Alice's Restaurant"; Sydney Pollack, "They Shoot Horses, Don't They?" George Roy Hill, "Butch Cassidy and the Sundance Kid."

Best Actor: John Wayne, "True Grit."

Others Nominated: Richard Burton, "Anne of the Thousand Days"; Dustin Hoffman, "Midnight Cowboy"; Peter O'Toole, "Goodbye, Mr. Chips"; Jon Voight, "Midnight Cowboy."

Best Actress: Maggie Smith, "The Prime of Miss Jean Brodie."

Others Nominated: Genevieve Bujold, "Anne of the Thousand Days"; Jane Fonda, "They Shoot Horses, Don't They?"; Liza Minnelli, "The Sterile Cuckoo"; Jean Simmons, "The Happy Ending."

Best Supporting Actor: Gig Young, "They Shoot Horses, Don't They?"

Others Nominated: Rupert Crosse, "The Reivers"; Elliott Gould, "Bob & Carol & Ted & Alice"; Jack Nicholson, "Easy Rider"; Anthony Quayle, "Anne of the Thousand Days."

Best Supporting Actress: Goldie Hawn, "Cactus Flower."

Others Nominated: Catherine Burns, "Last Summer"; Dyan Cannon, "Bob & Carol & Ted & Alice"; Sylvia Miles, "Midnight Cowboy"; Susannah York, "They Shoot Horses, Don't They?"

Best Screenplay adapted from another medium: Waldo Salt, "Midnight Cowboy."

Others Nominated: John Hale, Bridget Boland & Richard Sokolove, "Anne of the Thousand Days"; Arnold Schulman, "Goodbye, Columbus"; James Poe & Robert E. Thompson, "They Shoot Horses, Don't They?"; Jorge Semprun & Cost-Garvas, "Z."

Best Original Screenplay: William Goldman, "Butch Cassidy and the Sundance Kid."

Others Nominated: Paul Mazursky & Larry Tucker, "Bob & Carol & Ted & Alice"; Nicola Badalucco, Enrico Medioli & Luchino Visconti, "The Damned"; Peter Fonda, Dennis Hopper & Terry Southern, "Easy Rider"; Walon Green, Roy N. Sickner & Sam Peckinpah, "The Wild Bunch."

Directors Guild Of America

1969 Best Director: John Schlesinger, "Midnight Cowboy."

Writers Guild Of America
(Awards given for pictures released in 1969)

Best Written Comedy Written Directly for the Screen: Paul Mazursky & Larry Tucker, "Bob & Carol & Ted & Alice."

Best Written Comedy Adapted from Another Medium: Arnold Schulman, "Goodbye Columbus."

Best Written Drama Written Directly for the Screen: William Goldman, "Butch Cassidy and the Sundance Kid."

Best Written Drama Adapted from Another Medium: Waldo Salt, "Midnight Cowboy."

Golden Globe Awards
(For 1969 Releases)

Best Picture-Drama: "Anne of the Thousand Days."
Best Picture-Musical/Comedy: "The Secret of Santa Vittoria."
Best Director: Charles Jarrott, "Anne of the Thousand Days."
Best Actress-Drama: Genevieve Bujold, "Anne of the Thousand Days."
Best Actor-Drama: John Wayne, "True Grit."
Best Actress-Musical/Comedy: Patty Duke, "Me Natalie."
Best Actor-Musical/Comedy: Peter O'Toole, "Goodbye Mister Chips."
Best Supporting Actress: Goldie Hawn, "Cactus Flower."
Best Supporting Actor: Gig Young, "They Shoot Horses, Don't They?"
Best Screenplay: John Hale, Bridget Boland & Richard Sokolove, "Anne of the Thousand Days."

National Society Of Film Critics
(Awards for films released in 1969)

Best Picture: "Z."
Best Director: Francois Truffaut, "Stolen Kisses."
Best Actor: Jon Voight, "Midnight Cowboy."
Best Actress: Vanessa Redgrave, "The Lovers of Isadora."
Best Supporting Actor: Jack Nicholson, "Easy Rider."
Best Supporting Actress: Sian Phillips, "Goodbye Mister Chips."
Best Screenplay: Paul Mazursky & Larry Tucker, "Bob & Carol & Ted & Alice."

New York Film Critics
(Awards for 1969 Releases)

Best Picture: "Z."
Best Director: Constantine Costa-Gavras, "Z"
Best Actor: Jon Voight, "Midnight Cowboy."
Best Actress: Jane Fonda, "They Shoot Horses, Don't They?"
Best Supporting Actor: Jack Nicholson, "Easy Rider."
Best Supporting Actress: Dyan Cannon, "Bob & Carol & Ted & Alice."
Best Screenplay: Bob & Carol & Ted & Alice (As a film, not to the individual writers)

Cannes Film Festival
(May of 1970)

Best Picture: "M*A*S*H"
Best Director: John Boorman, "Leo the Last."
Best Actor: Marcello Mastroianni, "Drama of Jealousy."
Best Actress: Ottavio Piccolo, "Metelo."
Best Screenplay: (Not awarded)
International Critics Prize: (Not awarded)
(No awards for "Best Supporting" categories until 1979)

Los Angeles Film Critics
(First awards presented in 1977)
Independent Spirit Awards
(First presented in 1986)

1970

1969

Best Picture: "Oliver!," Romulus-Columbia.
Others Nominated:
"Funny Girl," Rastar-Columbia.
"The Lion in Winter," Avco-Embassy.
"Rachel, Rachel," Warner Bros.-Seven Arts.
"Romeo and Juliet," Zeffirelli-Paramount.

Best Director: Carol Reed, "Oliver!"
Others Nominated: Anthony Harvey, "The Lion in Winter"; Stanley Kubrick, "2001: A Space Odyssey"; Gillo Pontecorvo, "The Battle of Algiers"; Franco Zeffirelli, "Romeo and Juliet."

Best Actor: Cliff Robertson, "Charly."
Others Nominated: Alan Arkin, "The Heart is a Lonely Hunter"; Ron Moody, "The Fixer"; Peter O'Toole, "The Lion in Winter."

Best Actress: Katharine Hepburn, "The Lion in Winter."
Others Nominated: Barbra Steisand, "Funny Girl"; Patricia Neal, "The Subject Was Roses"; Vanessa Redgrave, "Isadora"; Joanne Woodward, "Rachel, Rachel."

Best Supporting Actor: Jack Albertson, "The Subject Was Roses."
Others Nominated: Seymour Cassel, "Faces"; Daniel Massey, "Star!"; Jack Wild, "Oliver"; Gene Wilder, "The Producers."

Best Supporting Actress: Ruth Gordon, "Rosemary's Baby."
Others Nominated: Lynn Carlin, "Faces"; Sondra Locke, "The Heart is a Lonely Hunter"; Kay Medford, "Funny Girl"; Estelle Parsons, "Rachel, Rachel."

Best Screenplay adapted from another medium: James Goldman, "The Lion in Winter."
Others Nominated: Neil Simon, "The Odd Couple"; Vernon Harris, "Oliver!";Stewart Stern, "Rachel, Rachel"; Roman Polanski, "Rosemary's Baby."

Best Original Screenplay: Mel Brooks, "The Producers."
Others Nominated: Franco Solinas, & Gillo Pontecorvo, "The Battle of Algiers"; John Cassavetes, "Faces"; Ira Wallach & Peter Ustinov, "Hot Million"; Stanley Kubrick & Arthur C. Clarke, "2001: A Space Odyssey."

Directors Guild Of America

1968 Best Director: Anthony Harvey, "The Lion in Winter."

Writers Guild Of America
(Awards given for pictures released in 1968)

Best Written American Comedy: Neil Simon, "The Odd Couple."
Best Written American Drama: James Goldman, "The Lion in Winter."
Best Written American Musical: Isobel Lennart, "Funny Girl."
Best Written Original Screenplay: Mel Brooks, "The Producers."

Golden Globe Awards
(For 1968 Releases)

Best Picture-Drama: "The Lion in Winter."
Best Picture-Musical/Comedy: "Oliver!"
Best Director: Paul Newman, "Rachel, Rachel."
Best Actress-Drama: Joanne Woodward, "Rachel, Rachel."
Best Actor-Drama: Peter O'Toole, "The Lion in Winter."
Best Actress-Musical/Comedy: Barbra Streisand, "Funny Girl."
Best Actor-Musical/Comedy: Ron Moody, "Oliver!"
Best Supporting Actress: Ruth Gordon, "Rosemary's Baby."
Best Supporting Actor: Daniel Massey, "Star!"
Best Screenplay: Stirling Silliphant, "Charly."

National Society Of Film Critics
(Awards for films released in 1968)

Best Picture: "Shame."
Best Director: Ingmar Bergman, "Shame" & "Hour of the Wolf."
Best Actor: Per Oscarsson, "Hunger."
Best Actress: Liv Ullmann, "Shame."
Best Supporting Actor: Seymour Cassel, "Faces."
Best Supporting Actress: Billie Whitelaw, "Charlie Bubbles."
Best Screenplay: John Cassavetes, "Faces."

New York Film Critics
(Awards for 1968 Releases)

Best Picture: "The Lion in Winter."
Best Director: Paul Newman, "Rachel, Rachel."
Best Actor: Alan Arkin,
    "The Heart is a Lonely Hunter."
Best Actress: Joanne Woodward, "Rachel, Rachel."
Best Screenplay: Lorenzo Semple, Jr., "Pretty Poison."
(No awards for "Best Supporting" categories until 1969)

Cannes Film Festival
(May of 1969)

Best Picture: "If"
Best Director: (tie)
    Glauber Rocha, "Antonio Das Mortes"
    Vojtech Jasny, "My Dear."
Best Actor: Jean-Louis Trintignant, "Z."
Best Actress: Vanessa Redgrave, "Isadora."
Best Screenplay: (Not awarded)
International Critics Prize: Andrei Roubloy, USSR.
(No awards for "Best Supporting" categories until 1979)

Los Angeles Film Critics
(First awards presented in 1977)
Independent Spirit Awards
(First presented in 1986)

1969

1968

40th Annual Academy Awards
(Oscars given for pictures released in 1967)

Best Picture: "In the Heat of the Night," Mirisch-United Artists.
> *Others Nominated:*
> "Bonnie and Clyde," Warner Bros.-Seven Arts.
> "Doctor Dolittle," 20th Century-Fox.
> "The Graduate," Embassy.
> "Guess Who's Coming to Dinner?," Kramer-Columbia.

Best Director: Mike Nichols, "The Graduate."
> *Others Nominated:* Richard Brooks, "In Cold Blood"; Norman Jewison, "In the Heat of the Night"; Stanley Kramer, "Guess Who's Coming to Dinner?"; Arthur Penn, "Bonnie and Clyde."

Best Actor: Rod Steiger, "In the Heat of the Night."
> *Others Nominated:* Warren Beatty, "Bonnie and Clyde"; Dustin Hoffman, "The Graduate"; Paul Newman, "Cool Hand Luke"; Spencer Tracy, "Guess Who's Coming To Dinner?"

Best Actress: Katharine Hepburn, "Guess Who's Coming to Dinner?"
> *Others Nominated:* Anne Bancroft, "The Graduate"; Faye Dunaway, "Bonnie and Clyde"; Dame Edith Evans, "The Whisperers"; Audrey Hepburn, "Wait Until Dark."

Best Supporting Actor: George Kennedy, "Cool Hand Luke."
> *Others Nominated:* John Cassavetes, "The Dirty Dozen"; Gene Hackman, "Bonnie and Clyde"; Cecil Kellaway, "Guess Who's Coming to Dinner?"; Michael J. Pollard, "Bonnie and Clyde."

Best Supporting Actress: Estelle Parsons, "Bonnie and Clyde."
> *Others Nominated:* Carol Channing, "Thoroughly Modern Millie"; Mildred Natwick, "Barefoot in the Park"; Bea Richards, "Guess Who's Coming to Dinner?"; Katharine Ross, "The Graduate."

Best Screenplay adapted from another medium: Stirling Silliphant, "In the Heat of the Night."
> *Others Nominated:* Don Pearce & Frank R. Pierson, "Cool Hand Luke"; Calder Willingham & Buck Henry, "The Graduate"; Richard Brooks, "In Cold Blood"; Joseph Strick & Fred Haines, "Ulysses."

Best Original Screenplay: William Rose, "Guess Who's Coming to Dinner?"
> *Others Nominated:* David Newman & Robert Benton, "Bonnie and Clyde"; Robert Kaufman & Norman Lear, "Divorce American Style"; Jorge Semprun, "La Guerre est Finie"; Frederic Raphael, "Two for the Road."

Directors Guild Of America

1967 Best Director: Mike Nichols, "The Graduate."

Writers Guild Of America
(Awards given for pictures released in 1967)

Best Written American Comedy: Calder Willingham & Buck Henry, "The Graduate."
Best Written American Drama: David Newman & Robert Benton, "Bonnie and Clyde."
Best Written American Musical: Richard Morris, "Thoroughly Modern Millie."
Best Written Original Screenplay: David Newman & Robert Benton, "Bonnie and Clyde."

Golden Globe Awards
(For 1967 Releases)

Best Picture-Drama: "In the Heat of the Night."
Best Picture-Musical/Comedy: "The Graduate."
Best Director: Mike Nichols, "The Graduate."
Best Actress-Drama: Dame Edith Evans, "The Whisperers."
Best Actor-Drama: Rod Steiger, "In the Heat of the Night."
Best Actress-Musical/Comedy: Anne Bancroft, "The Graduate."
Best Actor-Musical/Comedy: Richard Harris, "Camelot."
Best Supporting Actress: Carol Channing, "Thoroughly Modern Millie."
Best Supporting Actor: Richard Attenborough, "Doctor Dolittle."
Best Screenplay: Stirling Silliphant, "In the Heat of the Night."

New York Film Critics
(Awards for 1967 Releases)

Best Picture: "In the Heat of the Night."
Best Director: Mike Nichols, "In the Heat of the Night."
Best Actor: Rod Steiger, "In the Heat of the Night."
Best Actress: Dame Edith Evans, "The Whisperers."
Best Screenplay: David Newman & Robert Benton, "Bonnie and Clyde."
(No awards for "Best Supporting" categories until 1969)

Cannes Film Festival
(May of 1968)

(Festival Closed)

National Society Of Film Critics
(Awards for films released in 1967)

Best Picture: "Persona."
Best Director: Ingmar Bergman, "Persona."
Best Actor: Rod Steiger, "In the Heat of the Night."
Best Actress: Bibi Andersson, "Persona."
Best Supporting Actor: Gene Hackman, "Bonnie and Clyde."
Best Supporting Actress: Marjorie Rhodes, "The Family Way."
Best Screenplay: David Newman & Robert Benton, "Bonnie and Clyde."

Los Angeles Film Critics
(First awards presented in 1977)
Independent Spirit Awards
(First presented in 1986)

1968

1967

39th Annual Academy Awards
(Oscars given for pictures released in 1966)

Best Picture: "A Man for All Seasons," Columbia.

Others Nominated:
"Alfie," Paramount.
"The Russians Are Coming, The Russians Are Coming," United Artists.
"The Sand Pebbles," 20th Century-Fox.
"Who's Afraid of Virginia Woolf?, " Warner Bros.

Best Director: Fred Zinnemann, "A Man for All Seasons."

Others Nominated: Michelangelo Antonioni, "Blow-Up"; Richard Brooks, "The Professionals"; Claude Lelouch, "A Man and a Woman"; Mike Nichols, "Who's Afraid of Virginia Woolf?"

Best Actor: Paul Scofield, "A Man for All Seasons."

Others Nominated: Alan Arkin, "The Russians Are Coming, The Russians Are Coming"; Richard Burton, "Who's Afraid of Virginia Woolf?"; Michael Caine, "Alfie"; Steve McQueen, "The Sand Pebbles."

Best Actress: Elizabeth Taylor, "Who's Afraid of Virginia Woolf?"

Others Nominated: Anouk Aimee, "A Man and a Woman"; Ida Kaminska, "The Shop on Main Street"; Lynn Redgrave, "Gregory Girl"; Vanessa Redgrave, "Morgan."

Best Supporting Actor: Walter Matthau, "The Fortune Cookie."

Others Nominated: Mako, "The Sand Pebbles"; James Mason, "Georgy Girl"; George Segal, "Who's Afraid of Virginia Woolf?"; Robert Shaw, "A Man for All Seasons."

Best Supporting Actress: Sandy Dennis, "Who's Afraid of Virginia Woolf?"

Others Nominated: Wendy Hiller, "A Man for All Seasons"; Jocelyn Lagarde, "Hawaii"; Vivien Merchant, "Alfie"; Geraldine Page, "You're a Big Boy Now."

Best Screenplay adapted from another medium: Robert Bolt, "A Man for All Seasons."

Others Nominated: Richard Brooks, "The Professionals"; William Rose, "The Russians Are Coming, The Russians Are Coming"; Ernest Lehman, "Who's Afraid of Virginia Woolf?"; Bill Naughton, "Alfie."

Best Original Screenplay: Claude Lelouch (S), Pierre Uytterhoeven and Claude Lelouch (SP), "A Man and a Woman."

Others Nominated: Michelangelo Antonioni, Tonino Guerra & Edward Bond, "Blow-Up"; Billy Wilder & I.A.L. Diamond, "The Fortune Cookie"; Clint Johnston & Don Peters, "The Naked Prey"; Robert Ardrey, "Khartoum."

Directors Guild Of America

1966 Best Director: Fred Zinnemann, "A Man for All Seasons."

Writers Guild Of America
(Awards given for pictures released in 1966)

Best Written American Comedy: William Rose, "The Russians Are Coming, The Russians Are Coming."

Best Written American Drama: Ernest Lehman, "Who's Afraid of Virginia Woolf?"

Best Written American Musical: (No award presented)

Best Written Original Screenplay: (category first presented in 1968)

Golden Globe Awards
(For 1966 Releases)

Best Picture-Drama: "A Man for All Seasons."
Best Picture-Musical/Comedy: "The Russians Are Coming, The Russians Are Coming."
Best Director: Fred Zinnemann, "A Man for All Seasons."
Best Actress-Drama: Anouk Aimee, "A Man and a Woman."
Best Actor-Drama: Paul Scofield, "A Man for All Seasons."
Best Actress-Musical/Comedy: Lynn Redgrave, "Gregory Girl."
Best Actor-Musical/Comedy: Alan Arkin, "The Russians Are Coming, The Russians Are Coming."
Best Supporting Actress: Jocelyn La Garde, "Hawaii."
Best Supporting Actor: Richard Attenborough, "The Sand Pebbles."
Best Screenplay: Robert Bolt, "A Man for All Seasons."

National Society Of Film Critics
(Awards for films released in 1966)

Best Picture: "Blow-Up."
Best Director: Michelangelo Antonioni.
Best Actor: Michael Caine, "Alfie."
Best Actress: Sylvie, "The Shameless Old Lady."

New York Film Critics
(Awards for 1966 Releases)

Best Picture: "A Man for All Seasons."
Best Director: Fred Zinnemann, "A Man for All Seasons."
Best Actor: Paul Scofield, "A Man for All Seasons."
Best Actress: (tie) Elizabeth Taylor, "Who's Afraid of Virginia Woolf?" and **Lynn Redgrave**, "Georgy Girl."
Best Screenplay: Robert Bolt, "A Man for All Seasons."
(No awards for "Best Supporting" categories until 1969)

Cannes Film Festival
(May of 1967)

Best Picture: "Blow-Up."
Best Director: Ferenc Kosa, "Ten Thousand Suns."
Best Actor: Odded Kotler, "Three Days and a Child."
Best Actress: Pia Degermark, "Elvira Madigan."
Best Screenplay: (Not awarded)
International Critics: (Not awarded)
(No awards for "Best Supporting" categories until 1979)

Los Angeles Film Critics
(First awards presented in 1977)
Independent Spirit Awards
(First presented in 1986)

1967

1966

38th Annual Academy Awards
(Oscars given for pictures released in 1965)

Best Picture: "The Sound of Music"
  Others Nominated: "Darling"; "Doctor Zhivago";
  "Ship of Fools"; "A Thousand Clowns."
Best Director: Robert Wise, "The Sound of Music."
Best Actor: Lee Marvin, "Cat Ballou."
Best Actress: Julie Christie, "Darling."
Best Supporting Actor: Martin Balsam, "A
Thousand Clowns."

Best Supporting Actress: Shelley Winters, "A
Patch of Blue."
Best Screenplay adapted from another medium:
  Robert Bolt, "Doctor Zhivago."
Best Original Screenplay: Frederic Raphael,
  "Darling."

Directors Guild Of America

1965 Best Director: Robert Wise, "The
Sound of Music."

Writers Guild Of America
(Awards given for pictures released in 1965)

Best-Written American Comedy: Herb Gardner,
"A Thousand Clowns."
**Best-Written American Drama: Morton Fine &
David Friedkin,** "The Pawnbroker."
Best-Written American Musical: Ernest Lehman,
"The Sound of Music."

Golden Globe Awards
(For 1965 Releases)

Best Picture-Drama: "Doctor Zhivago."
Best Picture-Musical/Comedy: "The Sound of
Music."
Best Director: David Lean, "Doctor Zhivago."
Best Actress-Drama: Samantha Eggar, "The
Collector."
Best Actor-Drama: Omar Sharif, "Doctor Zhivago."
Best Actress-Musical/Comedy: Julie Andrews, "The
Sound of Music."
Best Actor-Musical/Comedy: Lee Marvin, "Cat
Ballou."
Best Supporting Actress: Ruth Gordon, "Inside
Daisy Clover."
Best Supporting Actor: Oskar Werner, "The Spy
Who came in from the Cold."
Best Screenplay: Robert Bolt, "Doctor Zhivago."

New York Film Critics
(Awards for 1965 Releases)

Best Picture: "Darling."
Best Director: John Schlesinger, "Darling."
Best Actor: Oskar Werner, "Ship of Fools."
Best Actress: Julie Christie, "Darling."
Best Screenplay: (not presented)

Cannes Film Festival
(May of 1966)

Best Film: "A Man and a Woman."
Best Director: Serge Youtkevitch, "Lenin in Poland."
Best Actor: Per Oscarsson, "Hunger."
Best Actress: Vanessa Redgrave, "Morgan."
Best Screenplay: (Not awarded)
International Critics Award: "Young Torless" &
  "La Guerre est Finie."
Best Supporting: (category first presented in 1979)

National Society Of Film Critics
(First awards presented in 1967)
Los Angeles Film Critics Assoc.
(First awards presented in 1977)
Independent Spirit Awards
(First presented in 1986)

37th Annual Academy Awards
(Oscars given for pictures released in 1964)

1965

Best Picture: "My Fair Lady"
  Others Nominated: "Becket"; "Dr. Strangelove"; "Mary Poppins"; "Zorba the Greek."
Best Director: George Cukor, "My Fair Lady."
Best Actor: Rex Harrison, "My Fair Lady."
Best Actress: Julie Andrews, "Mary Poppins."
Best Supporting Actor: Peter Ustinov, "Topkapi."

Best Supporting Actress: Lila Kedrova, "Zorba the Greek."
Best Screenplay adapted from another medium: Edward Anhalt, "Becket."
Best Original Screenplay: S.H. Barnett, (S); Peter Stone & Frank Tarloff (SP), "Father Goose."

Directors Guild Of America

1964 Best Director: George Cukor, "My Fair Lady."

Writers Guild Of America
(Awards given for pictures released in 1964)

Best-Written American Comedy: Stanley Kubrick, Peter George & Terry Southern (SP), Peter George (S), "Dr. Strangelove."
Best-Written American Drama: Edward Anhalt, "Becket."
Best-Written American Musical: Bill Walsh, & Don Da Gradi, "Mary Poppins."

Golden Globe Awards
(For 1964 Releases)

Best Picture-Drama: "Becket."
Best Picture-Musical/Comedy: "My Fair Lady."
Best Director: George Cukor, "My Fair Lady."
Best Actress-Drama: Anne Bancroft, "The Pumpkin Eater."
Best Actor-Drama: Peter O'Toole, "Becket."
Best Actress-Musical/Comedy: Julie Andrews, "Mary Poppins."
Best Actor-Musical/Comedy: Rex Harrison, "My Fair Lady."
Best Supporting Actress: Agnes Moorehead, "Hush, Hush, Sweet Charlotte."
Best Supporting Actor: Edmond O'Brien, "Seven Days in May."
Best Screenplay: (Not awarded)

New York Film Critics
(Awards for 1964 Releases)

Best Picture: "My Fair Lady."
Best Director: Stanley Kubrick, "Dr. Strangelove."
Best Actor: Rex Harrison, "My Fair Lady."
Best Actress: Kim Stanley, "Seance on a Wet Afternoon."
Best Screenplay: Harold Pinter, "The Servant."

Cannes Film Festival
(May of 1965)

Best Film (Palme d'Or): "The Knack."
Best Director: L. Ciulei, "The Lost Forest."
Best Actor: Terence Stamp, "The Collector."
Best Actress: Samantha Eggar, "The Collector."
Best Screenplay: (Not awarded)
International Critics Award: "Tarahumara"
Best Supporting: (category first presented in 1979)

National Society Of Film Critics
(First awards presented in 1967)
Los Angeles Film Critics Assoc.
(First awards presented in 1977)
Independent Spirit Awards
(First presented in 1986)

1964

36th Annual Academy Awards
(Oscars given for pictures released in 1963)

Best Picture: "Tom Jones"
  Others Nominated: **"America, America";
  "Cleopatra"; "How the West Was Won"; "Lilies
  of the Field."**
Best Director: Tony Richardson, "Tom Jones."
Best Actor: Sidney Poitier, "Lilies of the Field."
Best Actress: Patricia Neal, "Hud."

Best Supporting Actor: Melvyn Douglas, "Hud."
**Best Supporting Actress: Margaret Rutherford,
  "The V.I.P.s."**
**Best Screenplay adapted from another medium:
  John Osborne, "Tom Jones."**
**Best Original Screenplay: James R. Webb, "How
  the West Was Won."**

Directors Guild Of America

1963 Best Director: Tony Richardson, "Tom Jones."

Writers Guild Of America
(Awards given for pictures released in 1963)

**Best-Written American Comedy: James Poe, "Lilies
  of the Field".**
**Best Written American Drama: Harriet Frank, Jr.
  & Irving Ravetch, "Hud."**
Best Written American Musical: (No Award)

Golden Globe Awards
(For 1963 Releases)

Best Picture-Drama: "The Cardinal."
Best Picture-Musical/Comedy: "Tom Jones."
Best Director: Elia Kazan, "America, America."
**Best Actress-Drama: Leslie Caron, "The L-Shaped
  Room."**
**Best Actor-Drama: Sidney Poitier, "Lilies of the
  Field."**
**Best Actress-Musical/Comedy: Shirley MacLaine,
  "Irma La Douce."**
**Best Actor-Musical/Comedy: Alberto Sordi, "To
  Bed or Not to Bed."**
**Best Supporting Actress: Margaret Rutherford,
  "The V.I.P.s."**
**Best Supporting Actor: John Huston, "The Cardi-
  nal."**
Best Screenplay: (Not awarded)

New York Film Critics
(Awards for 1963 Releases)

Best Picture: "Tom Jones."
Best Director: Tony Richardson, "Tom Jones."
Best Actor: Albert Finney, "Tom Jones."
Best Actress: Patricia Neal, "Hud."
Best Screenplay: (Not awarded)

Cannes Film Festival
(May of 1964)

**Best Film (Palme d'Or): "The Umbrellas of
  Cherbourg."**
Best Director: (Not awarded)
Best Actor: (tie)
  Antal Pager, "Pasirta"
  Saro Urzi, "Seduced and Abandoned"
Best Actress: (tie)
  Anne Bancroft, "The Pumpkin Eater."
  Barbara Barrie, "One Potato, Two Potato."
International Critics Award: "The Passenger."
Best Supporting: (category first presented in 1979)

National Society Of Film Critics
(First awards presented in 1967)
Los Angeles Film Critics Assoc.
(First awards presented in 1977)
Independent Spirit Awards
(First presented in 1986)

35th Annual Academy Awards
(Oscars given for pictures released in 1962)

1963

Best Picture: "Lawrence of Arabia"
Others Nominated: "The Longest Day"; "The Music Man"; "Mutiny on the Bounty"; "To Kill a Mockingbird."
Best Director: David Lean, "Lawrence of Arabia."
Best Actor: Gregory Peck, "To Kill a Mockingbird."
Best Actress: Anne Bancroft, "The Miracle Worker."
Best Supporting Actor: Ed Begley, "Sweet Bird of Youth."

Best Supporting Actress: Patty Duke, "The Miracle Worker."
Best Screenplay adapted from another medium: Horton Foote, "To Kill a Mockingbird."
Best Original Screenplay: Ennio de Concini, Alfredo Giannetti & Pietro Germi, "Divorce-Italian Style."

Directors Guild Of America

1962 Best Director: David Lean, "Lawrence of Arabia."

Writers Guild Of America
(Awards given for pictures released in 1962)

Best-Written American Comedy: Stanley Shapiro & Nate Monaster, "That Touch of Mink."
Best-Written American Drama: Horton Foote, "To Kill a Mockingbird."
Best-Written American Musical: Marion Hargrove, "The Music Man."

Golden Globe Awards
(For 1962 Releases)

Best Picture-Drama: "Lawrence of Arabia."
Best Picture-Musical/Comedy: "That Touch of Mink."
Best Director: David Lean, "Lawrence of Arabia."
Best Actress-Drama: Geraldine Page, "Sweet Bird of Youth."
Best Actor-Drama: Gregory Peck, "To Kill a Mockingbird."
Best Actress-Musical/Comedy: Rosalind Russell, "Gypsy."
Best Actor-Musical/Comedy: Marcello Mastroianni, "Divorce-Italian Style."
Best Supporting Actress: Angela Lansbury, "The Manchurian Candidate."
Best Supporting Actor: Omar Sharif, "Lawrence of Arabia."
Best Screenplay: (Not awarded)

New York Film Critics
(Awards for 1962 Releases)

(None)

Cannes Film Festival
(May of 1963)

Best Film (Palme d'Or): "The Leopard."
Best Director: (Not awarded)
Best Actor: Richard Harris, "This Sporting Life."
Best Actress: Marina Vlady, "The Conjugal Bed (a.k.a. "Queen Bee)."
Best Screenplay: (Not awarded)
International Critics Prize: "This Sporting Life."
Best Supporting: (category first presented in 1979)

National Society Of Film Critics
(First awards presented in 1967)
Los Angeles Film Critics Assoc.
(First awards presented in 1977)
Independent Spirit Awards
(First presented in 1986)

1962

34th Annual Academy Awards
(Oscars given for pictures released in 1961)

Best Picture: "West Side Story"
  Others Nominated: "Fanny"; The Guns of Navarone"; "The Hustler"; "Judgment at Nuremberg."
Best Director: Robert Wise & Jerome Robbins, "West Side Story."
Best Actor: Maximilian Schell, "Judgment at Nuremberg."
Best Actress: Sophia Loren, "Two Women."

Best Supporting Actor: George Chakiris, "West Side Story."
Best Supporting Actress: Rita Moreno, "West Side Story."
Best Screenplay adapted from another medium: Abby Mann, "Judgment at Nuremberg."
Best Original Screenplay: William Inge, "Splendor in the Grass."

Directors Guild Of America

1961 Best Director: Robert Wise & Jerome Robbins, "West Side Story."

Writers Guild Of America
(Awards given for pictures released in 1961)

Best-Written American Comedy: George Axelrod, "Breakfast at Tiffany's."
Best-Written American Drama: Sidney Carroll & Robert Rossen, "The Hustler."
Best-Written American Musical: Ernest Lehman, "West Side Story."

Golden Globe Awards
(For 1961 Releases)

Best Picture-Drama: "The Guns of Navarone."
Best Picture-Comedy: "A Majority of One."
Best Picture-Musical: "West Side Story."
Best Director: Stanley Kramer, "Judgment at Nuremberg."
Best Actress-Drama: Geraldine Page, "Summer and Smoke."
Best Actor-Drama: Maximilian Schell, "Judgment at Nuremberg."
Best Actress-Musical/Comedy: Rosalind Russell, "A Majority of One."
Best Actor-Musical/Comedy: Glenn Ford, "Pocketful of Miracles."
Best Supporting Actress: Rita Moreno, "West Side Story."
Best Supporting Actor: George Chakiris, "West Side Story."
Best Screenplay: (Not awarded)

New York Film Critics
(Awards for 1961 Releases)

Best Picture: "West Side Story."
Best Director: Robert Rossen, "The Hustler."
Best Actor: Maximilian Schell, "Judgment at Nuremberg."
Best Actress: Sophia Loren, "Two Women."
Best Screenplay: (Not awarded)

Cannes Film Festival
(May of 1962)

Best Film (Palme d'Or): "The Given Word."
Best Director: (Not awarded)
Best Acting: (Given collectively to two films) Katharine Hepburn, Ralph Richardson, Jason Robards Jr., & Dean Stockwell, "Long Day's Journey Into Night"; Rita Tushingham, "Murray Melvin, A Taste of Honey."
Best Screenplay: (Not awarded)
International Critics Prize: "The Exterminating Angel."
(No awards for "Best Supporting" categories until 1979)

National Society Of Film Critics
(First awards presented in 1967)
Los Angeles Film Critics Assoc.
(First awards presented in 1977)
Independent Spirit Awards
(First presented in 1986)

33rd Annual Academy Awards
(Oscars given for pictures released in 1960)

1961

Best Picture: "The Apartment."
  Others Nominated: **"The Alamo"; "Elmer Gantry"; "Sons and Lovers"; "The Sundowners."**
Best Director: Billy Wilder, "The Apartment."
Best Actor: Burt Lancaster, "Elmer Gantry."
Best Actress: Elizabeth Taylor, "Butterfield 8."

Best Supporting Actor: Peter Ustinov, "Spartacus."
Best Supporting Actress: Shirley Jones, "Elmer Gantry."
Best Screenplay adapted from another medium: Richard Brooks, "Elmer Gantry."
Best Original Screenplay: Billy Wilder & I.A.L. Diamond, "The Apartment."

Directors Guild Of America

1960 Grand Award for Direction: Billy Wilder, "The Apartment."

Writers Guild Of America
(Awards given for pictures released in 1960)

Best-Written American Comedy: Billy Wilder & I.A.L. Diamond, "The Apartment."
Best-Written American Drama: Richard Brooks, "Elmer Gantry."
Best-Written American Musical: Betty Comden & Adolph Green, "The Bells Are Ringing."

Golden Globe Awards
(For 1960 Releases)

Best Picture-Drama: "Spartacus."
Best Picture-Comedy: "The Apartment."
Best Picture-Musical: "Song Without End."
Best Director: Jack Cardiff, "Sons and Lovers."
Best Actress-Drama: Greer Garson, "Sunrise at Campobello."
Best Actor-Drama: Burt Lancaster, "Elmer Gantry."
Best Actress-Musical/Comedy: Shirley MacLaine, "The Apartment."
Best Actor-Musical/Comedy: Jack Lemmon, "The Apartment."
Best Supporting Actress: Janet Leigh, "Psycho."
Best Supporting Actor: Sal Mineo, "Exodus."
Best Screenplay: (Not awarded)

New York Film Critics
(Awards for 1960 Releases)

Best Picture: (tie)
  "The Apartment" & "Sons and Lovers."
Best Director: (tie)
  Billy Wilder, "The Apartment."
  Jack Cardiff, "Sons and Lovers."
Best Actor: Burt Lancaster, "Elmer Gantry."
Best Actress: Deborah Kerr, "The Sundowners."
Best Writing: Billy Wilder & I.A.L. Diamond, "The Apartment."

Cannes Film Festival
(May of 1961)

Best Film (Palme d'Or): "Viridiana."
Best Director: Yulia Solntzeva, "History of the Flaming Years."
Best Actor: Anthony Perkins, "Goodbye Again."
Best Actress: Sophia Loren, "Two Women."
Best Screenplay: (Not awarded)
International Critics Prize: "Hands in the Trap."
Best Supporting: (category first presented in 1979)

National Society Of Film Critics
(First awards presented in 1967)
Los Angeles Film Critics Assoc.
(First awards presented in 1977)
Independent Spirit Awards
(First presented in 1986)

1960

32nd Annual Academy Awards
(Oscars given for pictures released in 1959)

Best Picture: "Ben-Hur."
 Others Nominated: **"Anatomy of a Murder"; The Diary of Anne Frank"; "The Nun's Story"; "Room at the Top."**
Best Director: William Wyler, "Ben-Hur."
Best Actor: Charlton Heston, "Ben-Hur."
Best Actress: Simone Signoret, "Room at the Top."
Best Supporting Actor: Hugh Griffith, "Ben-Hur."

Best Supporting Actress: Shelley Winters, "The Diary of Anne Frank."
Best Screenplay adapted from another medium: Neil Paterson, "Room at the Top."
Best Original Screenplay: Russell Rouse, Clarence Greene (S) Stanley Shapiro & Maurice Richlin (SP), "Pillow Talk."

Directors Guild Of America

1959 Grand Award for Direction: William Wyler, "Ben-Hur."

Writers Guild Of America
(Awards given for pictures released in 1959)

Best-Written American Comedy: Billy Wilder & I.A.L. Diamond, "Some Like It Hot."
Best-Written American Drama: Frances Goodrich & Albert Hackett, "The Diary of Anne Frank."
Best-Written American Musical: Melville Shavelson & Jack Rose (SP), Robert Smith (S), "Five Pennies."

Golden Globe Awards
(Foror 1959 Releases)

Best Picture-Drama: "Ben-Hur."
Best Picture-Comedy: "Some Like It Hot."
Best Picture-Musical: "Porgy and Bess."
Best Director: William Wyler, "Ben-Hur."
Best Actress-Drama: Elizabeth Taylor, "Suddenly Last Summer."
Best Actor-Drama: Anthony Franciosa, "Career."
Best Actress-Musical/Comedy: Marilyn Monroe, "Some Like It Hot."
Best Actor-Musical/Comedy: Jack Lemmon, "Some Like It Hot."
Best Supporting Actress: Susan Kohner, "Imitation of Life."
Best Supporting Actor: Stephen Boyd, "Ben-Hur."
Best Screenplay: (Not awarded)

New York Film Critics
(Awards for 1959 Releases)

Best Picture: "Ben-Hur."
Best Director: Fred Zinnemann, "The Nun's Story."
Best Actor: James Stewart, "Anatomy of a Murder."
Best Actress: Audrey Hepburn, "The Nun's Story."
Best Writing: Wendell Mayes, "Anatomy of a Murder."

Cannes Film Festival
(May of 1960)

Best Film (Palme d'Or): "La Dolce Vita."
 *(The Virgin Spring" and "The Young One" were announced as too good to be judged)
Best Director: (Not awarded)
Best Actor: (Not awarded)
Best Actress: (tie)
 Melina Mercouri, "Never on Sunday."
 Jeanne Moreau, "Moderato Cantabile."
Best Screenplay: (Not awarded)
International Critics Prize: "The Virgin Spring."
Best Supporting: (category first presented in 1979)

National Society Of Film Critics
(First awards presented in 1967)
Los Angeles Film Critics Assoc.
(First awards presented in 1977)
Independent Spirit Awards
(First presented in 1986)

31st Annual Academy Awards
(Oscars given for pictures released in 1958)

1959

Best Picture: "Gigi."
  Others Nominated: "Auntie Mame"; "Cat on a Hot Tin Roof"; "The Defiant Ones"; "Separate Tables."
Best Director: Vincente Minnelli, "Gigi."
Best Actor: David Niven, "Separate Tables."
Best Actress: Susan Hayward, "I Want to Live!"
Best Supporting Actor: Burl Ives, "The Big Country."

Best Supporting Actress: Wendy Hiller, "Separate Tables."
Best Screenplay adapted from another medium: Alan Jay Lerner, "Gigi."
Best Original Screenplay: Nathan E. Douglas & Harold Jacobs Smith, "The Defiant Ones."

Directors Guild Of America

1958 Grand Award for Direction: Vincente Minnelli, "Gigi."

Writers Guild Of America
(Awards given for pictures released in 1958)

Best-Written American Comedy: S.N. Behrman & George Froeschel, "Me and the Colonel."
Best-Written American Drama: Harold Jacob Smith & Nathan E. Douglas, "The Defiant Ones."
Best-Written American Musical: Alan Jay Lerner, "Gigi."

Golden Globe Awards
(For 1958 Releases)

Best Picture-Drama: "The Defiant Ones."
Best Picture-Comedy: "Auntie Mame."
Best Picture-Musical: "Gigi."
Best Director: Vincente Minnelli, "Gigi."
Best Actress-Drama: Susan Hayward, "I Want to Live!"
Best Actor-Drama: David Niven, "Separate Tables."
Best Actress-Musical/Comedy: Rosalind Russell, "Auntie Mame."
Best Actor-Musical/Comedy: Danny Kaye, "Me and the Colonel."
Best Supporting Actress: Hermione Gingold, "Gigi."
Best Supporting Actor: Burl Ives, "The Big Country."
Best Screenplay: (Not awarded)

New York Film Critics
(Awards for 1958 Releases)

Best Picture: "The Defiant Ones."
Best Director: Stanley Kramer, "The Defiant Ones."
Best Actor: David Niven, "Separate Tables."
Best Actress: Susan Hayward, "I Want to Live!"
Best Writing: Nathan E. Douglas & Harold Jacob Smith, "The Defiant Ones."

Cannes Film Festival
(May of 1959)

Best Film (Palme d'Or): "Black Orpheus."
Best Director: Francois Truffaut, "The 400 Blows."
Best Actor: (Collectively)
  Dean Stockwell, Bradford Dillman & Orson Welles, "Compulsion."
Best Actress: Simone Signoret, "Room at the Top."
Best Screenplay: (Not awarded)
International Critics Prize: (tie)
  "Hiroshima Mon Amour"
  "Araya"
Best Supporting: (category first presented in 1979)

National Society Of Film Critics
(First awards presented in 1967)
Los Angeles Film Critics Assoc.
(First awards presented in 1977)
Independent Spirit Awards
(First presented in 1986)

1958

30th Annual Academy Awards
(Oscars given for pictures released in 1957)

Best Picture: "The Bridge on the River Kwai."
Others Nominated: "Peyton Place"; "Sayonara"; "Twelve Angry Men"; "Witness for the Prosecution."
Best Director: David Lean, "The Bridge on the River Kwai."
Best Actor: Alec Guinness, "The Bridge on the River Kwai."
Best Actress: Joanne Woodward, "The Three Faces of Eve."

Best Supporting Actor: Red Buttons, "Sayonara."
Best Supporting Actress: Miyoshi Jmeki, "Sayonara."
Best Screenplay adapted from another medium: Pierre Boulle, "The Bridge on the River Kwai."
Best Original Screenplay: George Wells, "Designing Woman."

Directors Guild Of America

1957 Most Outstanding Directorial Achievement: David Lean, "The Bridge on the River Kwai."

Writers Guild Of America
(Awards given for pictures released in 1957)

Best-Written American Comedy: Billy Wilder & I.A.L. Diamond, "Love in the Afternoon."
Best-Written American Drama: Reginald Rose, "Twelve Angry Men."
Best-Written American Musical: John Patrick (SP) Vera Casary (S), "Les Girls."

Golden Globe Awards
(For 1957 Releases)

Best Picture-Drama: "The Bridge on the River Kwai."
Best Picture-Musical/Comedy: "Les Girls."
Best Director: David Lean, "The Bridge on the River Kwai."
Best Actress-Drama: Joanne Woodward, "The Three Faces of Eve."
Best Actor-Drama: Alec Guinness, "The Bridge on the River Kwai."
Best Actress-Musical/Comedy: Kay Kendall, "Les Girls."
Best Actor-Musical/Comedy: Frank Sinatra, "Pal Joey."
Best Supporting Actress: Elsa Lanchester, "Witness for the Prosecution."
Best Supporting Actor: Red Buttons, "Sayonara."
Best Screenplay: (Not awarded)

New York Film Critics
(Awards for 1957 Releases)

Best Picture: "The Bridge on the River Kwai."
Best Director: David Lean, "The Bridge on the River Kwai."
Best Actor: Alec Guinness, "The Bridge on the River Kwai."
Best Actress: Deborah Kerr, "Heaven Knows, Mr. Allison."
Best Writing: (Not awarded)

Cannes Film Festival
(May of 1958)

Best Film (Palme d'Or): "The Cranes Are Flying."
Best Director: Ingmar Bergman, "Brink of Life."
Best Acting: Paul Newman, "That Long Hot Summer."
Best Actress: (Collectively) Eva Dahlbeck, Ingrid Thulin, Bibi Andersson, Babro Ornas, "Brink of Life."
Best Script: Mauro Bolognini, "Newlyweds."
International Critics Prize: "Vengeance."
Best Supporting: (category first presented in 1979)

National Society Of Film Critics
(First awards presented in 1967)
Los Angeles Film Critics Assoc.
(First awards presented in 1977)
Independent Spirit Awards
(First presented in 1986)

29th Annual Academy Awards
(Oscars given for pictures released in 1956)

1957

Best Picture: "Around the World in 80 Days."
  Others Nominated: "Friendly Persuasion";
  "Giant"; "The King and I"; "The Ten Commandments."
Best Director: George Stevens, "Giant."
Best Actor: Yul Brynner, "The King and I."
Best Actress: Ingrid Bergman, "Anastasia."
Best Supporting Actor: Anthony Quinn, "Lust for Life."

Best Supporting Actress: Dorthy Malone, "Written on the Wind."
Writing (Motion Picture Story): Dalton Trumbo, "The Brave One."
Writing (Best Screenplay-Adapted): James Poe, John Farrow, S.J. Perelman, "Around the World in 80 Days."
Writing (Best Screenplay-Original): Albert Lamorisse, "The Red Balloon."

Directors Guild Of America

1956 Most Outstanding Directorial Achievement: George Stevens, "Giant."

Writers Guild Of America
(Awards given for pictures released in 1956)

Best-Written American Comedy: James Poe, John Farrow & S.J. Perelman, "Around the World in 80 Days."
Best-Written American Drama: Michael Wilson, "Friendly Persuasion."
Best-Written American Musical: Ernest Lehman, "The King and I."

Golden Globe Awards
(For 1956 Releases)

Best Picture-Drama: "Around the World in 80 Days."
Best Picture-Musical/Comedy: "The King and I."
Best Director: Elia Kazan, "Baby Doll."
Best Actress-Drama: Ingrid Bergman, "Anastasia."
Best Actor-Drama: Kirk Douglas, "Lust for Life."
Best Actress-Musical/Comedy: Deborah Kerr, "The King and I."
Best Actor-Musical/Comedy: Cantinflas, "Around the World in 80 Days."
Best Supporting Actress: Eileen Heckart, "The Bad Seed."
Best Supporting Actor: Earl Holliman, "The Rainmaker."
Best Screenplay: (Not awarded)

New York Film Critics
(Awards for 1956 Releases)

Best Picture: "Around the World in 80 Days."
Best Director: John Huston, "Moby Dick."
Best Actor: Kirk Douglas, "Lust for Life."
Best Actress: Ingrid Bergman, "Anastasia."
Best Writing: S.J. Perelman, "Around the World in 80 Days."

Cannes Film Festival
(May of 1957)

Best Film (Palme d'Or): "Friendly Persuasion."
Best Director: Robert Bresson, "A Condemned Man Escapes."
Best Actor: John Kitzmiller, "Valley of Peace."
Best Actress: Guilietta Massina, "Nights of Cabiria."
International Critics Prize: (category first presented in 1958)
Best Script: (category first presented in 1958)
Best Supporting: (category first presented in 1979)

National Society Of Film Critics
(First awards presented in 1967)
Los Angeles Film Critics Assoc.
(First awards presented in 1977)
Independent Spirit Awards
(First presented in 1986)

1956

28th Annual Academy Awards
(Oscars given for pictures released in 1955)

Best Picture: "Marty."
Others Nominated: "Love is a Many-Splendored Thing"; "Mister Roberts"; "Picnic"; "The Rose Tattoo."
Best Director: Delbert Mann, "Marty."
Best Actor: Ernest Borgnine, "Marty."
Best Actress: Anna Magnani, "The Rose Tattoo."
Best Supporting Actor: George Chakiris, "West Side Story."

Best Supporting Actress: Jo Van Fleet, "East of Eden."
Writing (Motion Picture Story): Daniel Fuchs, "Love Me or Leave Me."
Writing (Best Screenplay-Adapted): Paddy Chayefsky, "Marty."
Writing (Best Screenplay-Original): William Ludwig & Sonya Levien, "Interrupted Melody."

Directors Guild Of America

1955 Most Outstanding Directorial Achievement: Delbert Mann, "Marty."

Writers Guild Of America
(Awards given for pictures released in 1955)

Best-Written American Comedy: Frank S. Nugent & Joshua Logan, "Mr. Roberts."
Best-Written American Drama: Paddy Chayefsky, "Marty."
Best-Written American Musical: Daniel Fuchs & Isobel Lennart (SP); Daniel Fuchs (S), "Love Me or Leave Me."

Golden Globe Awards
(For 1955 Releases)

Best Picture-Drama: "East of Eden."
Best Picture-Musical/Comedy: "Guys and Dolls."
Best Outdoor Drama: "Wichita."
Best Director: Joshua Logan, "Picnic."
Best Actress-Drama: Anna Magnani, "The Rose Tattoo."
Best Actor-Drama: Ernest Borgnine, "Marty."
Best Actress-Musical/Comedy: Jean Simmons, "Guys and Dolls."
Best Actor-Musical/Comedy: Tom Ewell, "The Seven Year Itch."
Best Supporting Actress: Marisa Pavan, "The Rose Tattoo."
Best Supporting Actor: Arthur Kennedy, "The Trial."
Best Screenplay: (Not awarded)

New York Film Critics
(Awards for 1955 Releases)

Best Picture: "Marty."
Best Director: David Lean, "Summertime."
Best Actor: Ernest Borgnine, "Marty."
Best Actress: Anna Magnani, "The Rose Tattoo."
Best Writing: (category first presented in 1956)

Cannes Film Festival
(May of 1956)

Best Film (Palme d'Or): "World of Silence."
Best Director: Serge Youtkevitch, "Othello."
Best Actor: (Not awarded)
Best Actress: Susan Hayward, "I'll Cry Tomorrow."
International Critics Prize: (category first presented in 1958)
Best Script: (category first presented in 1958)
Best Supporting: (category first presented in 1979)

National Society Of Film Critics
(First awards presented in 1967)
Los Angeles Film Critics Assoc.
(First awards presented in 1977)
Independent Spirit Awards
(First presented in 1986)

27th Annual Academy Awards
(Oscars given for pictures released in 1954)

1955

Best Picture: "On the Waterfront."
Others Nominated: "The Caine Mutiny"; "The Country Girl"; "Seven Brides for Seven Brothers"; "Three Coins in the Fountain."
Best Director: Elia Kazan, "On the Waterfront."
Best Actor: Marlon Brando, "On the Waterfront."
Best Actress: Grace Kelly, "The Country Girl."
Best Supporting Actor: Edmond O'Brien, "The Barefoot Contessa."

Best Supporting Actress: Eva Marie Saint, "On the Waterfront."
Writing (Motion Picture Story): Philip Yordan, "Broken Lance."
Writing (Screenplay): George Seaton, "The Country Girl."
Writing (Story & Screenplay): Budd Schulberg, "On the Waterfront."

Directors Guild Of America

1954 Most Outstanding Directorial Achievement: Elia Kazan, "On the Waterfront."

Writers Guild Of America
(Awards given for pictures released in 1954)

Best-Written American Comedy: Billy Wilder, Samuel Taylor & Ernest Lehman, "Sabrina."
Best-Written American Drama: Budd Schulberg, "On the Waterfront."
Best-Written American Musical: Albert Hackett, Frances Goodrich & Dorothy Kingsley, "Seven Brides for Seven Brothers."

Golden Globe Awards
(For 1954 Releases)

Best Picture-Drama: "On the Waterfront."
Best Picture-Musical/Comedy: "Carmen Jones."
Best Director: Elia Kazan, "On the Waterfront."
Best Actress-Drama: Grace Kelly, "The Country Girl."
Best Actor-Drama: Marlon Brando, "On the Waterfront."
Best Actress-Musical/Comedy: Judy Garland, "A Star Is Born."
Best Actor-Musical/Comedy: James Mason, "A Star Is Born."
Best Supporting Actress: Jan Sterling, "The High and the Mighty."
Best Supporting Actor: Edmond O'Brien, "The Barefoot Contessa."
Best Screenplay: Billy Wilder, Samuel Taylor & Ernest Lehman, "Sabrina."

New York Film Critics
(Awards for 1954 Releases)

Best Picture: "On the Waterfront."
Best Director: Elia Kazan, "On the Waterfront."
Best Actor: Marlon Brando, "On the Waterfront."
Best Actress: Grace Kelly, "The Country Girl"; "Rear Window"; "Dial M for Murder."
Best Writing: (category first presented in 1956)

Cannes Film Festival
(May of 1955)

Best Film (Palme d'Or): "Marty."
Best Director: (tie)
    Jules Dassin, "Riffi."
    Serge Vasiliev, "Heroes of Shipka."
Best Actor: (tie)
    Spencer Tracy, "Bad Day at Black Rock"
    Ernest Borgnine, "Marty."
Best Actress: Betsy Blair, "Marty."
International Critics Prize: (category first presented in 1958)
Best Script: (category first presented in 1958)
Best Supporting: (category first presented in 1979)

National Society Of Film Critics
(First awards presented in 1967)
Los Angeles Film Critics Assoc.
(First awards presented in 1977)
Independent Spirit Awards
(First presented in 1986)

1954

26th Annual Academy Awards
(Oscars given for pictures released in 1953)

Best Picture: "From Here to Eternity."
Others Nominated: "Julius Caesar"; "The Robe"; "Roman Holiday"; "Shane."
Best Director: Fred Zinnemann, "From Here to Eternity."
Best Actor: William Holden, "Stalag 17."
Best Actress: Audrey Hepburn, "Roman Holiday."
Best Supporting Actor: Frank Sinatra, "From Here to Eternity."

Best Supporting Actress: Donna Reed, "From Here to Eternity."
Writing (Motion Picture Story): Ian McLellan Hunter, "Roman Holiday."
Writing (Screenplay): Daniel Taradash, "From Here to Eternity."
Writing (Story & Screenplay): Charles Brackett, Walter Reisch & Richard Breen, "Titanic."

Directors Guild Of America

1953 Most Outstanding Directorial Achievement: Fred Zinnemann, "From Here to Eternity."

Writers Guild Of America
(Awards given for pictures released in 1953)

Best-Written American Comedy: Ian McLellan Hunter & John Dighton (SP); Ian McLellan Hunter (S), "Roman Holiday."
Best-Written American Drama: Daniel Taradash, "From Here to Eternity."
Best-Written American Musical: Helen Deutsch, "Lili."

Golden Globe Awards
(For 1953 Releases)

Best Picture-Drama: "The Robe."
Best Director: Fred Zinnemann, "From Here to Eternity."
Best Actress-Drama: Audrey Hepburn, "Roman Holiday."
Best Actor-Drama: Spencer Tracy, "The Actress."
Best Actress-Musical/Comedy: Ethel Merman, "Call Me Madam."
Best Actor-Musical/Comedy: David Niven, "The Moon is Blue."
Best Supporting Actress: Grace Kelly, "Mogambo."
Best Supporting Actor: Frank Sinatra, "From Here to Eternity."
Best Screenplay: Helen Deutsch, "Lili."

New York Film Critics
(Awards for 1953 Releases)

Best Picture: "From Here to Eternity."
Best Director: Fred Zinnemann, "From Here to Eternity."
Best Actor: Burt Lancaster, "From Here to Eternity."
Best Actress: Audrey Hepburn, "Roman Holiday."
Best Writing: (category first presented in 1956)

Cannes Film Festival
(May of 1954)

Best Film (Palme d'Or): "Gate Of Hell."
Best Director: Rene Clement, "Monsieur Ripois."
Best Actor: (Not awarded)
Best Actress: (Not awarded)
International Critics Prize: (category first presented in 1958)
Best Script: (category first presented in 1958)
Best Supporting: (category first presented in 1979)

National Society Of Film Critics
(First awards presented in 1967)
Los Angeles Film Critics Assoc.
(First awards presented in 1977)
Independent Spirit Awards
(First presented in 1986)

25th Annual Academy Awards
(Oscars given for pictures released in 1952)

1953

Best Picture: "The Greatest Show on Earth."
Others Nominated: "High Noon"; "Ivanhoe"; "Moulin Rouge"; "The Quiet Man."
Best Director: John Ford, "High Noon."
Best Actor: Gary Cooper, "High Noon."
Best Actress: Shirley Booth, "Come Back, Little Sheba."
Best Supporting Actor: Anthony Quinn, "Viva Zapata!"

Best Supporting Actress: Gloria Grahame, "The Bad and the Beautiful."
Writing (Motion Picture Story): Frederic M. Frank, Theodore St. John & Frank Cavett, "The Greatest Show on Earth."
Writing (Screenplay): Charles Schnee, "The Bad and the Beautiful."
Writing (Story & Screenplay): T.E.B. Clarke, "The Lavender Hill Mob."

Directors Guild Of America

1952 Annual Award: John Ford.

Writers Guild Of America
(Awards given for pictures released in 1952)

Best-Written American Comedy: Frank S. Nugent, "The Quiet Man."
Best-Written American Drama: Carl Foreman, "High Noon."
Best-Written American Musical: Betty Comden & Adolph Green, "Singin' in the Rain."

Golden Globe Awards
(For 1952 Releases)

Best Picture-Drama: "The Greatest Show on Earth."
Best Picture-Musical/Comedy: "With a Song in My Heart."
Best Director: Cecil B. DeMille, "The Greatest Show On Earth."
Best Actress-Drama: Shirley Booth, "Come Back, Little Sheba."
Best Actor-Drama: Gary Cooper, "High Noon."
Best Actress-Musical/Comedy: Susan Hayward, "With a Song in My Heart."
Best Actor-Musical/Comedy: Donald O'Connor, "Singin' in the Rain."
Best Supporting Actress: Katy Jurado, "High Noon."
Best Supporting Actor: Millard Mitchell, "My Six Convicts."
Best Screenplay: Michael Wilson, "High Noon."

New York Film Critics
(Awards for 1952 Releases)

Best Picture: "High Noon."
Best Director: Fred Zinnemann, "High Noon."
Best Actor: Ralph Richardson, "Breaking the Sound Barrier."
Best Actress: Shirley Booth, "Come Back, Little Sheba."
Best Writing: (category first presented in 1956)

Cannes Film Festival
(May of 1953)

Best Film (Palme d'Or): "Wages of Fear."
Best Director: Walt Disney, For his work as a whole.
Best Actor: Charles Vanel, "Wages of Fear."
Best Actress: Shirley Booth, "Come Back, Little Sheba."
International Critics Prize: (category first presented in 1958)
Best Script: (category first presented in 1958)
Best Supporting: (category first presented in 1979)

National Society Of Film Critics
(First awards presented in 1967)
Los Angeles Film Critics Assoc.
(First awards presented in 1977)
Independent Spirit Awards
(First presented in 1986)

1952

24th Annual Academy Awards
(Oscars given for pictures released in 1951)

Best Picture: "An American in Paris."
Others Nominated: "Decision Before Dawn"; "A Place in the Sun"; "Quo Vadis"; "A Streetcar Named Desire."
Best Director: George Stevens, "A Place in the Sun."
Best Actor: Humphrey Bogart,"The African Queen."
Best Actress: Vivien Leigh, "A Streetcar Named Desire."
Best Supporting Actor: Karl Malden, "A Streetcar Named Desire."

Best Supporting Actress: Kim Hunter, "A Streetcar Named Desire."
Writing (Motion Picture Story): Paul Dehn & James Bernard, "Seven Days to Noon."
Writing (Screenplay): Michael Wilson & Harry Brown, "A Place in the Sun."
Writing (Story & Screenplay): Alan Jay Lerner, "An American in Paris."

Directors Guild Of America

1951 Annual Award: George Stevens, "A Place in the Sun."

Writers Guild Of America
(Awards given for pictures released in 1951)

Best-Written American Comedy: Frances Goodrich & Albert Hackett, "Father's Little Dividend."
Best-Written American Drama: Michael Wilson & Harry Brown, "A Place in the Sun."
Best-Written American Musical: Alan Jay Lerner, "An American in Paris."

Golden Globe Awards
(For 1951 Releases)

Best Picture-Drama: "A Place in the Sun."
Best Picture-Musical/Comedy: "An American in Paris."
Best Director: Laslo Benedek, "Death of a Salesman"
Best Actress-Drama: Jane Wyman, "The Blue Veil."
Best Actor-Drama: Fredric March, "Death of a Salesman."
Best Actress-Musical/Comedy: June Allyson, "Too Young to Kiss."
Best Actor-Musical/Comedy: Danny Kaye, "On the Riviera."
Best Supporting Actress: Kim Hunter, "A Streetcar Named Desire."
Best Supporting Actor: Peter Ustinov, "Quo Vadis."
Best Screenplay: Robert Buckner, "Bright Victory."

New York Film Critics
(Awards for 1951 Releases)

Best Picture: "A Streetcar Named Desire."
Best Director: Elia Kazan, "A Streetcar Named Desire."
Best Actor: Arthur Kennedy, "Bright Victory."
Best Actress: Vivien Leigh, "A Streetcar Named Desire."
Best Writing: (category first presented in 1956)

Cannes Film Festival
(May of 1952)

Best Film (Palme d'Or): (tie)
   "Othello."
   "Two Cents Worth of Hope."
Best Director: Christian-Jaque, "Fanfan la Tulipe."
Best Actor: Marlon Brando, "Viva Zapata!"
Best Actress: Lee Grant, "Detective Story."
International Critics Prize: (category first presented in 1958)
Best Script: (category first presented in 1958)
Best Supporting: (category first presented in 1979)

National Society Of Film Critics
(First awards presented in 1967)
Los Angeles Film Critics Assoc.
(First awards presented in 1977)
Independent Spirt Awards
(First presented in 1986)

23rd Annual Academy Awards
(Oscars given for pictures released in 1950)

1951

Best Picture: "All About Eve."
Others Nominated: "Born Yesterday"; "Father of the Bride"; "King Solomon's Mines"; "Sunset Boulevard."
Best Director: Joseph L. Mankiewicz, "All About Eve."
Best Actor: Jose Ferrer, "Cyrano de Bergerac."
Best Actress: Judy Holliday, "Born Yesterday."
Best Supporting Actor: George Sanders, "All About Eve."

Best Supporting Actress: Josephine Hull, "Harvey."
Writing (Motion Picture Story): Edna Anhalt & Edward Anhalt, "Panic in the Streets."
Writing (Screenplay): Joseph L. Mankiewicz, "All About Eve."
Writing (Story & Screenplay): Charles Brackett, Billy Wilder, D.M. Marshman, Jr., "Sunset Boulevard."

Directors Guild Of America

1950/51 Annual Award: Joseph L. Mankiewicz, "All About Eve."

Writers Guild Of America
(Awards given for pictures released in 1950)

Best-Written American Comedy: Joseph L. Mankiewicz, "All About Eve."
Best-Written American Drama: Charles Brackett, Billy Wilder & D.M. Marshman, Jr., "Sunset Boulevard."
Best-Written American Musical: Sidney Sheldon, "Annie Get Your Gun."
Best-Written American Western: Michael Blankfort, "Broken Arrow."

Golden Globe Awards
(For 1950 Releases)

Best Picture-Drama: "Sunset Boulevard."
Best Director: Billy Wilder, "Sunset Boulevard."
Best Actress-Drama: Gloria Swanson, "Sunset Boulevard."
Best Actor-Drama: Jose Ferrer, "Cyrano de Bergerac."
Best Actress-Musical/Comedy: Judy Holliday, "Born Yesterday."
Best Actor-Musical/Comedy: Fred Astaire, "Three Little Words."
Best Supporting Actress: Josephine Hull, "Harvey."
Best Supporting Actor: Edmund Gwenn, "Mister 880."
Best Screenplay: Joseph J. Mankiewicz, "All About Eve."

New York Film Critics
(Awards for 1950 Releases)

Best Picture: "All About Eve."
Best Director: Joesph L. Mankiewicz, "All About Eve."
Best Actor: Gregory Peck, "Twelve O'Clock High."
Best Actress: Bette Davis, "All About Eve."
Best Writing: (category first presented in 1956)

Cannes Film Festival
(May of 1951)

Best Film (Palme d'Or): "Miracle in Milan."
Best Director: Luis Bunuel, "Los Olvidados."
Best Actor: Michael Redgrave, "The Browning Version."
Best Actress: Bette Davis, "All About Eve."
International Critics Prize: (category first presented in 1958)
Best Script: (category first presented in 1958)
Best Supporting: (category first presented in 1979)

National Society Of Film Critics
(First awards presented in 1967)

Los Angeles Film Critics Assoc.
(First awards presented in 1977)

Independent Spirit Awards
(First presented in 1986)

1950

22nd Annual Academy Awards
(Oscars given for pictures released in 1949)

Best Picture: "All the King's Men."
Others Nominated: "Battleground"; "The Heiress"; "A letter to Three Wives"; "Twelve O'Clock High."
Best Director: Joseph L. Mankiewicz, "A Letter to Three Wives."
Best Actor: Broderick Crawford, "All the King's Men."
Best Actress: Olivia de Havilland, "The Heiress."
Best Supporting Actor: Dean Jagger, "Twelve O'Clock High."

Best Supporting Actress: Mercedes McCambridge, "All the King's Men."
Writing (Motion Picture Story): Douglas Morrow, "The Stratton Story."
Writing (Screenplay): Joseph L. Mankiewicz, "A Letter to Three Wives."
Writing (Story & Screenplay): Robert Pirosh, "Battleground."

Directors Guild Of America

1949/50 Annual Award: Robert Rossen.

Writers Guild Of America
(Awards given for pictures released in 1949)

Best-Written American Comedy: Joseph L. Mankiewicz, "A Letter to Three Wives."
Best-Written American Drama: Robert Rossen, "All the King's Men."
Best-Written American Musical: Betty Comden & Adolph Green, "On the Town."
Best-Written American Western: Lamar Trotti (SP) W.R. Burnett (S), "Yellow Sky."

Golden Globe Awards
(For 1949 Releases)

Best Picture-Drama: "All the King's Men."
Best Director: Robert Rossen, "All the King's Men."
Best Actress: Olivia de Havilland, "The Heiress."
Best Actor: Broderick Crawford, "All the King's Men."
Best Supporting Actress: Mercedes McCambridge, "All the King's Men."
Best Supporting Actor: James Whitmore, "Battleground."
Best Screenplay: Robert Pirosh, "Battleground."

New York Film Critics
(Awards for 1949 Releases)

Best Picture: "All the King's Men."
Best Director: Carol Reed, "The Fallen Idol."
Best Actor: Broderick Crawford, "All the King's Men."
Best Actress: Olivia de Havilland, "The Heiress."
Best Writing: (category first presented in 1956)

Cannes Film Festival
(May of 1950)

(No festival)

National Society Of Film Critics
(First awards presented in 1967)
Los Angeles Film Critics Assoc.
(First awards presented in 1977)
Independent Spirit Awards
(First presented in 1986)

21st Annual Academy Awards
(Oscars given for pictures released in 1948)

1949

Best Picture: "Hamlet."
Others Nominated: "Johnny Belinda"; "The Red Shoes"; "The Snake Pit"; "Treasure of Sierra Madre."
Best Director: John Huston, "Treasure of Sierra Madre."
Best Actor: Laurence Olivier, "Hamlet."
Best Actress: Jane Wyman, "Johnny Belinda."

Best Supporting Actor: Walter Huston, "Treasure of Sierra Madre."
Best Supporting Actress: Claire Trevor, "Key Largo."
Writing (Motion Picture Story): Richard Schweizer & David Wechsler, "The Search."
Writing (Screenplay): John Huston, "Treasure of Sierra Madre."

Directors Guild Of America

1948/49 Annual Award: Joseph L. Mankiewicz.

Writers Guild Of America
(Awards given for pictures released in 1948)

Best-Written American Comedy: F. Hugh Herbert, "Sitting Pretty."
Best-Written American Drama: Frank Partos & Millen Brand, "The Snake Pit."
Best-Written American Musical: Sidney Sheldon, Frances Goodrich & Albert Hackett (SP), Frances Goodrich & Albert Hackett (S), "Easter Parade."
Best-Written American Western: John Huston, "Treasure of Sierra Madre."

Golden Globe Awards
(For 1948 Releases)

Best Picture-Drama: "Treasure of Sierra Madre."
Best Director: John Huston, "Treasure of Sierra Madre."
Best Actress: Jane Wyman, "Johnny Belinda."
Best Actor: Laurence Olivier, "Hamlet."
Best Supporting Actress: Ellen Corby, "I Remember Mama."
Best Supporting Actor: Walter Huston, "Treasure of Sierra Madre."
Best Screenplay: Richard Schweizer, "The Search."

New York Film Critics
(Awards for 1948 Releases)

Best Picture: "Treasure of Sierra Madre."
Best Director: John Huston, "Treasure of Sierra Madre."
Best Actor: Laurence Olivier, "Hamlet."
Best Actress: Olivia de Havilland, "The Snake Pit."
Best Writing: (category first presented in 1956)

Cannes Film Festival
(May of 1949)

Best Film (Palme d'Or): "The Third Man."
Best Director: Rene Clement, "Au Dela des Grilles."
Best Actor: Edward G. Robinson, "House of Strangers."
Best Actress: Isa Miranda, "Au Dela des Grilles."
International Critics Prize: (category first presented in 1958)
Best Script: (category first presented in 1958)
Best Supporting: (category first presented in 1979)

National Society Of Film Critics
(First awards presented in 1967)
Los Angeles Film Critics Assoc.
(First awards presented in 1977)
Independent Spirit Awards
(First presented in 1986)

1948

20th Annual Academy Awards
(Oscars given for pictures released in 1947)

Best Picture: "Gentleman's Agreement."
Others Nominated: "The Bishop's Wife"; "Crossfire"; "Great Expectations"; "Miracle on 34th Street."
Best Director: Elia Kazan, "Gentleman's Agreement."
Best Actor: Ronald Colman, "A Double Life."
Best Actress: Loretta Young, "The Farmer's Daughter."
Best Supporting Actor: Edmund Gwenn, "Miracle on 34th Street."

Best Supporting Actress: Celeste Holm, "Gentleman's Agreement."
Writing (Original Story): Valentine Davies, "Miracle on 34th Street."
Writing (Original Screenplay): Sidney Sheldon, "The Bachelor and the Bobbysoxer."
Writing (Screenplay): George Seaton, "Miracle on 34th Street."

Golden Globe Awards
(For 1947 Releases)

Best Picture-Drama: "Gentleman's Agreement."
Best Director: Elia Kazan, "Gentleman's Agreement."
Best Actress: Rosalind Russell, "Mourning Becomes Electra."
Best Actor: Ronald Colman, "A Double Life."
Best Supporting Actress: Celeste Holm, "Gentleman's Agreement."
Best Supporting Actor: Edmund Gwenn, "Miracle on 34th Street."
Best Screenplay: George Seaton, "Miracle on 34th Street."

New York Film Critics
(Awards for 1947 Releases)

Best Picture: "Gentleman's Agreement."
Best Director: Elia Kazan, "Gentleman's Agreement" & "Boomerang."
Best Actor: William Powell, "Life with Father" & "The Senator Was Indiscreet."
Best Actress: Deborah Kerr, "Black Narcissus" & "The Adventuress."
Best Writing: (category first presented in 1956)

Cannes Film Festival
(May of 1948)

(No festival)

Directors Guild Of America
(First awards for 1948/49 releases)
Writers Guild Of America
(First awards presented in 1948)
National Society Of Film Critics
(First awards presented in 1967)
Los Angeles Film Critics Assoc.
(First awards presented in 1977)
Independent Spirit Awards
(First presented in 1986)

19th Annual Academy Awards
(Oscars given for pictures released in 1946)

1947

Best Picture: "The Best Years of Our Lives."
Others Nominated: "Henry V"; "It's a Wonderful Life"; "The Razor's Edge"; "The Yearling."
Best Director: William Wyler, "The Best Years of Our Lives."
Best Actor: Fredric March, "The Best Years of Our Lives."
Best Actress: Olivia de Havilland, "To Each His Own."
Best Supporting Actor: Harold Russell,"The Best Years of Our Lives."

Best Supporting Actress: Anne Baxter, "The Razor's Edge."
Writing (Original Story): Clemence Dane, "Vacation from Marriage."
Writing (Original Screenplay): Muriel Box & Sydney Box, "The Seventh Veil."
Writing (Screenplay): Robert E. Sherwood, "The Best Years of Our Lives."

Golden Globe Awards
(For 1946 Releases)

Best Picture-Drama: "The Best Years of Our Lives."
Best Director: Frank Capra, "It's a Wonderful Life."
Best Actress: Rosalind Russell, "Sister Kenny."
Best Actor: Gregory Peck, "The Yearling."
Best Supporting Actress: Anne Baxter, "The Razor's Edge."
Best Supporting Actor: Clifton Webb, "The Razor's Edge."

New York Film Critics
(Awards for 1946 Releases)

Best Picture: "The Best Years of Our Lives."
Best Director: William Wyler, "The Best Years of Our lives."
Best Actor: Laurence Olivier, "Henry V."
Best Actress: Celia Johnson, "Brief Encounter."
Best Writing: (category first presented in 1956)

Cannes Film Festival
(May of 1947)

Best Film (Palme d'Or): (5 films)
 "Antoine et Antoinette"
 "Les Maudits"
 "Crossfire"
 "Dumbo"
 "Ziegfeld Follies"
Best Director: (Not awarded)
Best Actor: (Not awarded)
Best Actress: (Not awarded)
International Critics Prize: (category first presented in 1958)
Best Script: (category first presented in 1958)
Best Supporting: (category first presented in 1979)

Directors Guild Of America
(First awards for 1948/49 releases)
Writers Guild Of America
(First awards presented in 1948)
National Society Of Film Critics
(First awards presented in 1967)
Los Angeles Film Critics Assoc.
(First awards presented in 1977)
Independent Spirit Awards
(First presented in 1986)

1946

18th Annual Academy Awards
(Oscars given for pictures released in 1945)

Best Picture: "The Lost Weekend."
  Others Nominated: "Anchors Aweigh"; "The Bells of St. Mary's"; "Mildred Pierce"; "Spellbound."
Best Director: Billy Wilder, "The Lost Weekend."
Best Actor: Ray Milland, "The Lost Weekend."
Best Actress: Joan Crawford, "Mildred Pierce."
Best Supporting Actor: James Dunn, "A Tree Grows in Brooklyn."

Best Supporting Actress: Anne Revere, "National Velvet."
Writing (Original Story): Charles G. Booth, "The House on 92nd Street."
Writing (Original Screenplay): Richard Schweizer, "Marie Louise."
Writing (Screenplay): Charles Brackett & Billy Wilder, "The Lost Weekend."

Golden Globe Awards
(For 1945 Releases)

Best Picture-Drama: "The Lost Weekend."
Best Actress: Ingrid Bergman, "Gaslight."
Best Actor: Ray Milland, "The Lost Weekend."
Best Supporting Actress: Angela Lansbury, "Gaslight."
Best Supporting Actor: J. Carroll Naish, "Gaslight."

New York Film Critics
(Awards for 1945 Releases)

Best Picture: "The Lost Weekend."
Best Director: Billy Wilder, "The Lost Weekend."
Best Actor: Ray Milland, "The Lost Weekend."
Best Actress: Ingrid Bergman, "Spellbound" & "The Bells of St. Mary's."
Best Writing: (category first presented in 1956)

Cannes Film Festival
(May of 1946)

Best Film (Palme d'Or): (7 pictures)
   "La Bataille du Rail"
   "Symphonie Pastorale"
   "The Lost Weekend"
   "Brief Encounter"
   "Open City"
   "Maria Candelaria"
   "The Last Chance"
Best Director: Rene Clement, "La Bataille du Rail."
Best Actor: Ray Milland, "The Lost Weekend."
Best Actress: Michele Morgan, "Symphonie Pastorale."
International Critics Prize: (category first presented in 1958)
Best Script: (category first presented in 1958)
Best Supporting: (category first presented in 1979)

Directors Guild Of America
(First awards for 1948/49 releases)
Writers Guild Of America
(First awards presented in 1948)
National Society Of Film Critics
(First awards presented in 1967)
Los Angeles Film Critics Assoc.
(First awards presented in 1977)
Independent Spirit Awards
(First presented in 1986)

17th Annual Academy Awards
(Oscars given for pictures released in 1944)

1945

Best Picture: "Going My Way."
Others Nominated: "Double Indemnity"; "Gaslight"; "Since You Went Away"; "Wilson."
Best Director: Leo McCarey, "Going My Way."
Best Actor: Bing Crosby, "Going My Way."
Best Actress: Ingrid Bergman, "Gaslight."
Best Supporting Actor: Barry Fitzgerald, "Going My Way."

Best Supporting Actress: Ethel Barrymore, "None But the Lonely Heart."
Writing (Original Story): Leo McCarey, "Going My Way."
Writing (Original Screenplay): Lamar Trotti, "Wilson."

Golden Globe Awards
(For 1944 Releases)

Best Picture-Drama: "Going My Way."
Best Actress: Ingrid Bergman, "The Bells of St. Mary's."
Best Actor: Alexander Knox, "President Wilson."

New York Film Critics
(Awards for 1944 Releases)

Best Picture: "Going My Way."
Best Director: Leo McCarey, "Going My Way."
Best Actor: Barry Fitzgerald, "Going My Way."
Best Actress: Tallulah Bankhead, "Lifeboat."
Best Writing: (category first presented in 1956)

Cannes Film Festival
(First awards presented in 1946)
Directors Guild Of America
(First awards for 1948/49 releases)
Writers Guild Of America
(First awards presented in 1948)
National Society Of Film Critics
(First awards presented in 1967)
Los Angeles Film Critics Assoc.
(First awards presented in 1977)
Independent Spirit Awards
(First presented in 1986)

1944

16th Annual Academy Awards
(Oscars given for pictures released in 1943)

Best Picture: "Casablanca."
Others Nominated: "For Whom the Bell Tolls"; "Heaven Can Wait"; "The Human Comedy"; "In Which We Serve"; "Madame Curie"; "The More the Merrier"; "The Ox-Bow Incident"; "The Song of Bernadette"; "Watch on the Rhine."
Best Director: Michael Curtiz, "Casablanca."
Best Actor: Paul Lukas, "Watch on the Rhine."
Best Actress: Jennifer Jones, "The Song of Bernadette."

Best Supporting Actor: Charles Coburn, "The More the Merrier."
Best Supporting Actress: Katina Paxinou, "For Whom the Bell Tolls."
Writing (Original Story): William Saroyan, "The Human Comedy."
Writing (Original Screenplay): Norman Krasna, "Princess O'Rourke."
Writing (Screenplay): Julius J. Epstein, Philip G. Epstein & Howard Kock, "Casablanca."

Golden Globe Awards
(Awards for 1943 Releases)

Best Picture-Drama: "The Song of Bernadette."
Best Actress: Jennifer Jones, "The Song of Bernadette."
Best Actor: Paul Lukas, "Watch on the Rhine."

New York Film Critics
(Awards for 1943 Releases)

Best Picture: "Watch on the Rhine."
Best Director: George Stevens, "The More the Merrier."
Best Actor: Paul Lukas, "Watch on the Rhine."
Best Actress: Ida Lupino, "The Hard Way."
Best Writing: (category first presented in 1956)

Cannes Film Festival
(First awards presented in 1946)
Directors Guild Of America
(First awards for 1948/49 releases)
Writers Guild Of America
(First awards presented in 1948)
National Society Of Film Critics
(First awards presented in 1967)
Los Angeles Film Critics Assoc.
(First awards presented in 1977)
Independent Spirit Awards
(First presented in 1986)

15th Annual Academy Awards
(Oscars given for pictures released in 1942)

1943

Best Picture: "Mrs. Miniver."
Others Nominated: "The Invaders"; "The Magnificent Ambersons"; "The Pied Piper"; "Pride of the Yankees"; "Random Harvest"; "Talk of the Town"; "Wake Island"; "Yankee Doodle Dandy."
Best Director: William Wyler, "Mrs. Miniver."
Best Actor: James Cagney, "Yankee Doodle Dandy."
Best Actress: Greer Garson, "Mrs. Miniver."
Best Supporting Actor: Van Heflin, "Johnny Eager."

Best Supporting Actress: Teresa Wright, "Mrs. Miniver."
Writing (Original Story): Emeric Pressburger, "The Invaders."
Writing (Original Screenplay): Michael Kani & Ring Lardner Jr., "Woman of the Year."
Writing (Screenplay): George Froeschel, James Hilton, Claudine West & Arthur Wimperis, "Mrs. Miniver."

New York Film Critics
(Awards for 1942 Releases)

Best Picture: "In Which We Serve."
Best Director: John Farrow, "Wake Island."
Best Actor: James Cagney, "Yankee Doodle Dandy."
Best Actress: Agnes Moorehead, "The Magnificent Ambersons."
Best Writing: (category first presented in 1956)

Golden Globe Awards (First presented in 1944)
Cannes Film Festival (First awards in 1946)
Directors Guild of America
   (First awards for films released in 1948/49)
Writers Guild of America *(First awards in 1948)*
National Society of Film Critics
   (First awards presented in 1967)
Los Angeles Film Critics Association
   (First awards presented in 1977)
Independent Spirit Awards
   (First presented in 1986)

14th Annual Academy Awards
(Oscars given for pictures released in 1941)

1942

Best Picture: "How Green Was My Valley."
Others Nominated: "Blossoms in the Dust"; "Citizen Kane"; "Here Comes Mr. Jordan"; "Hold Back the Dawn"; "The Little Foxes"; "The Maltese Falcon"; "One Foot in Heaven"; "Sergeant York"; "Suspicion."
Best Director: John Ford, "How Green Was My Valley."
Best Actor: Gary Cooper, "Sergeant York."
Best Actress: Joan Fontaine, "Suspicion."

Best Supporting Actor: Donald Crisp, "How Green Was My Valley."
Best Supporting Actress: Mary Astor, "The Great Lie."
Writing (Original Story): Harry Segall, "Here Comes Mr. Jordan."
Writing (Original Screenplay): Herman J. Mankiewicz & Orson Welles, "Citizen Kane."
Writing (Screenplay): Sidney Buchman & Seto I. Miller, "Here Comes Mr. Jordan."

New York Film Critics
(Awards for 1941 Releases)

Best Picture: "Citizen Kane."
Best Director: John Ford, "How Green Was My Valley."
Best Actor: Gary Cooper, "Sergeant York."
Best Actress: Joan Fontaine, "Suspicion."
Best Writing: (category first presented in 1956)

Golden Globe Awards (First presented in 1944)
Cannes Film Festival (First awards in 1946)
Directors Guild of America
   (First awards for films released in 1948/49)
Writers Guild of America *(First awards in 1948)*
National Society of Film Critics
   (First awards presented in 1967)
Los Angeles Film Critics Association
   (First awards presented in 1977)
Independent Spirit Awards
   (First presented in 1986)

1941

13th Annual Academy Awards
(Oscars given for pictures released in 1940)

Best Picture: "Rebecca."
Others Nominated: "All This and Heaven Too"; "Foreign Correspondent"; "The Grapes of Wrath"; "The Great Dictator"; "Kitty Foyle"; "The Letter"; "The Long Voyage Home"; "Our Town"; The Philadelphia Story."
Best Director: John Ford, "The Grapes of Wrath."
Best Actor: James Stewart, "The Philadelphia Story."
Best Actress: Ginger Rogers, "Kitty Foyle."

Best Supporting Actor: Walter Brennan, "The Westerner."
Best Supporting Actress: Jane Darwell, "The Grapes of Wrath."
Writing (Original Story): Benjamin Glazer & John S. Toldy, "My Love."
Writing (Original Screenplay): Preston Sturges, "The Great McGinty."
Writing (Screenplay): Donald Ogden Stewart, "The Philadelphia Story."

New York Film Critics
(Awards for 1940 Releases)

Best Picture: "The Grapes of Wrath."
Best Director: John Ford, "The Grapes of Wrath", "The Long Voyage Home."
Best Actor: Charles Chaplin, "The Great Dictator."
Best Actress: Katharine Hepburn, "The Philadelphia Story."
Best Writing: (category first presented in 1956)

Golden Globe Awards (First presented in 1944)
Cannes Film Festival (First awards in 1946)
Directors Guild of America
   (First awards for films released in 1948/49)
Writers Guild of America *(First awards in 1948)*
National Society of Film Critics
   (First awards presented in 1967)
Los Angeles Film Critics Association
   (First awards presented in 1977)
Independent Spirit Awards
   (First presented in 1986)

1940

12th Annual Academy Awards
(Oscars given for pictures released in 1939)

Best Picture: "Gone With the Wind."
Others Nominated: "Dark Victory"; "Goodbye, Mr. Chips"; "Love Affair"; "Mr. Smith Goes to Washington"; "Ninotchka"; "Of Mice and Men"; "Stagecoach"; "The Wizard of OZ"; "Wuthering Heights."
Best Director: Victor Fleming, "Gone With the Wind."
Best Actor: Robert Donat, "Goodbye, Mr. Chips."
Best Actress: Vivien Leigh, "Gone With the Wind."

Best Supporting Actor: Thomas Mitchell, "Stagecoach."
Best Supporting Actress: Hattie McDaniel, "Gone With the Wind."
Writing (Original Story): Lewis R. Foster, "Mr. Smith Goes to Washington."
Writing (Screenplay): Sidney Howard, "Gone With the Wind."

New York Film Critics
(Awards for 1939 Releases)

Best Picture: "Wuthering Heights."
Best Director: John Ford, "Stagecoach."
Best Actor: James Stewart, "Mr. Smith Goes to Washington."
Best Actress: Vivien Leigh, "Gone With the Wind."
Best Writing: (category first presented in 1956)

Golden Globe Awards (First presented in 1944)
Cannes Film Festival (First awards in 1946)
Directors Guild of America
   (First awards for films released in 1948/49)
Writers Guild of America *(First awards in 1948)*
National Society of Film Critics
   (First awards presented in 1967)
Los Angeles Film Critics Association
   (First awards presented in 1977)
Independent Spirit Awards
   (First presented in 1986)

11th Annual Academy Awards
(Oscars given for pictures released in 1938)

1939

Best Picture: "You Can't Take It With You."
Others Nominated: "The Adventures of Robin Hood"; "Alexander's Ragtime Band"; "Boys Town"; "The Citadel"; "Four Daughters"; "Grand Illusion"; "Jezebel"; "Pygmalion"; "Test Pilot."
Best Director: Frank Capra, "You Can't Take It with You."
Best Actor: Spencer Tracy, "Boys Town."
Best Actress: Bette Davis, "Jezebel."

Best Supporting Actor: Walter Brennan, "Kentucky"
Best Supporting Actress: Fay Bainter, "Jezebel."
Writing (Original Story): Eleanore Griffin & Dore Schary, "Boys Town."
Writing (Adaptation): Ian Dalrymple, Cecil Lewis & W.P. Lipscomb, "Pygmalion."
Writing (Screenplay): George Bernard Shaw, "Pygmalion."

New York Film Critics
(Awards for 1938 Releases)

Best Picture: "The Citadel."
Best Director: Alfred Hitchcock, "The Lady Vanishes."
Best Actor: James Cagney, "Angels with Dirty Faces."
Best Actress: Margaret Sullavan, "Three Comrades."
Best Writing: (category first presented in 1956)

Golden Globe Awards (First presented in 1944)
Cannes Film Festival (First awards in 1946)
Directors Guild of America
(First awards for films released in 1948/49)
Writers Guild of America *(First awards in 1948)*
National Society of Film Critics
(First awards presented in 1967)
Los Angeles Film Critics Association
(First awards presented in 1977)
Independent Spirit Awards
(First presented in 1986)

10th Annual Academy Awards
(Oscars given for pictures released in 1937)

1938

Best Picture: "The Life of Emile Zola."
Others Nominated: "The Awful Truth"; "Captains Courageous"; "Dead End"; "The Good Earth"; "In Old Chicago"; "Lost Horizon"; "100 Men and a Girl"; "Stage Door"; "A Star Is Born."
Best Director: Leo McCarey, "The Awful Truth."
Best Actor: Spencer Tracy, "Captains Courageous."
Best Actress: Luise Rainer, "The Good Earth."
Best Supporting Actor: Joseph Schildkraut, "The Life of Emile Zola."

Best Supporting Actress: Alice Brady, "In Old Chicago."
Writing (Original Story): William A. Wellman & Robert Carson, "A Star Is Born."
Writing (Screenplay): Heinz Herald, Genza Herczeg & Norman Reilly Raine, "The Life of Emile Zola."

New York Film Critics
(Awards for 1937 Releases)

Best Picture: "The Life of Emile Zola."
Best Director: Gregory La Cava, "Stage Door."
Best Actor: Paul Muni, "The Life of Emile Zola."
Best Actress: Greta Garbo, "Camille."
Best Writing: (category first presented in 1956)

Golden Globe Awards (First presented in 1944)
Cannes Film Festival (First awards in 1946)
Directors Guild of America
(First awards for films released in 1948/49)
Writers Guild of America *(First awards in 1948)*
National Society of Film Critics
(First awards presented in 1967)
Los Angeles Film Critics Association
(First awards presented in 1977)
Independent Spirit Awards
(First presented in 1986)

1937

9th Annual Academy Awards
(Oscars given for pictures released in 1936)

Best Picture: "The Great Ziegfeld."
Others Nominated: "Anthony Adverse"; "Dodsworth"; "Libeled Lady"; "Mr. Deeds Goes to Town"; "Romeo and Juliet"; "San Francisco"; "The Story of Louis Pasteur"; "A Tale of Two Cities"; "Three Smart Girls."
Best Director: Frank Capra, "Mr. Deeds Goes to Town."
Best Actor: Paul Muni, "The Story of Louis Pasteur."

Best Actress: Luise Rainer, "The Great Ziegfeld."
Best Supporting Actor: Walter Brennan, "Come and Get It."
Best Supporting Actress: Gale Sondergaard, "Anthony Adverse."
Writing (Original Story): Pierre Collings & Sheridan Gibney, "The Story of Louis Pasteur."
Writing (Screenplay): Pierre Collings & Sheridan Gibney, "The Story of Louis Pasteur."

New York Film Critics
(Awards for 1936 Releases)

Best Picture: "Mr. Deeds Goes to Town."
Best Director: Rouven Mamoulian, "The Gay Desperado."
Best Actor: Walter Huston, "Dodsworth."
Best Actress: Luise Rainer, "The Great Ziegfeld."
Best Writing: (category first presented in 1956)

Golden Globe Awards (First presented in 1944)
Cannes Film Festival (First awards in 1946)
Directors Guild of America
(First awards for films released in 1948/49)
Writers Guild of America *(First awards in 1948)*
National Society of Film Critics
(First awards presented in 1967)
Los Angeles Film Critics Association
(First awards presented in 1977)
Independent Spirit Awards
(First presented in 1986)

1936

8th Annual Academy Awards
(Oscars given for pictures released in 1935)

Best Picture: "Mutiny on the Bounty."
Others Nominated: "Alice Adams"; "Broadway Melody of 1936"; "Captain Blood"; "David Copperfield"; "The Informer"; "Les Miserables"; "The Lives of a Bengal Lancer"; "A Midsummer Night's Dream"; "Naughty Marietta"; "Ruggles of Red Gap"; "Top Hat."
Best Director: John Ford, "The Informer."
Best Actor: Victor McLaglen, "The Informer."

Best Actress: Bette Davis, "Dangerous."
Writing (Original Story): Ben Hecht & Charles MacArthur, "The Scoundrel."
Writing (Screenplay): Dudley Nichols, "The Informer."

New York Film Critics
(Awards for 1935 Releases)

Best Picture: "The Informer."
Best Director: John Ford, "The Informer."
Best Actor: Charles Laughton, "Mutiny on the Bounty" & "Ruggles of Red Gap."
Best Actress: Greta Garbo, "Anna Karenina."
Best Writing: (category first presented in 1956)

Golden Globe Awards (First presented in 1944)
Cannes Film Festival (First awards in 1946)
Directors Guild of America
(First awards for films released in 1948/49)
Writers Guild of America *(First awards in 1948)*
National Society of Film Critics
(First awards presented in 1967)
Los Angeles Film Critics Association
(First awards presented in 1977)
Independent Spirit Awards
(First presented in 1986)

1935

7th Annual Academy Awards
(Oscars given for pictures released in 1934)

Best Picture: "It Happened One Night."
 Others Nominated: "Barretts of Wimpole Street"; "Cleopatra"; "Flirtation Walk"; "The Gay Divorcee"; "Here Comes the Navy"; "The House of Rothchild"; "Imitation of Life"; "One Night Of Love"; "The Thin Man"; "Viva Villa"; "The White Parade."
Best Director: Frank Capra, "It Happened One Night."
Best Actor: Clark Gable, "It Happened One Night."
Best Actress: Claudette Colbert, "It Happened One Night."
Writing (Adaptation): Robert Riskin, "It Happened One Night."
Writing (Original Story): Arthur Caesar, "Manhattan Melodrama"

1933

5th Annual Academy Awards
(Oscars given for pictures released in 1931/32)

Best Picture: "Grand Hotel."
 Others Nominated: "Arrowsmith"; "Bad Girl"; "The Champ"; "Five Star Final"; "One Hour with You"; "Shanghai Express"; "Smiling Lieutenant."
Best Director: Frank Borzage, "Bad Girl."
Best Actor: Wallace Beery, "The Champ."
Best Actress: Helen Hayes, "The Sin of Madelon Claudet."
Writing (Adaptation): Edwin Burke, "Bar Girl."
Writing (Original Story): Frances Marion, "The Champ."

1934

6th Annual Academy Awards
(Oscars given for pictures released in 1932/33)

Best Picture: "Cavalcade."
 Others Nominated: "A Farewell to Arms"; "Forty-Second Street"; "I Am A Fugitive from a Chain Gang"; "Lady for a Day"; "Little Women"; "The Private Life of Henry VIII"; "She Done Him Wrong"; "Smilin' Through"; "State Fair."
Best Director: Frank Lloyd, "Cavalcade."
Best Actor: Charles Laughton, "Private Life of Henry VIII."
Best Actress: Katharine Hepburn, "Morning Glory."
Writing (Adaptation): Victor Herman & Sarah Y. Mason, "Little Women."
Writing (Original Story): Robert Lord, "One Way Passage."

1932

4th Annual Academy Awards
(Oscars given for pictures released in 1930/31)

Best Picture: "Cimarron."
 Others Nominated: "East Lynne"; "The Front Page"; "Skippy"; "Trader Horn."
Best Director: Norman Taurog, "Skippy."
Best Actor: Lionel Barrymore, "A Free Soul."
Best Actress: Marie Dressler, "Min and Bill."
Writing (Adaptation): Howard Estabrook, "Cimarron."
Writing (Original Story): John Monk Saunders, "The Dawn Patrol."

1931

3rd Annual Academy Awards
(Oscars given for pictures released in 1929/30)

Best Picture: "All Quiet on the Western Front."
Others Nominated: "The Big House"; Disraeli";
"The Divorcee"; "The Love Parade."
Best Director: Lewis Milestone, "All Quiet on the
Western Front."
Best Actor: George Arliss, "Disraeli."
Best Actress: Norma Shearer, "The Divorcee."
Writing: Frances Marion, "The Big House."

1929

1st Annual Academy Awards
(Oscars given for pictures released in 1927/28)

Best Picture: "Wings."
Others Nominated: "The Last Command"; "The
Racket"; "Seventh Heaven"; "The Way of All
Flesh."
Best Director: Frank Borzage, "Seventh Heaven."
Best Comedy Director: Lewis Milestone, "Two
Arabian Knights."
Best Actor: Emil Jannings, "The Last Command"
& "The Way of All Flesh."
Best Actress: Janet Gaynor, "Seventh Heaven",
"Street Angel" & "Sunrise."
Writing (Adaptation): Benjamin Glazer, "Seventh
Heaven."
Writing (Original Story): Ben Hecht, "Underworld."

1930

2nd Annual Academy Awards
(Oscars given for pictures released in 1928/29)

Best Picture: "The Broadway Melody."
Others Nominated: "Alibi"; "Hollywood Revue";
"In Old Arizona"; "The Patriot."
Best Director: Frank Lloyd, "The Divine Lady."
Best Actor: Warner Baxter, "In Old Arizona."
Best Actress: Mary Pickford, "Coquette."
Writing: Hans Kraly, "The Patriot."

New York Film Critics Circle
(First awards presented in 1936)
Golden Globe Awards
(First presented in 1944)
Cannes Film Festival
(First awards presented in 1946)
Directors Guild of America
(First awards for films released in 1948/50)
Writers Guild of America
(First awards presented in 1949)
National Society of Film Critics
(First awards presented in 1967)
Los Angeles Film Critics Association
(First awards presented in 1977)
Independent Spirit Awards
(First presented in 1986)

INDEX

Movies in Section 9: Top Film Rentals (which are listed in alphabetical order) are <u>not</u> included in the index.

Movies in Section 9: Top Film Rentals (which are listed in alphabetical order) are <u>not</u> included in the index.

Movies in Section 9: Top Film Rentals (which are listed in alphabetical order) are <u>not</u> included in the index.

Flashback 33
Flatliners 31
Fleischer, Charles 10
Fleisher, Richard 5
Fleming, Victor 98, 178
Fletch Lives 37
Fletcher, Charlie 7
Fletcher, Louise 98, 134, 135
Flight of the Intruder 26
Flintstones, The 7, 14
Flirtation Walk 181
Flirting 22
Flock, John 11
Florek, Dann 7
Fly II, The 38
Flynn, John 85
Foley, Dave 8
Foley, James 13
Folks 21
Folsey Jr., George 7
Fonda, Bridget 6, 88
Fonda, Henry 98, 122, 123
Fonda, Jane 98, 112, 122,
  126, 128, 129, 130, 131,
  142, 143, 146, 147
Fonda, Peter 146
Foner, Naomi 108, 109
Fontaine, Joan 99, 177
Fools of Fortune 35
Foote, Horton 114, 115, 118,157
For a Lost Soldier 16
For All Mankind 40
For Keeps 44
For Love or Money 16
For Queen & Country 41
For Sasha 23
For the Boys 26,102, 103
For Whom the Bell Tolls 176
Foray, June 12
Forbes, Michele 11
Forbidden Dance, The 34
Ford, Glenn 158
Ford, Harrison 6, 86, 92, 114
Ford, John 97, 98, 167, 177,
  178, 180
Foreign Correspondent 178
Foreman, Carl 140, 167
Foreman, John 114
Forever Young 19
*Forgotten Tune for the Flute, The
  48*
Foriani, Claire 10
Forman, Milos 97, 116, 117,
  134, 135
Forrest, Frederic 10, 126, 127
Forrest Gump 7, 14
Forslund, Bengt 140
Forsyth, Bill 119
Fortress 16
Fortune Cookie, The 152
Forty-Second Street 181
Fosse, Bob 97, 126, 128,
  136, 140
Foster, David 7, 11
Foster, Jodie 9, 88, 91, 98, 102,
  103, 108, 109, 132, 133
Foster, Lewis R. 178
*Four Adv.s Of Reinette & Mira
  41*

Four Daughters 179
Fourth War, The 34
*Fox and the Hound (Re), The
  44*
Fox, Edward 131
Fox, Michael J. 7, 12, 86
Frances 120
Franciosa, Anthony 160
Franco, Ramon 11
Frank, Frederic M. 167
Frank, Harriet 156
Frank, Melvin 138
Franken, Al 11
Frankenhooker 35
*Frankenstein, Mary Shelley's
  9, 14*
Frankenstein Unbound 35
Frankie & Johnny 26
Franklin, Carl 101
Franklow, Morton 93
Frantic 44
Fraser, Brendan 5
Frears, Stephen 85, 104
Freddie As F.R.O.7. 22
*Freddy's Dead: Final Nightmare
  26*
Free Soul, A 99, 181
Free Willy 16
Freejack 20
Freeman, Morgan 11, 86, 106,
  107, 110, 111
Freeway 48
Freeze-Die-Come to Life 36
*French Connection, The
  97, 98, 142, 143*
*French Lieutenant's Woman,
  The 122, 123*
Fresh Horses 45
Freshman, The 32
Frey, Leonard 142
Freyermuth, Ortwin 11
Fricker, Brenda 5, 106, 107
Friday The 13th Part VII 44
Friday the 13th Pt VIII 38
Fried Green Tomatoes 25, 102
Fried, Rob 7
Friedenberg, Richard 100
Friedkin, David 154
Friedkin, William 6, 97, 138,
  139, 142, 143
Friedman, Bruce Jay 116, 117
Friendly, David 9
Friendly Persuasion 163
Fright Night: Part II 39
Froeschel, George 161, 177
From Here to Eternity 97, 166
Front Page, The 181
Front, The 132
Frozen Assets 23
Frydman, Marc 9
Fuchs, Daniel 164
Fuchs, Fred 9
Fugitive, The 1, 16
Full Fathom Five 35
Full Metal Jacket 110
Full Moon in Blue Water 47
Fuller, Charles 116
Funny About Love 33
Funny Farm 44

Funny Girl 148, 149
Furlong, Edward 87
Furlong, John 13
FX2 26

G

Gable, Clark 99, 181
Gaby-A True Story 110
Galatea 7, 14
Galati, Frank 108
Gale, Bob 114
Gallienne, Eva Le 124
Gammon, James 6, 9
Gandhi 97, 98, 120, 121
Ganis, Sid 93
Ganz, Lowell 6, 7, 92, 116,
  117
Garbo, Greta 179, 180
Garcia, Andy 11, 87, 104
*Garden of the Finzi-Continis
  142*
Gardenia, Vincent 110, 138
Gardner, Herb 154
Gardner, Pierce 7
Garland, Judy 165
Garner, James 9, 114
Garofalo, Janeane 11
Garr, Teri 120
Garson, Greer 99, 159, 177
Gas, Food, Lodging 22, 101
Gaslight 99, 175
Gassman, Vittoria 137
Gasso, Michael V. 136
Gate II 22
Gate Of Hell 166
Gay Desperado, The 180
Gay Divorcee, The 181
Gaylin, Michael 10
Gaynes, George 10
Gaynor, Janet 99, 182
Gayton, Joe 6, 7
Geary, Cynthia 8
Geer, Richard 86
Geffen, David 8, 91
Geissler, Dieter 10
Gelbart, Larry 120, 121, 128,
  130
*Gentleman's Agreement
  97, 172*
George, Chief Dan 144, 145
George, Peter 155
George's Island 30
Georgy Girl 153
Gereghty, William 9
Germi, Pietro 157
Gerolmo, Chris 10
Get Back 30
*Get Out Your Handkerchiefs
  101, 129*
Getaway, The 7, 14
Getchell, Robert 6, 132, 136
Getting Even With Dad 7, 14
Getting It Right 40
Gettysburg 16
Ghia, Fernando 112
Ghost 1, 31, 82, 104, 105
Ghost Dad 32
Ghostbusters 1

Ghostbusters II 3, 37, 82
Ghosts Can't Do It 36
Giacomo, Laura San 88, 107
Giannetti, Alfredo 157
Giannini, Giancarlo 132, 141
Giant 97, 163
Gibney, Sheridan 180
Gibson, Henry 135
Gibson, Mel 9, 86, 91
Gibson, Thomas 12
Gideon, Raynold 11, 112
Gielgud, John 115, 122, 123,131
Gigi 97, 161
Gilbert, Brian 12
Gilford, Jack 138
Gille, Francois 93
Gilliam, Terry 6, 85, 114, 115
Gilliatt, Penelope 142, 143
Gilroy, Dan 6
Ginger Ale Afternoon 42
Gingold, Hermione 161
Girl in a Swing, The 40
Give 'em Hell, Harry! 134
*Give My Regards to Broad
  Street 117*
Given Word 158
Givens, Robin 5
Gladiator 21
Gladys Hill 134
Glattes, Wolfgang 6
Glave, Matthew 5
Glazer, Benjamin 178, 182
Gleaming The Cube 39
Glengarry Glen Ross 21, 100
Glenn, Scott 12
Gloria 124
Glory 38, 106, 107
Glotzer, Liz 11
Glover, Danny 5, 86, 105
Glynn, Victor 11
Go-Between, The 142, 145
*Godfather, The 1, 97, 98,
  140, 141*
Godfather, The, Part II 97, 136
Godfather, The, Part III 31,104
Gods Must Be Crazy II, The 33
Going My Way 97, 99, 175
Gold, Eric 5
Goldberg, Whoopi 6, 10, 88,
  92, 104, 105, 114, 115
Goldblum, Jeff 86
Golden, Annie 10
Golden Child, The 4
Golden Globe Awards 95
Goldman, Bo 100, 101, 124,
  125, 134, 135
Goldman, Gary 10, 12
Goldman, James 148
Goldman, William 8, 9, 132,
  146
Goldmann, Bernie 6
Goldschmidt, Ernst 10
Goldsman, Akiva 5, 6
Golin, Steve 6
Golino, Valeria 88
Gollaher, Kevin 12
Gomez, Jose-Luis 135
*Gone With the Wind 2, 98, 99,
  178*

Movies in Section 9: Top Film Rentals (which are listed in alphabetical order) are <u>not</u> included in the index.

Movies in Section 9: Top Film Rentals (which are listed in alphabetical order) are <u>not</u> included in the index.

Movies in Section 9: Top Film Rentals (which are listed in alphabetical order) are <u>not</u> included in the index.

Movies in Section 9: Top Film Rentals (which are listed in alphabetical order) are <u>not</u> included in the index.

Movies in Section 9: Top Film Rentals (which are listed in alphabetical order) are <u>not</u> included in the index.

Movies in Section 9: Top Film Rentals (which are listed in alphabetical order) are <u>not</u> included in the index.

Movies in Section 9: Top Film Rentals (which are listed in alphabetical order) are <u>not</u> included in the index.

No need to worry about buying out-of-date statistics!

To receive <u>one</u> *FREE* update to your
1994 Hollywood Power Stats Book
Just mail or fax your name, address and

update number* | 401356 | to:

POWER STATS "UPDATE"
4804 Laurel Canyon Blvd., Suite #203
Valley Village, CA 91607

or Fax to (818) 509-1349

*This number is good for only <u>one</u> free update and is valid for
requests postmarked or faxed no later than September 1, 1994.
Thereafter updates or additional updates are $6 apiece and are available until November 1, 1994.
Update number must accompany all orders.
Make checks or money orders payable to Cineview Publishing.
(Updates contain information on film grosses since the publication of this book.)